VOLCANO SANTORINI

JAMES FREW

LMH Publishing Limited

Edited by Louise Cogan, B.A.

Cover Design by Keith Frew

Book Design & Layout by Michelle M.A. Mitchell

Published by LMH Publishing Limited
7 Norman Road,
LOJ Industrial Complex
Building 10
Kingston C.S.O., Jamaica
Tel: 876-938-0005; 938-0712
Fax: 876-759-8752
Email: lmhbookpublishing@cwjamaica.com
Website: www.lmhpublishingjamaica.com

Printed in the U.S.A.   ISBN 976-8184-81-7

Dedication

To my son, the late James Keith Frew,
wherever he may be.

By the same Author

~ Bahamas Passage ~

The most devastating explosion known to mankind blew the heart out of the Aegean island of Santorini one black after noon in 1628 B.C., dismembering Minoan culture with a blast of worldwide ramifications. Stratification of their civilization was mercifully instantaneous. No life remained on the tiny island, nor on the exposed flanks of neighboring Crete, Helos, Naxos, Ios, Anafi, Amorgos or Astiplea. An immense fireball rolled from the collapsing volcano, vaporizing all protein matter in its path. The rapidly expanding ring of super-heated gas fired the temples of Knossos ninety miles to the south, cinderized villages bordering the sea, flamed forests to the mountain tops. As for those fortunate souls who escaped the initial blast – those beyond its searing perimeter, sheltered by crags and valleys – there was more to come.

The opening phase of the gigantic eruptions consisted of a violent continuum of vented gas, pumice and fragmented rock, expelled vertically to the stratosphere. As the mixture rose cold air was dragged into the column to become heated by the venting particles which expanded rapidly into a gigantic mushroom cloud. The venting grew with its own momentum, spewing six cubic miles of gut matter from the 3000 foot peak, leaving an immense, white-hot cavity in the center of the tiny island.

The island convulsed. Those who had yet to flee were incinerated alive when the emptied volcano imploded. The cold Mediterranean waters rushed in to fill the enormous cavity, resulting in a water magma explosion with a force equal to the devastation of forty Hiroshimas.

The mixture of intensely hot gas and incandescent material shot into the air as only an eruption could, with an intensity so great the cloud collapsed of its own weight, sending dense avalanches of pumice cascading over the island. A monstrous melange of debris and noxious gas, spreading outward at a speed in excess of 400 miles per hour, decimated the island with a hurricane of fire. The ensuing envelopment of eastern Crete guaranteed instant death in a widening ring over the outlying Aegean.

The sea continued to rush into the newly-formed caldera. Secondary explosions spewed sheets of pumice skyward, the towering inferno clawing upward to 30 miles, darkening the sun. The saucer-shaped caldera overflowed from the inward momentum of invading sea, creating a massive wave that overwhelmed the neighboring islands, assaulting the hills of Crete, sweeping into the Sahara, shearing the cliffs of Asia Minor, surging the flatlands of prehistoric Athens and ravaging the coast of the eastern Mediterranean.

Its fading crest marched through the Straits of Gibraltar and spent itself in the mid-Atlantic. In the Aegean, devastation was complete. Europe's finest Bronze Age civilization had been erased in a matter of hours.

There were survivors, of course, on the outlying islands. On Crete, those who heeded months of intensifying earthquakes and fled to the heights; grape gatherers tending vines on the hillsides; shepherds quieting their flocks in the mountain valleys. But the spirit that nurtured their remarkable culture was gone. The Minoans were not a warlike people, and the dazed few who returned to their sheltered temples were easy prey.

The Myceneans, who came from the north to pillage their weakened friends, remained for 300 years, absorbing the Minoan culture and legends, inspiring a golden age and the winged words of Homer. They, in turn, were overcome by the Dorian tribes from the highlands. The Minoans and the Myceneans were not Greek, but their legends endured as the germ of ancient Greek classics. Homer described from what he had never seen, but modernity has viewed the Minoan ruins and knows the truth in his descriptions – of palaces with golden riches, spacious halls and vibrantly echoing porticos.

But there is yet another story.

Survivors of the cataclysmic holocaust who did not elect to remain in the nooks and valleys, nor to intermarry with the conquering Myceneans, drifted eastwards to Rhodes, to Kos and to Anatolia, from whence their ancestors had come. There were others who found sanctuary in the clouded peaks. Others, called Eteocretans, near about the fourth century B.C. left inscriptions written with the Greek alphabet and in the Greek manner, but strangely not in the Greek language. What language, this? A language of palaces, of gods?

Above the vale of Lasithi, in the heartland of Crete, towers Karphi, the Nail. Here, onto this pinnacle of stone, moved the Minoan refugees. They established a settlement of 150 rooms and lived there for possibly a century; little of the ancient ruins remain today.

Beyond the pass, however, in an isolated valley, there is a cluster of stone dwellings, active to this day. Smoke rises from chimney places, goats flock there and vines are tended. The cottages are simplistic, the furniture constructed from olive wood stretched with hide. An open heart serves as a kitchen, water toted from the spring in highly decorative clay urns. Oil lamps suffuse the night. Their mode of living not unlike that of provincial Crete, including paths that lead to the villages below, but there is a difference in the people who live in this secluded valley.

The walls of their cottages are frescoed with scenes of ancient time – highly colored, precise in detail, the work of master craftsmen. The earrings they wear, minutely inscribed, are hammered from gold. Their clothes are coveted by the lowlanders; woven from virgin wool, dyed with vivid colors – indigo, brilliant red, crystalline green. They produce no somber colors to frock the aged. Women move freely about, bare to the waist when the sun is warm, draped with shawls when clouds obscure the glare and after twilight. Children are slimmer and somewhat taller than the aboriginal Mediterraneans. They speak a language that is not quite Greek and worship a deity adorned with the horns of a bull.

Menfolk seek their brides from faraway places, not from the villages below the valley, not always from the hinterlands of Crete…often from the mainland of modern day Greece, down the coast to Sounion where they barter their ancient crafts. Questing, observing, sailing away during the night…more often not alone.

And here, near Kavouri, adjacent to Athens, a crimson sail appeared at dusk while volcano Santorini was spoiling the Aegean. Quietly approaching the cliffs with the moon-drawn tide, a mysterious stranger furled his sail and cast an anchor of stone. And there he silently awaited his quest in the darkness before dawn.

Strange vessel was this – graceful, with a blade of oak for a tiller, triangularly rigged with a lateen sail. Similar to the fishermen's craft that ply the Aegean today…more like the Minoan depicted on the walls of ancient Akrotiri. Planked with cedar, fastened with bronze, a pierced stone for an anchor tethered to the bow. The gaunt stranger waited on a pathway hewn from the cliff, peering patiently at a darkened villa to which he was mysteriously drawn.

While the volcano was raising a warning pillar of fire, the crimson sail was unfurled and westerly bent, passing to the leeward on the second day of dawn…fleeing to the headlands of Crete as if the stranger and his companion, a slender girl with a shawl, had an ungodly premonition of the catastrophe to come.

When all was done, when the island of Santorini was reduced to a tremulous mass of seething steam, when the massive sea that enveloped coastline cities retreated from the hills and the Mediterranean once again became navigable...the "Searcher" traced the course of the crimson sail to where the vessel was found torn from its moorings, on a hillside near Karphi.

He climbed the rocky precipices that had escaped the deluge, sought guidance from villagers who had seen them pass during the night – a young girl with long, raven hair and her mysterious companion, who seemed cut from the grave. From there he followed a rugged pathway leading to an escarpment beneath Karphi. And here, carved in stone, were inscriptions from another time, an ancient monument commanding a secluded valley where ancestral Minoans live to this day. From there leads a faint trail, seldom followed, seldom trod...a place of antiquity. Here the searcher, a haggard man in tattered khakis, would search for his wife.

And thus commences the ending. The beginning answers to a wisp of steam surfacing the caldera of Santorini during the preceding year. There are three stories, in fact...curiously interwoven with the occult and an ironic twist of fate...of which the last can be told – but not explained.

CHAPTER 1

y late September, a boil of mud and sulfurous smoke announced a new arrival near the southern rim of the ancient caldera. Day by day it rose from the 1200 foot depth, until the seething mass broke surface in the early spring. Thus a boisterous monster was born to Santorini, with an awesome rumbling from her subterranean maw. A cindery cone rose steadily until it enveloped the shanks of Nea Kameni and the sister islet of Palaeo. On the eve of Easter the volatile thing had attained a height of 100 meters and displaced a cubic mile of its watery crib. Molten lava streaked its flanks, compounding layer upon layer, glowing ruby red by night as it tumbled to the boiling sea.

During the early dawn of Easter Sunday, a series of muffled explosions occurred. Then a geyser of fire erupted and flung flaming gut matter to the sky; the morning sun came to darkness in a pall of descending ash, interrupting the service of the Community Church. All became still as a drift of snow-white pumice swirled softly to the streets. Mass resumed on a gentle note, the townsfolk questing their beads.

At first the villagers of Thera were fascinated by the newborn volcano; wary but unafraid, despite the haze that filmed their groves and automobiles. Inns were filled to capacity as more and more tourists arrived to observe the pyrotechnics and sip the excellent wines.

Had not Nea Kameni calmed to a whimper when it erupted in 1950? Athens raised a cautionary warning, but tourists took little heed and the media was immersed in politics.

Others viewed the event more seriously. A learned group of meteorologists and volcanologists, attending a seminar in Geneva, expressed their concern to the United Nations, noting the possibility of a paroxysmal explosion if the volcano continued to rise, as well as the consequential spread of ash to the troposphere that would blot out the sun for years to come. A legacy of spectacular sunsets...of long winters and decimated crops.

By mid-April the magma chamber was expelling a 40,000-foot column of smoke and ash from its conical vent, forming an immense anvil head cloud that dispersed to the southeast over Egypt and the Sudan. The asheous fallout was of little concern in the eastern Aegean Sea, but the minute particles transcending the crop dependent sub-Sahara immediately raised eyelids in the Third World. And, when the stratospheric haze drifted west with the jet stream, there was further consternation in the mid-Caribbean. The expanding haze had little effect on mean temperatures at that moment, but the accelerating outflow of ash and the possibility of a magma water explosion of unthinkable magnitude, brought a degree of response from the UN.

An environmental studies group sponsored by a Third World committee — a splinter group drawn from the environmental and meteorological agencies — was accompanied by an immediate plea for funds. With the Arab bloc abstaining, a petition was sent to NASA requesting the services of a high-flying U-2, a non-military version equipped with dust-collecting pods, to sample the volume of ash from its source and determine its path over the sensitive Middle East, together with an "on-site" analysis of the fuming volcano by the learned group from Geneva.

* * * * * *

Project WHITE DOVE was hatched by the United nations in early May, when NASA made available a late model U-2 recalled for servicing after lengthy missions over volcanic Colombia and Mexico. The aircraft was a stretch-wing version of the original concept, highly modified to accommodate a raised rear cockpit with dual controls, equipped for high altitude screening with ash-collecting pods linked to sensoring devices, and an onboard computer, but not capable of in-flight refueling and a lengthy flight to the Aegean. It would be necessary to disassemble for transport by military airlift, together with a ground crew, wing hoists, and a 90-day supply of spares.

The ground crew would maintain the aircraft for the duration of its mission, the pilot drawn from NASA's resources, the project administered by the United Nations and supervised by a Third World appointee. Meteorological and volcanic research, however, would be programmed to include fact-finding missions of the far-reaching U-2.

The limitations of the administrative authority, however, were ill defined and bureaucratic ineptness would emerge in the months to come. The plum, of course, was the supervisory role, and initially the bickering was unanimous. The incessant haze over Africa, however, brought a subdued response. A Nigerian was appointed to the latter position when his government agreed to fund the ground operation. A Swedish volcanologist nominated to captain the research team, together with a Canadian meteorologist suggested by the group from Geneva. The Europeans insisting the in-flight observer be one of their own, a condition imposed by the Russians when the flight schedule, with its routing intersecting their former border with Iran, became generally known. A Polish meteorologist subsequently approved by the UN, although the conditions were amended to include a German technician who would monitor communications with the pilot in command.

Curiously, no objections were raised when the aircraft was closeted by Lockheed for wing removal, although the facility was adjacent to the highly secret "Skunk Works" and its pool of advanced technology. And no objections were voiced when the Aegean island of Kos was approved by the UN as its operational base, aside from a protest by the wary Turks who had ruled the island prior to the war of 1912.

Kos was selected for its non-military status and proximity to Santorini. The narrow, 112-kilometer island's northerly reach, penetrated the Turkish archipelago; its seaward flank lay 120 kilometers to the northeast of the volatile volcano. Since the prevailing winds were drawn to the southwest, the island was marginally apart from the soaring ash.

In ancient times, the golden years of Kos came to tragedy when Thera's (Santorini's) convulsions toppled the temples, wasted the groves and fouled the streets with pumice. The bulls offered to the sacrificial knife, their severed heads raised by pagan priests failing to placate the volcano, a failing compounded by terror during the ensuing fiery years, leading to the ultimate demand – human sacrifice.

The Phoenix-like glow from Thera was observable for months on end and from lands apart. As chronicled by the Egyptians, it possibly concurred with Moses' flight across the 'Sea of Reeds', although the biblical accounting differs by years. Historians believe the total wave that swept the marshlands and inundated the pursuing Egyptian chariotry resulted from the paroxysmal explosion of 1628 BC, the bright flash in the northern sky that decimated the Aegean.

Tremors preceding the catastrophe occurred over a period of years. The timing is obscure, but a Minoan temple at Arhannes in Crete was destroyed and ravished by fire. An archeological inspection of the ruins revealed the first

3

known evidence of human sacrifice...the bones of a young man on a slab of stone, his legs drawn and tied to his back, his carotid artery severed by a bronze knife.

The bones of a young girl were found by an adjacent wall; an attendant, perhaps...possibly the young man's betrothed, her presence unexplained. Subsequent findings revealed ornaments befitting a princess of high standing, priceless, intricately-fashioned jewelry secreted in a crevice by the dying girl's hand. Earrings of hammered gold, a serpent ring, and a necklace fastened to a miniature figure cast in gold – the likeness of a young girl with long braided hair, faceted with emeralds depicting her eyes. Eyes that sparkled with fury when brought to light, contemptuous of the beholders, glowering as if they guarded her grave.

The earrings and serpent's coil were retained by a collector of Minoan artifacts. A native Greek of Anatolian extraction, a well-intentioned man, he sponsored the findings while visiting the site when Santorini was clearing its throat. He was accompanied by his daughter, a pretty little girl of eight with startling green eyes and long braided hair caught with a scarf...a likeness that gave pause to the archeologists on site when the pendant was passed from the dig. The likeness was observed by the curious child, who was hurried away to field her dreams – dreams of a Minoan princess with eyes such as hers, a forbidding dream that endured throughout her childhood years when she was often mysteriously withdrawn.

Schooled in Switzerland and later at Berkeley to obtain a degree in economics (a degree that escaped her father who dealt in edible oils), she graduated with honors in June while project White Dove was resolved at the UN. Slender, with the height and poise of a mannequin, with classic features and long black hair, a sparkling personality and the ability to speak many languages, a teller of anecdotes spiked with expletives from dockside Piraeus. A superb athlete with an inherent interest in the sea to which she sometimes withdrew, she favored long walks beneath the cliffs at Big Sur – usually towards sunset when beach goers and surfers had returned from whence they came.

It was here, one late Sunday afternoon, that she chanced to meet the pilot selected to fly the U-2. A lone man seemingly engrossed with his thoughts, a shaggy dog bounded to greet him when he descended the pathway to the narrow stretch of beach. He was tall and gaunt, deeply tanned, with a hawk-like nose and a hank of sun-bleached hair, garbed in tattered shorts and skivvy shirt, but no necklaces dangling from his chest she was quick to note. The dog's owner, no doubt, although the animal had been into the trash bin when she parked her convertible atop the cliff.

4

Thirtyish, she thought, knotting a towel around her hips so as not to draw further attention to her brief bikini. Curious, but not the usual beach bum, she concluded. Quickening her pace, she indicate she wasn't to be followed, not wanting to engage in conversation. The shadowing twilight and deserted beach presented a compounding problem, however; aside from turning about, there was no alternate pathway for a graceful exit to the cliff and her gleaming red Mercedes. Moreover, she'd been unable to spring the rag top and left it ajar! 'God in heaven, the beastly thing's unlocked! My bag...my keys, did I leave them under the seat?' she fretted, loosening a torrent of expletives best left untold and fortunately unheard. 'Stupid Greek!' she chided herself, casting a nervous glance over her shoulder. 'Half-naked, no robe and...Jesus, I forgot my wallet! So what happens if he steals my car or intends to rape and rob me?' she gasped, looking about for a handy stick.

He'd made no attempt to follow or interfere with her privacy, she noticed, gathering her wits; hesitant to display anxiety much less make a bloody run for it! He'd maintained a respectful distance, at the moment casting a stick to the surf for the Labrador to retrieve, the delighted animal in flop-eared pursuit, grinning as Labs are prone to do, their antics far removed from her grievous thoughts.

The twosome were aware of her presence, however, the dog bounding alongside when she decided they were no threat and turned to retrace her footprints in the sand. His master offered a polite smile when their eyes met briefly...and held momentarily. 'Good grief, I believe we've met before!' she thought, puzzling an episode of years ago?

He called softly for the Lab to fetch the stick to hand. The receptive animal wagged gleefully, eyes alert when he pointed to the surf in her nearby proximity.

"Lordy!" Nina murmured, at odds with his lack of interest when she offered a redeeming smile, loosening her towel a hitch when he chanced to look back. 'He's either blind or I'm lacking', she determined, tossing her hair to display what she had.

His marksmanship was unerring, the spiraling stick glinting in the sun as it plunged to the sea. The Lab went airborne, as if shot from a gun, slashing the surf, utilizing his tail for a rudder when he emerged with his prize, which he immediately delivered to the young lady's feet. His tail wagged furiously as he cast an eye to gauge his master's approval of a mission well done!

Call it the name of the game, with improvisations, of course, but that's how they chanced to meet that fateful afternoon at Big Sur. The story is best told from the eyes of the beholder, however.

CHAPTER

t was a last second decision to turn off the highway at Big Sur that fateful Sunday afternoon. Normally the cliff-top area was cluttered with vans and two-wheelers, but the sun was waning and the lot relatively clear aside from a departing jitney bus and a low-slung convertible parked by the path to the beach. The convertible was a spanking new Mercedes, its rag top unsecured and half-mast I noted when I drew alongside. The jitney long gone when I exchanged my longies for a pair of shorts, intending to wade the surf and give my future judicious thought.

Flying part-time with NASA, I had the weekend free from test-hopping a two-seat version of the U-2 at Moffet Field pending a contract with the UN to contemplate – essentially a three month contractual stint with project White Dove in the Aegean. My part involved high altitude ash collecting data from the super-active volcano on the island of Santorini, inclusive of tracking the drift over Africa and the Middle East. The risky part necessitating low-altitude close-up scans of the volcano's cone velocity and temperature readings for the scientists in the field.

I also was to accommodate a rear-seat observer, a renowned Polish meteorologist lately appointed by the committee at the UN…at the moment standing by at Mountain View, waiting on my decision to come to terms with the UN. To that end, the Air Force had agreed to provide a two-seat hybrid version of their current U-2R, duly equipped with an updated engine and extended wing tips; at the moment under wraps at Lockheed, but not dissimilar to the U–2 I'd test-hopped the previous day. Further, I was to give the "doctor" a series of familiarization rides to acquaint him with the basics and confinement of a pressure suit, necessary above 40,000 feet. For my part, the raised cockpit two-seater was a brand new experience; hence, my test flight to determine how it flew. Later, the weight and drag of the immense underwing pods would prove to be another factor; the hybrid's untried engine, yet another.

My immediate concern, however, was an unsolicited early morning call from my former commander during Desert Storm.

Wounded in combat, disqualified from high-performance jets, I'd opted for a civilian career, although the love of flying was ingrained in my soul. Later, wounds on the mend, I'd rehabilitated myself sufficiently to qualify with the U-2 and fly high altitude volcanic research for NASA. My motivation conceivably of interest when I was nominated to White Dove. My wartime familiarization with the Middle East, as well as my civilian status, most likely the deciding factors. Available U-2 pilots mostly retired Air Force types, and the project was apolitical!

White Dove held my keen interest; my motivation was the opportunity to join and participate with a group of learned scientists in the Aegean. The volatile volcano was a challenge to all parties, a dedication of unselfish services; so be it. But now there was apparent interest of a high-ranking general in the Pentagon.

Classmate of my dad (they'd flown together in 'Nam), he'd advised on my service with NATO, saved my life over Iraq. But I hadn't seen the old rascal since he pinned the Purple Heart on my pillow at Walter Reed. And now, years later, when I'd made my own way, what was the underlying motive for his sudden interest in White Dove?

Such were my dithers when I locked my Porsche, noting the status of the Mercedes alongside; the beach bag on its seat, the keys in the ignition! Its owner, apparently trusting all to luck, was possibly nearby, although there was no presence on the path ascending the cliff. The surfers were long gone, but a nondescript van cruised the lot, pausing by the lead to the highway. The red convertible an apt target, I thought.

Presumptuous, perhaps, although I was met by a friendly Labrador on the beach I assumed was companion to the convertible. Abandoning all for a swim, most likely...although he had no collar and his hide was a tangle of burrs, a creature of neglect, judging from the condition of the car. Then again, possibly a stray? Playful, however, his yellowish eyes pleading for a game of sticks, narrowing when he dropped a well-chewed morsel by my side. No harm, I thought, looking about for his owner. The gleeful animal streaked the surf when I hurled his stick between a pair of combers, my attention given to a solitary figure in the distance.

Up the beach, silhouetted by the sun, a lanky, solitary girl was striding the stretch where it narrowed by the escarpment. The dog's owner, I assumed, although she was seemingly disinterested or unaware of his antics when the Lab

7

crested an incoming roller and fetched his stick to my hand. Content to remain by my side, he showered brine and teased for another try. The Mercedes a lapse of memory, if she'd left it in his care!

Long of limb, superbly tanned, wearing a red bikini partly draped with a towel, she was seemingly absorbed with thoughts apart. Her long raven hair glistened recently of the sea, casually gathered to her neck with a flouncy silken scarf. Her facial features obscured by the sun, although I was aware of her golden earrings when she chanced to look back, obviously startled, hitching the towel around her waist. Frowning when our eyes met, it was as if my presence was neither wanted nor appreciated.

Frightened, I assumed, sensing her quandary when she eyed the cliffs. Myself at odds when she made no attempt to summon the dog, and not wanting to frighten her further, I shrugged and returned my attention to the puzzled Labrador, his curiosity seemingly kin to mine, begging to get on with our game. 'So, what the hell!' I decided, determining to try a deflection shot before she scurried for the hill. The animal perked his ears while I flung the stick sideways, boomerang style, to where he'd gain it in her proximity. Off again, full body in the surf, no longer puzzled when he emerged from the boil; he dutifully deposited his gamy stick at her feet!

"Haven't you the sense to rein your dog?" she shouted, pointing to a weathered sign, appraising my appearance in general terms but not retreating, her chin jutting angrily...until I assured her the dog did not belong to me.

Most likely my NASA skivvy shirt from Moffet Field helped matters along, her eyes softening when she gandered my limp while I hastened from the beach. Also noticeably at ease when she bent to tousle the Lab's floppy ears.

"Lost or abandoned?" she commented, eyeing me curiously with her startling green eyes. Her accent was "pukka" English, not American, although she had the tan of a native Californian.

Tall and exquisite, with wide-sprung legs and sexy hips, her ample breasts tempted her bikini's close tether. Her emerald eyes slanted somewhat, not quite oriental, but in keeping with her classic profile and sensuous lips, her sparkling teeth no less an asset. Possibly Greek, I thought, wondering if we might have met somewhere before?

"Most likely starved," she added, testing the Lab's depleted hindquarters. "Might you have thought to bring a sandwich, or a snack from Seven Eleven?" she added mischievously, dimpling her square-toothed smile.

"Not really," I said, sensing her warmth and laid-back sense of humor. "But there's a trash barrel up the cliff...perhaps we could sort it out?"

"My, what a sordid thought!" she countered, arching her eyebrows. "Wretched thing, hungry to the bone, shivering from the sea...obviously abandoned and needing a home! In fact, I've a blanket in my car should you decide to take him in?"

"Red convertible, California plates?"

"My graduation present, no less! Lordy, don't tell me I left it unlocked?"

"Keys on the seat, top half-mast, beach bag and blanket rear slab...which I'll be pleased to fetch if you insist?"

"God in heaven, my wallet! Did you find that as well?"

"Stashed the lot in the boot! The rag top an easy target, what with a van cruising nearby."

"Lordy, you must think I'm a bloody fool! Might you have thought to bring along my keys?" she stammered, her expressive eyes softening somewhat.

"You'll find your keys under the mat! Like I had no way of knowing if you belonged to the Mercedes, until you offered the blanket and set me right! The initials on the beach bag of little help, assuming they also belong to you?"

Station break whilst she studied my face, my scruffy T-shirt from Moffet Field...my heart quickening when she tossed her raven hair and displayed a mischievous grin. Her eyes straightforward to mine, seemingly allowing a moment of trust.

"NHM? Short for Nina Helena Maris, if you'd chosen to inspect my wallet! I'm a graduate student at Berkeley...a Greek national with a Green Card, although I spread my time between Athens and my parent's home in the Bahamas. And I do believe we've met, long ago, but I can't rightly recall where or when? I also have a tendency to forget my belongings when I hike the beach at sunset to clear my mind! Now then," she furthered, her emerald eyes softening again, "now that you've appeared out of nowhere and set me right, I also have a right to inquire your name and from whence you came?"

Her surname lofted a memory of a braided youngster at Lyford Cay whilst I was recovering from my wartime wounds, but that was eons ago and no way she could be the beautiful girl that set my heart straight that wondrous afternoon at Big Sur.

"Keith Slater, Nina...moderate means, rental condo in New York, monthly payments for my car. And now you know my statistics! I fly part-time for NASA, high-altitude volcanic research over Central America and the like. I'm also acquainted with an excellent restaurant in Palo Alto, if you'll do me the honor to have dinner there?"

She eyed me keenly, her interest obviously drawn, but not by my choice of restaurants, apparently.

"Volcanic research? Such as that hideous monster in the Aegean? No doubt you're aware of the bloody thing! We've family in Athens and they're worried there might be a Plinian eruption, scared shitless in fact! We've olive groves at Naxos and I was recently there with papa...our seedlings blighted with ash, to say nothing of the countryside! We could see its horrendous smoke on the horizon, its fire at night, but there's little attention from the media aside from a columnist with The Examiner," she added, visibly shaken by her thoughts.

Typically Greek, she was straightforward and not lacking for words to express her concern for the Aegean. Nor were her fears unfounded. Fortunately, I'd done my homework and the scientists in Geneva held like concern. I was hesitant to remark on my pending affiliation with the project, however, although my interest was whetted when she mentioned having close family on the island of Kos; a maiden aunt she'd promised to visit later on.

"Quaint place," she said, not knowing my state of mind while she described the Crusaders' fortress and her auntie's nearby cottage. Our conversation drifted to her childhood experiences at Arhannes in Crete. Nina gave free run to her innermost thoughts while we walked together, Lab by our side, the sun a red ball on the horizon. My spirits soared when she offered her hand along the way, warm and complacent with mine...When the beach went no further, we reluctantly turned back.

Seemingly at ease with our companionship, Nina deliberately slowed our pace to disclose the source of the mysterious dreams she'd been plagued with since childhood. To that end, she chose her solitary walks when her dreams recurred, and she sought the solitude of Big Sur to fathom the depths of her mind. Most likely my research with NASA was a catalyst to her unwinding. Her chums at Berkeley disinterested, or out of touch with events in the Aegean.

Intelligent and low key, not prone to rambling with the sun low on the horizon, she explained her dreams were drawn from her emotional experiences as a child in the lowlands of Crete. Her father, a dilettante archeologist with an interest in Bronze Age Minoans, had funded the dig at Arhannes...taken Nina and her mother along when they discovered the ruins of a palace and probed what lay beneath.

"We stayed aboard the Helena," she explained, the 'Helena' being a motor ketch named for her mother. Nina's mother was of English extraction, her grandfather the former ambassador to Greece. "Papa came from nothing," she continued, pausing to flip the stick again to the sea. "In his early twenties he owned and captained a coastal tanker, later developed our olive groves and a small fleet to transport the oils. A seaman at heart, he's always had this thing about the Minoan culture. Believed his family blood strain was seeded from Anatolia, that his ancestors founded the Minoan civilization in the Aegean long before the birth of Jesus of Nazareth, near about the time the Egyptians were raising pyramids to entomb their kings.

"Hence his interest, Keith. The Minoan civilization was destroyed by catastrophe, as you know, but their shattered palaces spurred the legends of mythical Greece, although Greek they were not. A unique race apart, according to Papa. Their frescoes and artifacts the only evidence of their being. Their inscriptions and language lack a Rosetta stone to identify, apart from their lifestyle, when the Greeks were Stone Age on the archipelago.

"Their lifestyle was evident from the dig at Arhannes," she continued. "Also at Akrotiri, when I visited with Papa the previous year. But at Arhannes there was evidence of their fears...the first known indication of human sacrifice, the active volcano at Thera a hideous thing to behold. Erupting day and night, months or years on end, who knows? The poor souls were obviously terrified when they resorted to the thing they did...

"So maybe you'll understand the reason for my fears, Keith. Thirty-five hundred years later, the volcanic scenario is much the same. Tremors in the Aegean, Thera's rumbling once again. At Arhannes, Papa said there was evidence of massive tremors, although the temple's beams were charred by fire, most likely set by their oil lamps...not the Plinian explosion, as they first thought.

"Beneath the debris they discovered the skeletons, the remains of a young man on a sacrificial slab, a bronze knife nearby, a shattered vase by an altar containing a residue of human blood. In a far corner, the skeleton of a young girl, her hand by a crevice in the wall, apparently alive when the walls collapsed. The young man's betrothed, I'll forever believe!"

"Not a pleasant sight for a child of eight. Did you identify with the girl, perhaps?"

Nina frowned, not wanting to commit.

"At Arhannes I'd witnessed the scene of factual findings...the Minoans in real life, their wondrous lifestyle, and the dreadful fears they'd expressed at the end. The evidence was there, so like the frescoes Dr. Marinatos uncovered at Akrotiri. I was mesmerized, Keith. They were so bloody real! The young man and the girl waiting their turn in the afterlife. I was reminded of the legend of Deucalion and Pyrrha – when I was led away in tears – of Prometheus' warning of an impending deluge when they sought refuge in the ark. I dreamt of them that very night, a wondrous dream then, later a recurring nightmare, but I'll not allude to that any further."

"So maybe you elaborated; did you bend your books at school?"

"The classics, yes, but I became a non-believer when I studied Papa's notes. The Greeks were barbarians, Keith. Warlike, unkempt, until they subdued a dying civilization. The seeding of their mythology a Minoan thing, not Grecian until the golden fables were glorified a thousand years later, their wispy past drawn from half truths by the scholars. Plato, for instance, fabilized Atlantis from an accounting by his grand uncle Solon, a dealer in olive oils who'd visited Egypt and retold a story attributed to their Saite priests. So maybe Plato elaborated when he described a civilization he'd never seen."

"Do you consider yourself a Minoan throwback? You seem to have a thing about aboriginal Greeks."

"Possibly. My eyes are green, my mother's blue and Papa's somewhere in between. Greek I am, although sometimes I sense the 'in between'," she added, fingering her earrings. "Why else would I fantasize the fears they held so many years ago?"

"Association with the artifacts, most likely. Shall we discuss the possibility of dinner for two?" She grinned at the note, tossed her lovely hair aside. Hand in hand, we ascended the pathway to the cliff, the shaggy dog at our heels, the depth of her reflections as yet untold.

The sun had slipped from the horizon when we reached the summit, the golden sky in vivid contrast with the dark gray sea – a typical California sunset. But not for long, with darkness fast approaching and a chilly breeze lofting from the cliffs.

Sparse words passed between us while we retrieved Nina's keys and unlocked the trunk of her car, awkward words when she slipped into a loose-hanging shirt and shorts from her bag. Myself in a quandary...was it possible I might hold this beautiful creature to my heart? Or might she haul off and clobber where it hurt?

"So I did most of the talking," she declared, adjusting her sandals. "I'm prone to that! So let's wait dinner until Saturday night. I must bend to my exams until then. Zonicle's my favorite restaurant in Silicon Valley. Do you know where it is?"

"Approximately."

"Say around eight then, but call me to confirm, Keith. My numbers aren't listed, but I'll jot them down if you tend to forget."

We located her note pad in the trunk with a flashlight from my Porsche. Nina in a hurry to be off to study for her exams. Unable to prompt her ragtop, her exasperation was voiced in dockside Greek.

"Fucking fuse!" she exclaimed. "Same damn thing when I went to the beach! Might you have a sweater, Keith? I'm shivering cold!"

In the end I loaned her my A-2 flight jacket. The Lab had sought the sanctuary of my Porsche when I reached inside. Ready for a quiet nap, his work done for the day, Nina nodded approval when I volunteered to take him along. Her landlord not keen on shaggy animals -- neither two nor four legged varieties she implied.

I saw her off with a long, enduring kiss, the scent of her lavender on my cheek when she spun gravel towards the highway, her scarf trailing behind. Tail lights aglow when she stopped briefly to wave from the intersection, disappearing with a beep of her horn.

Staggered by the hour we'd shared, more so by the remarkable twist of luck that caused me to pull off the highway that unforgettable afternoon, I spurred the Porsche to my digs at Mountain View. My contract with the UN decided when she mentioned visiting Kos when the Helena was off charter. As yet unaware of my pending contract or my itinerary once approved.

Unfortunately, I'd wadded her telephone numbers with my currency; the slip of paper discarded with my receipt when I stopped briefly at a convenience store for a beer, a sandwich for the Lab.

* * * * *

I faxed my contractual acceptance to the UN early Monday morning, not certain if White Dove was in operation at the time. The dog, my constant companion when I checked in with NASA at Moffet Field, was happy with a bowl of Gravy Train and the air-conditioned lounge. Nina's numbers of immediate concern when I retrieved my shorts from the laundry and turned the pockets inside out. Pacific Bell of no help, her numbers unlisted at her request.

At noon I met Dr Gomulaka for lunch at the Officer's Club across the field. Gomulaka, the appointee meteorologist, designated to be my rear-seat observer once we were based in the Aegean. A pleasant type, fortyish, short and stocky, with a neatly clipped beard. Polish, but apt with English; we got along immediately. A member of the group from Geneva, he'd recently arrived from Warsaw to undertake his physical, inclusive of the altitude test chamber at Beale Air Force Base and a mini flight aboard the 'wild horse' simulator -- the acid test for air sickness, which he passed with no problem.

In the days to come, I gave the doctor ten hours of familiarization flights in the two-seater U-2, capped off with a high-altitude flight above 40,000 feet, where we would wear space suits similar to the astronauts. At the doctor's insistence, an off-the-shelf suit in the process of refabrication was tailor made to fit his stature. A non-pilot, his familiarization to acquaint him with the U-2's mannerisms at low and high altitudes, not to fly the bloody thing...although he'd gain sufficient feel to maintain power off descent and possibly a survivable crash landing in lieu of ejecting should the pilot become incapacitated. To that end, I sent him along with a declassified copy of the U-2's flight manual to study at his hotel.

Dr Gomulaka in turn presented me with a sheaf of notes from his colleagues who would join us in the field, an update of the volcano's activity from Athens, and the heavily worded synopsis from Dr Sigurdesson, the group's mainstay geophysicist/volcanologist, warning of an imminent paroxysmal explosion should the moon tides cause a rupture in the volcano's venting tube and magma chamber.

I received my confirmation from the UN Tuesday morning, with a copy note to White Dove, which had yet to establish its infrastructure or a viable office. Most likely waiting the arrival of Dr Nokomo, the project administrator from Nigeria.

My contract binding, I spent the afternoon examining charts of the areas we were to reconnoiter with our dust-collecting U-2. Later, I collected Gomulaka from his hotel and we walked around NASA's current U-2, inspecting the ash-collecting version I'd recently flown over Colombia. Fascinated by the updated electronics array, he spent an hour or so in the cockpit on a question and answer basis, making copious notes, admitting to reading glasses.

The following day the doctor underwent a lengthy session in the U-2 simulator. An instructor coaching whilst he familiarized himself with the controls, saving hours in the air. Basic maneuvers mostly, simulated from level flight at 10,000 feet, a video screen providing the horizon. No landings or take-offs; the simulator's primary purpose to provide a close-up instrument orientation given the conditions for an instrument landing. The sensitive controls sufficient to allow 'feel' of the U-2 in flight, with an occasional air bump thrown in so he wouldn't think it a piece of cake.

Later I placed a call to Berkeley and was put on to a crusty lady with negative thoughts, when I asked if she would put me in touch with Nina, repeating her full name and she placed me on indefinite hold.

"Sorry, Miss Maris is taking her exams," another voice replied when I tried again. "You might try her at home after five," she offered, adding that it was against regulations to divulge students' numbers or addresses short of an emergency. Emergency for my part, but I didn't want to frighten Nina unnecessarily! Maris? I mused again, thinking back to a misadventure of recent years. The scrawny girl in pigtails who'd slammed the gate in my face when her daddy crashed his Mercedes and I gave him a lift to Lyford Cay? Has to be, I thought, remembering her angry green eyes and unfounded accusations.'

Determined to give it a try, I dialed Bahamas information. The operator immediately responded, yes, there were two Maris listed in Nassau. Cable Beach or Lyford Cay? I dialed the latter, calculating the three hour time difference when a native Bahamian picked up.

"Yeah, man, got the right place, but Missy 'way to school! Might axe who's callin'?" he questioned politely. I handed off my name, inquiring if she attended school in California.

"Yes, suh, but don't rightly know where she stay. Have her daddy's numbers handy, but come to think they's travelin' overseas. Best to call Noo York, suh! Office open 'til five."

I declined the idea, thinking it unwise. Gave him my phone numbers in the event she called in.

"Ain't likely," he said. "seems I recollect your name, though, Mistah Slater. Same party have cottage Cable Beach?" I admitted to that, although I'd leased it out a couple of years back. Inquired of the weather, missing the warm clear sea and groupers swimming amongst the reefs.

"All the same, Mistah Slater. Most time sun, sometimes rain. Pleased if'n you reach Neenie say Audley remark everyt'ing all right at home!"

Frustrated, but satisfied Nina was one and the same, I researched Palo Alto's yellow pages for a lead, recalling we were to confirm our dinner date at Zonicle's for Saturday night. Might she have made reservations, or inquired if I had? Zonicle's listing paramount: Four stars, offering Greek cuisine and a splendid view of the valley. Reservations only, dinner jackets suggested, casual dress accepted in the upstairs bar.

The morning manager picked up. "Nina Maris? Yes, of course!" he said. "Just a moment," he added, scuffling with his book. "Yes, I have it here, reservations for two, Saturday night at eight. In fact we've reserved her favorite window table. Might you be Mr. Slater, sir?"

"Affirmative," I replied, inquiring whether he might have Nina's telephone number's at hand?

"No, sir, we're not permitted to divulge our patrons' telephone numbers, sir! I suggest you try information, but I'll make a note that you called, Mr. Slater.

Might you be late?"

"Negative," I allowed, determined to be on hand promptly at eight, with jacket as suggested.

* * * * * *

The doctor and I met later in the day for a scheduled interview by a columnist from the examiner, an interview I'd nearly forgotten due to searching for my blazer. Project White Dove apparently gathering interest from the media. I suspected Dr Nokomo's public relations staff when his status was mentioned frequently while we were video taped and photographed alongside a vintage U-2. Gomulaka smiling with his flight helmet underarm, his glasses reflecting the sun. Myself ill at ease in cut-off shorts, but fortunately we were imaged from waist up.

The columnist, an environmentalist of sorts, got along immediately with Dr Gomulaka. Fortyish, with a bushy beard, his bifocal spectacles perched on his nose, he wore a safari jacket and a fisherman's cap, which was somewhat odd but not out of keeping with Gomulaka's mismatched socks and flannel shirt. The twosome intellectually bent, obviously unconcerned with whatever came first from the rack. Well traveled, a freelance journalist with the International Herald Tribune on occasion, he'd recently returned from Egypt where he'd learned of the UN's project in the Aegean.

He was well informed, acquainted with Santorini's history and current status; describing its volatile activity and the possibility of a paroxysmal explosion such as occurred in 1628 BC, with no attempt to disguise his concern. His apt remarks provided a running commentary for the video screening while he produced an illustrated map of the Aegean. Doctor Gomulaka added comments pursuant to the present outfall of sulfurous ash, the project's prime concern he noted, not the copious public relations release promoting Dr Nokomo's agricultural reforms in Nigeria and equatorial Africa.

The columnist commenting about the dangers involved with close-up viewing of the volcano whilst we monitored the temperature of the cone with our infra-red sensors, the U-2's wingtip barely an eyelash from the unholy upheaval. My interest further drawn when he produced a recent photo of the airstrip at Antimahia, my first sight of the project's 'operational base' on Kos. An active bulldozer in the process of lengthening the facility for our needs.

Once the video crew had packed their gear and disappeared, the columnist decided to join us at Hennessey's tavern to further our conversation over a beer.

The Lab, shampooed and rid of his fleas, my self-appointed guardian since the afternoon at Big Sur, quick to bound aboard the Porsche's rear seat!

'Hennessey's', a popular bistro at Mountain View, its woodsy tavern a gathering spot for off-duty pilots from Moffet Field; Hennessey, a retired Air Force type, commanding the bar. The woody walls decorated with photographs of vintage aircraft and military pilots of multiple wars (collectors' items but not for sale). His enormous fireplace and hearty meals a draw for the kindred souls from Mountain View.

Gomulaka, pleased with his simulator ride, at ease with the surroundings and a stein of lager, sat ear to ear with the columnist whilst I queried my answering machine for word from Nina...with negative response. There was, however, a congratulatory message from Major General T.S. O'Brien having to do with my assignment with White Dove? The Lab, content with a sausage and a saucer of beer, asleep at my feet when I reminded the doctor of his early morning moment of truth! Gomulaka, buoyant but steady on his feet when I dropped him to his hotel.

* * * * * *

Dawn was appropriate for Gomulaka's solid-ass two-hour familiarization ride over the Pacific. Heat thermals not yet a factor when we suited up in the change room, Gomulaka wearing a standard flight suit when we were belted aboard the Air force tandem seat U-2, a goodwill loan from Beale. We communicated on intercom whilst taxiing to the business end of the runway to wait clearance from the tower. A pair of jeeps collected our pogo struts (wingtip wheels) when we rotated from the strip.

Takeoff with the unwieldy U-2 was not altogether an easy go, the high-riding rudder demanding heavy input when I juiced the power package upon centering the strip. The lightly loaded U-2 rotated immediately, airborne with a roll of 600 feet and wanting to climb. Sensing his hand on the stick, I reminded the doctor to contain his feet from the rudder while we climbed over the Pacific, choosing to level off at 20,000 to avoid commercial traffic in the area.

Our air work was of a basic nature -- shallow turns and the like I'd learned from my dad years before -- 60 degree turns in sequence, reminding the doctor to maintain altitude until we blunted our thrust wash. The altitude factor difficult to contain, the U-2 more or less reacted as a powered glider, incessantly wanting to climb. The two of us on oxygen while we tried a series of mushy power stalls. Later we climbed to 40,000 feet and leveled off. My intention to acquaint Gomulaka with the feel of high altitude, where the U-2 flew like a gentle bird; also, to acquaint him with the auto pilot we'd utilize later on.

Our descent another matter, with the doctor gasping on intercom while we spiraled over the coast with our speed brakes and gear extended. At low altitude the U-2 flew like a barn door – a bastard to contain when we crossed the threshold at 70 knots. Our ground crew racing alongside with their jeeps, calling our altitude by radio until we stalled and our gear grounded the macadam. The rudder and ailerons ineffective until the pogo struts were reattached , stabilizing our wingtips, short of grounding their skids. The ashen-faced doctor staring fretfully from my mirror while we were drawn to the ramp.

* * * * *

Gomulaka was not averse to a beer at Hennessey's later in the day. I remember the occasion well, recalling how it all began. A 'two-steiner' at the most, Gomulaka was on to his second when he encountered his former classmate from Warsaw at the bar. Stash Obolensky, a tall, friendly character of sorts, a computer analyst in Silicon Valley, had recognized the doctor from our video screening on local TV.

The back-slapping pair, grinning from ear to ear, exchanged memories in Polish while I routinely checked my answer phone. The Lab, with his saucer of brew, had become a member of Hennessey's family of friends, bounding to the Porsche when Obolensky saw Gomulaka to the door. The pair would meet again at Hennessey's in days to come, although I wasn't present when Stash allowed to the reason for his presence at Mt. View.

Our air work continued much the same. Friday we rotated to midday to acquaint Gomulaka with the thermals over northern California and a roundabout scan of volcanic Mt. St. Helen's in its dormant phase.

Not so Santorini! Molten lava cascading her shanks, she'd showered the village of Thera with pumice and rocks, loosing a series of massive tremors to awaken Athens and Rhodos, reminding of her proximity. The morning newscast supplemented with videos of a stratospheric column of smoke.

Gomulaka commented of this while we scheduled his flights for the remainder of the week.

"Frankly, I fear the worst," he said, producing a fax transmissions he'd received from Geneva and Athens earlier in the day. "There is definite indication of increasing cone velocity. Best we proceed to Kos as quickly as possible, Keith. Otherwise our efforts may be for naught."

18

He had yet to undertake his high-altitude familiarization (above 40,000 feet) where we'd wear the ungainly pressure suits in part to acquaint him with the ponderous gloves he'd require to conduct his research. He also needed exposure to the necessary facts of U-2 life...our liquid food and body waste disposal during a ten or twelve hour flight span.

Briefly inspecting his newly arrived gear, the doctor begged off for the remainder of the day; skipping Hennessey's to call his wife in Poland, catching a ride while I checked my mail at operations.

A telephone message in my box caught my attention, but it was not what I'd hoped for. The message, from Air Force operations across the way, indicated I was to contact the tower before five. An Air Force sergeant picked up when I phoned from the desk. Apparently Nina had managed to contact the tower, and they'd taped her conversation as a matter of form.

"Man, she was really pissed off!" the sergeant said. "Like she reached operations, thinking you were Air Force, so the Captain switched her to the tower, thinking it was an emergency, knowing you were in the air with that fella from the UN."

"So what did she say?"

"I'll feed it back, Keithy, but you ain't gonna like it!" he added, prompting the recording. The background chatter indicating Nina was at school.

"Have you a Major Keith Slater thereabouts?" she inquired, obviously referring to the name patch on the front side of the jacket I'd loaned at Big Sur.

"Keithy flies for NASA, sweetie...like they're on the opposite side of the field."

"Don't you dare address me as such!" she snapped with her icy british accent. "I'm not his sweetie, you asshole!"

"Sorry, got me with that one! Keithy's ex-Air Force, Lady Thatcher. Flies U-2s for NASA, like he was off at 1200 with a fella from the UN."

"U-2s?"

"Affirmative! The U-2's a high-flyer and trips volcanoes, like that firecracker in Greece. We can cycle their frequency," he offered. "No sweat, they're flyin' close in...180 miles out on our scan."

"Heavens no, it's not that urgent! But then, if he's that available he should have called! Furthermore," she added, her tone frosty, "I'd be pleased if you would tell him Nina's had it! And I'm returning his jacket UPS!" There was a short pause, the muffled roar of a turbo jet exerting reverse thrust on the runway.

"Cool it, sweetheart! I'm not about to lay a heavy on Keithy!" the sergeant snapped back. "Have you fanned the Examiner lately? Like the morning edition, section B?"

"Not really," Nina retorted. "Now, if you'll accept my apology, I've better things to do!"

"Okay, so do your homework, baby! Keith's respected hereabouts!" Nina apparently had more to say, but the sergeant hung up.

"Man, I'd hose the package in a pail before you open it!" he commented. "Like she had herself a hissy fit, Keithy, usin' words I ain't never heard before! Greek, I take it?" I agreed to that.

"Did you catch her numbers?"

"No, man, sounded like she was on a pay phone. Inquirin' around for change."

Curious, of course, I picked up a copy of The Examiner from a newsstand, scanned the front page and flipped to section B — and there we were, a four-column picture of Gomulaka and myself standing next to the U-2. I was in definite need of a haircut, the doctor gripping his helmet as if we'd recently arrived from outer space.

Datelined Moffet Field, the caption read: Ex-Air Force pilot volunteers for hazardous high-altitude research over the eastern Mediterranean. The doctor was identified as Dr George Gomulaka, the esteemed Polish meteorologist who will monitor the volcanic haze over the Middle East from their highly-modified U-2.

Mid-text, an apparently post-dated press release from the UN included a brief summary of Santorini's recent activity and the concern expressed by a group of environmental scientists attending a conference in Geneva. Their findings resulted in the appointment of an environmental studies team for on-site analysis. Obviously P.R., the article dealt at length with White Dove's infrastructure, emphasizing the credentials of Dr Jomo Nokomo, the renowned Nigerian agriculturist, authorized by the UN to supervise the project's logistics from the capital city of Kos. More to the point, the columnist's personal interview with Gomulaka (no mention of Hennessey's, I noticed). The doctor expressed his anxiety for the populace of the Aegean area should the volcano turn Plinian (the terminology drawn from Pliny the Elder's description of the paroxysmal explosion at Pompeii, later told by his son, Pliny the Younger; the elder was asphyxiated by the fumes.)

The article terminated with a brief synopsis of myself: Severely wounded in combat, Slater overcame his injuries to fly privately in the Bahamas. An Academy graduate, the ex-major pursued a career in construction engineering. Honing his skills as a jet pilot, Slater joined NASA on a part-time basis, piloting U-2s over volcanic Mexico and Colombia, a voluntary endeavor considered favorably by the selection committee at the UN.

The ex-major, consumed with frustration, returned to his flat to await Nina's package of rejection!

* * * * *

Saturday morning, NASA's operations received the package from UPS. Nina had checked the address, not offering hers, but paying the extra charge for Saturday delivery. She'd apparently worn the jacket to class, judging from a library slip in the side pocket, together with a wad of Kleenex scented with her lavender, and a match folder from Zonicle's.

Promptly at eight that evening, I parked the Porsche in Zonicle's commodious lot. Lowering the windows to benefit the Lab, I shouldered my blazer and checked the rooms inside.

And there she was, filmed in a red silk dress to her lovely knees, a matching scarf caught in her hair. Ignoring my presence when I waved from the bar, she was seated with a group of five and a magnum of wine. Graduate types, judging from their newly sprung beards and corduroys. They seemed to be pleasant chaps, obviously friends, apparently surprised when I approached their table and Nina deliberately turned her back.

Baffled, I horsed a chair at a nearby table, waiting patiently while she capped her Greek anecdote with a dockside expletive. The grads bent with laughter while I jarred her chair with my size 12 shoe. Startled, Nina spun about to skewer me with her defiant green eyes.

"So what's your problem?" she said. "The gentlemen's loo is past the bar, but there's a bed of roses outside!"

"I stopped on my way in." I said.

"Then perhaps you should see a urologist!"

"Come off it, Nina! I thought we had a date tonight."

"Heavens! What made you think that? You seem to know my name, however. Did you bribe the maitre d'?"

"I lost your numbers and your phone's unlisted. Have you had a problem with Pacific Bell?"

"With jocks I do!"

Weary of the game, I got to my feet. The grads exchanged glances, but Nina relented.

"I read The Examiner, Keith. We discussed the bloody volcano but you never mentioned the UN nor the cottage you inhabited near Lyford Cay!"

"Who told you that?"

"Our gardener! Have you forgotten the day Papa was smashed and you dropped him off at our gate? I remembered your silly grin when I saw your picture in The examiner."

"Nick's daughter...figured as much!"

"Plus ten and wary! The gardener warned me about the likes of you!"

"Your gardener's a shrink?"

"He said you staged orgies at your cottage on Saturday nights. For shame! You had a nice face...were your orgies much fun?" I grinned.

"Sundays were better. We screened porno and gave prizes for acrobatics."

"Good heavens! Is that why you limp?"

"Your table is ready, ma'am," the maitre d' interrupted with an oily smile. "Has the gentleman arrived? Should I hold the wine?" Nina blushed, the grads raised their glasses and cheered.

"A magnum for the gentlemen and Taittinger for the madam and myself," I said. The maitre d' fluttered his menu.

"Yes, of course, sir! And tonight, I suggest our Arni Avgolemono with a feta cheese salad on the side."

* * * * * *

Nina did not return to her apartment that night, nor the following night, nor did I to mine. She had foreseen the possibility and brought an overnighter in the trunk of her car, leaving the Mercedes in Zonicle's care. And somewhere down the coast we encountered a lovely inn, a veranda suite with a view of the silvery pacific, a splendid enclosure set privately apart with a low-burning fire to void the nightly chill. The Lab free to roam the beach, but not to wander far.

Continents away, 7000 miles to the east, Volcano Santorini loosed a dazzling display of pyrotechnics, showering the cliffside village of Thera with sulfurous rock and ash. Athens and Crete, the entire eastern Aegean, were jolted with convulsive shock waves from its epicenter, crevicing an orgasm of molten lava from its flanks to the steaming sea; quieting at dawn. Unfortunately, the seething monster was not yet asleep.

Monday, cruel Monday, did not lack for a tender departing kiss. Nina returned to Berkeley to gauge the results of he final exams, hopefully sufficient for a master's degree in economics. For myself, the good doctor peering from his helmet at 40,000 feet.

Gomulaka had the aptitude; the makings (in time) of a good pilot...exercised

22

good judgement and had a natural feel for the controls, which eased the mind. His stability a prime factor; a dependable observer was mandatory during our hazardous flights over the Aegean. He performed beautifully, obviously pleased with himself when I signed his log book the following day, justifiably proud of his 16 hours flight time, went to Hennessey's to celebrate.

Nina joined us later for a grinder and beer, meeting Gomulaka for the first time. And later, Stash Obolensky arrived for the occasion. He seemed at odds, however, bending Gomulaka's ear, Gomulaka frowning in return. I would have reason to recall the significance of their conversation in later weeks. The Lab, fast becoming a bar regular, an integral part of the celebration we scheduled for the following night.

A farewell party in honor of Gomulaka's return to Poland, including a pre-paid long-distance call to his wife, together with a video copy of our U-2 interview, the latter recapped in Polish. Lastly, the Lab given a proper name – Hennessey the elder officiating with a saucer of Heineken that the Lab lapped contentedly, ears perked when he was proclaimed 'Hennessey the Wagger' forevermore.

Following Nina's graduation ceremony, an announcement appeared in the society section of the Sunday Times: Mr. and Mrs. Nicholas Maris of Athens and New York announce the engagement of their daughter, Nina Helena, to James Keith Slater, currently affiliated with a volcanic research project sponsored by the United Nations. The Marises are well known to international society, the article continued, with mention of Nicholas' credits as a philanthropist in the field of archeology. The bridegroom-to-be, a US Air Force Academy graduate, is the son of Major General James 'Jimmy' Slater (retired) and the late Melinda Fraser-Slater of Memphis, Tennessee. The article was accompanied by a photograph of Nina in her graduation gown, her winsome smile, and her golden earrings that she wore to please her papa.

Not to be outdone, I arranged a quickie engagement party at the Fairmont Hotel. Inviting Nina's circle of friends and my buddies from Moffet Field, inclusive of Dr Gomulaka and Stash Obolensky his childhood friend. And paradoxically, General T.S. O'Brien, who'd arrived unexpectedly to 'inspect the 99th at Beale AFB' for reasons undisclosed? Nevertheless, a close family friend, although I hadn't seen the old fart for a number of years.

Our wedding plans were accelerated by the conditions in the Aegean, however. Volcano Santorini had compounded its fiery growth in a matter of months. No longer a geyserous mound emerging from the ancient caldera, the volcano had built upon itself a mountain of lava streaming seaward from its cone. No longer a tourist attraction from the village of Thera, the volcano's nightly glare was observable from Athens and Rhodes. Its towering plume spiked with lightning; discharging super-heated ash to the stratospheric winds, blighting the Cyclades with its gritty residue. All of which, together with the rising fears of a Plinian explosion, hastened the UN's decision to marshal their scientists to the scene.

White Dove's timetable was shortened by weeks, the modified U-2 readied for shipment to Kos, faxes dispatched to essential personnel. Allowing ten days to gather all hands, an expeditious briefing scheduled. Apprised of this in California, Nina and I revised our plans accordingly and proceeded to New York with the Porsche. Arrangements had been made at the Greek Orthodox Church; guests invited to a reception at the Olympic towers, but fortunately no questions were asked when our nuptials were updated by a week.

There remained an ironic twist of fate that would forever alter our lives, however. Anxious to meet their daughter's betrothed, unable to book an earlier flight from Athens, Nina's parents arranged to charter a corporate jet from Athens to New York.

I'd shipped my flight gear with the U-2 and, forwarding our belongings, we traveled the interstate with minimal luggage and Hennessey rear ledge. We were on our second day out when the tragedy occurred in the hills of Athens; a heart-rending calamity post the morning newscast, when Nina's parents were supposedly en route to New York. Later in the day came the terse message received by Nick's corporate office in Manhattan: Confirming Air Traffic Control, Athens International. Private charter, outbound to JFK via London, exploded midair at 1320 Greenwich Mean Time. There are no survivors. Advise Nina to contact us immediately. The fax a roundabout relay from her elderly uncle in Greece.

The shock was irreversible to the lanky girl who idolized her papa; more often disturbed by her mysterious dreams, of which I was unaware at the time. Nor was I aware of her psychic nature, inflamed with suspicion of the circumstances...clouding the dreadful occurrence of her parents' death.

CHAPTER 3

*W*e'd crossed the Great Divide with our luggage topside and Hennessey backside. We were on the down slope to Denver when Nick's chartered jet flamed the hills east of Kavouri. I remember the occasion so vividly; the bright, sunny afternoon, the Shell station we'd passed, when Nina paled and came upright in her seat.

"Oh my God!" she gasped, gripping my arm with her fingers. "Something terrible's happened; Mama's screaming! Please turn back, there's a phone at the petrol station, Keith!"

I braked the Porsche and turned around, down-shifted to the station. As I recall, it was almost to the minute when their jet exploded and impacted a low-lying hill. A half-hour passed until the facts were confirmed, and Nina cradled the phone in tears. How she knew I'll never understand, but I was to remember the mysterious side of her psychic mind in days to come...so like the dark side of the moon, a worldly view we'll never see or understand.

Nina boarded a flight from Denver that night, continuing to Athens while I traversed the eastbound interstate with Hennessey curled up in her seat. She was, however, determined to carry on with our wedding plans. We had sufficient time, although her stay was lengthened by the funeral proceedings and the chaotic state of Nick's financial affairs. Apparently the latter issue came to light while she was away at school. Confronted with this, Nina was nervously at ends when she briefed me nightly from her uncle's home in Kavouri.

Nick was a high-flyer in commodities, over-extended due to the blight shrouding their groves at Naxos. Pressed by the banks, he'd mortgaged their storage tanks in Piraeus, anticipating the rising price of edible oils. Except for her uncle, and a brother prone to the tables, Nina alone had to deal with this and liquidate other equities, all of which contributed to her state of mind when she booked her return to New York.

There was another matter she was unwilling to confide or discuss at the time. Suspicious of the circumstances surrounding the jet's erratic takeoff from Athens International, she'd prompted an investigation of her own. This coincided with suspicions I held when I requested the accident report and confidential analysis from the FAA.

There remained, however, a bright spot when we furthered our plans, and Nina looked forward to this. Nick's vintage motor-sailer, the Helena, would be off charter when we arrived at Kos. Documented in Nina's name, captained by a family retainer of many years, we planned to stay aboard while the U-2 was reassembled at Antimahia. Conditions permitting, Nina would commute to Athens to deal with her financial affairs.

* * * * * *

Interstate 80 was a long haul, although the Porsche was a delight when the radar was quiet. I was reminded of Steinbeck's 'Travels with Charley'...Hennessey's interest in the sights and scents of the Midwest, his friendly overtures and obedience when we were accepted by motels along the way.

New York was something else. Confused by the thunderous traffic, bewildered by the Lincoln Tunnel and the lack of receptive trees, his head rested on my shoulder when we stopped briefly at my apartment building on East 55th, where he was declared persona non grata by the surly doorman on duty. Hennessey was neither a lapdog nor a cat, according to the rules of the condominium, although I suspect O'Reilly would have let him in if I'd offered him a twenty. Hennessey, not keen to his scent, seemed anxious to move on.

It was on to six when I scanned the yellow Pages and located a kennel in Queens. I booked the dog until the following Monday, when we'd trip to Nassau with Nina after a White Dove briefing at the UN, hopefully to enjoy a week in the sun before we proceeded to London and Greece. As for Hennessey, he wasn't unhappy with his temporary digs, tugging at his leash, sensing a female in heat in the kennel next to his.

Bone tired, weary of the six o'clock crush on the bridge, I stabled the Porsche in the condo garage, collected my mail, and keyed the dank apartment, helping myself to a beer. It was after seven before I'd aired the place and showered, verging eight when I scanned the bills and phoned my office in Fort Lauderdale. Promptly on the hour, the elevator clanged, the doorbell buzzed, and an envelope containing a fold of hotel stationery was slipped beneath my door.

'2100 hrs, suite 601, Carlyle Hotel, urgent!' the message read. No explanation, no signature aside from the initialed T.S. scrawled with a ballpoint pen. I poured myself a bracer in the kitchen, contemplated the phone, and gave it up. The general wouldn't acknowledge a spurious response. As to how he tracked my arrival, I'll never know. His timing uncanny!

* * * * * *

"Light-skin nigger came by a while back," O'Reilly muttered when I inquired in the lobby. "Kept bangin' on me door with her flashy rings! Ain't taken with them high-nose Jamaicans," he added. "Seein' you been travellin', I figured you was wantin' to change your luck!" Collectively, I'd had it...sent him reeling with a fist to his bloated liver, arm-locked his head until he gasped an apology and stumbled to a lavatory down the hall. Bad vibes I'd have reason to regret, but that was my state of mind when I shouldered my blazer and made straight away to Clarkes on the corner of Third and 55th.

Although fond of the General, I was suspicious of his motivation, of the impromptu call I'd received while I was pondering my contract with White Dove. Suspicious of his hand in the UN's quick acceptance. Had I known what was in the offing, I'd have watched the Mets with my buddies at the bar, but instead, at 2100, the desk clerk at the Carlyle inquired my name and buzzed suite 601.

* * * * * *

My former wing commander met me at the door with the ever-present cigar clamped in his jaw. He was garbed in a business suit, although his military haircut was at odds with posh Manhattan. There were others present. I was introduced to a deputy director of the Defense Department, a top dog from Hughes Research Lab, and a short, balding man I recognized from a tabloid spread...Rex Keenan, formerly a lieutenant general with the Air Force, intellectually bent, a high-level confidante of the Security Council.

There were no drinks to hand, none offered, although they were available on a service trolley. Judging from the lack of small talk, they'd gathered to discuss a policy matter...an issue unresolved at the moment. The answer forthcoming, however. Keenan had but an hour to spare, a limousine waiting, and a speech in the offing at a black tie affair. He flexed his fingers, nodded impatiently when T.S. flourished his cigar to draw attention, and spelled it out the way it was.

27

The session was lengthy, highly complex, and futuristic, dealing with advanced technology and covert activities. Awesome at first, unbelievable in a sense.

"We've reason to believe the Soviets were experimenting with a series of robot tanks in Turkmenistan, prior to the break up of the USSR," T.S. offered when we'd settled in our chairs. "Specifically, an all-terrain vehicle capable of operating at night, utilizing stealth anti-radar technology, battery driven to avoid infra-red detection by our 'Lantern' equipped F-15s. They're controlled internally by terrain-reading computers and artificial intelligence," he added. "Most likely programmed in advance, with a feedback to their C-3 command stations in the field."

"So what happens if their batteries fade the last nine?" I quipped, picturing a ponderous Ez-Go with cannons. T.S. was not amused.

"From what we know, the batteries are good for five or six hours," the deputy asided with the trace of a smile. "Sufficient to penetrate an enemy minefield with devastating fire power, and the capability to self-destruct in command. In the latter instance, we believe they're designed to carry a low-yield neutron device with a kill radius of ten kilometers."

"Jesus Christ!"

"The tanks are lightweight and carry no personnel. Molded from titanium with a shield of armor underside, they're designed to move quickly at night before their shadows can be detected by satellite. Or by the infrared optics we employed in Iraq. We've a similar version at White Sands," he added, "but at the moment we're baffled by their communications link with the tanks."

I sat back, visualizing a line of futuristic monsters advancing miles apart, terrifying enemy bunkers, immune to optics and heat-seeking rockets. High-riding robots belching electro-magnetic cannon fire and fuel-air explosives...detonating a nuclear device if the attack was indecisive.

"Shades of a regional war?" I asked.

"The possibility of a thrust by hard nosed factions in Turkmenistan to seize the oilfields of Azerbaijan!" Keenan corrected.

"Now then," the deputy continued as I squirmed in my chair, "our priority is the means to intercept and record their mode of communication. Given this, we can analyze the state-of-art and devise a window to their microlink with the tanks, objectively to access the mode for information that's presently unavailable to military intelligence. The transmissions are short range, limited to the line of sight, computer encoded, inaccessible to our long-range electronics. Added to this, the proving grounds are contained to a remote desert region in Turkmenistan, bordering the western Caspian and the boundary with northern Iran!"

I had a gut feeling of what they were about when the deputy extracted a folder from his briefcase and spread a series of satellite photos on the marble tabletop. My suspicions confirmed when I stared at T.S. and he averted his eyes to examine his cigar.

"We came about our information initially from an ex-KGB defector in California," the deputy reported with a sidelong glance to focus my attention. "Frankly, we gave it little heed until we upped the satellite over Iraq to observe the truce in the Persian Gulf, which in turn gave us a view of suspect activities in the border region of Turkmenistan and Iran. Apparently there's a cadre of hard-line generals and elements of the de facto KGB who might be tempted to dictate a sovereign state of their own.

"Now then," he added, "politics aside, note the rail spur terminating west of Ashkhaded, Slater. Newly constructed, the spur came to our attention when we detected a series of camouflaged sheds adjacent to the railhead, together with a fleet of empty flat cars and heavy-duty cranes. Then, day by day, we observed a series of gigantic tank tracks extending from the sheds. Lately, a pattern of maneuvering tracks indicate they were testing the tanks in the field. Always at night," he added. "Come daylight, the tanks are housed in sheds and our surveillance is ineffective...aside from the width and depth of the tracks, from which we computerized a reasonable facsimile and realized what we had."

The satellite photos were remarkably clear, magnified to a bird's-eye view of the sheds, enhancing a soldier relieving his bladder in the midday sun. Photographed in chronological sequence, although swept by the drifting sands, there was evidence of widespread maneuvering tracks extending west to the Caspian...widespread in that the tracks were triple the width of the tanks we utilized in Kuwait!

"Note the maneuvering tracks when they tested a range of 50 kilometers...the erratic movements before they turned about and returned straightaway to the sheds," the deputy continued.

"The erratic movements suggest the robots are controlled by frequencies limited to the line of sight or roughly 50 kilometers," the wizard from Hughes interjected. "Beyond that, the inboard computers are seemingly confused or lacking input, directing the tanks to 'hold' and wait for the command stations to advance from the rear. From this we detected a time lapse when they're receptive to counter command, which is intriguing," he added reflectively. "At the moment, however, we're confronted with their micro-link which we've yet to totally comprehend."

Thirtyish, pale and withdrawn, a top-drawer analyst, nervous in the presence of T.S.'s intimidating cigar – he cleansed his bifocals and addressed the problem in rudimentary terms: the transmissions were apparently encoded in radar-type pulsations, which in turn were demodulated by the computers controlling the C-3 tactical commanders.

"The pulsations short span" he continued, "lasting a fraction of a second, like the Sparks from an anvil. Lately, however, they've altered the wavelengths with minute bursts of power, most likely to accommodate the terrain. The transmissions were scrambled, of course, and short-lived, but we fielded a bounce from the tropopause and gained a fragmentary view. So we enhanced the signal at Hughes and established the mode, but we're lacking further input to develop a hypersensitive amplifier capable of detecting the signals by satellite, wherein we'd have the means to demodulate the pulsations remotely and access their channels of command."

The technology beyond me, but I could read between the lines; realizing he was on to the finale when he turned to Keenan who was impatiently studying his watch, and avoiding T.S.'s beady blue eyes, he favored the Department of Defense. The deputy shrugged and urged him to carry on. And with this, he retreated behind his bifocals and dropped the other shoe.

"Okay, so we pooled our research and devised a spectrum analyzer to detect and record the mode. The instrument is compact and self-sustaining," he continued. "Coupled to a scrambler, it has the capacity to transmit the recording to an AWACS MD-11 or retain the disc for ground retrieval. In the latter instance, we've employed a safeguard, should the platform be compromised or disabled," he added nervously," in that the disc is triggered to erase on command if the situation so demands.

"Our optimum range is the line of sight," he continued, keying an equation to the visual display. "Or roughly 80 kilometers from our altitude factor where the reception is least distorted. But then, our platform would be subject to radar surveillance…"

"…and surface-to-air missiles!" I retorted. "Assuming your *platform* is an apolitical U-2 cruising naively off course at 70,000 feet, where it definitely shouldn't be!"

"I'm not certain what you mean," he stuttered, obviously taken aback. I was sorry for the chap; he was well intentioned, but apparently not apprised of my apolitical status with the UN. Flustered, he shed his glasses and peered anxiously at T.S., whom I'd fixed with a gesture the general would visually comprehend!

"Let him off the hook!" I exploded, confronting the group. "If you're referring to White Dove, call your shots and lay it the way it is!"

An icy silence ensued, a reactive silence aside from Keenan who seemingly was bemused and onto his cellular. I stared at the ceiling, waiting for the chandelier to fall. I hadn't long to wait. Red of face, T.S. ripped the binding from a fresh cigar with his teeth.

"A golden opportunity exists for the taking," he growled, containing his Irish temperament. "Turkmenistan agreed to the UN's request and you'd be flying scot-free along their boundaries with northern Iran. This would align the analyzer with the proving grounds when you make your westerly turn from Mashhad, Keith."

In essence, they intended I fly my turn over Iran and covertly penetrate the suspect area in Turkmenistan with a long sweeping turn to the west! All of which was a violation of the flight plan approved by the UN! I gave instant thought to the maps and directives I'd compiled at Moffet; the uncanny parallel to the area they had in mind.

"Subject to the addendum they filed with White Dove, T.S.?"

"How's that?"

"Worrisome, come to think of it! Call it sixth sense, but I've a kinky feeling they've read the scenario and have alternate plans for the little black box!"

"Spell it!" Keenan interjected.

"The swing over Iran was authorized when White Dove was hatched by the UN; I wasn't under contract at the time."

"And subsequently approved by the representative from Turkmenistan," Keenan asided.

"Okay, so maybe they had second thoughts. In any event, they forwarded an addendum to the UN, fixing our westerly leg to an inviolate 50-kilometer corridor paralleling their border with Iran; together with 'way points' we're to monitor from Mashhad to Trabiz (Iran). Which is a damn thin line, considering winds aloft and the conditions we'd face if we play games over Koppeh Dagh!"

"Aside from that," Keenan countered, puzzling his chart, "were you advised of the directive when you signed with White Dove?"

"Negative," I retorted. "The transcript was forwarded after Dr Gomulaka arrived at Mountain View. Struck me as odd at the time," I added. "The fax, an updated copy of the addendum, apparently misfiled or gathered dust at White Dove."

"What struck you as odd, Slater?"

"The copy was overlaid with deletions and frequency changes that differed from the addendum...bold face, heavily scored, as if someone had been at it with a ballpoint pen! The caption date also was amended and initialed in the margin, same hand, no confirming documentation."

"Authorization by whom?"

"Dr Nokomo, although it was initialed by his secretary. More to the point, there was no indication of prior approval by the Turkmenistan ambassador to the UN. As to where and by whom the addendum was corrected, I haven't the vaguest. Nokomo's infrastructure was disorganized at the time and I assumed this created a mix-up in communication. Frankly, the addendum didn't surprise me," I added. "Having flown with NATO, I realized their sensitivity to order intrusions and gave it little thought, but the changes didn't make sense when I checked their charts."

"How such?" Keenan asked.

"The addendum corresponded with our current charts, but the overlay was marked with frequency vectors that were either outdated or don't exist! Ashkhabad was vectored with a frequency similar to the mobile decoys we encountered in Iraq! There also was a pattern to the frequency additions, corresponding with the highway from Ashkhabad to Kizi-Arvat and Nebit-Dag. If the transmitters were moved about and we abided by the vectors, we'd have a 'balls up' in Turkmenistan with the U-2 up for grabs."

"Were you aware of this?" Keenan thundered, turning to T.S. "I'm referring to the change of addendum, General, Slater's comments aside!"

"Negative, sir! We – uh – it never crossed my desk!"

"In other words, intelligence was out to lunch!"

"I'm not in a position to answer that, but apparently there was a mix-up at the UN or we'd have it first lick when I reviewed the concept with TAC."

"Unbelievable!" Keenan sputtered. "You're suggesting the corrected addendum passed your desk, unseen until it was delivered to White Dove...revised and corrected with a ballpoint pen! Someone obviously had access to communications and I've a gut feeling there's a link with an incident in Palo Alto, General! Have White Dove's staff members been screened?"

"Affirmative, sir! The report was compiled by the AFOSI and the CIA."

"As of when?" Keenan questioned. T.S. reached for his glasses and scanned his file.

"Couple of weeks back, Rex...when Nokomo was given quarters at the UN. I presume the report is up to date, although there's a footnote pertaining to an open slot in communications which previously was assigned and amended to accommodate a Russian nominee."

"Read on, General! Was the nominee identified?"

"Not at the time, apparently, but the footnote refers to a memo attached to the report." Flustered, T.S. struggled with a paper clip. "Okay, I have it now."

"Read on," Keenan politely suggested.

"The memo suggests a possibility," T.S. continued. "Specifically, a former East German officer who served with the former Soviet consulate in New York. I quote the AFOSI: Reprimanded by the State Department for visa violations (unauthorized travel), inclusive of suspect activities in Palo Alto. Duties herewith confined to metropolitan New York. There's no reference to an incident, but his moniker rings a bell," T.S. added. "Think back, Rex. Vietnam, communications, the radar specialist who served with the Russian contingent at Hanoi?"

Startled, Keenan motioned to the deputy and they examined the memo, conversing privately. Palo Alto was mentioned, seemingly in context with an ongoing investigation of which, judging from his questions, T.S. hadn't been apprised. Disturbed by the lapse of liaison, Keenan suggested the deputy 'knock a few heads!' And, glancing at his watch, he asked if I'd copied NASA with the transcript when they shipped my gear to Kos?

"It's included with my file at Moffet Field," I replied.

"Would you tend to that?" Keenan furthered, turning to the deputy. "Have the AFOSI run a computer analysis of the 'subject initials' and advise if he's one and the same! Have the findings hot-lined to General O'Brien and Air Force intelligence. I would also suggest they further the investigation from this end," he continued. "The agent or agents who compiled the report obviously are acquainted with the rank and file at the UN. At the moment, we're confronted with a post-dated addendum that presumably was altered between the Russian secretariat and Nokomo's desk, which would indicate we have reason to suspect an inventive hand whilst Nokomo was absent from his desk!"

"I'm concerned by the clumsy effort to subvert or misdirect the U-2." Keenan asided. "The Russians are much too clever to condone a diplomatic flap, so I suspect we're dealing with a de facto residue of their KGB. Perhaps a covert network aligned with military hard-liners who would have much to gain from a confrontation. Such a possibility lends credence to Slater's remarks!"

"Enough said," Keenan continued. "The concept was approved by the Security Council per your recommendation, General! We're looking to you to determine the flaws and circumvent a misadventure! You also will have an active volcano to contend, atmospheric conditions that will affect the timing. There also is the factor of support personnel when the U-2 is ramped at Kos; most likely a mixed bag of unknowns drawn from the locals and Greek militia, inclusive of the 'communications nominee', who may have thoughts of his own! Do you read me loud and clear, T.S.? Provided Slater agrees to the concept, it's up to you to see it through!"

T.S. looked up and smiled, cherishing the responsibility. An ace pilot in 'Nam, he'd earned his third star as a brilliant tactician with Desert Storm. His desk at the Pentagon frustrated the old war-horse, nibbling at straws in the waning days of his career. Had he proposed the concept to advance his seniority, to teeth another challenge, I wondered.

It was after 10.00 p.m. when Keenan's chauffeur buzzed the suite from the lobby. Nodding to the remainder of the group, Keenan gathered his notes, motioned T.S. to carry on, conferred briefly with the deputy and disappeared to the lavatory with his tux under his arm. In the interim, the wizard from Hughes was cordially excused by the deputy; the discs he'd ejected from his laptop computer remaining in the custody of the department of Defense!

"For security reasons," the deputy allowed. "The knucklehead was programming your comments for analysis, Slater! Let's get on with it, General. Rex is running late and our bridegroom is loose on the vine!"

T.S. gripped the arm of my chair and laid it bluntly on the line.

"There's no need to summarize further, Keith. You know exactly what we're about, so hear me out and decide for yourself! Frankly, we need your expertise," he added. "You've flown long-term missions for NASA; you're also an experienced combat pilot, acquainted with conditions in the field and our state-of-the-art technology. All of which led me to seek you out when you were selected to recon Santorini.

"Obviously there's an element of risk," he continued. "Possibly a communications flap, but it would be illogical to think in terms of missiles with a UN observer aboard. Moreover, the UN-marked U-2 is easy to identify, an unlikely target for interception. If there were an attempt to seize the U-2, they'd want it intact. Why, or how, remains a moot question," he added. "Most likely, disrupting or querying your navigational system at a definitive time and place...possibly internally incapacitate the U-2, or remotely, to where you'd attempt an emergency landing."

"So we land wheels up and bleed from the nose!"

"Come off it, boy! I'm postulating possibilities; we've no intention to cut you short! You could encounter an attempt to divert the U-2, which you could override or challenge if you're awake at the stick. Tampering with the bird is another matter, but we'll have operatives in the field to avert such a thing. Your crew chief, for instance, is an old hand from the 99th, ex-service like yourself.

Moreover, the analyzer is undetectable from the ground. Implanted in the starboard wingtip, the unit's coupled to a sensing antenna in the vertical stabilizer; the recording triggered from a pressure point beneath the pilot's seat."

"At a definitive time and place?"

"When you turn west to intercept the corridor, Keith."

"Meaning a long, wide turn while they paint the U-2 on radar?"

"At 70,000 feet! I wouldn't worry it, boy! The analyzer, slaved to a digital recording of the C-3 transmissions, will activate a blinking light on your console until you out-range the signal; the recording terminates automatically. From thereon, the disc is self-contained until the AWACS establishes your 'blip' and prompts a coded transmission."

"Automatically?"

"Hands off! The disc will self erase when it's transmitted to the AWACS MD-11."

"What happens if they miss my turn?"

"There's an interim of risk," a voice behind me said. I looked back from my chair. Keenan had combed his wisp of gray and freshened his face with a complimentary lotion from the Carlyle. "Officially, the AWACS MD-11 will be monitoring Iraq from our base in Saudi Arabia," he added. "Factually, they'll be tracking your position by satellite, inclusive of your return to Kos. They're prohibited to overfly Iran, unfortunately, and you'll be 900 miles apart when you turn west to intercept the corridor from Mashhad.

"The problem's two-fold," T.S. interjected. "AWACS will pinpoint your position electronically, track your heading and ground speed, monitor the critical area. They will, however, refrain from radio contact. The analyzer's output is limited to line of sight, again 150 miles! In other words, you'd be on your own for give or take a couple of hours, provided you hose 450 knots, at which point the MD-11 will establish you on radar, prompting the coded transmission."

There was 'an interim of risk' as Keenan aptly put it. Long hours of sweat while we sufficed on oxygen, subject to unknown conditions while we traversed the target and the murky Caspian!

"Okay, so let's say we pull it off and intercept a westerly heading until we vector Trabiz(Iran) – on our return leg to Kos," I added. "Now then, if I recall the coordinates, Trabiz is roughly 300 miles north of Baghdad, on a mean line with our base at Ar-Riyadh(Saudi Arabia), 600 miles to the south. Which would place the MD-11 somewhere in between while they're scanning Iraq. In other words, we'll be 300 miles apart at our closes juncture once we vector Trabiz."

"More or less," T.S. Admitted. "Your position will be known to the MD-11, however. They'll change heading or advance throttles until they close and acquire your 'blip' on radar."

"I realize that, but prior to that we'll be hours apart! Hard put to maintain a true course once we encounter the prevailing winds; possibly crabbing 300 knots while we're laboring the corridor and point for Trabiz! In the meantime, what happens if Santorini erupts and blankets communications? It's not that I'm negative, T.S., but it's a tricky deal at best. I'll also have a wife to consider if there's a flash in the sky and the volcano turns Plinian!"

"Valid point," T.S. allowed. "But remember this: if Santorini erupts, the airborne MD-11 would be a mainstay of communications! Alternatively, you'll have access to our NATO base at Incirlik in Turkey if you elect to set down. The disc can be safely removed at this point, or again at Antimahia should you decide to plod on!"

I eyed the tray for a bracer, realizing that come what may, T.S.'s mind was wired to the little black box!

Realizing I was at odds, Keenan lingered to express his point of view. A former general with a grasp for detail, he also was a sensitive human being, receptive to my thoughts and, fortunately, the apolitical nature of my contract with the UN.

"Your duties with White Dove are foremost," he said. "Ours is a mission you can draw from your boot if conditions are favorable when you traverse Iran. The analyzer was installed at Lockheed when the concept was suggested by TAC, prior to your appointment. Self-contained, completely automatic, the device was programmed for retrieval by our ground crew operative at Kos. The coverage was limited, however, and when the tanks were discovered in Turkmenistan, we realized the necessity of a close up view. That's how it came to be, Keith. Your credentials advanced and approved by the Security Council; your appointment suggested by our ambassador to the UN without his knowledge of the situation at hand!

"There are mitigating circumstances, however," Keenan continued. "Lending to an escape clause should you decide to terminate this matter as of now, or at any set time or place. Firstly, we weren't aware of your interim plans when the format was introduced. Secondly, we hadn't realized the status of the hyperactive volcano, which could lead to your preoccupation if there's chaos in the Aegean. Thirdly, we've hung a bummer on your conscience with respect to your integrity. I've no quarrel with that, Keith, but there are circumstances that have come to light in recent weeks, a matter of regional security. We also believe Moscow shares our concern!"

"Hard to believe they'd abandon an arsenal of high-tech tanks they could sell to the Chinese," I commented, tongue in cheek.

"At the moment, the tanks are controlled by a mixed bag of ex-Soviet militants who might feast on the Muslim ideology and consolidate a power sphere in Turkmenistan and northern Iran. The area has been rife with sword since the days of Genghis Khan," Keenan added. So let's put a note from ancient history together with the lesson we learned in Iraq. Given the tools of war, a cult of inspired personalities may have studied the text for an opportunity in the twentieth century!"

"Given the micro-link, we can take them out overnight!" T.S. growled.

"They could be on the move at any time," Keenan cautioned. "All they'd need is a publicized flap to justify a cause. Have you given thought to that, General O'Brien?"

In the end, I agreed to carry on, subject, of course, to the conditions we'd discussed. I had misgivings, however. Deception wasn't my thing and I had Nina to consider; also Dr Gomulaka, who would be an unwitting accessory.

The deputy, surprisingly well informed, rose to the occasion when Keenan was out the door and gone. He suggested a one-to-one briefing session in suburban New Jersey, after which communication would be limited to public telephone, via a series of coded numbers he'd thoughtfully brought along.

"Should we encounter information best exchanged by hand, we'll arrange a drop at the UN," he allowed. "I also suggest you maintain an open ear at the UN, a watchful eye on conditions that might warrant your suspicion. If you discover anything, avoid a confrontation and report to an agent at first opportunity. In the latter instance, be cautious," he warned. "Intelligence is segmented for security reasons, and no one person, aside from tonight, is totally versed in the subject we've discussed."

We dispersed independently. Although I promptly offloaded my misgivings whilst I tagged T.S. in the elevator that unfortunate evening at the Carlyle Hotel.

CHAPTER

I collected the Times from the corner newsstand the next morning, called Nina at her office at 0800...mid-afternoon Athens time. Preoccupied with business, she asked if I'd air the family suite at the Olympic Towers, touch base with the caterers and, please would I visit with the priest at the Orthodox Church. In short, she'd arrive at JFK Friday afternoon, but the arrangements were left to me.

I followed through, spoke with the caterers, visited the priest. As for the Olympic Towers, a C-note took care of the superintendent. The limousines, flowers and champagne I charged to American Express, surprised by the enormity of the thing!

This completed, I checked in with the environmental studies group at the UN. A proper English accent responded when I inquired if our briefing was scheduled as planned for Monday morning? Crisply efficient, apparently anticipating the call, she advised me of an accelerated change of venue. Following Monday's briefing, the operational group would proceed directly to Athens. An advisory seminar scheduled whilst we waited transport to Kos.

"A week from Monday's our target date," she added. "Within a fortnight we should commence our studies from Antimahia." There were 'ifs' of course, mainly the status of the group's scientific equipment, their state-of-the-art computers and sounding devices, and a reassembled and flyable U-2.

Shades of the Persian Gulf, I thought as I cradled the phone and considered the logistics. Plans afar and Murphy's Law combined with bureaucratic naiveté? In a contemporary sense the natives were friendly and, despite T.S.'s interference, I'd play it by ear when the U-2 was available at Kos.

Our honeymoon was shot to hell, however, limited to a three-day stopover in the Bahamas and a day in London, allowing for time en route. Nina had family in Athens, so she was not altogether disappointed by the turn of events...able to rationalize cheerfully when I contacted her in Kavouri.

"Perhaps it's best," she said. "Auntie will be pleased; she's a special delight and we'll have a few days to meet with my friends. You will love our old home by the sea," she added. "Kavouri's a half-hour drive from Athens and I'll have time to tend to business while you meet at the Grand Bretagne."

It was late night in Kavouri and Nina was obviously tired...and I suspected business was getting the upper hand, a little too much for a high-strung girl. She also asked if I would check the invitation list; she had a cousin in Manhattan she'd nearly forgotten.

"She's originally from Naxos, Keith. Her surname is Garfinkle, 21st Street I think. Would you call her? It's important to me."

I understood. Nina had no other relatives in New York, nor did I, aside from cousins I'd never seen. The list inclusive of family acquaintances, the Greek consul and the like, together with Nina's friends from Berkeley and a circumspect selection of my buddies from Moffet Field.

I wrapped matters up the following day, checked Hennessey...then, knowing the Porsche's unforgiving electronics, I parked the car in the condo garage and disconnected the battery for the duration of our stay in the Aegean. And, stomaching my misgivings, dialed 1-800 and a series of numbers from a nearby phone, pressing the numbers of my birth date when a mechanical phone voice picked up and inquired of such.

"Require voice identification for our record," it said. I repeated my numbers, upping the volume.

"Confirmation correct," it said. "Please stand by while we contact your advisor." I waited a long minute whilst the computer exchanged blips with another. Then a friendly voice picked up.

"Slater?"

"Affirmative!" I replied.

"Colonel Forsythe here, Keith. Would you be free tomorrow morning, say until noon?"

"My fiancée's arriving at JFK tomorrow afternoon at three," I replied, thinking he intended to meet somewhere nearby.

"Excellent, Keith! I promise we'll make a quick nip of it and get you back on time! Would you be an early riser?"

"Depends..."

"Then make careful note of where and when it's best we meet, Keith! At the moment I'm in Palo Alto, which is also nip and tuck!"

* * * * * *

And promptly come morning, at 7.00 AM, I boarded the commuter train to suburban New Jersey. Minding the first stop past Newark, come what may?

I'd attended intelligence briefings in Riyadh, been apprised of battle conditions and missile concentrations when we flew cover for our A-10s, but my briefing in New Jersey was apart from all of that...a one-time mission dealing with covert activities, in peacetime?

Thoughts such as these crossed my mind as the train passed through Newark. The abandoned tenements, stark and featureless, focused the indifference of moral decay. It was then I realized my innermost concern...the deceit clouding my commitment with T.S., as opposed to the vows I'd express when I'd stand with Nina in the Orthodox Church.

* * * * * *

The seedy motel near the railroad station sat ambiguously in the morning gloom. The unshaven manager shrugged and pointed with the stub of a moist cigar when I inquired for room 103. A rental Ford with Jersey plates parked adjacent to the door, the only vehicle in the immediate vicinity.

I tapped on the door, stepped aside as the curtain was drawn, nodding when I was scrutinized by a pair of owlish bifocals that tallied with my advisor's descript. He opened the door quickly, scanned the walkway and beckoned me in. I checked the room visually when he stood back to acknowledge my presence.

"Colonel Forsythe, Slater. I'm quite alone as you can see."

Satisfied when he displayed his ID, I closed the door. The room was orderly; he obviously hadn't spent the night. His briefcase lay unopened on the dresser, together with a portable slide projector, a manila envelope and a pair of paper coffee containers.

Smallish, forty-odd, dressed in jeans and short-sleeved shirt, he'd pass for a shopper in the mall. Slim of waist, of athletic build, he was an Academy graduate with a Doctorate in psychology. A brigadier general selectee with expertise in counter-intelligence, he studied me briefly with his penetrating eyes. Then, offering coffee dispensed with idle chatter and came quickly to the point.

"I reviewed your file on the plane," he said. "I'm also acquainted with your background and combat credits...remembered your name when I was assigned to NATO. There is a lapse in your file, however, following your discharge from

Walter Reed, although a memo was included in recent weeks, initialed by general O'Brien," he added, extracting a page from the envelope.

The run down dealt with my recovery and flights with NASA leading to my contract with the UN. Minutely detailed, I was surprised by the observance of my career since the Persian Gulf, the disability I'd overcome and my current status and time with the U-2.

"I'm apprised of your meeting with Keenan and General O'Brien, Keith. Although I wasn't favored with a copy of the minutes, I understand it had to do with your pending flights in the Aegean...possibly a covert maneuver in the vicinity of the Caspian. I'm also aware of your apolitical contract with the UN and of your hesitancy in the latter matter, which is understandable," he continued. "So be it; I'm not here to rationalize the subject. Your tour with White Dove is inclusive of Europe and the Middle East, areas I dealt with as an intelligence analyst. And to this end I'm familiar with a recent development, suggestive of a penetration by a former officer with the East German army in Berlin.

"Now then," the Colonel continued when I settled into a creaky chair, "our information stems from an impromptu bender in a bar...a chance meeting of old friends, producing an ex-KGB operative wanting out. Needless to say, we had him when he sobered up," the Colonel added, "together with a detailed disclosure of a KGB capo we've had under surveillance for many years. His name is Horst Gunnar." The Colonel studied my reaction. "Does his moniker ring a bell?"

"Vaguely, Colonel, although I don't know where or when."

"He was known to Air Force Intelligence until he dropped from sight in the 90s, Keith, but NATO maintained a watch and we've had reason to update his file."

The Colonel unlatched his briefcase and removed a ribbon-bound folder containing a computer readout of multiple pages. Then, adjusting his glasses, he quoted the contents: "An expert in counter surveillance...a brilliant technician...Gunnar served with the Viet Cong, advisor to a forward radar missile complex during the war as a civilian, although he was known to intelligence as a colonel in the East German Army. Obscure in later years, presumably to computerize their communications systems, involving frequent visits to their consular offices...until his clearance was curtailed by the State Department."

"The CIA and AFOSI were on to him at the time," Forsythe commented, "having reason to suspect he was instrumental in a computer leak at Hughes. Our office was alerted when he was stopped for speeding near Palo Alto, where he shouldn't have been. He claimed diplomatic immunity and, rather than tip his ear, a decision was made to press the clearance violation and request his activities be confined to New York. For security reasons the State Department was not advised of our informant. Aside from the visa violation, Gunnar's movements have been circumspect, until he suddenly hauled ass and tripped for parts unknown."

"When was this?" I asked, sensing a link with White Dove.

"Early this month, following Dr. Gomulaka's transition at Moffet Field! Obviously something came up, most likely a high-level briefing dealing with the project's infrastructure abroad. Are you aware of the interplay at the UN? Have you been contacted recently?" he asked abruptly.

"Negative, Colonel, except for a meeting scheduled for Monday at 10."

The Colonel puzzled his notes for a moment, extracted a memo from his file and examined it minutely.

"Odd," he commented. "I've a fax of the proceedings and assumed you knew when you met with T.S."

"In reference to what?"

"Horst Gunnar, Keith. I've fixed the cart before the horse, I think! In any event, he was nominated to fill the communications slot, presumably while you were en route to New York."

"Was the nomination approved?"

"Unfortunately, yes! Frankly, we were caught off guard," Forsythe commented, "but there was little we could do, short of raising a fracas with the State Department and acknowledging what we know. That, together with the complexities involving your ex-service career. Tit for tat, so to speak. In essence, the Russians had us by the balls."

"Meaning my contract was on the hinge?"

"Your assignment wasn't challenged, Keith! The Russians have a knack for leverage and the decision was rendered by Third World factions, with Dr. Nokomo capping the vote. Apparently they had second thoughts and demanded the communications post when the project was extended to the Caspian; or shortly thereafter, coinciding with the U-2's modification at Lockheed, which possibly compounded a decision to monitor the flight from Kos."

Lockheed? The Caspian? I stared bleakly at the window. Was the Colonel aware of the analyzer? Had T.S. avoided mention of Gunnar knowing there was a skunk in the basement? Was Keenan aware of all this when we met at the Carlyle?

The express to Washington roared by while I considered the objective of my impromptu briefing...the emphasis of Gunnar's past activities, the informant they had in tow. Was there a link to White Dove that intelligence hadn't resolved yet?

Was I subject to a game of musical chairs?

"Level with me, Colonel," I said abruptly. "I'm under contract as a civilian to evaluate Santorini. My observer's a Polish meteorologist, the project apolitical. And until we met at the Carlyle, I wasn't party to fun and games. Okay, so T.S. played hard ball, but where's the middle road? Like, all of a sudden, I'm up to my ass with intrigue. Do you follow me?"

The Colonel removed his glasses and rubbed his eyes. We'd been at it for an hour and he obviously was beat.

"Not completely," he admitted, sipping his coffee. "Although we're investigating the lead I mentioned earlier, which partly explains the urgency. I'm aware of your misgivings, but I'm not here to console you, Slater. Nor am I privy to T.S.'s strategy at the moment. In fact, I received a hurry-up call on my cellular and reviewed my files on the plane." He declined to comment when I repeated my question, although he answered roundabout with a classified document dealing with de facto KGB activity in Europe and the Middle East.

"I'm not authorized to divulge the content, Keith, other than an analysis of their ways and means. I advise you to take judicious heed," he added. "Despite glasnost, they haven't changed their ways."

We spent a blood-curdling hour while I agonized what he had to say; matters I'd previously attributed to fiction...'jinks' in high places, torture, drugs and deadly poisons! I was repulsed and the Colonel was aware of my thoughts.

"Quandary, Keith?"

"Wary, Colonel! Provided the volcano holds tight, I agreed to a minimal risk maneuver when we circuit the Caspian...a westerly leg along the Turkmenistan border with Iran, a fifty kilometer corridor. No sweat! We'd be traversing a thin, hazy line, however, with the possibility of a navigational error. I was mentally prepared for this," I continued, "until you laid a heavy on Gunnar and dropped the other shoe! Do you follow me, Colonel? Are you familiar with the area?"

Forsythe fixed me with an owlish stare, seemingly confused, searching for words.

"I'm remotely acquainted with North Arabia," he admitted, "but wasn't advised to bring a map of the area."

"Okay, so I brought one along! Studied it after I rapped with Keenan and T.S." I unfolded an aeronautical chart I had at the apartment. It was long outdated, but there was sufficient information to sketch the corridor from Mashhad to the Caspian. I'd extended this with a pencil to include our MD-11 rendezvous near Tabriz.

"Note the adjacency of Turkmenistan Bases at Aschabad and Nabit-Dag,

Colonel. Also, the proximity of Baku and Yerevan, west of the Caspian; all of which are equipped with surface to air missiles, their air space off limits should we over-fly our turn to the west! Now then, all the while...the U-2 will maintain contact with our base at Kos via our RON data link! Which in turn will be monitored by the Russian nominee stationed at Kos...the Russian nominee conceivably an ex-military hot shot with known de facto KGB affiliations. Namely one Horst Gunnar, if I hear you rightly?"

"Correct!"

"Well now, Colonel, I wasn't made aware of this until you filled me in, and there could be mitigating circumstances as an end result! Like, with the winds aloft, the U-2 might be *temporarily blown off course while we make out turn over Iran.* Comprehend what I mean, Colonel?"

"Yes and no, Keith!" I shrugged my shoulders, realizing he hadn't been apprised of the action, although he was obviously piecing it together. Myself, noteworthy of Keenan's parting words: 'Intelligence is segmented for security reasons, Keith. No one part knowing of the other.'

"Okay. So let's say we *inadvertently* wander off course and he challenges our position for all to hear! And, what with a threat of being shot down, I'm faced with my options? Alternatively, he might command we track a series of kinky waypoints, recently added to our current charts? All of which would lead us to points astray...to where we'd be forced to set down, which might cause an international flap. Possibly juice a punitive expedition by militant forces towards the Caspian! Conjecture, of course, but there's also an ingredient that foxes me, Colonel."

"Out with it, Keith!"

"Well now, let's say hypothetically, the U-2 has means to decipher electronic communications from singular sources on the ground...the ability to immediately relay their GPS locations to AWACS by satellite. And let's say there could be a covey of stealth B-2s, equipped with precision guided bombs, winging nearby. In other words, if the U-2's a patsy to lead a 'surgical operation in the field', I'd damn well like to know!"

Obviously shaken by the thought, the Colonel's reaction was surprising for a mature psychologist. Florid, he groped blindly about, grappling with the chart, until I retrieved his specs with the point of my shoe. We shared a moment of silent confrontation whilst the Colonel collected his wits. Then, realizing my briefing was contained to elementary matters, that I'd overstepped his guidelines, I let it go at that!"

"That's not for me to say!" he commented, however. "Although I understand your concern for rampant possibilities, Keith.

"At the moment we're not sure of we're dealing with Moscow or a paranoid individual. There are xenophobic factions who'd parlay an incident to embarrass all parties…the UN, the USA and the Russians no less." And with that, he shed his glasses and waxed philosophic, reminiscent of Keenan's parting words.

"Historically, the military is the same worldwide. Constantly on guard, assessing opportunities, and invariably there's a loose cannon who'd take license with his authority. Gunnar, for instance…old school, Silesian-Prussian with Stalinist leanings. Introverted and dangerous if we analyze his past. But frankly, I wasn't advised to the extent of your undertaking. The U-2's turn over Iran was mentioned, but I assumed your involvement was contained to maintain a watchful eye of undisclosed matters. Your prognosis sheds a glimmer of light, however?"

"Could be we've been misled, for reasons also undisclosed, Colonel! But once we gander the edge of space, I intend the options to be up to me!"

Forsythe declined to comment. Apparently Gunnar's assignment was closer to the bone. In any event he warmed up, laying his cards on the table.

"Take note of our screening," he commented. "He'll cast a long shadow when you meet at Kos." The Colonel inserted a slide in the projector…a photograph of Gunnar emerging from a long, gray building, focusing a saber scar effected during his university years, his military stance, and his elongated neck.

"There's no way he can disguise himself, so he's above all that; depends on his mistress to ferret what he needs." The Colonel focused the projector on Gunnar's companion, a heavy-set woman in tweeds.

"We know her as Amalia," he said. "High German, a suspect widow, prone to limousines and social functions in Berlin and New York. In early years, she operated a brothel in Brussels; serviced NATO until she married a German diplomat, who later shot himself…and she moved to higher ground. Financially secure, a slippery bitch, she moves about with impunity. Portrays a matronly type, although she's as hard as nails and packs a Biretta." I squirmed in my chair.

"On with it, Colonel. I'm not into widows and tweeds!"

"Of course not, but there's a possibility she'll track your movements to Athens and Kos, Keith! Back seat and discreet, a remote face in the distance, perhaps a schoolmarm on holiday or a dowager at the marketplace. In other words, be wary. If there's an occasion to meet with an operative, inspect your surroundings very carefully. Should you spot Amalia nearby, avoid eye contact, play it cool and wait for another day."

I was mentally exhausted, thoughts in a quandary when I caught the 11.30

to New York. My conscience low ebb when I hailed a cab and collected Nina at JFK, near about three that afternoon.

CHAPTER 5

ina was radiant in her white wedding gown...tall, proud, her green eyes shining from beneath the veil. The consul accompanied her down the aisle, stood by while we exchanged crowns and golden rings. The elderly priest blessed us in her native Greek, stepped forward to clasp Nina about the waist, and pressed her hand to his bearded lips.

The crowd parted and a gray limousine with diplomatic plates waited to whisk us from the showering rose petals to the Olympic Towers, where we joined the reception on the upper rise. Champagne with caviar, splendid gowns and gales of laughter, lingering hands and gracious blessings, faces I'd never seen before. Small talk, wine talk, cablegrams from Athens, the tiny lady who had taken the subway from south Manhattan.

"I've known Nina as a child," she whispered as I bent to buss her cheek. And then we had portioned the wedding cake and toasted one and all; Nina took me quietly by the arm, led us to the library down the hall and latched the door.

"This we must do," Nina said, as she knelt before the portraits of her late father and mother. "I miss them so, but I know they are here." I dropped to my knees beside her and clasped her hand when she displayed her wedding band and bowed her head.

The portrait of Nick had been painted when he was in his 40s...a broad-shouldered man of medium height, with a full head of hair graying at the temples. The artist had caught his kindly face, easy grin and intense gray eyes probing from the canvas. A shaft of sunlight pierced the room just then, briefly silhouetting Nina's classical features. Her eyes glistened with tears when she crossed herself and bowed to the portrait of her mother.

The resemblance to Nina was uncanny: her blue eyes, her strong dark hair caught with a tiara. Thinly tall, gowned for the portrait in evening dress, seated in a Gainsborough chair. The setting a richly paneled room with a view of the English countryside. She would be in her early 30s, I guessed. A gray-haired man stood beside her, wearing a military uniform with many ribbons. Tall and bent, with aging eyes, Nina's grandfather, the late Sir Harold, former ambassador to Greece.

"My grandmother was Anatolian, from the island of Kos. They met in Athens before the war," Nina said. "She died before Mama's portrait was completed. She was a remarkable woman, high-spirited, mysterious in a way. I have her photograph somewhere," she added. "Grandfather was devastated when she died. He purchased a cottage in Kos to be near her grave; he's buried nearby. She had a likeness to my mother, her eyes and olive skin, but I'm told she was very naughty." Nina turned to me then, loosening her impish grin. "She had a fling with an artist in Crete; my bloodline is a bit obscure, I think."

She paused by her father's desk to finger an ancient terracotta figure, a bare-breasted lass in a bell-shaped skirt, holding a golden serpent in each hand, a tiny cat perched on her head.

"Papa's favorite statuette," she murmured. "He found her in Arhannes when I was a little girl. Late Minoan, the cat represents royalty, Papa said." And it was here, when Nina opened a drawer in her father's desk that I had a glimpse of a golden pendant, an ancient thing with emerald eyes, staring from the depths. She closed the drawer quickly, shaking her head as if it wasn't meant for her to see. Visibly shaken, her voice quavered when she pointed to an early Picasso adjoining a priceless Cézanne, but she caught herself and went on.

"We'll sell Papa's collection to pay the death taxes, Keith. He intended it so. The majority will be shipped to Sotheby's for auction. I'll forward the remainder when we close the house in Nassau. We'll need every penny to hold our groves in Naxos," she added.

We departed an hour later; Nina tossed her bouquet to the frantic spinsters and we discreetly exited to the lobby floor. Our limousine was missing when we stepped outside. Traffic was heavy, taxis committed, but Nina was a sport. She hitched her gown to her knees and we struck out for my apartment at 55th and 2nd, arm in arm, exchanging banter with the passers-by, halting traffic at Lexington Avenue when a fascinated lady cop blew her whistle and waved us across. We sprinted the final blocks when my bride removed her slippers and flashed her beautiful legs. The wide-eyed attendant spun about when we parted his polished brass doors and darted inside.

There are moments of anticipation difficult to suppress, frenzied moments of truth known to every bride and groom...the significance of legality, the release of emotions when the door to privacy is close at hand. Such were ours when I gathered Nina in my arms to wait the elevator's slow ascent. We managed zippers and snaps while the cab lifted from 1 to 10, trailed our formal dress along the spotless marbled halls, spoke softly to one another while I fumbled with the double lock, and carried my naked bride to our wedding bed.

Such moments are treasured by lovers, the pitfalls taken in stride when one has a hand to seek during the night. As years go by, the growth of mutual understanding supercedes all else.

Five thousand miles to the east the forces of nature, forces that would arouse the mystique in the souls of those who were spawned by the seeds of antiquity were rumbling beneath the quiescent Aegean.

During the night, while Nina slept, I was awakened by the sounds of pre-dawn Manhattan...trash cans and rumbling trucks, hoarse voices, a siren whining down York Avenue, a dog barking from the street below. Introspection takes over in these moments when one studies the shadows and reflects upon the days ahead...responsibilities, realities one must face in the light of dawn; the covert mission thrust upon me. Did she know? As I look back on it, I believe she did!

CHAPTER 6

The usual brightness was not at our window when I awakened Sunday morning. I inched the blinds, checked my watch. It was after ten, but lights were aglow in the adjacent buildings, faces at the windows, a dog howling mournfully from the street below. The sky strangely overcast the sun a blood red orb...like the planet Mars seen from one of its moons. I raised the window and experienced a blast of stifling humidity. The sill was coated with a thin, gritty film. Acid to the tongue, the residue of pumice and sulfurous ash had been deposited by the evening rains.

This was something new to a city accustomed to blizzards and sizzling heat...an alien thing from the distant Aegean. Old-timers perhaps would remember the inescapable grit and sulfurous smog from the coal-burning era, when thrusting chimneys and elevated trains spewed their residue to the streets. I closed the window softly, gave thought to the consternation in Central Park, the grimy faces at Yankee Stadium and the party-prone Hamptons. I collected the Sunday Times from the hall.

Nina was fast asleep, unmindful of the eerie morning, her long raven hair strewn across our pillows. A thunderclap sounded from the north, rousing her momentarily. I drew a blanket to shield her buff from the air conditioning, lingered to savor the scent of her lavender, hesitated when her sensuous fingers stroked my arm and drew me back to our bridal bed.

It was after eleven when I extricated myself from the tangle sheets to answer the intercom squawking intermittently in the darkened foyer.

"Cablegram, Mr. Slater. Came a while back, but I figured you was busy and slipped it under the door!" I saluted his esprit de corps, replaced the phone and gathered the envelope, most likely a congratulatory, which I tossed aside in favor of the Times.

I showered and shaved, brewed a pot of coffee, and spread the news on the kitchen table. Front page, Russia at odds with her former republics in East Asia. No mention of Santorini or the volcanic haze inundating the city, although at press time the ash would have fouled the streets! Headlines confined to politics in Moscow, the European community, the Middle East, the Japanese Diet, or wherever there was opposition universally it seemed. No mentions of the devastating blight in the Aegean.

There was mention of our wedding in the society section, however...which I set aside for Nina to see: her graduation photograph from Berkeley, her startling beauty and impish smile! I held the paper at arm's length and blessed my luck! There also was mention of the guest list: the Greek consul among others but, more importantly to Nina's liking, Ms. Garfinkle from South Manhattan, her matron of honor!

Concerned by the haze and diminished sunlight, I scanned the satellite weather report and studied a comment advanced by the meteorology department at Penn State University:

'Stratospheric westerlies have enveloped the Caribbean with the fallout from Santorini, overriding a tropical trough moving north along the eastern coast. An unexpected turn accompanied by a downpour of acid rain (the residue I'd tested from our windowsill!). A cold front over New England is on a collision course, however, moving south with heavy thunder- storms predicted by mid-afternoon.'

An inkling of things to come, I thought. Santorini's high-riding dust was on the move, drawn to the equatorial regions. Flowing to the north with the pressure gradient, traversing the Northern Hemisphere...multi-fold, if the volcano turned Plinian. It would screen the sun, decimating crops for years to come; days of total darkness, comparable to the onslaught from Krakatoa when the volcano blew its core in 1883. That explosion was heard in Australia, 2200 miles to the south; an explosion magnified twice by Thera's lethal eruption in 1628 BC!

Casting the section aside, I gave thought to the Swedish volcanologist's doomsday prediction when we viewed her videotape at Moffet Field. "I warn you," she said, "if the lunar tides draw the Aegean from the mantle over Santorini's hot spot, the weakened chamber will most likely collapse and we will experience a paroxysmal explosion that will rock the world!"

Dark thoughts for a groom with his bride trilling 'Summertime' in her shower, calling for a towel to turban her hair, pouting for a kiss that led to a steamy embrace and the sanctuary of our rumpled bed. And there we found tenderness, suppressed with understanding while we explored our sensitivity. Until, thoroughly aroused, we shared a splendid orgasm, clinging together, oblivious to time and place, until we were emotionally and physically spent.

Much later, while we drowsed midst the tangled sheets, Nina teased my ear with a strand of her dampish hair. Giggling when I raised my head from her breasts, she demanded I fetch a tumbler of juice from the fridge, spiked with the Taittinger we'd tapped the night before, suggesting we share the cup together..."Greek custom" she said.

Equal to the occasion, I stumbled naked to the kitchen, hesitating when she pointed to the steaming bathroom and shouted,

"We forgot to turn off the bloody shower!" Detouring momentarily to shut the thing down, I spied the hand-delivered cablegram on the floor while I struggled with a can of concentrate and our depleted bottle of wine. Puzzled by the instructions stapled to the envelope – 'Deliver by hand, receipt requested' (initialed by the doorman at 0800), I scanned the message to identify the sender, intending to take it along with the section of the Times. I had second thoughts, however, assuming there was a mix-up with ITT, when I attempted to unravel the text.

The garbled message was not the usual congratulatory I'd anticipated, although there was reference to our wedding and other matters which I thought best not to mention when Nina beamed her pleasure and we sipped my concoction from the fridge. Later, however, while she sat cross-legged with the newspaper strewn over the bed, I returned to the kitchen and examined the cable for a clue, wondering if the cryptic message was meant for eyes aside from mine.

The cable was addressed to my digs in Manhattan, to Mr. and Mrs., although our RSVP invitation applied to the Olympic Towers. The cable was datelined Vienna, however, and lacking a mailed invitation the sender might have referred to ITT's directory service or possibly my card from another time.

'Regards to Nina. Sorry unable to attend. G.G. under intensive care. Bypass imminent; advise T.S. Particulars en route by messenger. Signed Harry B. Hennessey.'

The only Hennessey I knew was biding time in his kennel. But Harry B. rang a bell. Was he someone we'd met at Mountain View? 'Regards to Nina' tallied with her presence, but who was G.G.? And then there was the familiarity with the General's initials, T.S.?

An icy feeling coursed my spine. Was the message an urgent warning, spuriously coded in desperation by an overseas operative on the lam? I circled 'Harry B.' with a pencil, Hennessey apart. The dog was in attendance at Hennessey's Bar when we celebrated Gomulaka's transition in the tandem U-2! We called him Doc, but the initials G.G. corresponded with the logbook he'd proudly brought along. Who else had been there, other than Nina and a gaggle of pilots from Mountain View?

I flexed my memory, thinking back. Focused a possibility...the rangy Pole of recent citizenship, the childhood friend of Dr Gomulaka. The computer analyst from Silicon Valley, he'd joined us late, saucered a beer for our thirsty dog. What was his name? Had I invited him to our engagement party, tendered my card when we called it a night?

An arm circled my shoulder; the scent of lavender and the touch of slender fingers announced the presence of my mischievous bride. Dressed in filmy silk that offered a glimpse of her pretty knees, she trailed my throat with a lingering kiss...demanding I dress immediately.

"I'm famished!" she said. "You promised lunch at the Plaza, my love. If you don't feed me .promptly, I shall faint!"

* * * * * *

The afternoon was hot and oppressive when we took to the street. The greenhouse effect had trapped a dome of humidity over the sweltering city; depressed the listless breeze to eddies of gritty ash. Taxis were few and far between, avoiding side streets, favoring the avenue with their lights ablaze, unmindful of the doorman's whistle. I tipped the old fellow for his efforts and slipped him a ten-spot to accept an important envelope should a courier arrive before five.

"Hold it in your desk," I cautioned, indicating I'd collect it when we returned.

"I'm off duty at four," he said, "but I'll leave word with O'Reilly." O'Reilly was notorious, inclined to lock the door and snooze in a cushy chair, but Nina was pacing the lobby and I was reluctant to express my concern. 'Particulars en route by messenger' did not necessarily mean they'd been forwarded by Federal Express.

"Do you talk to yourself often?" Nina inquired. I spun around and found her frowning her displeasure, a palm cupped beneath her mouth, as would an urchin begging for food.

"You told the doorman you'd call back. Do you intend to sublet the apartment to pay for lunch?"

"Depends on your appetite, sweetie. We'll sell my class ring if you order strawberries and cream!" She arched an eyebrow and flounced the avenue with abandon, disregarding the rank humidity, pointing to the outrageous gowns

53

she'd buy if we sold the Porsche! Her high-spirited, mischievous demeanor sparked with her inherent beauty, turned heads of pedestrians for an envious look see. Nina warm to my hand, warm to my heart, clinging to my arm when eyes were cast to observe the 'lucky guy'!

We sipped Taittinger and dined on Eggs Florentine in the Edwardian Room, fresh strawberries and heavy cream. We watched the surreys clopping by while we talked of many things. Central Park was alive, despite the smog. The usual Sunday carnival...bikers, hawkers, a monkey on a chain. Elderly people relaxed on the benches, heads festooned with newspaper to shield from the clinging ash. Sidewalk magicians plucking endless scarves from old silk hats, joggers, Hispanics, children with balloons, young men hand in hand, a bag lady prodding bins...a typical summer Sunday, a release for the cooped and lonely. A patchwork of color amongst the heavy green trees and leaden sky.

"Monet would have loved it," Nina observed. "He'd paint the sky a lovely blue, I think."

"Beer cans and stereos?"

"Humanity, Keith. Common folk on parade."

"Coffee, madam?" Nina looked up and smiled.

"Ice with a shot of ouzo, please!" The waiter frowned.

"For two?" I nodded; why not? Nina's tapered fingers reached across the table and clasped my hand.

"You seem worried, Keith. Is it the cable, or your wallet, my love?"

"You read it?" I blurted. She arched her eyebrows.

"You needn't shout! It was addressed to Mr. and Mrs., silly!"

I wrestled with my thoughts. How much had she read; how to deal with it in terms of husband and wife? The answer was forthcoming. Nina reached into her purse and unfolded the damnable thing.

"I have friends in Vienna, Keith, but the initials are a mish-mash and Hennessey hasn't the funds!" I closed my eyes; she'd deciphered the cable in part!

"Okay, so we juiced it at Hennessey's Bar. Do you remember the fellow who bought the Lab a beer?"

"Are you suggesting I was there?" she twinkled.

"Aside from that!" She studied the cablegram.

"Doctor Gomulaka, what a lovely man. G.G.?" I nodded.

"Gomulaka's friend...he stood a round of drinks?" She shook her head.

"Sorry, Keith. I took Hennessey for a walk to straighten him out. Poor animal, I do think he should join the AA"

"Later on, our engagement party at the Fairmont Hotel?"

"Oh, yes, I was definitely there!"

"Same fellow, arrived with the doctor. Damned if I can remember his name." Nina thought back. The guests were mostly her college friends and those motley pilots from Moffet Field! Her eyes narrowed. The older pilots with the balding man in a tight-fitting blazer!

"The man with the odious cigar!" She eyed me closely, pointing to the cablegram. "Your whatever-he-was in Riyadh? You introduce him as General O'Brien, but they called him T.S.!"

"They?"

"Your rackety friends; you know who I mean!" I fidgeted with my collar.

"I was referring to Gomulaka's buddy, honey. The tall European with a ring in his nose!"

"Slim like yourself, devilish blue eyes? You would make a good pair!"

"Compliments aside, do you remember his name?"

"Now I do, silly! He was off in a corner with T.S. most of the night. I have his card somewhere; he was very polite, said we invited him the night we leveled Hennessey's Bar? Keith, it isn't nice to stir ouzo with a knife!"

"It's not that important, honey! Shall we call it a day and go back to bed?" Nina smiled demurely. Her bridegroom was an incorrigible tease.

"Stanislas Obolensky, love! Dr Gomulaka called him Stash; does the name ring a bell?"

I gulped the ouzo and sneezed. "Obolensky!"

"Good heavens, Keith, now you've done it!" Nina exploded with laughter. The fiery liquid channeled my esophagus and detonated a mist of ouzo and ice! The waiter rolled his eyes and brought napkins to sop the linen.

"Ouzo is meant to be sipped, silly! Have you forgotten the meltdown at Chernobyl?"

I red-eyed the bending trees; a freshing breeze from the north was scattering newspapers and loose debris. Obolensky was mentioned briefly by Colonel Forsythe, although he declined to elucidate when he checked his notes. I assumed there was a connection with Gunnar's activities in Palo Alto, possibly a recent update he was unwilling to say. Suddenly, a segment fell into place. Obolensky had conversed at length with 'G.G.' at Hennessey's Bar! Lifelong friends, reacquainted, they'd most likely discussed the doctor's pending trip to Warsaw. 'G.G. under intensive care. Bypass imminent'? Was Obolensky aware of Gomulaka's schedule? Post a fortnight with his family in Poland, he was to join our group at the UN. Did the cable imply information to the contrary? Was

Obolensky the sender?

"...Chernobyl?" I became aware of Nina's voice in the distance. Nina shrugged; her groom was mouthing words, staring at the window. Was it the 'flounce' with spiked heels or the cable that had him at odds? She fingered her wedding band, pointing to the surreys flanking the street.

"Clippety-clop, why not? We could shop Madison Avenue and exercise your American Express!" She peered mischievously between her fingers. "A dress for me and a towel for thee?"

"The old gray mare with her nose in oats?"

Nina nodded. "The dilapidated rig with the sleepy old man!"

"You're on!"

She excused herself to powder her nose, drawing eyes as she skirted the tables. I crumpled the cablegram into my pocket, paid the tab, nodded to the disapproving dowagers and made haste to the downstairs phones. The doorman's answer was negative. I pressed the series of numbers I'd memorized at the Carlyle; the answer was a beep tone similar to a recording machine and to that I voiced my birth date. A vocal computer answered immediately.

"Your question please. Speak slowly and enunciate with clarity." I did what it said, requesting my call be relayed to General T.S. O'Brien. The computer responded, "Voice pattern identified; call in progress." I jingled the change in my pocket, searching for quarters while the call was transferred by satellite.

"Yes, Major!" I gripped the phone, picturing a lass with dimples and curls.

"I've a problem, honey. Is General O'Brien available?" There was a pause while she checked.

"Not at the moment, sir. Would you state your message, please!" I assessed my thoughts.

"Would you try his cell phone, honey? He plays golf at Congressional." There was another pause. I could hear a computer spooling nearby.

"You accessed a classified line, Major Slater; I've checked your file and find you 'inactive with a medical discharge'!"

I studied the graffiti scrawled on the wall. I'd been spooked by the general, endured an intensive briefing, and my file had been post-dated to desert Storm.

"Would you copy O'Brien, sweetie? I've an urgent from Vienna and I'm short of change!" She put me on hold. I applied my last quarter when the telephone beeped; gritted my teeth, in need of a pee.

"Roger, Major. I've your update from AFIA."

"AFIA?"

"Never mind! Would you repeat your code name, please?" I searched my mind.

"Turtle Dove, honey! I'm new to this," I added.

"Verified, Major. Your message, please?" I spieled off the cablegram word for word. She'd contact O'Brien immediately, she said. "Is Hennessey a personal friend?"

"Try Obolensky, first name Stash, Ames Research Lab. Talk to AFIA and see what they have." She fingered her computer.

"Stanislas S. Obolensky, computer analyst, high-tech communications. Okay, he's one of ours, but Hennessey doesn't show!"

I explained the circumstances to help her along. Submitted Gomulaka for G.G. and O'Brien for T.S. " Read it back and see what you have."

There was a long pause, conversation in the background, and then an older voice commanded the phone. I eyed the men's room and winced. My benefactor was obviously upset. I was treated to an earful from the open line; high voltage questions to someone apart, ill-defined answers, the bips and squeaks of a laboring computer. In part a follow-up of Obolensky's itinerary. Opted, Warsaw, Rpt'd, Vienna 1805, all clear!" And then, "No further contact 72 hours, the hell you say?" followed by expletives seldom expressed by ladies in air force blues.

I clung desperately to the phone, and made headlong for the shadows when Nina swished by. I'd gained a measure of credibility, however, an apology of sorts.

"Was the cable relayed to your apartment by fax machine?"

"Negative, sweetie! Delivered by hand." She expressed her relief, told me bluntly that my line might be tapped!

"Is there a pay phone adjacent to your apartment building?" she asked. Fortunately, I remembered the numbers.

"Excellent! Contact us immediately upon interception. I'm referring to the particulars, Major Slater." She handed off the 800 numbers. "Ask for Charlie, and for God's sake safeguard the package until we establish a drop! You've a 10 o'clock with the UN tomorrow, I believe?"

"That's right."

"Okay, now hear me loud and clear! We'll post a watch on your building as of 1800. That is the best we can do, Keith! Fortunately, there's a smog delay at JFK, but the messenger is unknown and there's a chance he'll be tailed by the KGB!" My neck hair curled.

"Jesus Christ!"

"Don't worry it, Keith. Play it cool and avoid a confrontation by all means. If there's a problem, we'll handle it off-street." She lowered her voice, as if she had a hand on my shoulder. "You're new to this, Keith. It's not your choice to be involved with a shitty situation. We apparently have an operative running scared with vital information, unable top contact our agency, but it would be folly to think he'd send wolves to your door."

"Aside from that, have we met before?"

"It's Colonel Pettigrew, sweetie! General O'Brien's aide de camp. I'm married now, but I ferried F-16s to Riyadh when you were a hot stick on the make!"

We were cut off for lack of change, but I remembered the non-combatant reserve major as I sped for the men's room; a wispy blonde with icy blue eyes, who'd buzzed the strip inverted while we were refueling our F-15s.

CHAPTER 7

Awnings were whipping, the breeze spinning debris from the street when the mare clopped to a stop and would go no further. We were at Madison and 70th; a curl of gray cloud moved swiftly overhead, a roll of thunder echoed from the north. The fast-moving cold front was almost upon us.

"Sorry folks! She's sensin' the rain and wantin' her barn." The old man fingered his hat. He'd promised us an hour, and was uncertain of his tip.

"He could drop us at Fifth," Nina suggested. "There's a café at the Stanhope and the museum across the way." The old man brightened.

"Anywhere on Fifth, ma'am. Long's she got the wind behind." I shrugged; we had the afternoon to ourselves. Nina's eyes sparkled.

"A glass of iced tea for the hot and weary?"

"Why not?" I responded, nodding to the old man. The mare jawed her lines, eyed traffic, and trotted peacefully through the light.

The nippy wind was a welcome change from the sultry afternoon when we dropped the surrey. The approaching front had lifted the smog. The residue of ash would be washed to the gutters with the rain. It would be bright by early morning; the volcanic grit long forgotten as it swirled the rivers and joined the outgoing tide.

"Why so quiet, Keith?"

"Thinking, Nina. New Yorkers are an insulated lot."

"I know! Volcanoes are so remote; they should witness the havoc in Naxos and Paros, the olive groves crusted with ash!"

"Rain! Hike your dress and let's go!"

Nina took off like a Thomson gazelle, her long legs gathering momentum as she darted between the startled pedestrians. I was yards behind when she averted the Stanhope, gambling traffic fronting the Met.

"Sanctuary, Keith! The Stanhope's crowded, shall we try the museum?" She pointed to the long gray building shouldering the park, vising my arm when a bolt of lightning illuminated the edifice. We'd climbed the granite steps and gained the revolving doors when a peal of thunder jolted the avenue, and I then realized she was no longer beside me.

The memory of that moment haunts me now; that and the incident that followed. Had fate turned the wrong page when we aborted the Stanhope for the Metropolitan? Was Nina drawn by her psychic dreams to the unholy thing that lay inside, spurred by the volatile storm that came so suddenly upon us?

I found her by the desk where they take donations and clip a tab to one's lapel. She was pale and withdrawn, shivering from the air conditioning, her long black hair clinging to her shoulders. Disoriented, I thought, when I gripped her arm and led her past the sharp-eyed attendant. She brightened when we climbed the inner stairway, on to her light-hearted self when we strolled the westerly wing, admiring the Art Nouveau, Weiner Werstatte, and the Scandinavian drawings of recent times.

"It's fantastic, Keith! They have it so much together, and the lighting is superb, so unlike the Prince Albert Museum and the dreadful Prado in Madrid!"

She slung my jacket to her shoulders and we wandered the Renaissance section; gloomy oils, the heroic scenes of long ago. We spent an hour in the southerly room, with Winslow Homer and his contemporaries, with the French Impressionists and their vivid colors. It was a peaceful afternoon, and Nina was completely absorbed, aside from a nervous hand on my wrist when the halls echoed with distant thunder.

It was nearing closing time when it happened. The crowd had thinned; the guards were shepherding stragglers to the foyer, when a jagged bolt of lightning neonized the window, followed by a horrendous clap of thunder.

Children screamed and clung to their elders; outsiders re-emerged from the revolving doors. There was mayhem of sorts, then the hard-driving rain and a spatter of hail. I was conscious of Nina's icy fingers on my arm, but when I eased through the pressing crowd she was no longer there!

"Closing time, mister," a guard reminded me as I circled the foyer. "The storm's calmed down a bit and we lock the doors at five."

"I know, but my wife's still inside!" I pointed to the Greco-Roman section. He followed me in; we passed through the maze of marbled heads from Roman times, and chronologically we found her, clinging to a display of artifacts preceding the days of Ancient Greece.

Nina was kneeling by the illuminated display, clawing the glass as if the unyielding substance was an incomprehensible barrier. The guard's hand tightened on my arm.

"Jesus, man, she been smoking the weed?" I brushed him aside and went immediately to Nina. She was rigid to my touch, eyes fixed to an ancient serpent ring with emerald eyes...carded Arhannes, 1628 BC

Nina sobbed when I pulled her away, chanting all the while in a language I'd never heard before, pointing to the unearthly thing that glared from the case. Then, shaking her head as if awakening from a trance, she yielded to my arm and I led her gently to the foyer, pausing until the onlookers thinned at the revolving doors.

"She pregnant?" the guard inquired.

"Not yet," I said, shielding Nina with my blazer.

"We had a weirdo last week," he commented. "Same thing...she played a flute to that fucking snake. Creepy, man! Took four of us to carry her outside. Resembled your wife, come to think...long hair, but not so pretty."

Well meaning, aware of my problem, the guard held the emergency exit door open while I guided my trembling bride to the outside. And it was here that I noticed we'd been followed by a stout woman in tweeds! I'd observed her earlier in the foyer, but gave her scant thought when she entered a waiting limousine and disappeared in the pelting rain.

The tweedy lady was Amalia, of course. Discreet and remote, she'd apparently tracked us from the Plaza, observed us from a distance, presumably to acquaint herself with our faces. I was preoccupied with Nina at the time, although I was aware of her presence in weeks to come.

The raw wind brought a measure of color to Nina's cheeks when we descended the granite steps. Her dispirited stumbling gave way to her long-legged stride when we bolted the avenue for lack of an accommodating cab. I caught up with her between Madison and Lex when she steered for an awning to shake the moisture from my blazer.

Dusk by then; the rain had abated to an occasional splatter. Volatile lightning illuminated New Jersey while the cold front traversed the Hudson. To the west, skies were clearing, offering a glimpse of golden sunshine when I flagged an off-duty cab.

"I can drop you at 58th and Third," the driver stated, apparently en route to his stable in Queens. "55th heads west, and I'd be roundabout to tackle the fuckin' bridge!" I produced a tenner and he agreed to the extra blocks.

"Why am I so drained?" Nina whispered, her eyes glistening with tears as she slumped in the rear seat. "Was I hysterical, Keith? Tell me!" she pleaded, staring blindly at the trendy shops.

I gripped her icy hand, realizing she had no recollection of the eerie scene at the Met.

"You panicked, honey! A bolt clipped a tree and you split for ancient history."

"Don't tell me I freaked out!"

"Frightened, Nina. Children were screaming, the outsiders crashed the doors, and we had a Chinese fire drill until they reasoned it wasn't a bomb."

She closed her eyes momentarily, groping for an answer. Her eyes turned to the window, puzzled by the reflection of her earrings in the glass.

"Is it possible they might have come from the wall?" she said.

I gripped her arm, realizing she'd dislodged an incident from the past. We were stalled with traffic at 57th Street at the time, the disgruntled cabby eyeing us from his mirror.

"Papa gave me the earrings when I was eighteen," Nina murmured. "Said I'd worn them before, although he didn't say where or when. I assumed they were replicas," she added, "until recently, when Auntie told me they'd come from Arhannes." Nina paused for a moment, collecting her thoughts. Then, clasping my hand, she related a curious story.

"I've had a dreadful fear of lightning since I visited the dig at Arhannes, Keith. We stayed aboard the Helena and papa took me ashore when they uncovered the Minoan temple. The archeologists, excited after months of digging, had sent a messenger to the yacht. Papa wasn't aware of what they'd discovered until we reached the site and it was all too late! God love him, he tried to shield me when I saw the skeletons, said it happened long ago, explained as best he could."

"Scary, hey?"

"Ghastly, Keith! Thera was rampant at the time, but judging from the sediment, the tragedy preceded the catastrophe. There was evidence of a heavy tremor; most likely their torches set the timbers ablaze. At nightfall, when the volcano was a dreadful glow in the sky, its horror combined with the awesome rumbling they'd endured for months on end! The Minoans were peaceful, Anatolian people who worshiped the bull, offering the heads ritualistically. Towards the end, they obviously were terrified and resorted to human sacrifice."

Nina paused for a moment, fingered her earrings. I gripped her arm again, glancing at the cabby staring wide-eyed from his mirror, and urged her to continue when he spurted the light.

"There was something more," Nina mused, seemingly relaxed with the slow-moving traffic. "Macabre, and yet so beautiful. 'So like the legend of Amor and Psyche' Papa said when I was reduced to tears. Huddled in a corner, buried alive, they discovered the skeleton of a girl in her teens, most likely a Minoan princess or a priestess attending the young man's obeisance. Close by her hand, as if she intended to return in future time, they found her jewelry in a crevice she'd gouged in the wall; rings and bracelets, earrings, and a necklace with a pendant of solid gold.

"The necklace you saw in my father's drawer, out of sight until I searched for his tax receipts. He said I wasn't to wear it," she added. "But that was long ago, never again mentioned when he was alive."

"The ring?"

"Donated first off! Papa was disdainful of the hideous thing; superstitious, perhaps, but in retrospect he exercised good reasoning. I remember the occasion vividly," she continued. "The archeologists' sweaty shirts, the workmen staring at my braids. Papa took the jewelry aboard that night for safekeeping. The gold artifacts were tagged, the serpent ring glaring from the fold."

The cabby was visibly interested, so I nodded to his mirror, indicating he was to pull aside momentarily. He obliged at once, punching his meter to 'hold'.

"Aside from the ring, I was fascinated by the figurine attached to the necklace," Nina continued, caught up in her thoughts, oblivious to the changing lights as she clutched my hand. "Carved from a chunk of gold, it depicted a bare-breasted girl wearing a bell-shaped skirt; hair gathered with a strand of silver. I vividly remember her eyes...so lifelike – green like mine – set with emeralds. The archeologists said the resemblance was uncanny, Keith, but I wasn't aware of what they meant. It didn't register until that evening when I experienced a curious dream."

"You identified with the princess?" Nina nodded.

"As would any child," she reasoned. "Perhaps I exercised my imagination, but the circumstances were unusual and I was bloody scared! A terrible storm roared from the highlands while we were hurrying to board the Helena," she added. "The sky was hazy blue, electric; workmen were jittery, talking amongst themselves. The cyclone appeared from nowhere, weird and ominous. It seemed to follow us, curling like an angry snake, churning the sea, striking the Helena's mast. It was as if we'd penetrated a sacred lair!"

"Cyclones in Crete?" the cabby chided. "I'm a generation Greek, ma'am, but Arhannes lays me down!"

Nina smiled and spoke to him briefly in his native language.

"Captain Stavos said it was very unusual," she said. "In fact, the Cretans refused to work the dig the next day. Said the storm was a bad omen, that there were matters best left undisturbed."

"So what happened next? Like, I gotta tell my wife!"

Nina turned to question me with her eyes. I urged her to continue; the cabby was well meaning, family by then.

"I dreamt of the princess that very night," Nina said. "The dream I mentioned earlier was long and mysterious, as if I'd entered another world while we sat and talked. She was beautiful, Keith. Tall and slender, bare to the waist, so like the frescoes I'd seen at Akrotiri. She was older than I, although her eyes were similar and she wore earrings of hammered gold.

"Later that night, long after midnight, Papa found me on the stern deck where I'd wandered in my sleep. I was wearing her necklace, her earrings, the ring on my finger...chanting words of a dialect he'd never heard before! Or so he said, when he pulled me from the railing and shook me awake!

"Papa was furious," Nina continued with a reflective smile. "Frightened, more likely, realizing I was unaware of my closeness to the sea. God love him, Keith, he embraced me tenderly when I told him of my dreams. I slept between them until we returned to Athens. I'd no recollection as to how I found her things in total darkness, much less the key to Papa's desk!"

"That will be $5.80," the cabby commented when he circled our block. "Forget the ten spot," he added, helping Nina to the curb. "I'm acquainted with Deucalion and Pyrrha, sir...the legend...but never dreamed she'd share me cab!"

I had an inkling of Nina's psychic mind when he sped away to enlighten his wife, but I placed my thoughts on hold when O'Reilly unlatched the lobby doors.

CHAPTER

'Reilly bowed over-politely whilst I guided Nina to the elevator and pressed the floor. Realized something was up (in addition to his ingestion of vodka) when he leered from his desk, pointing to the inner lobby as if he'd admitted an unwelcome guest. Kissing Nina soundly, I said I'd follow her up in a few minutes then, turning to O'Reilly, I inquired of his problem. He loosed a woozy grin.

"O'Malley said you was expectin' an envelope."

"That's right."

"Well, it came a while back and' I let him in." I scanned my watch, wondering if 'Charlie' had had time to contact and brief an operative familiar with the case?

"Messenger?"

"Probably. He was bangin' on the glass and callin' your name. Left his bag outside, but someone came and got it, I think."

"Where is he now?" O'Reilly refocused his eyes, pointed to the high-back chairs.

"Over there, but he ain't communicatin'. You forgot me Christmas gratuity, Mr. Slater. Been meanin' to ask."

The stranger was slouched in a chair by a column. He wore an unlikely jacket of wrinkled tweed, a sweaty shirt and a knotted tie loosened at the collar. A hank of brownish hair clung damp to his forehead, his arms were limp and hanging from the chair, his eyes fixed to the vaulted ceiling. I thumped his shoulder, attempting to bring him about, but his head fell forward and lolled to the side. I fingered his wrist for a pulse; there was none. Pressed an ear to his chest...a gaseous gurgle greeted me from his abdomen, but no heartbeat. The man was obviously dead!

"Is there a doctor in the building?" I shouted. O'Reilly lunged from his desk.

"S'matter? He drunk?" I motioned him back, mindful of the circumstances, remembering the quiet little man who sometimes nodded in the elevator.

"Dr. Liebman…10B! Would you please call him; tell him it's an emergency!" O'Reilly shrugged and turned about; I moved quickly to frisk the stranger's jacket while he muddled with the intercom.

His pocket divulged a wad of Kleenex, a fiver, several ones, as if he'd pocketed recent change. Replacing the contents, I explored the opposite side…surfaced a pack of cigarettes and a math folder from the *Palace Hotel in Wien*! My pulse quickened. I scanned the lobby, searching his inner pockets with an eye to the door. The left inner side was ripped from the lining, visibly forced, as if wrested from behind. The contents of the right pocket seemingly intact, yielding a leather passport folder, but not what I was seeking. Curious as to why the jacket was undone, drawn by the missing buttons and dangling threads, I lifted the tail of his jacket and there it was! A long brown envelope jammed sideways beneath his belt, lodged against his hip.

Withdrawing the envelope quickly, I examined it by the lamp. The sealed contents bore a thumbprint on the closure, smeared but legible, as if hurriedly applied from a felt tip pen. The envelope was not addressed, damp, as if he'd crammed it in his waistband while exposed to the rain. He'd been followed, I assumed, manhandled and robbed before he hammered the door.

O'Reilly's voice echoed in the distance. The intercom squeaked, the door opened and closed, and a tenant bustled by with a bag of groceries while I gathered my wits. Turning quickly to shield the dead man from her view while she waited for the elevator, I probed his backside cautiously with my fingers, my suspicions confirmed when I snagged a sliver of metal embedded in the tweeds! A shiver iced my spine when I realized the circumstances that had sent him reeling to his chair. An outsized needle was lodged in his back; he'd been struck by a deadly dart while he waited at the door!

The elevator clanged to a stop whilst I removed the needle by its shaft and, heeding a voice from days before, I inserted the lethal thing in my tie. '*Now then,*' Colonel Forsythe had added in closing, '*the devices you may encounter on a quiet street…a furled umbrella triggered from the handle; a walking cane; a fountain pen. The CO_2 cartridge discharges a dart the size of a sewing needle; the penetrating point excretes a deadly poison upon rupturing the victim's skin… a massive heart seizure results. The countdown is three minutes; there is no antidote. Recin leaves no residual trace and is twice as deadly as cobra venom. The needle usually falls away, or is lost when the victim's cloth-*

ing is removed at the morgue.'

"He has no heartbeat; call an ambulance at once," a calm voice intoned. The thin-nosed doctor applied a stethoscope to the stranger's chest and fingered his eyes. "He's been dead for at least an hour; suffered a massive seizure. Is he a friend?" he added, looking up.

"I've never seen him before," I answered truthfully.

"Shoutin' your name when I let him in!" O'Reilly interjected. The doctor nodded impatiently.

"I'll need his name and address. Would you check his pockets for identification, please?"

I checked his passport, together with his KLM ticket. The passport was American, a multi-page commercial type. The ticket, issued in Vienna, showed he'd caught the morning flight...arrived around 5 p.m.

"Stanislas Obolensky, male, birthplace Warsaw, Poland," I noted, staring at the photograph. The likeness matched the dead man, but he was not Obolensky!

"Passport issued?"

"San Francisco, November '97." I rattled off the information...who was this man who'd cleared immigration?

"Check his trousers for an address, his wallet, a driver's license," the doctor suggested.

His pockets were cold and clammy, yielding a roll of currency...so he hadn't been robbed!

"That's it," I said, pointing to the wad of currency, "except for loose change."

"No wallet?"

"Negative, doctor." Liebman looked up, adjusted his glasses.

"10D?" I nodded

"Mr. and Mrs. as of yesterday noon!" He offered a smile.

"You're assigned to the UN?" I nodded again; he'd read the Times.

"Did either of you witness the seizure?" he queried.

"Negative! He was here when we returned from the museum, and my wife went directly upstairs." Liebman fingered his bifocals; was he staring at my tie?

"Do you recall the time?"

"Six-thirty, give or take. So what's the drill?"

Liebman lowered his eyes and continued to make notes on a medical form. 'European, Caucasian male, age 35-38, approximately five eight, blue eyes, brown hair. No indication of alcohol or barbiturates, medical history unknown. No identification aside from passport attached.' He thumbed the photograph, tested the seal.

"Are you acquainted with Stanislas Obolensky?" he asked abruptly. I steeled myself. Was he referring to the fraudulent photo or to O'Reilly's remarks?

"The man's a total stranger, Doctor! I'm cold and wet. Might we call it a day?" His eyes darted to O'Reilly's desk, but O'Reilly was closeted somewhere with his bottle. Liebman shrugged and signed the form.

"There's a possibility the police will request your statement when they question the doorman, he said, pointing to the beacons flashing outside. "Although, considering his condition, they'll put it off until tomorrow, I think." He hesitated for a moment, studied my reaction, and lowered his voice.

"Frankly, I'm puzzled, but I'm impressed by your commitment to serve with the UN and I'm omitting your name from my notes. I strongly suggest you join your bride," he added with a dour smile. And, with that, he closed his bag and hurried to unlock the door, standing aside while a stretcher was trundled from the ambulance. Inclining his head towards the elevator when a burly lieutenant followed behind.

* * * * * *

Nina was fast asleep, clutching her pillow. She'd bathed, stretched my blazer with her dress to dry, and savaged the fridge, exploding our remaining bottle of champagne. Left the residue for me, together with a frosted glass and a napkin, both with her lip imprint.

I stripped in the kitchen so as not to disturb her. Encountering the envelope, I eyed the tie draped on a chair and spied the deadly needle glinting from the carpet. Drained of Recin? Most likely not, I thought. Mindful of Nina's early hours and her inquisitive nature, I slipped the dart inside the envelope, folded the lot in the realty section of the Sunday Times and parked it on a closet shelf she'd be hard put to reach. Come morning I had a ten o'clock at the UN...a prearranged briefing with the meteorological group who would staff our project in Kos. We'd be long gone, squared away in Nassau, if questions were asked when O'Reilly came on duty at five. Pleasant thoughts were short-lived, however, when the phone rang from the kitchen wall.

I reached quickly to subdue the thing, thankful it wasn't the intercom.

"Is that you, Keith?" a female inquired.

"Possibly," I answered, thinking she was a friend from the past. The caller giggled.

"It's Maggie, sweetie! Sorry to call late, but we were caught in traffic and just got back. Is tomorrow okay for lunch?" she added, suggesting the Giraffe at 58th. I nodded to myself, realizing 'Maggie' was a covert operative waiting my cue. She prattled on for a moment, remarking of the weather while I gave thought to Charlie's coded instructions. 'Lunch' was keyed to collecting the envelope, if I had received such? They'd apparently sped the action and needed confirmation. 'Giraffe' indicated a caution light, suggesting a secondary time and place!

"Tomorrow's okay!" I allowed. Then, opening my briefcase, I attached a transistor to the receiver. A red light glowed immediately; we had a silent listener and my bride was sound asleep!

"You're mumbling, Keith!" I cut the conversation short, confirming lunch at the Giraffe was also okay, observing the transistor light dimmed and blinked off shortly after Maggie hung up! My phone obviously tapped since God knows when?

CHAPTER 9

*N*ina was her lively self the next morning, expressing delight while she tilted the shades to the sun; giggling, offering   sudsy lips when we embraced in the shower. No hint of yesterday when we shared a Danish with coffee, no remorse when she arched her lovely eyes and waxed enthusiastic for the days ahead.

Sprightly dressed in clinging silk, she was off to collect Hennessey when I retrieved the realty section from the closet shelf. Gone with the clanging elevator, the scent of her lavender lingering as if she'd read my grievous thoughts.

The sun was bright, sidewalks gritty, but the streets were freshly swept when I purchased the morning Times at Second Avenue. Santorini front page...'Volcanic Ash Inundates New York', highlighting a report from their correspondent at Penn State. I hailed a southbound taxi and read on, shrugging when we fronted the UN. There was little of note, aside from a pithy remark on the editorial page suggesting the *inconvenience* be blasted at its source.

At nine-thirty I collected my pass from security and caught an elevator to room 821. Per Dr. Nokomo's request, our briefing session was scheduled for 10 o'clock. I had reason for arriving early, however, nodding to the tall black standing by the conference room door. He had me tagged by my limp; flashed his AFIS ident when I asked if he was a friend of Charlie's?

"Slater?"

"Right!"

"Sorry for last night," he said. "We were stalled in traffic," he added, stepping aside to avoid a trio of waiters with the coffee and croissants. "Like, they're setting up your meeting, hey?"

The clatter was a little much, and I had questions to ask. I spied the gent's room down the hall and tried the entry. The agent followed me in and listened patiently while I unloaded my misgivings.

"Okay, so you came along late," I said. "The doorman was smashed, my wife's upstairs, and I'm nursing a corpse with a dart in his spine! I'm new to this," I added. "By rights, I'm a material witness; should we sneak out with the trash?"

"Don't worry it, you're clean," he replied. "We copied the police report and there's no way they'd get back to you, man."

Ex-FBI, multi-lingual, field grade officer with the AFIS, he'd teamed with Maggie when they were alerted to the case, he allowed.

"We were on to a security leak at the time," he added. "Bartending at Andrews Air Force Base, like we're a couple of no count blacks fixin' drinks for a loudmouth from overseas." Called on the cellular, they'd been briefed by 'Charlie' and caught the 4 o'clock shuttle to New York.

"We circled the smog until six," he continued. "Now it's rainin' frogs and the cabbies don't like us, so we hike it to the marine terminal for a government car. Then comes the traffic...like the weirdoes from the Hamptons are blastin' their horns, and all we see is tail lights until we cross the Queensborough Bridge."

They'd apparently cruised by when the police arrived, monitored the situation on the emergency band, and tailed the ambulance to the morgue.

"We spotted you in the lobby," he added. "Pieced things together when we examined the stiff's credentials."

"Did you identify the corpse?" I asked abruptly.

"He wasn't Obolensky, if that's what you mean. Slavic, same build, that's all we know."

"Did they perform an autopsy?"

"Sort of. The coroner had a row of stiffs to do, and signed the certificate while we were there. I couldn't handle it," he admitted, "but Maggie stood by to see if they detected homicide."

"Negative, hey?" The agent nodded.

"Thanks to Liebman's notes...we suspected he knew, but we weren't about to muddy the water. Obolensky's officially dead...for the record, that is. So maybe he doesn't know it yet, but his obit will draw them off if he's hiding out in Vienna."

"KGB?" The agent nodded again.

"KGB's old hat, but tell that to someone else! So now we have a half dozen breakaway republics to screen and the operatives haven't changed their spots! Same old faces, cozy with the hard-liners in the military who may be planning a coup d'etat! So, let's say Obolensky came onto something heavy. Judging from his wire he's running scared, desperate to make contact. Aware of your wedding plans and your address in New York, he fires it off, knowing you'd decipher the contents and contact T.S. We doubt if they had means to intercept the cable," he added, "much less decode the thing. Unfortunately, there was a glitch when he prompted a courier to deliver the package."

"You checked it out?"

Prompted by Charlie, the AFIS had obtained a feedback from the airline's computerized passenger list, cross-checked with Vienna. The ticket had been issued minutes before the flight, paid with cash, no prior reservation! The passenger hand-carried his luggage, requested a seat in the smoking section and boarded the flight without incident.

"Okay, so they've a watch for Obolensky, but he doctors his passport to match an unknown. Most likely a friend or acquaintance; possibly an illegal immigrant wanting to join the Polish community in New York. Normally, it would have worked, seeing as he breezed stateside immigration. But Charlie figured he was tagged when he presented Obolensky's passport in Wien...most likely by a departure clerk, a confidant with a hotline to the KGB, but it's too late to field a strong arm. So they panic, thinking Obolensky's slipped by, and arrange a reception committee at JFK."

"So he hails a cab and heads for my flat?"

"Exactly, but there's no indication they knew your address, or they'd have staked your street in advance! It was strictly a hit. They had the hots for Obolensky and spiked his descript."

"Bugged my phone in advance?"

"Come off it, man, the shoe doesn't fit! Your line was needled weeks back; when, we're not sure. Most likely has to do with the UN. Like the Russkies are paranoid," he added. "They Okayed White Dove, but they're long in the tooth when it comes to U-2s."

Since the hybrid was closeted at Lockheed, why the bloody caper they'd laid at my door, I wondered to myself.

"The connection with Obolensky?"

"I'm not authorized to answer that!" I flushed my urinal.

"Okay, so I'm walking out!" He fingered his left incisor.

"Cool it, man! We'll have a better picture when we analyze what you have!" I clung to the envelope for leverage, curious of what he knew.

"Look, fella, we've labored Obolensky, but the cable's the issue and I can read between the lines. We've a project briefing scheduled for ten," I added, "so don't cut me short if he's into a nasty scene!"

"Are you acquainted with the man?"

"Affirmative!" I admitted. "He bought our group a round at Hennessey's Bar, came along late, wiped us out! We were celebrating my observer's transition in the U-2!"

"Dr. Gomulaka, right?" I nodded, realizing he was referring to G.G. "They were childhood friends in Silesia. Hadn't seen one another in years. He recognized the doctor from an article in the examiner, and NASA told him where we were likely to be."

"Okay, so we've established a link with G.G., and Hennessey indicates a time and place. Is Hennessey your dog? We've wondered about that."

"Alcoholic of late. So what's the pitch?" The agent grinned.

"The wording and timing's important, man! Like, you meet an old friend who's hacked it and you wonder where you've been? Gomulaka was the catalyst," he added, "straight, happily married, an apolitical scientist dedicated to his work. There's a new generation in Poland and Obolensky came to heel."

"KGB operative?"

"De facto, Slater! Now you know why they have the hots for his ass. Obolensky was assigned to Silicon Valley; his forte...computer technology. He was into export-import of micro-chips, but was mainly a computer hack analyzing over-the-shoulder information for the KGB. He's a naturalized citizen and traveled extensively, no questions asked, but the AFIS spooled his number when he cracked the computer bank at Ames. So he shows up at Hennessey's Bar like he has a premonition and is giving it thought." I stared at the marble walls.

"Christ, I invited him to our engagement party! He was off in a corner with T.S."

"Right, but we had him by then. He could be tried for treason, but the old man played it cool and cut a deal, knowing Obolensky had access to the KGB. He put him to the test, turned him loose with a covert assignment! We weren't clued to the specifics, not then. T.S. was closemouthed; the decision top drawer."

"Had it to do with White Dove?"

"You're giving me fits, man!"

"I'm flying the U-2, goddammit!"

The agent groomed his hair in the mirror, shrugging when I eyed my watch.

"Okay, so there's a link; but it's strictly offbeat and I'm asking you to hold your mouth. Do we have an understanding?" I agreed, listening carefully when he laid it on the line.

"Obolensky was last seen near Ramenskoye, where the Russkies are testing high-altitude recon in the class of the advanced U-2...a Ram-M. Something like that. Ring a bell?"

"Right! It's a stretch-wing Mystic M-17-B; long range, loaded with high-tech radar, strictly experimental."

"Okay, so the flights are top secret, the area restricted to high-level brass. Obolensky was observed driving a Lada with Soviet Polkovnik front seat. We have it from a reliable source with a connection to the CIA. Interesting, hey? Like, he tripped with the braid, or penetrated the base with his KGB credentials."

"And they found him out?"

"Later, we think; but we hadn't a clue until you contacted Charlie. Obolensky was on his own, mind you. Like I said, T.S. was closemouthed and Ramenskoye a thing apart. So Charlie plays your hunch and checks Gomulaka independently, knowing T.S. was playing golf. Took a while, but the gal hung in and had word back from Warsaw around 3 a.m."

"Confirming?"

"Affirmative! The doctor disappeared Thursday last, and it reeks of KGB! Seems his wife phoned the university when he didn't show for lunch. Knows he's absent-minded and due at the UN, maybe caught the wrong flight? But they located his car in the university parking lot with the keys inside, his glasses nearby. So she's off the wall, checked the hospitals, and the agency picked it up from there."

"Is T.S. in the know?"

"As of now, he is! Said to haul ass with what you have. He was steaming, man! Said to tell you to clam it and he'd contact you in London; more like he was worried you'd confide in your bride. Do you know him well?"

I passed the envelope to the agent, cautioning him to be careful with the lethal dart. He turned abruptly when an Arab bustled by and hurried to a stall...inclined his head to the doorway when the Muslim spread his skirts.

"Gotta tell you something, Slater. I didn't know you from shit, but you gave me a straight eye and loosened me up. So I'm asking you politely to forget what I said, seeing you're up to your ass in something you don't like. Now, I'll put it personal," he added. "Maggie and I will be watching the tube when you tackle that fucking volcano!"

We shook hands on that. I waited until he was out the door, washed my face to clear my thoughts, and joined the conference down the hall.

CHAPTER

"Gentlemen, please be seated," the secretary said, when we'd downed the croissants, doughnuts and coffee. She was tall and bony, wore a short-clipped afro and a colorful gown to her sandled toes. She spoke with a British accent when she unfurled a chart of the staff's configuration.

"Your team captain is Dr. Louis Nokomo," she continued, pointing to the chart with a lighted wand. "Dr. Nokomo is a graduate of the University of Edinburgh, a long-time member of the Nigerian Agriculture Planning Committee, and a recipient of the OBE!" She looked about, frowning when an English type said:

"The doctor's detained, Miss Obtrui; his press conference, you know." Obtrui shrugged apologetically and referred again to her chart.

"And now, our staff meteorologist, Dr. Allen Winner, who will accompany the group to Kos. Dr. Winner is on leave of absence from McGill University in Toronto, Canada, a valued member of our environmental studies group."

"McGill is in Montreal," the English girl asided. Obtrui was unflappable. She commended the podium!

"Yes, of course! Would the doctor please stand?" Winner was a pleasant type, bearded, square of shoulder, forty odd. We'd talked for a while before we sat down.

Obtrui continued with her chart, naming Dr. Nokomo's designated priorities in his chain of command. Dr. Ingrid Sigurdesson, the Swedish volcanologist, would join us in Athens, as would Dr. Edwards, who would accompany her there. The Nigerian checked her notes, scanning the room. Was Dr. Gomulaka present?

"The doctor's wife called this morning, Miss Obtrui," her companion informed her. "She asked if we'd seen him; she'd apparently checked his hotel."

I walked to the window and stared at the East River while the English lass conversed with Obtrui. An oil barge careened by with the outgoing tide; FDR was alive with bumper-grinding traffic. I wished I were somewhere else, with Nina on a solitary island!

"Dr. Gomulaka has been detained," Obtrui explained. "More likely missed his plane and will join the group at Kos," she surmised. "The pilot commanding White Dove's U-2 is among those present, I believe." She scanned her notes. "Keith Slater, formerly with NASA, and Air Force graduate with a degree in aeronautical engineering. Should I address you as Major?" she questioned. "Dr. Nokomo cites you as a civilian contract pilot?"

I saluted the group from the window, realizing I was low on Nokomo's totem pole, a 'necessary American' assigned to the leased U-2.

The remainder of the assembly was mainly clerical, assigned to desks and pencils, none with the expertise to define our objectives, I was quick to learn.

"Overpaid, overstaffed and demanding," the English girl commented when Obtrui adjourned the meeting and disappeared with the rank and file. She joined Winner and myself when we tarried to examine his meteorological charts...lent an ear, made notes while we plotted the winds aloft over North Africa and the Persian Gulf. She was also helpful; genuinely interested when we calculated the U-2's flight path over Iran. An Oxford graduate, she was assigned to logistics.

"The wherewithal to transport Nokomo and his staff to Kos, housing arrangements...a bloody waste of funds, considering three could do the work of twenty and the scientists will make do with tents," she allowed.

"You sound bitter," Winner commented. She forced a smile, displaying square white teeth and a stubborn chin. Twentyish, her auburn hair was sensibly cut pageboy style.

"Disappointed," she replied, saying she'd majored in ecology...taken the UN job when a position was offered in environmental studies, not realizing she'd be burdened with unrelated paperwork. "I do wish I could join you in Kos," she added. "I requested field studies, as assistant to Dr. Edwards, in fact. And he agreed, but then Dr. Nokomo turned it down."

"Why?" I countered.

"In lieu of a bevy of secretaries," Winner interjected, indicating he'd had a similar problem and would make do on his own. "Nokomo's long on administration, short in the field; juices his staff with Third World appointees. They mean well," he added, "but by and large, they lack the expertise to assist our analysis...the nitty-gritty on site, and that's what it's all about! True...it's Maureen, is it not?"

76

She dimpled rosy cheeks, explaining the setup as she saw it. Nokomo and his staff would be quartered in the capital city, miles from the aerodrome at Antimahia, "Where you'll make do with goats and rocks," she pointed out. Abandoned barracks would house the scientists and their monitoring devices, plus an isolated ramp to service the U-2.

"Fortunately, your complement is to be serviced by NASA, Mr. Slater, except for a local ground crew and your petrol requirements." Communications, the satellite link, and mainstay computers were assigned to the aerodrome as a precautionary measure.

"In the event of an emergency," she explained. "The aerodrome is located on relatively high ground."

"And God forbid," Winner asserted, "but historically the hills were swept by the deluge."

"Yes, and Dr. Sigurdesson warns it may happen again! She predicts a Plinian explosion following a series of flood tides on the eve of the full moon! The tidal draw on the tectonic plates crevassing Santorini's hot spot, I believe. Her personal theory, of course, bit it brings to point a serious flaw in Dr. Nokomo's planning, as I see it," she added. "Although I shan't be there if it comes to be."

"Out with it, honey. We'll keep it to ourselves," Winner prompted.

She brightened, and said she appreciated the confidence. Sensible, dedicated to the project …frustrated, shorn of her input. She'd apparently flown to Kos to arrange Nokomo's accommodations in early June, booking his entourage at a harbor-side hotel.

"Full fare, per his instructions," she added, "although the city is low-lying with a tenuous link to the aerodrome at Antimahia; a suspect telephone line and little more. Buses are available for transport over the rocky road to high ground. We had a mild quake while I was there," she went on. "The streets flooded and I was booties deep…struck by the absurdity."

"Did you inform the good doctor?" Winner asked.

"Of course. In fact, I backpacked to Antimahia and there were villas available on higher ground, minutes from the aerodrome. Offices were available in the terminal building across the field. The choice made sense to me, and Dr. Edwards concurred when we spoke on the phone."

"And Nokomo turned it down?"

"I should never have mentioned Dr. Edwards," she said. "They apparently had words, and I was ordered home."

"You breached his chain of command, homey. Take it from a fractured Air Force type."

"I know, but it's hard to believe he'd segment the project for sake of comfort. Dr. Nokomo's not a scientist, Mr. Slater. He's an administrator, and there's a resentment of sorts; delves with figures, but not their source. Perhaps you're better off," she added. "His staff is ass-heavy with untrained technicians. Your field computers, for instance, are programmed in German! So they'll pick their teeth and bug off!" She stopped short and frowned, noticing I was staring blankly at her cleavage.

"If I was to complain, I'm a bloody Brit!" she continued, when I averted my eyes to the river. "Worse still, a racist, which I'm definitely not!" Winner picked up, aware of my thundering thoughts.

"Obtrui, for instance, is she party to this shit?" Maureen scrutinized her nails.

"In a sense, Dr. Winner. She was a fashion model in Lagos, a close friend of a Nigerian cabinet minister who visits often," she added wryly. "But fortunately, he's a purser to our funds and we take it in stride. She tries, I must add, but there's a distrust in her demeanor I find difficult to overcome."

"Programmed in German!" I sputtered. The twosome spun about.

"Sorry," I allowed. "I was onto something else." Maureen stared at Winner; Winner stared at me.

"Computers, Allen. Are you fluent in German?"

"Not really," he admitted. "I had a problem with Kant."

"Come off it," Maureen said. "Our computers were programmed several weeks ago."

"By whom?" we chorused. She evidenced surprise.

"The Soviet contingent; I thought you knew. They've come and gone," she added. "Closeted themselves in our computer room. I hardly saw them, aside from the chap who is to monitor communications with theU-2. Strange person," she reflected, "older than yourselves; has a nasty scar on his cheek, piercing eyes, an aggressive personality. I was uncomfortable in his presence, as was Dr. Nokomo, I think. Matter of fact, he inquired about you, Mr. Slater. Seemed curious as to your whereabouts the early part of last week."

"Gunnar's our Russian counterpart," Winner asided, seeing I was unwound. "Seems he was put onto us by the Russians when the program was extended to include the Caspian. Like, they're wary of a border intrusion should the U-2 wander off. We met briefly, mainly to update the frequencies you're to monitor when you corner Ashhad in northeastern Iran, more so the corridor bordering Turkmenistan and Azerbaijan."

"He was on to that, too?"

78

"You'd better believe it! Capped their frequencies with a memo to Nokomo, in fact. Red-lined our aeronautical charts...for the record, I think. You're to straddle a mean course when you cross the Caspian. Interesting, hey, the way he took over and hammered our guidelines? So, we'll share our lot with goats or whatever. Our feedback is metric and it really doesn't matter if he spools our computers in German. It's our collective analysis that counts."

I backtracked the subject.

"Did he mention Dr. Gomulaka?" Winner thought back.

"Not that I remember, although he asked if we had a diagram of the U-2's electronics. Never once mentioned Santorini or our primary flights over the Aegean. He was preoccupied with Iran. Sorta got my dander up. Hell's fire, the volcano's our big stick!"

"Okay, so Gunnar freaked the computers and meddled with our charts. When did he leave? Do you know where he went?"

"Thursday last, and aside from that I really don't give a shit!"

"We vouchered his ticket to Warsaw, Mr. Slater," Maureen interjected. "And you needn't be crude, Dr. Winner! We weren't discussing your stool!"

We parted in the hallway and said our goodbyes on a lesser note. Winner I'd see in Athens and Kos, but Maureen was helplessly caught with the tapestry in New York. She had a crush on Edwards, I suspected, and they'd make an excellent team.

* * * * * *

Nokomo's infrastructure didn't concern me at the time, although I was surprised by his preoccupation with the press during the urgent meeting he'd scheduled weeks before. Despite the fax I'd received at Mountain View, together with a scrawled notation: 'Suite 821, promptly at ten, wherein we shall define your duties and meet together with our staff.' Copies sent to Edwards, Sigurdesson, Winner and Gomulaka. None to Gunnar, I recalled, but then he was late to the game!

Fiasco in past, but not a total waste of time. Thanks to Maureen, I'd gained an inside view of the project. Her candid observations fragmented and incomplete, but invaluable during weeks to come. The U-2 was mine to command, per NASA's contract with the UN...subject to the whims of the volcano. Although Dr. Nokomo would captain our wherewithal, the scientists would call the shots!

CHAPTER 11

ina dozed while Cape Hatteras slipped past out starboard wing. Hand clasped with mine, the golden ring on her finger evidence of the vows we'd exchanged the previous Saturday. Hennessey was asleep in the hold; tranquilized by the beer he'd consumed to ease the discomfort of his cage. A family together, we were en route to the Bahamas to relax and enjoy the sparkling sea. We had matters to attend, of course. Nick's estate, his lovely home at Lyford Cay, foremost in Nina's mind; memories would be difficult to suppress while she collected the family belongings and placed the house up for sale.

My cottage was better suited to our future needs. Compact, with a view of the sea and lovely beach for the Lab to roam, an idyllic retreat from furthering careers...eventually a place where a child might splash with naked abandon.

Juiced with complimentary wine, I triggered my seat full length and gave continued thought to such things. Thoughts shadowed with apprehension when I considered our future weeks in the Aegean; my tenure with White Dove when the U-2 was fitted and we'd test the volcano close range.

Designed for high altitude recon (where air is relatively calm), the U-2 wasn't stressed for the violent thermals we'd encounter. Nor would its engine cope indefinitely with the sulfurous grit when we sampled the density of the plume. Highly corrosive, the ash could induce compressor stall; failing a restart, we'd depend on our glide ratio to make it back to Kos. All of this while confined to an unwieldy pressure suit, sipping oxygen, flying instruments with an observer who might panic and grab the dual controls!

I inched the window shade up for a glimpse of the westing sun, pondering its shimmering reflection on the Boeing's massive wing. To the south, the sky was brilliant blue, the pensive gray sea below hosting a covey of shrimpers trawling the shoals off South Carolina. The yellowish haze had yielded to the cold front that lay behind us. It's ashy residue dispersing with the drizzle along the eastern seaboard, most likely to the discomfort of the posh resorts and bewildered farmers tending their fields.

I drowsed, fell asleep, and slipped into a recurring dream of the fiery missile that streaked from the desert and stroked my F-15, dreamed of the gloating face of a man I'd yet to meet, of Amalia nodding in the distance when I hastened Nina from the Met, of the insidious ground fire that seared my leg when I was cabled from the rocky terrain.

"Heavens, Keith, you're mumbling to yourself!" Nina exhorted, nudging my leg. I winced, raising an eye to the window. Grand Bahama had passed beneath us, the Boeing 777 on a rumbling descent to Windsor International.

"Sorry, I was somewhere else, I think?"

"Aren't you always, my sweet? Is it the stewardess with the boobs and the stringy hair?"

"May I have your glass, please?" the stewardess interrupted, uprighting my chair.

"Let her have it, Keith," Nina chided. "We've more at the house!"

"You may keep the bottle if you wish, ma'am. Compliments of Delta and the crew! It's your honeymoon, I believe. Do you plan to visit Paradise Island?"

"If he makes it through Immigration," Nina asided as she peeked from the window. "My, what a beautiful day!"

* * * * * *

New Providence Island appeared on the horizon. The 20-mile, low-lying island a disappointment first view, but when it closed we could see the white of its cresting reefs, the turquoise of the shoals, and sugary beaches that lay beyond. Portside from our cabin we had a bird's-eye view of Delaporte and the teeming harbor to the east of Paradise Island and its spindly bridge to the mainland of Nassau proper and the garish hotels commanding Cable Beach. To starboard we were rewarded with the elegance of Lyford Cay…of towering palms and splendid villas capping the ridge, the vivid green of a golfer's dream! More so, a rambling pink house amidst a stand of casuarinas by the sea, of which Nina was quick to point when she sprawled headlong across my knees.

We were on our final approach by then, gear extended, flaps rumbling as we crossed the highway and flared for the runway. I braked instinctively when the nose wheel touched. The terminal flashed by, the pilot applying reverse thrust when he ground to near stop and steered for the turnoff to the terminal.

Nina was first off, of course, grinning from ear to ear, sprinting for immigration while I limped behind, burdened with her valise, my briefcase, her camera and our captured bottle of champagne!

* * * * * *

The family retainer, a courteous Bahamian by the name of Audley, met us at the terminal with Nick's vintage Mercedes. Apparently he'd come along at an odd moment when his mother was hard put to recall who his father might be. A kindly old man with a leathery face and a crown of gray, he'd served the family since Nina was a child. He called her 'Neenie' and adored her as if she was his own. They talked at length while we drove the short distance to Lyford Cay. The reunion was joyous, although he expressed concern for his garden when Hennessey eyed the passing trees.

The Maris residence was a rambling affair set in a low-lying grove of feathery casuarinas on an isolated stretch of beach. The house was dank from oppressive humidity; the furniture shrouded since early spring. Nina moved quickly to open the doors and air the rooms. Memories known only to her; family photographs hazed with salt in the paneled library; Nick's chestnut desk and the models of his coastwide fleet; an aged copy of the Wall Street Journal; his score card from the course at Lyford Cay; her mother's garden hat; a letter from Nina posted from Berkeley months before.

The old man directed us to 'Neenie's' room and followed along with her luggage. Uneasy in my presence, he pointed to the adjoining dressing room, where I offloaded our suitcases...lingering to unlatch the veranda doors, tidying this and that until Nina appeared to air her closets with the freshing breeze. I realized his concern was not of me, however, when she fingered her dresses from another time...the clinging gown she'd worn the previous New Year's Eve, judging from the conical paper hat on the shelf...memories best left to herself. Audley nodding silently when he withdrew to the kitchen to acquaint with and feed our famished dog.

Wobbly at first, released from his leash, Hennessey lapped a beer to aid his digestion. Then, sensing Nina's presence, he circuited the house, barking when he cornered her bedroom, followed by a moment of explosive redress whilst he tagged us to the veranda and sprinted the surf. Nina's nostalgia a thing apart when she shed her clothes along the beach and bare-assed the afternoon sea!

Audley and I set about getting acquainted. Dubious, the old man eyed me warily when I tasted the conch salad he'd prepared for our arrival. Brightening, however, when I mentioned my cottage at Love Beach, my adventures as a charter pilot whilst nursing my lacerated leg. Audley recollecting I'd flown him to Cat Island when his eldest son was married at Old Bight.

"Missed the mail boat," he chuckled, "but, sure enough, you came along right time, man! Got a scat of gran'chillen to thank for that!" I was unsure of the occasion, but we were friends by then, more so when he produced a brace of towels to redeem my naked bride from the beach.

The old man was long gone, prompted by his calling to the Baptist church, while we tossed coconuts and sticks for Hennessey to fetch from the surf. It was reminiscent of Big Sur... the fading sun; Nina clasping towels for warmth; the Lab alongside when we climbed the steps to the house, nuzzling pour legs to determine his status quo.

Audley had thoughtfully spread a table on the veranda, replete with flowering hibiscus surrounding our plates, long-stemmed glasses and a chilled bottle of Nick's favorite Santorini wine, which Nina quickly exchanged for Delta's complimentary; close to tears when she returned the Santorini to the fridge.

"Don't worry about it," she said, searching my eyes for understanding. "Audley means well, but it will take a few days to adjust to all of this. Sort of like coming home from school," she added, clasping her wedding band next to mine. "Everything in place, except for their presence, Keith. God love them, wherever they are!"

Later, at dusk, when the sun had slipped beneath the horizon, leaving a path of gold on the ever-moving seas, I checked the doors and latched the screens, looking in to Nina and the sprawling dog at her bedside. She was fast asleep, clutching her pillows like a teenager home from school, secure with her surroundings from another time. Not to disturb her, I switched off the lights and slipped beside her, turning up the ceiling fan when the ocean breeze faltered. She slept the night without a murmur, nuzzling my shoulder when the winds took a westerly turn to herald the cold front lingering off Cape Canaveral.

* * * * * *

Come morning, while the sky was shades of orange in the east, we slipped from the house to loosen our bones along the deserted stretch of beach, jogging, walking, and conversing until the sun emerged from a casuarina and cast its glow on the sea. Breakfast on the veranda included coffee and the newscast from Miami WINZ, our eyes on a fishing smack rounding the reefs off Lyford Cay. Relaxed by her measure of sleep, Nina was her lively self, talkative, eyes sparkling, giggling when we spied a land crab puzzling Hennessey's inquisitive paw.

I was busy clearing our dishes to the kitchen when the phone shrilled. Nina, disturbed by the early morning call, paced the veranda with the phone cupped to her ear, her eyes narrowing with disbelief, obviously at odds with whatever they were discussing. Assuming it was her attorney, I motioned her to cool it when she loosened an expletive that caused me to wince.

"My lawyer!" she snapped, casting the phone aside. "Has to do with the estate, and a ridiculous offer for the house! I told him to screw it," she added vehemently. "Stupid ass! He had the audacity to ask me to appear at his office by ten!"

"Hell, he hasn't had time to shave, Nina. Call him back later and sweeten things up. Better tomorrow morning, when you've had time to unbend and give it some thought. This day is ours, honey! It's not up for grabs. Let's play it by ear and have ourselves a ball."

We did just that; explored the reefs until we were exhausted, basked in the sun with the phone off its hook. We inspected Audley's gardens when he appeared late morning...his plot of sweet potatoes, avocado and grapefruit trees, earthy things kin to the tropics with a measure of care...all of this bordering the pristine beaches and crystal clear waters of the nearby sea.

Later we fired up the Mercedes and drove to town, and had lunch at the Poop Deck, meeting friends and acquaintances from other times. At the Sailing Club we met with old friends of Nina's parents, an elderly Greek couple from cable beach. Nina was delighted, of course, waxing enthusiastic while we shared a sundowner at Traveller's Rest.

Dressing for the occasion, we ventured to Paradise Island...dined at the Radisson, danced the merengue beneath the stars, and capped the evening with ouzo and ice...privately, following a shoeless stroll along the beach. Hand-in-hand we whispered anticipation when we latched the screens and dimmed the lights.

* * * * * *

Our second morning was a mixed bag of business and moments of pleasure. Following an early morning swim and breakfast, Nina drove to Nassau to meet with her lawyer and the realtor who'd appraised the house. Pale and distraught when she reappeared at lunch, nibbling a sandwich while she conversed with a representative of the cartage company who'd come to crate the contents of the house, pointing to this and that, while Audley pleaded with the van driver to spare his immaculate lawn.

Nick's paintings, lofted for crating to Sotheby's in London, came down from the walls, among them his favorite Matisse, an early Picasso and a certified Monet he'd purchased in France. Items of a personal nature we decided to store at my cottage...Nick's desk, his ship models, the family portraits of Nina and Helena, his loving wife.

I visited my cottage to clear storage space and tidy matters with my tenants, extending their lease until we returned from the Aegean. Close friends, they agreed to accept Hennessey for the duration, squeezed a little on the rent until the Lab exercised his personality and they let it go at that.

"No leash," I warned. "He's road-wise, so let him romp and play with your kids and he'll guard the house!"

When I returned to Lyford Cay, the movers had removed the articles for auction and I found Nina face down on her bed...tears in her eyes, prodding her temples as I sat down beside her and cradled her head to my chest.

"I feel like I've kicked an old friend in the ass," she said, pointing to the wall where the Matisse had been. "I love this old house, but we need the bloody cash! Thompson appraised it for two million four," she added. "Thinks he has a buyer, a Canadian on an ego trip. If Sotheby's comes up with the rest, we'll have the banks off our backs! Papa's storage tanks are mortgaged to the hilt," she continued. "He left things in a terrible mess!"

"He didn't realize it was curtain time, honey."

"I know. Business was booming and he was dealing in futures...or was, until Santorini blighted our groves. We'll be all right if the auction comes off in London," she added. "Olive oil's premium at the moment, and we've adequate in storage once the liens are lifted. We stand to lose the tankers, however." Nina pointed to a letter on her dresser. "Addressed to my lawyer, and I refuse to deal with it, Keith! Seems my brother signed a note due the first of the month; pledged his equity in the fleet and blew it at the tables!"

"Is the estate responsible?" I asked. She shook her head.

"No way! In fact, my brother was excluded from the will. Papa had a premonition, I guess. He tendered the ships in total and paid the gift tax, hoping the asshole would measure up! No matter, we'll lease what we need. The Helena is documented in my name," she exclaimed, a faraway, wistful smile appearing on her lips. "She's old and grotty, Keith, but she has good engines and our charters pay the bills. Thanks to Captain Stavos! You'll love the old man, my sweet!"

Nina was looking forward to cruising the Aegean, her Papa's yacht dear to her heart. She had a sharp mind; wasn't destined to shop supermarkets or mend clothes. If she wanted to perpetuate the family holdings, which apparently was her father's wish, it was up to her. We had that understanding, provided I could afford the loose change!

Our third and last day in the tropics was fraught with emotions, however. The morning bright and seasonably pleasant, conducive to a cooling swim, but the casuarinas were listless; the sea, dead calm, lacked the slightest breeze, the air was heavy with humidity. Mare's tails clouds feathered the sky from the north; Sunday's cold front would be on us by late afternoon, its volatile air mass on a collision course with the southeasterly trades. We were in for an evening of pyrotechnics, I thought.

"Why are they so skittish?" Nina questioned, pointing to a pair of land crabs slinking sideways to the bush.

"Barometric," I answered. "If they sense a storm they head for high land."

She nodded apprehensively, shed her bikini top and spumed the mirror-like sea. Diving as a pair, we gathered our gear and separated a grouper from his reef. Adding another from a coral head to our net bag, we swam leisurely to shore, discussing how best to marinate the fillets.

"We could broil them on the charcoaler like Papa used to do," Nina said, staring at the rambling veranda facing the sea. "His gloves and tongs are beneath the broiler." She averted her eyes from the picturesque setting, immersed in memories of family gatherings when she was visiting from school. "Audley could steam peas and rice and fetch vegetables from the market. It's our last night in the Bahamas, Keith. I'll miss the old place."

The phone sounded as we climbed to the veranda with our catch. Nina picked up the extension, pacing the veranda as she talked, scribbling notes and casting them about. I was out of earshot, but realized she was upset when she cradled the phone in a spate of anger. I retrieved her bikini top from the beach and helped her tie its devious strings.

The conversation was spiked with expletives (best known in Piraeus) and her lawyer's silent response.

"I don't give a damn for the bloody note!" Nina thundered. "It's nothing to do with the estate and Metaxas can go to hell! The house? Okay, if Thompson comes up with a big number. Mind you," she added, "the collateral is assigned to our commodities and not up for probate or my brother's sleazy debts!"

They discussed Nick's insurance policy while I filleted the grouper. The policy wasn't a problem, it seemed, but my ears perked when the tragedy in Athens was mentioned. She'd apparently demanded an investigation of the conditions relating to the crash, reflecting suspicions akin to mine.

Deep in thought, frowning all the while, Nina paced the veranda and stared intermittently at the sea. She considered this and that, as she often did when she was upset or indecisive. Cornering the notes she'd flung aside, she examined the lot, then dialed a number she apparently intended to forget afterwards. When the party picked up, she added a middle-finger gesture.

The ongoing conversation was conducted in rapid-fire Greek. Initially circumspect, Nina employed her icy accent when the party labored the line. Sensing her mounting anger, knowing she was at odds and hanging a juicy response, I hauled in the extension cord until I had my bride face up!

The phone dangling unattended while we had words of other sorts, soft words she understood when I applied a finger to her lips. A knowing smile graced her lovely face when she signed off, and I suggested we bare-ass the pool.

Long of limb, superbly tanned to the outline of her discarded bikini, Nina cleft the pool like a nymph. Surfaced beside me, tossing her hair aside while we lingered for a watery kiss. We lapped the pool together, but her unlikely frown returned when we swam to the ladder and searched the chaises for towels.

"Problems, honey?"

She nodded, searching for words. "You're not going to like this, Keith!"

"I like what I see!" She forced a smile.

"I've invited company for dinner, darling. There's something I must know."

"Friend or foe? Is our evening up for grabs?"

"Possibly. Papa's ex-banker is staying at the Ocean Club and called my lawyer to discuss my brother's note; invited us to dinner while the nitwit had me on the conference phone! I told him to shove it up his..."

"Hey, there!"

"We owe him money, Keith, or so he says! He has a lien on our tanks and presented my brother's note. He's not very nice...alcoholic, slobbers when he drinks. I never liked the son of a bitch!"

"Greek?"

"The worst, a barbarian from Kostoris!"

"Pressing?"

"Definitely! Keith, he's been calling my lawyer since he arrived, out of turn, inquiring about Papa's insurance and the title to the house. Legally, my attorney has nothing to say until we settle the estate."

"Your attorney's an executor, I assume."

"Locally, yes, but the executors are four square; our attorney is in Athens, Papa's brother and myself. My uncle is old and somewhat out of it, Keith. Our attorney a trusted retainer, so it's mainly up to me to decide, which I believe was Papa's desire."

"In other words, he's cutting corners and laying a heavy to force a settlement."

"Exactly, darling, and I won't have any part of it! Moreover, my lawyer's a wimp; talks irrelevant nonsense, suggested I make a deal! So, I decided to tackle the bastard head on. Stand by me, Keith. There's a reason beyond all this, something I must know."

I let it go with that, realizing the back of her mind was attuned to her psychic nature. I ventured a question, however, more or less to satisfy my curiosity.

"Is he after the house, Nina? You mentioned a ridiculous offer; is he forcing your brother's note to pick up equity?"

"You're absolutely right. He'd like to wear Papa's shoes and join the club! But there's more than meets the eye, my love. He's after me, God forbid! Badgered me since they died, sent a nasty note when we didn't invite him to the funeral, roses later on.

"But that's not what unsettles me, Keith, it's something else. He's evil, darling! I sensed it long ago." She looked up with tears in her eyes, clasped my hand and said, "I love you, Keith; most of all your beautiful soul!"

"That's all that matters, honey. We'll feed him frozen caraivides if he doesn't behave!"

Nina slithered her hand the length of my thigh. I rolled my eyes; she was very naughty. A bird twittered in the distance.

"He wouldn't know the difference," she whispered. "He drinks!" she added, nuzzling my shoulder. I checked the surroundings, noticing a nearby chaise.

We kissed passionately, furiously, her tongue trailing my throat. I ran my fingers into her hair, felt her temples throbbing on my chest, her hot moist mouth on my belly. The sun blurred, the sea lapsed into silence, the casuarinas bowed as Nina dropped to her knees and looked up...eyes hot with passion, hair disheveled, her tongue lolling when she raised her head to take my rise.

The dizzy world swirled about as I eased her gently to the chaise and sought her mouth. I kissed the length of her splendid body; she tensed, arched her spine, raised my head to her breasts, and clawed my buttocks as she drew me deep inside her. We lay together for a moment, holding back, gently stroking, verging an incredible orgasm then and there.

CHAPTER

A pair of teenagers roused us from our nap. High noon; Audley hadn't arrived as yet and they'd buzzed the gate-side bell, parking their Jeep by the door. Gathering a towel, Nina peered from the window and recognized the twosome from a summer before…a blonde girl with braids together with a husky lad in a skivvy shirt…both from landlocked houses in Lyford Cay. They asked if they might use the grove by the beach that night. Had a bonfire and friends in mind, a case of beer in the Jeep. They'd completed their exams and were fresh from the north, the boy a sophomore at Dartmouth, the girl from Smith.

Nina said it would be okay if they didn't fire the bush; informed of the planned dinner party, they were told not to park their cars in the drive. Then, loosening her smile, she said they could store their beer in the fridge if they wanted, and to help themselves to a case of Pepsi gathering dust in the garage. The boy grinned, the girl thanked her, and then their Jeep spun gravel and disappeared.

The telephone rang before we could reassemble our nap…Nina's lawyer was requesting an appointment in his chambers after lunch. She nodded sleepily, talked to him briefly, then fluffed a pillow and buried her face to ward off her thoughts.

"Bloody nitpicker!" she groaned. "He wants an inventory of Papa's art collection. Thank God we shipped the lot. He wouldn't know a Monet from a ten dollar print! Odd he should ask," she added, raising her head to stare at the walls. "The Monet was Papa's pride and joy; someone's tipped him off!"

We gave it up when Audley's Ford rumbled the drive and he appeared with a folder of household bills. Stood by while Nina signed the checks, inspected our catch in the kitchen pantry, and voiced his approval of the dinner party when

I said I'd broil the fillets.

I borrowed his car to check on Hennessey, stopping briefly to acquire a case of his favorite brew and a recent copy of the Times. When I returned, Nina had showered and tripped to town, leaving a note with her lipstick imprinted on the fold. 'Have an appointment with my lawyer, Keith. Back by six. Don't forget we have guests at eight...the SOB from Athens, love!'

With her guests in mind, I helped Audley set up the library bar, chose the red wine to be uncorked later and iced the white. Helping myself to a beer from the fridge, I spread the Times to view the world news.

The front page was given to unrest in Armenia and Azerbaijan, resulting from the autonomous local governments rigged by Moscow as a breakaway buffer with Iran. Little of personal interest, aside from a photograph featuring the ash-polluted New York harbor with a caption asserting there was more to come.

Page eight stroked the gist of Keenan's rationale, however, and I gave thought to his remarks. A Reuters dispatch questioned tank movements bordering the Caspian to the east. 'Shrouded with secrecy, transported by rail at night', the article stated, confirming a satellite scan of the railhead extending to Daku and Ashkabad. The dispatch queried a huge warehouse complex under construction in the Kara-Kum desert nearby. 'For what purpose?' the article continued, although the columnist gave lip service to Turkmenistan's flat-out assertion that the complex was agriculturally oriented and nothing more than a fertilizer plant!

I scanned the section for news of Iran; there was none, but an editorial suggested the Commonwealth swap their ethnic problems with Tehran. *Better we focus attention on the possibility of a natural calamity* the editor opined. *If the weekend disaster gives an indication, let's not make noises in the war room and hide our heads in the closet.*

A distant roll of thunder echoed from the Berry Islands. I put the newspaper aside and studied the sky. A heavy band of clouds darkened the horizon; a land crab scurried from the beach and disappeared beneath a clump of palmetto. A fishing smack spread sail to catch the westing wind and steered full bent for the sanctuary of Nassau harbor.

The quartering breeze flapped the newspaper, turning pages one by one. I reached over to collect it, then recognized the photo adjoining the obituary section. Bent forward for better light, I sat heavily in my chair, completely stunned.

'Dr. George Gomulaka, Polish meteorologist recently appointed to the UN'. The notice was dated Monday, an INS dispatch from Warsaw. The obituary mentioned his wife and two children, listed his academic background, his research credits, and dealt at some length with his controversial prediction of an agricultural calamity in the Middle East. 'Dr. Gomulaka was 44. Cause of death undisclosed.'

I re-read the column, remembering the bearded man who had so recently peered from the rear seat of my U-2…scholarly, enthusiastic, apolitical. I shuddered, staring at a tumultuous swell pounding the reef. *Cause of death undisclosed.*

His medical had been approved by the flight surgeon. He'd undergone the pressure chamber tests to 100,000 feet. I'd scanned his cardiogram. There was no indication of a coronary insufficiency. What then…an unfortunate accident of the sidewalks of Warsaw? I balled the page and flung it to the wind, then helped myself to a jigger of rum from the pantry shelf.

The poor bastard! Was he an innocent pawn in the game we were playing? Had they set him up and knocked him down? Readied his substitute while he was still alive? Had someone talked when the package was assembled at Lockheed? A heavy guess, of course; but two inter-related deaths in the past few days?

"Needing vegetables for salad, Mr. Slater." I spun around, replacing the bottle on the shelf.

Audley fingered his black bow tie.

"Mind goin' to the store, suh? Farm truck usually park nearby. Old man Hepburn sell tomato and cucumber from the field. Go myself if'n it cause you problem. Ya looks worry, man. Miss Neenie been fussin' wid her lawyer again?"

I shook my head and smiled. I told him I was upset by something I'd read. He handed me the list and car keys; I drove to the market deep in thought.

* * * * * *

The door chime sounded at eight that evening. I caught Audley's eye when he hurried to the foyer, motioning him to show our guests to the library, suggesting he serve them a drink from the bar. Nina was running late and closeted in the shower. Overwrought and edgy, flinging expletives from the steam; she'd had a nasty session with her attorney. I called in to quiet her, but she was undeterred.

"Nervy bastard!" she screamed. "He insisted I sign over the house to Metexas to clear my brother's note. Had the damned papers ready, would you believe it? The mercenary pig! I told him to shove them up his…is someone at the door?"

I flashed the bathroom lights, closed the door softly, and donned my blazer. And checking the charcoal fire on the veranda, I went to the library to make amends.

Metexas was a powerfully built man of medium height, slim at the belt with an overhanging belly. He had a full head of greasy hair, streaked at the temples, marcelled to his collar. A faltering Adonis reeking of Aramis, he wore an immaculate raw silk suit tapered to his shoes, red tie, dark glasses, a ruby-studded ring and a gold Rolex. Heavy handed, a knuckle crusher, crude, belligerent and impolite, I thumbed the backside of his grip, tightening my fingers. He showed his teeth and retracted his hand.

"So you're the lucky bridegroom, hey? Fly aeroplanes, I understand." He turned abruptly to his companion before I could answer and flashed his dentures.

His choice for the evening was a middle-aged, frizzled blonde with china blue eyes, who hiccuped when she reached for my hand. Her shoulders glowed from overtime at the beach; her forehead beaded with perspiration, her mascara smudged and unattended. She'd squeezed herself into an undersized Pucci, wore an enormous diamond on her finger, displaying it when I winked and asked what she'd have.

"Dewar's on the rocks, honey. Tony will have the same...we're old friends from Cannes," she added. "My, what a lovely home you have!" She eyed the white rattan, the cypress-paneled walls, the hand-carved bar, while I added a splash to their drinks.

"Alice and I came upon one another at the Club," Metexas interjected. "She's in the market for a winter residence; I understand you're up for sale."

I eyed the man, figured he had a translation problem, and let it pass.

"Tony means he understands the house is for sale, don't you, darling?" Metexas spread his teeth.

"It's listed," I countered. "If you're interested, I'd suggest you discuss the matter with Nina. She'll be along in a few minutes. She was late from town; had a rough day."

The Greek scanned the vacant walls, the shadowy outlines where Nick's paintings had been, as if he'd inventoried the lot and wondered where they'd gone.

"What a shame," he said, peering inquisitively into the living room. "In Greece, we men make the decisions. But then, I suppose it's what one is accustomed to, or can afford." I tensed. He smirked and raised his glass; the blonde frowned and looked away.

An errant wave exploded against the outer reefs; an icy silence descended. I set my glass on the bar. Fortunately, Nina made her entrance before I invited him to smell the flowers.

Nina was exquisite. She wore a loose-fitting gown of Indian cotton that featured the length of her sensuous body to her lacquered toes. Her dampish hair flowed uninhibited about her shoulders, her golden earrings on display. A simple necklace accented her throat...an ancient necklace clasping a pendant of solid gold, a figurine with emerald eyes!

She entered the library with her animal-like stride. Graceful, feline, proud of her heritage...inwardly seething. I braced myself. There was a certain glint, a tightness to her lips that warned of her volcanic temperament when she was thoroughly aroused.

Metexas raised his tints and stared, readied his arms for an embrace. Nina came beside me and bussed my cheek, nodded politely to acknowledge his presence, then turned to the wide-eyed blonde, led her quietly to the veranda to admire the fading sky. The Greek dropped his arms and fidgeted with his glasses. I upped his drink with Dewars and excused myself to tend the fire.

Dinner began with a mixed bag of chatter. Metexas attempted a conversation in Greek, Nina responded in English. He plied himself with wine and glowered. I turned to pamper the weepy blonde; recently divorced, her husband had split with his secretary. But she'd captured the townhouse at Sutton Place and the summerhouse in the Hamptons. She studied the dining room hazily, as if planning to rearrange the furniture. Asked if Audley came with the house, eyeing Metexas reproachfully when he glared her to silence.

Dinner ended abruptly while Audley was serving the entree!

Metexas was in trouble. Leaning on the table with his elbow in the salad, he wagged a finger at Nina, growling in English. Told her point blank she should honor her brother's note with title to the house! Her eyes sparked, she poised her fork; I angled my head to caution her. She nodded, put her fork aside, calmly removed his finger from beneath her nose, crooked it, and told him politely to stick it up his ass!

Off came his tints. I had a frightening glimpse of murderous eyes. Down came his fist. Tableware shuddered and I warned him to back off! He got to his feet unsteadily, gripping the table for purchase. I balled my fist to warn him again. Fortunately, he was overcome by the weight of gravity; settled in his chair, glowering, mouthing threats while he cast about for means to wipe the salad dressing from his sleeve. Visibly upset, his companion belched and bent beside her plate. I hurried her outside immediately, led her to the terrace and the flowering jasmine.

The breeze had picked up, felt cool to my face when I examined the sky. The palm fronds overhead were whipping and bending to the south. To the north a heavy cloud roll was fast approaching from the sea. The inky sky neonized with lightning, reflecting the ominous build-up that had followed us from New York.

The sweet smell of pot mingled with the aroma of the nearby bonfire. A guitar strummed, a drum applied the beat. There was singing and laughter in the distance when I handed Alice my napkin and guided her across the terrace. She lurched along, holding my arm while I sped to the dining room to quiet a nasty scene.

We were greeted by a barrage of dockside Greek. Nina was on her feet and levering a dripping bottle of wine. Audley stood saucer-eyed at the kitchen door with a hand to his mouth. The blonde simpered and sagged; I held her aside and leapt across the intervening space, grabbing the bottle from Nina before she hurled it in Metexas' face.

"Vromiko Skile! File! Fthee-Na bastard!" she screamed. "Out...out!"

The Greek backed away, spread his arms to placate her. She upended a candelabrum and went after him with a club of solid silver. I caught her by the wrist and hauled her in. the Greek tried his smile. She gathered what was in her mouth and spat! Metexas wiped his cheek; his face blooded with drunken rage. He charged us like a maddened bull!

It was over in seconds. I shouldered Nina away, caught his collar and levered his underarm. The acceleration sent him crashing to the floor. I straddled his back and added a karate chop. He breathed heavily, gagged, and fouled the carpet. The blonde began to cry as I released him and got to my feet.

Groping for his glasses, he crawled to his knees and staggered to a chair. I drew Nina to my side, the beat of her heart pounding against my chest, trying to calm her before she went after him again. Audley chose this moment to emerge from the kitchen with a tray of coffee. Trembling, he set it on the table. Speaking softly to Nina, he suggested she show the hysterical Alice to the lavatory, then backed away.

Metexas poured a heavy cup and slurped it down. Loosening his tie, he wiped his mouth with the back of his hand.

"I won't forget this, Slater," he muttered.

"You're lucky you weren't clobbered with the family silver, fella. Let's call it a night, okay?"

He lunged to his feet, stumbling into the living room without a word. I followed him short of the entryway, where he smashed the screen door and staggered to his rental, beeping the horn. I waited by the door until Alice emerged from the lavatory on Nina's arm, apologizing profusely, asking if we might locate her purse?

I found it beneath the dining room table and saw her to the outside, catching a glimpse of Metexas' face when she tumbled in beside him. He looked up as he keyed the ignition, saw me standing beneath the light, drew his hand across his throat muttering an obscenity, whilst he wheeled away with a clump of shrubbery from Audley's lawn.

* * * * * *

I helped Audley clean up the mess in the dining room and said goodnight, then went to the patio to smother the embers in the charcoal bier. A ragged flash of lightning punctured the blackness to the north; an ominous clap of thunder rolled from the horizon. I inhaled the refreshing breeze for a moment, latched the doors and extinguished the lights. The bonfire glowed intermittently through the windows as I crossed the darkened room; a guitar strummed 'Sloop John B', a bongo drum rattling a quickening beat.

Nina was stretched full-length across the bed, staring at the ceiling, when I entered the bedroom. I knelt by her side and nuzzled her cheek. She brought an arm around me, moistened her lips, and apologized for the ugly scene. I loosened her dress and rubbed her back; said it couldn't be helped that Metexas was three sheets to the wind when they arrived. I didn't probe, didn't ask what had flamed her temper at the very last. I'd drawn my own conclusions, reasoning it was better left unsaid.

I heated a saucepan of milk in the kitchen and slugged it with rum. When I returned to the bedroom, she was sitting on the edge of the bed with a photograph of her dad cradled in her lap. She looked up and smiled as I bunched her pillows. Leaning back, she sipped thoughtfully from her glass.

"He was a lovely person, Keith. I miss him so! Uncle tries, but he's old and afraid to face up to that damned barbarian." She stared wistfully at her mother's picture on the dresser, then turned and pressed my hand. "They were so full of life, like you and I. Often they would come home at night giggling and laughing while we were vacationing in the Bahamas. When I was young and my brother was away at college, they would wake me to tell me what had happened at the club. Sometimes Papa would come to my bedroom alone. He would sit in that chair over there, sip ouzo and discuss business. Never talked down to me as a child. And in the summer, when we cruised the Aegean, he'd take me ashore to

inspect the groves...to Crete when they were uncovering the temple at Arhannes."
She pressed her fingers to her forehead, closing her eyes momentarily.

A ripple of lightning washed the room with incandescence. Her eyes opened
wide; she recoiled against the headboard as if the bolt had stirred a terrible
memory, clasping the necklace to her throat. I sat beside her, fingering the
pendant; the bloody thing was icy to my touch!

"It's gone now," she gasped. "Jesus in heaven! Why do I have nightmares
when I'm awake? What's wrong with me, Keith?" She shivered and stared into
the night.

"I found the necklace in Papa's desk last winter when I stopped in New York
on my way to Berkeley. They were in Nassau at the time, and I had a terrible
dream that very night. Walls were tumbling; people screaming...a young man lay
on a sacrificial stone in the very next room, near to death. Someone I knew. A
priest, who had cut an artery below his neck and caught his blood in an urn,
rushed past me toward the altar chamber. Suddenly, the floor began to rise and
the beams began to fall; the doorway burst into flames."

She put her hands to her face, ran her fingers through her hair, pressed them
to her ears.

"When I awoke, I was lying in a corner by the window, aware of a subway
train rumbling down below. I had the necklace in my hand, although I was certain
I'd left it in the drawer. And then I remembered the key in Papa's shoe! I've told
you the story in part, Keith, but apparently there was a void locked in my
childhood memory that I'd suppressed until then!"

"Association?"

"Most likely; desks look much the same and I'd been warned. Papa let me
wear the necklace briefly when we boarded the yacht that evening. Realizing I
was upset, he told me a little story to divert my mind from what I'd seen, related
a golden fable from Greek mythology. Said the necklace once belonged to an
enchanted princess with raven hair and eyes like mine, who'd fled the catastrophe with her lover to a magical island, where they lived forever in happiness,
apart from the world we know.

"This I remember so vividly," Nina continued. "The story of the magical isle,
Papa's quieting smile when he put me to bed. But later, when the storm tossed
the Helena at anchor, I dreamed of the princess and her necklace. Suddenly she
was there beside me, my dream entangled with the terrible discovery at the dig!
The sacrificial stone, the shattered urn, that awful knife! I realized she was the
Minoan princess; she had eyes like mine and a scarf in her hair. She said she'd
fled to the magical island and left her jewelry in the temple wall."

"The necklace?"

"Childish eyes are observant, Keith! I found the key in Papa's shoe, the necklace locked away! I've told you what happened later...my wandering half-asleep, of the lightning and thunder so like the rumbling volcano she had fled in terror. And ever since, whenever there's a violent storm, this mysterious dream re-occurs."

I gave thought to the eerie scene at the Met when she had chanted words of an ancient language. Casting my thoughts aside, I comforted Nina as best I could, holding her closely until her tears subsided, until our heartbeats meshed and she fell asleep. The ceiling fan purred softly, the guitar strumming in the distance, the youngsters' bonfire eddying shadows across the walls.

I finally turned on my side and tried to sleep. The approaching cold front intermittently flashed the windows. Nina slipped a leg over my thigh and wrapped an arm around me, breathing deeply, her fingers twitching spasmodically. I thought again of the scene at the Met, her psychic dreams. Had they come when she was emotionally spent, during an alpha level of consciousness when she was neither asleep nor awake? When they were triggered by a childhood nightmare, seeded in Crete, when the meaning of the sacrificial bowl had been inadvertently disclosed? Had the ring at the Met been found on the skeletal finger of a sacrificial victim at Arhannes, a young girl with eyes like hers?

* * * * * *

A strobe of lightning and crash of thunder rending the roof brought me awake. I reached for Nina's hand, fanned the mattress and tumbled to my feet, grappling for a lamp.

The veranda door was ajar; the feisty breeze caught Nina's gown from the chair and whipped it across the empty bed. Her earrings were on the side-stand, but the necklace was gone! I agonized for a moment, grabbed a towel, and ran for the door.

The sky came apart as I searched the veranda; a massive bolt severed a nearby tree. House lights faded. The frontal cloud loomed dirty gray over the blackened sea; a spatter of rain iced my back whilst I raced along the wall, calling her name. Noting the transfixed teenagers huddled near the faltering fire in the grove.

I saw her then, her naked body silhouetted by the flames...I vaulted the wall and barefooted the bush. Nina was standing in the smoldering embers with her arms outstretched, the necklace dangling from her fingers. Shrilling a singsong chant as if she were beseeching the sky!

Parting the mesmerized group, I lunged to her side. But she arched her head to the sky before I could gather her in. Snaking her arms as if she were embracing a ghost, she hurled the necklace into the fire!

I caught her about the waist and yanked her from the embers as she fell to her knees; squelched her flaming hair with my fingers. She twisted away and ripped me with her nails. Saliva dribbled from her lips; a trickle of blood glistened her throat where she'd torn the chain. There was no hint of recognition in her eyes whilst I gathered her to my side!

I stepped back and belted her across the cheek with the flat of my palm. Her head snapped aside, her eyes widening as if she'd suddenly come awake. She brought her hand to her jaw and frowned, looking down at her naked body, thence to the dazed group fringing the fire. She quizzed me wordlessly with her lips when she slumped in my arms.

The bewildered kids followed us to the house with their flashlights and blankets. The heavens opened; a wall of rain sheeted the veranda while we fought the doors. I motioned the group to come inside, deposited Nina on the bed, and sent them to the kitchen for brandy and ice.

The biting edge of the front slammed the house, rattled the windows, and tried the doors, as if something inside was denied. And then it was gone, moaning and wailing as it traversed the island to the east.

The lights blinked and held while the blonde girl wrapped Nina's feet with a cold compress. She stayed when the rain subsided and her friends departed with the Jeep. Anointing Nina's swollen ankles with aloe cream, she held a glass to her lips while she swallowed aspirin to ease the pain. She nodded when I massaged Nina's temples, speaking softly in response to her questions.

I turned off the lamp when Nina's eyelashes fluttered and her fingers eased their grip on my hand.

"I've forgotten her name, but she was a sweet, level-headed girl. She said she'd tell her friends to clam up when I explained the family tragedy, the emotionalism, the nightmares that sent Nina adrift in her sleep. I thanked her for the attention she'd given and insisted she drive the Mercedes to her home.

It was after I'd dimmed the lights and lay by Nina's side, reflecting on the disastrous evening that I heard the Mercedes cough to a start and venture the drive, stopping momentarily with the taillights aglow, as if the girl had further thoughts.

I found an explanation on the doorstep in the morning; the necklace, care-fully wrapped in tissue with a sprig of hibiscus, the keys to the Mercedes, and a thank-you note for the use of the grove.

Nina was lying on her stomach with a pillow under her arm, not yet awake, when I placed the necklace (with the hibiscus) next to her earrings on the bedside table. Later I told her she'd walked in her sleep and blundered into the fire; I made no mention of her sacrificial offering, which she was never to know.

CHAPTER

*O*ur British Airways flight from Nassau to London was seemingly never-ending, what with a stopover in Bermudato exchange pas sengers and top the tanks. Dusk by then, we stayed aboard in deference to Nina's blistered feet; collected blankets and pillows for the mid-Atlantic while the transients stretched their legs in the lounge. Sedated by her doctor in Nassau, Nina drowsed when they returned from the terminal, together with the newcomers we'd collected en route. One of whom was apparently a problem...yet to be allowed aboard, judging from the Captain's comments to the purser waiting at the door?

Fortunately, I'd booked first class with Nina's injuries in mind. And we were somewhat apart from the door when a hassle erupted rear side. Last in, obviously not a part of the confusion, an elderly British couple with their packages and canes, settling in a pair of seats across from ours; promptly ordering a double gin and tonic, their hands clasped for the night.

The cabin lights dimmed when our power appendage was disengaged, and we were greeted with a video taped announcement whilst the purser checked our belts. The ground crew standing by with their illuminated batons, but unfortunately there was a momentary delay...confusion behind us when the mid door reopened to admit a late coming passenger and a blast of humid air! Verbally abusive, she shrilled her displeasure to the ramp attendant, demanding her valise!

I looked back, of course, but the lady was out of view...venting anger to the purser, who was on the intercom with the Captain. The subject, apparently, a sizeable shoulder bag the attendant handed from the ramp. The bag passed quickly to the purser's lock up, I observed! The tempest subsided when the purser informed the passenger she was welcome to return to the terminal or belt up! Which she eventually did, settling noisily in the business section when the doors were closed and latched?

My ears pointing aft all the while...her coarse German accent coinciding with the episode at the Met! My eyes trailing the purser when he ascended the stairs to the upper deck, her leather valise tagged and tucked beneath his arm.

Amalia? I pondered Forsythe's comments while the 747 vectored the taxiway and made a lumbering turn to the active. Discreet and apart, he'd said. She obviously knew we were aboard; discreet until she'd blown her cool! Had she prior advice of my contact at Heathrow, or tagged us to determine the possibility? Turbines whined, spooled full thrust, and the Boeing nosed up while I gave thought to means of averting the coincidence of our arrival. The lights of Hamilton harbor faded behind us while we banked to intercept our circuitous route to the UK. The 747 climbed for altitude whilst I considered the onboard telephones...who to call? But why panic? If intelligence skipped lunch, they'd know she was aboard and adjust accordingly.

Nina came awake when we attained cruise altitude and the throttles reduced to an overnight purr. Sparked by the Brits' request of gin and tonic, she said she'd have the same. Reminded of her throbbing feet, however, she settled for aspirin and wine with her dinner, then fell asleep on my shoulder while the Boeing droned on. Wide awake, I watched the stars from our window, giving thought to the U-2 penetrating the troposphere on a night such as this; miles above the double deckers plying their routes with 350 passengers and stewardesses serving drinks. At the edge of space, we'd sustain on oxygen and plastic tubes to attend our needs.

There was indeed, a sense of closeness with dimensions of another kind. Mostly at night, weary from long hours in the cockpit, pilots often hear an ethereal chorus rising in cadence with their engines. Splendid voices in song, orchestrated with magnificent violins and the throaty crescendo of an organ played by a masterful hand; a wondrous chorus, sometimes perceived, but difficult to explain.

Stretching my legs while Nina slept, I parted the curtains for a moment and peered aft to satisfy my curiosity. Amalia was seated near the mid-ship galley with her chair reclined, clad in overnight slippers and a mask to shield her eyes. She was awake, however, complaining to the stewardess for want of a blanket, prodding her seat companion for room to spread her knees.

Cabin lights at low ebb, I took the opportunity to better my view. Middle aged, matronly stout, she was garbed in a stylish business suit and silken blouse that she'd partially unbuttoned to free her breasts. Long of face, nose redone, her blondish hair was drawn tightly from her forehead and clasped behind. She'd been pretty once, but sensibly traded youth for mature sophistication. An exquisite diamond ring, not overly flashy, sparkled when she drew the blanket to her chin. I closed the curtain then, sensing I'd been observed from beneath her mask when she allowed a knowing smile and levered her chair to full repose.

* * * * * *

The cabin lights brightened and jolted me awake. A rosy glow from our window and the clatter of plates in the galley while the early risers yawned and looked about. Our stewardess passed scented towels to herald the morning, returning with a trolley of coffee and tea, offering the breakfast menu and taking note. Nina was yet asleep and I let her be while I journeyed to wash and shave. When I returned, she was blinking her eyes, puzzling the window to determine where we were. Seemingly relaxed by her momentous sleep, she offered a smile when I inquired of her feet.

"They itch," she said, bending to remove the bandages and test her toes. "I can make do with loafers, I think. Where are we, Keith? Seems like I remember a stopover somewhere. Dinner? Wine? Did you slip me a double Mickey? My God, how I slept! No bloody dreams!"

"We've passed the coast of Ireland," I said. "Heathrow in an hour. Time for breakfast...scrambled eggs or diced fruit?"

"I haven't the capacity, my love. Coffee maybe, if you'll pardon me while I visit the loo?"

I'd trayed Nina's coffee when the chief purser appeared quietly at my shoulder and beckoned me aft.

"Captain requests your presence on the flight deck," he whispered, indicating the spiral stairway. He stopped short of the curtain, however, suggesting I change aisles and proceed on my own.

"Captain's instructions, Mr. Slater. I'll tell your wife you're visiting the cockpit as a company accommodation," he added, fingering his cap. And with that, he parted the curtains and strolled aft, collecting pillows and such, while I traversed first class and managed the stairs to the upper salon.

The economy section was a scene of chaos; babies wailing, trolleys cluttering the aisles, rest rooms besieged from all sides. But fortunately, the upper salon was relatively quiet. The purser indicating I should go forward to the cockpit and I assumed there was a connection with the Captain's impromptu request.

The 747 was descending through 18,000 when the cockpit door was unlocked and I went forward to the console. The Irish Sea had slipped behind; the heavy green of Wales was rolling beneath us. The Thames' headwaters glinted between the patchy clouds, flowing ribbon-like through the quilted countryside towards the haze of industrial London.

The cockpit reeked of cigarettes and overnight sweat. The first officer, conversing with approach control, calculated the Boeing's weight for our final approach. The radar screen stroking the horizon, the guidance system exacting our longitude and latitude, computing our ground speed on the digital display. The controls were linked to the autopilot, the autopilot to the onboard computer. The crew, flying hands off, watched for wandering aircraft while they monitored the display. The Captain raised his sun visor and angled his head, sensing my presence when the first officer looked back.

"Slater?" I acknowledged; he unfolded the jump seat and motioned me to sit.

"Captain Furzer here! We've word from the company, you're to be first off with the Mrs. when they extend the gates at Heathrow," he said. "You're to unbelt when we full-stop the ramp; the purser will see you out when the door is unlatched. There will be transportation nearby," he added. "You will clear with immigration at General Aviation, but make certain you've filled out the entry forms before you disembark! Questions?"

"Are you sure you have the right party?" I asked. He smiled, reached in his pocket for a cigarette.

"Don't worry it, Slater. We've had you on tab since 0600! Our instructions were relayed by Scotland Yard as a priority accommodation. As to why, we don't know, but possibly there's a connection with a problem we encountered in Bermuda. Odd, what? Our manifest was questioned on a military channel."

The captain puzzled my face for a moment. Lowering his visor to shield the sun, he drew the manifest from his flight case and scanned the list. The passengers were listed by their seat numbers, fore to aft. Following his finger, I noticed our seats were underlined, as was a seat by the galley, which I assumed was Amalia's although her name was obscured by his thumb.

"J. Keith Slater, hey? Mr. and Mrs.?" he continued, returning the manifest to his case. "Seems I recall your name from across the way...might you have flown F-15s from Riyadh, Slater?"

I nodded, said I was ex-service, currently assigned to the UN. The Captain raised his visor and smiled.

"Right-o! I remember you now! You teamed with our Tornadoes for ground suppression, caught yourself some bloody flak, I think. In fact, we were called in to rescue when we spotted your 'chutes...strafed the bastards until the 'copter showed up! Suffice? Glad you made it, Slater! So, what's with the UN?"

I allowed to my stint with NASA and my contract with the UN to recon Santorini with a hybrid U-2, inclusive of testing high-altitude haze over Africa and the Middle Eas5t.

"Long hours in a pressure suit, Captain. No coffee breaks!"

"Or wailing babies," he added with a grin. "Transatlantic's a long grind, Slater; no fun for the wicked, like flying a bus. Time out with jetlag while my sweetie's at her best!"

The first officer toggled seat belts before we had time to reminisce. Concerned for Nina, I folded the jump seat and thanked the Captain, but he apparently had more to add.

"Something we believe you should know, Slater. We've held a cautionary watch on a passenger we boarded in Bermuda. She's seated aft of your section and we've been advised to delay mid-door until you exit with your wife. Seems she was relieved of her shoulder valise when she refused to disclose the contents for security inspection. They opened it later and we have it here," he added, pointing to the company lock-bag. "She carries a diplomatic passport of sorts and we allowed her to board, sending word ahead, but the UK frowns on handguns, so she can jolly well claim it from the Yard!"

Amalia! I was aware of her steely eyes when I descended the stairs, alert to her demands of a stewardess while I proceeded to the forward compartment. Nina had slipped into her loafers when I returned to my seat. Wide awake, scented with her lavender, pouting for a kiss...

"Heavens, you reek of cigarettes, Keith! Smoking the weed with the captain while I guard your earthly belongings?" I clued her to the situation in general terms, said the Captain had arranged for us to be first off as a company favor.

"Jeepers, do I look that bad?" She asked.

"They're loaded with passengers, honey. It's up to you, first off or last?" She glanced at the endless rows of faces and gave it thumbs up!

The chief purser came forward when we touched down and turned from the active. The Boeing rumbled to the ramp while I shouldered Nina's overnighter and toed my valise from beneath the seat. When we jolted full stop, he ushered us to the forward door while the ensemble collected their packages from the overhead bins.

"We'll have a wheelchair waiting at the gate," the purser volunteered. Nina frowned at the thought, suggesting a skateboard would do. The purser smiled politely, cautioned us to wait until the ramp was adjusted, then handed the company bag to the console operator. Extending his hand, he helped Nina to the ramp. Motioning us to hurry, he prudently closed the door whilst Amalia shrieked for her bag.

* * * * * *

Clearing Heathrow International is a long drawn out process. Initially, a navigational problem when one exits the ramp and confronts an endless series of gates, where one elects to carry on with the mainstream or be trampled underfoot. Then, a tedious walk to where the pier junctures an automated slideway, while the intrepid bound ahead. Congestion a matter of form by then; passengers converging to wait their turn with immigration. Luggage retrieval next; a spinning console of tumbling bags, means of cartage, and customs inspection. Congestion again. Beaming faces awaiting arrivals; some, not polite, necessitate a panzer thrust to gain access to transportation.

We fortunately were allowed to avoid all of that. A red-coated supervisor met us at the console enclosure and checked our names with his notes. A wheelchair stood by, but Nina shook her head and he proposed an alternate route, pointing to the exterior stairway leading directly to the tarmac. The tarmac slippery with grease and condensation...but we managed with Nina clinging between us.

We were greeted by a bright English morning, nipped by a blast of chilly air as we threaded the maze of ground equipment to where he pointed to a waiting van. The supervisor was polite and obliging, forging ahead with Nina's overnighter while she hobbled along on my arm.

"I'll need your luggage tabs," he said. "Hold on to your entry forms," he added, sliding the passenger door aside. "We've arranged to clear with immigration at their field office. Now then, if you'll kindly be seated, I'll identify your luggage and follow you along directly."

Mystified by the turn of events, Nina maintained her silence while I helped her to a seat and the driver closed the door. She sat stoically beside me, studying the teeming activity; gazing at the monstrous jets nesting side by side, pondering the low-slung AV truck darting underwing, the elevated vans loading provisions, and the salvage tankers pumping sewage from the Boeing's underbelly.

"So like the dockside at Piraeus," she commented. "Same scene...ships from sea, arrivals thirsting for fuel while their crews hit the pubs!"

"Sobriety tests when they re-board, I think!"

"Don't be a prude, Keith! So, maybe you can explain why we were expelled from our seats?" I had no ready answer, although I pondered the reason when

105

I observed an unlikely F-15 ramped near General Aviation; an advanced series, under guard! The familiar silhouette passed from view when our driver pulled to a stop by a low gray building housing immigration.

"UN, hey?" the rosy-cheeked inspector commented, when he examined my passport and applied the appropriate stamp. "And the young lady, I presume, is your wife?"

"As of Saturday last," I responded, presenting Nina's passport. "Mrs. Slater is a Greek national at the moment, she carries a stateside residency card."

The inspector smiled, declined to question the purpose of our stopover, and glanced momentarily at the window.

"Your entry states you're in transit to Athens, following a stopover in London," he said, "which is not a problem, but we've disturbing news from Greece. I suggest the Mrs. give her departure judicious thought!"

"In what way?" interjected Nina.

"We've word they're evacuating Santorini, ma'am. Now that's not Athens, but it's jolly close by, and we're advising our transits accordingly."

"I was there only last week!" Nina sputtered.

"I've observed the entries in your passport, Mrs. Slater, but recent advisories suggest passage for visitation be deterred."

Deterred? Recently advised? I gave thought to his source of instructions when he again peered to the window.

"Visitation!" thundered Nina, her temper aroused. "I've business in Athens, a conference with the authorities, Inspector! Moreover, I'm also my husband's wife," she stammered. "Where he goes I go, so don't you dare patronize me!"

The inspector grimaced, visibly shaken, but he collected himself before I could intercede. Then, shaking his head, he gave us a quick once-over and stamped her passport accordingly.

"Can't knock it, ma'am! That's the way it should be. Wish me wifey had your fire!" he added, enclosing Nina's entry form with mine. "Now then," he said, "you've transportation waiting outside, I believe. Yon Bentley, Mr. Slater. They came by earlier to facilitate your arrival," he asided when Nina spotted the limousine and split for the ladies lounge.

"Wasn't wanting the Mrs. to know," he added apologetically, "seeing she's upset as it is, but the gent in yon Bentley, American methinks, came by with a chap from our Foreign Office and laid a heavy on me shoulder! Said it was better the Mrs. stayed in the UK while you went about your business in Greece. Was inclined to agree," he added, "knowing the volcano's short fuse and we've advice from the ministry. Obliged as best I could, sir, until the Mrs. laid me down!"

"The American, Inspector...middle-aged, short and balding?"

"Mistook him for our gentry until he exercised his Irish temperament, Mr. Slater. We Brits have a thing about that! Chap from our Foreign Office was most polite, however. Upper class, judging from his Kentish accent. Matter of fact, he's offloading your luggage from the van, sir. Tall and lanky like yourself, dressed for the city, aside from his cap!" the inspector mused, while I peered from his window. "Nevertheless, I'll exempt your belongings from Customs inspection, seeing the Mrs. is hurrying to get on!"

I eyed the waiting Bentley and glanced warily at Nina when she emerged from the lounge. Trim and exquisite, she'd changed to a flouncy dress, abandoned her loafers for high-heeled shoes (testing for balance when she grasped my arm). Puzzled, she offered an icy smile when I thanked the inspector, and frowned when I pumped his hand. Shrugged her contempt when he saw us to the door, then wide-eyed the ensemble gathered outside!

Forest green, long and sleek, with chromium headlights, the vintage Bentley was appropriate for the times of Agatha Christie, as was the burly gentleman who emerged from the shadowy saloon. Comparatively garbed, he resembled the leading character from one of her mysteries. I was startled by his appearance but withheld my comments. Not so Nina, who expressed herself immediately.

"God in heaven!" she shrieked. "Could that be you, Timothy Shannon O'Brien?" The general winced, extending his hand.

"Greetings, Nina, did you have a nice flight?"

"Aside from my bloody feet," she replied, dipping a mock curtsey to his attire. "My, what a sight! I'd buss your cheek, T.S., if you weren't mouthing that terrible cigar!" Casting it aside, he prompted Nina to the rear seat, closing the door softly when she offered her impish grin.

Comical in a sense, appropriate to a proper English morning, T.S. wore a splendid tweed jacket, scarf at his throat, and plaid trousers befitting a gentleman at ease. His glossy shoes were somewhat at odds, however, as were the flight togs I observed when we piled our luggage in the boot.

"Eyes front!" he cautioned when I glanced at the F-15. "I'll have none of your lip," he rasped when I offered a left-handed salute. "We've an urgent matter to discuss in private, Keithy! So mind your tongue and play it the way it is!"

"Now then," he continued for Nina when she lowered the window to request her valise. "Had occasion to visit Farnborough and popped over to take you to lunch! Also, to offer my condolences in regards to your parents, Nina. Tragic thing! I've read the report, of course."

"Not to say it couldn't be helped," Nina commented when he slipped in beside her. "I've a theory of my own, T.S. Nevertheless, I appreciate your thoughts. Where are we off to for lunch? Strawberries and Devon cream, I'd fancy that...if you intend to drive us to your estate!"

"London, my dear! The butler's on holiday. I understand you've booked the Carlton Towers and they've an excellent restaurant with a view of Cadogan Square. I've an appointment at Sunningdale post lunch, but we'll have time for strawberries Chambord with vintage champagne on the side!"

"With an entrée of Eggs Benedict and bangers, perhaps? I'm famished, T.S., although I did so wish for a ride in the countryside. But then Sunnningdale's miles away, I suppose. In fact, Grandpa said it's better to play it with a four iron to avoid the nasty traps!"

"Grandpa?"

"On my mother's side, silly! He had a home nearby."

"Four iron, hey? But then you've time to visit! I understand you'll be staying on."

"What made you think that?" Nina retorted, helping herself to a brandy from the console. "Tell me, T.S., I've been wondering about this. Tweeds are out of season and Bentleys are strictly glitz! So, maybe you thought I was a ninny when you pulled the plug with immigration?"

T.S. was noncommittal, although his face was florid when he explored his jacket for a cigar (pausing mid-pocket when Nina expressed her fiery greens). There was little I could say, realizing the sham was a convenience to exit Heathrow while Amalia was having her do with Scotland Yard.

We proceeded to the security gate in silence...Nina with her feet on the jump seat, T.S. at odds. The Bentley had tinted windows, custom interior, rear seat TV and a cellular phone, most likely an accommodation for a gentleman of means. Not so the chauffeur, I thought, judging from the ill-fitting cap he apparently borrowed for the occasion. Thirtyish, groomed with a military haircut and sparse moustache, his pukka accent and easy demeanor suggested he was more than he seemed. My suspicions confirmed when he flashed his pass at the gate and was given a brisk salute (an action not lost on my keen-eyed bride)!

We threaded traffic to the underpass and joined the mayhem on the M$, accelerating to pace the Jaguars hell-bent for the morning tea. The general contained his conversation to matters at hand; idle chatter mostly...the brightness of the morning compared with the haze in the Aegean. I suspected he was waiting for a moment of privacy, as did Nina, who remained content to nurse her feet and bide the decanter of brandy.

"I borrowed the lot from Norman Barclay when I checked your itinerary," T.S. offered when we drew abreast of the city. "Norman's an old friend, and we planned to golf at Sunningdale when I opted to slip over for a chat. Okay, so I pulled a few strings to expedite matters, but don't lay me down, my sweet. Keith's dad was my classmate, and I've an interest in his career!"

"How sweet of you to say that," Nina commented as we rounded Harrods and pointed for Cadogan Square. "Come to think, I wasn't aware of your presence at our wedding, although we're grateful for the case of champagne!"

"I was checking stats in Saudi Arabia, my dear. Haven't retired as yet, and we've ongoing matters to decide in the Persian Gulf."

"Or possibly a collective venture with the U-2, unbeknownst to the UN? Come off it, Timothy Shannon! You've been after Keithy's hide since Mountain View, and most likely while I was detained in Greece! So explain your note from the Carlyle that he tossed in the kitchen bin, the screwy cable from ITT! Same damned initials, T.S.! Coded or otherwise, they continue to pop up whenever I'm invited to lunch!"

The general played it down, admitting to our impromptu meeting at the Carlyle.

"We had technical information to pass along to Keith," he said, prodding his pockets again. "Mostly an update by Lockheed in regard to the modified U-2. We also reviewed a communications package recently developed by Hughes," he added, "of which the Air Force has interest when we monitor its range in flight. As for the cable you mentioned, I'm puzzled by the analogy, my dear. Initials or otherwise, it never crossed my desk!" I squirmed at the near truth, but Nina smiled and carried.

"I regard that as an evasive answer," she retorted. "More so when you appear out of nowhere to discuss a matter you've already discussed! I'm also curious about the psychological reason for that insidious cigar, which you continue to favor whenever there's a contrary turn. Is it to salve for indecision, time out for calculation or a matter of conscience...provided you have such? I question your motivation, General! Have you reason to reach beyond all of this, an adversary from your past to equate? Is your alter ego involved, a matter you've buried in the back side of your mind?"

Granite jawed, short of an answer, T.S. cast about to eye the traffic, scanning the distance to the Carlton Towers, thinking the doorman would provide an end to the conversation. Silence, unfortunately, wasn't one of Nina's virtues, and she insistently elbowed his arm.

"Alright," he growled. We have, in fact, encountered a recent development in regard to White Dove and our monitoring devices in the Gulf. It is related in part to an unsigned memo from Dr. Nokomo's desk, contrary to the format agreed by our joint command, of which I'm part!" he added brusquely. "Specifically, for reasons unknown, the memo authorizes a change of radio frequencies Keith's to address when we monitor the U-2 over Iran. This includes our security zone, which we consider inviolate, my sweet!"

"So, let's ice it!" I interjected, realizing he was hedging. "Enough's enough, Nina! If there's a problem with communication, I'll deal with it later. Let's get on with lunch!" The Bentley entered the portico and the doorman waved us on. Taken aback, she turned abruptly to sort me out.

"It's unlike you to blow a fuse," Nina retorted. "I'm your wife, lest you forget, and I'm not accustomed to ambiguous answers! You might also have the courtesy to help me out," she snapped when the general made a hasty retreat. "My feet hurt, damn it! And aside from lunch, I've reason enough to visit the loo!"

That said, Nina grasped my arm, furthering her misgivings while she hobbled alongside. Her temper, usually short span, allowed a temporary truce. Apologies for my part, recourse on hers when she spied a boutique adjoining the lobby.

"I'll join you on the mezzanine," she announced, while I scrawled my signature on the registry pad. "Provided I've access to your American Express as your obedient and loving wife!"

* * * * * *

Lunch was a casual affair, fraught with double entendres (aside from Nina's niggling reminder of the scenario in the Edwardian Room when she compared our view with Central Park). T.S. was unheeding, taciturn, while he stirred his straw-berries and scanned his watch. He brightened when the waiter uncorked the champagne, however...toasted our future with the vintage he'd thoughtfully checked in advance. There was an undercurrent, of course, his lingering presence to which Nina alluded when she asked for the key to our room.

"I've business at Sotheby's," she said. "Papa's paintings, Keith! So have your chat while I shower and change. Should be back by six," she added. "Might we catch a show and dinner at Annabel's? I'd like that! In fact, I've arranged our reservations with the concierge. And lest you forget," she warned, confront-ing the general with her winsome smile, "we're booked for Athens tomorrow morning, promptly at ten, my sweet! Olympic will see us to Heathrow. There'll be a dearth of transportation when Barclay collects his Bentley!"

Mindful of her mood, I saw Nina to the elevator and impeded the door with my shoe until she turned to face me and I released the jangling thing.

"I love you dearly," she whispered while we clung together in the cab. "But lately, I'm worried about our future, my darling. Not of your dealings with that iron ass in tweeds; I can handle that, knowing you'll eventually confide in me. It's something else…a hateful matter, an ongoing suspicion that's disturbed me endlessly since I attended the funeral in Greece. Perhaps it's my psychic nature," she added, tightening her grip on my arm. "My fear of a dreadful bloodletting that fills me with a sense of dread. Good heavens!" she gasped when the door opened abruptly and we were greeted by the throng in the lobby!

"Honeymooners!" a waiting dowager complained, while we extracted ourselves. "Have you no sense of decency?"

"Don't knock it," Nina countered, adjusting her blouse while I set matters straight with the cab controls. "My husband has problems with elevators, but he's splendid when we're naked in bed!"

"Having your ups and downs?" T.S. commented when we met at the head of the stairs. "You appear a bit wan, my boy. Might you have settled accounts with the concierge?"

Unsettled was apt for my state of mind. Despite Nina's banter, she'd confirmed what I'd suspected since she'd wandered at the Met; her psychic suspicion of the circumstances that led to her family's death. I thought again of the nasty episode at Lyford Cay, of her response to the thunder when she submerged from reality and escaped to her confounding dreams. Metexas had set her off, but likened to the Met, it was the thunderous lightning that did her in! Was it related to the explosion she'd sensed at the Great Divide? I wondered about that, worried for Metexas if she had vengeance in her soul!

"Beautiful lady!" T.S. ventured when we returned to his table. "Intelligent, observant, although I'm not too keen for an impromptu analysis of the back side of my mind!"

"Intuition!" I corrected, attempting to shrug off my thoughts. 'Nina has an uncanny perception she can tune in; its multi-layered when she's upset and withdraws to another time."

"Multi-layered?"

"Uncommon perception, T.S.! Her dad had an interest in Greek mythology and Nina absorbed it as a child. She sometimes identifies with the story of Amor and Psyche. So let's get on with it!" I suggested, changing the subject. "Give or take a couple of days, ten at the most, I'll be circling the Goddamned volcano!"

Scanning his watch, T.S. produced an envelope from his jacket and fanned a series of photos on the table, addressing them one by one while I bent over to get a better view. Developed from the negatives I'd lifted from the corpse, I noticed they were stained but otherwise legible.

"Note the computerized enhancement," he said, comparing an enlargement with a mini shot. "Long range, but nevertheless they identify our suspect at Ramenskoye where the de facto KGB has a measure of control."

"Gunnar?" T.S. nodded.

"Long of neck, standing by a Mystic-B, their twin engine version of our advanced TR-2. They hadn't developed a two-seat trainer, as far as we know, but apparently he underwent high-speed taxi tests to familiarize his feel of the controls. We assumed this, noting his lack of pressure suit while seated in the cockpit, per photo number three! In fact, there's no indication he actually soloed the Mystic in flight."

"Is he a qualified pilot?" I asked.

"Not that I know, Keith, although there's a possibility he's flown gliders as a student in East Germany. Now then, photos four and five were snapped from a different angle, on a subsequent day judging from the shadows. Same scene, however...Gunnar in the cockpit, an instructor standing by; all of which indicates an intensive briefing over a short span of time."

"Recently?"

"Shortly after he hauled ass from New York. We had a knowledgeable person tracking his movements, although we were unaware of his whereabouts until he was sighted at Ramenskoye by a CIA informant; near about the time Gunnar was photographed on the line."

"Obolensky?"

"Affirmative, Keith! We acquired Obolensky as a turncoat and assigned him to determine Gunnar's intentions, more or less as a test, not knowing he'd traced him to Ramenskoye. We also knew he was a childhood friend of Gomulaka and would pursue the matter with a vengeance when the doctor disappeared. He held a measure of confidence with the de facto KGB, until he appeared at Ramenskoye...and Gunnar wondered why!"

"So Obolensky split the park!"

"With the help of a Russian colonel, most likely someone he'd known in Poland. But again, we had no knowledge of Gunnar's activities, until we enhanced the photos you removed from the stiff."

"Amen! Let's hope he didn't die in vain!"

"Sorry, lad! It happened so quickly we hadn't time to react. In fact, intelligence was completely baffled when you contacted Charlie. No one knew Stash was on the run with information, although they'd established a contact in Vienna. Which he obviously gave up, knowing the area was hot with unfriendlies and Gunnar was after his hide!"

"Aware of plans to replace Gomulaka?"

"Apparently! But judging from his wire, he wasn't aware of the aftermath! The doctor was murdered, Keith! The circumstances indicated suicide, but an autopsy proved otherwise. We had word of this from Interpol. In short, the autopsy revealed he was *unconscious* when he 'leapt' from the window."

"Two dead Poles and Stash on the run! Any feedback?"

"Not yet, but there's a possibility of inside help. The Polish authorities were cooperative, Keith. Aside from advising his widow, they withheld their findings from the media, indicating they may have information! Gomulaka had many friends, some with connections to the former Polish underground who may know of Stash's whereabouts."

"The Poles are a close-knit lot, my boy. If Stash sought their help, let's assume he's well protected."

"Where do we go from here, general? Judging from the photos, Gunnar has plans for the U-2, but he's not a meteorologist and the option would be up to me! I'm not uncomfortable with that," I added. "I'll have Winner or Edwards close in, but it's the turn over Iran that gives me the shits!"

T.S. reached for his glasses, sipping the last of his wine while the waiter cleared the table. He then spread the pictures face up, adding another from the envelope to judge my reaction.

"Note the bearded chap in the background," he said, pointing to photos one through three. Tall and blond, not Russian. "At first, we assumed he was ground crew, or an interpreter with Gunnar and his instructor. Now then, note photos four and five, again in the background while Gunnar's seated in the cockpit."

"Shaved his beard, hey?"

"Exactly, Keith. As you know, beards are an inconvenience when one is breathing oxygen at 70,000 feet."

"Wouldn't worry it," I said. "If Gunnar's sporting a ringer, they'll have to clear him at the UN. Sort of scary, though, if he has a hand for high-performance jets. Could be he's ex-Warsaw Pact, a Baltic type. Any leads?"

"None whatsoever, Keith. Intelligence screened their files and they haven't a clue! Could be he had no past affiliation, or possibly flew for another service. He couldn't have been known to Obolensky, in that he had Gunnar in focus all the while. I bring this to your attention should he surface in the future," T.S.

continued. "If he's a candidate for Gomulaka's vacancy you'll be apprised by the UN."

"Or Dr. Nokomo's secretary; she has a tendency to 'misfile' their addenda."

"Alright, so we had a flap about that! But you'll be joining his group in Athens, Kos later on, where you'll have access to information. More to the pint, Keenan's established an operative in the area who is privy to all we've discussed, who will report hereafter to our joint command. Unknown to Gunnar's generation, he was suggested by British Intelligence when Keenan determined we were in need of help."

"That's a switch!"

"True, but the Brits know the region better than we; the ins and outs in Greece and the Middle East, and Keenan thought it best to address the issue independently, while we concentrate on our objective. We'll be monitoring the situation from Riyadh, inclusive of your communications link with Kos. Also in touch indirectly if you encounter a flap with Gunnar. To that end, we've provided a measure of security, Keith. As you know, your crew chief was formerly with the 99th at Beale; fortunately at hand when he was assigned by NASA to maintain the U-2."

"An old friend?" T.S. nodded.

"Foresight, Keith! I arranged his security clearance when the sensor was installed at Lockheed, and later he agreed to carry on...voluntarily, of course!"

"Like our arm-twisting session at the Carlyle?"

"Call it what you like, but he's acquainted with U-2s and you'll need a top mechanic."

"Is he acquainted with the cloak and dagger part?"

"No, but he's aware of your part and knows what we have in mind. Gunnar's a new trick, however, so guide him confidentially. And for God's sake steer him away from Amalia if she sports for a brace of beer! In fact, we had her in mind when I rearranged our appointment to bring you up to date. She's a savvy bitch, would know us by sight. Sums it up, Keith!"

"Off to Sunningdale?"

"Damn it, boy! If I've the chance to relax, so be it! And what do you do on the side?"

"Make love to my lovely bride!"

"I've no quarrel with that, but I'm stuck with a can of worms, possibly a reprimand if I've fucked this thing up!"

"Problems with Keenan, T.S.?"

The general examined his class ring, turning it on his finger when he looked up to address me with his blues. He seemed overly tired, showing his age in the sunlight, his morning stubble flecked with gray. Squint wrinkles attested to years in the cockpit when he was a hot stick in Vietnam...a living legend, a pilot's pilot. He was troubled, I thought, when I urged him to open up.

"As a career officer, I'm stuck with my lot," he said. "Aside from Air Force intelligence, I've little knowledge of covert activities, of which I was reminded when the situation compounded beyond my means. Your mission stands...it's too late to undo my responsibility for your part. I initially thought there was minimal risk when I prompted your name to the Security Council. Now we're confronted with a global problem contrary to my point of view."

"So, get on with it, T.S.!"

"Call it instinct, Keith. I've earned my stars in combat and I've observed what we've had to contend. Likened to Kuwait and Kosovo, we have a similar situation that could develop overnight. So we sat on our asses, eventually amassed a half million troops, and now again we have a gaggle of erratics on the loose! No sweat until they round the Black Sea. What then? A massive confrontation? Whereas a pre-emptive strike with sensor-fused weapons could reduce the robot tanks to molten metal in a matter of seconds!"

"Keenan didn't take to it nicely?"

"Politics, Keith! He acknowledged my view, didn't question it, but he has the Third World to consider. They'd be prompt to cuss us out if we doused a spark before it flamed! So, I'm in orbit for the time being, but we'll have the means at hand if there's a decision to intervene!"

"Change of subject," the general abruptly added. "Do you hear something, boy? Are my ears shot to hell?"

"It's your cellular, I think." T.S. searched his blazer and silenced the thing; he checked the display.

"Scotland Yard! They were to let me know when they released Amalia."

"Close by?"

"Could be," he muttered, tipping the mystified waiter with a twenty-dollar bill. "Whitehall's nearby, but most likely they detained her at Heathrow. If she's on to your itinerary, it wouldn't do to be seen together, much less with the Bentley if she pulls up in a taxi."

"So split for the lobby and I'll haul ass to the elevator!"

"Makes for a problem, Keith! I hoped you could meet in private with your contact in Greece. Presumably you have a memory for faces, but I couldn't put it together with Nina back seat!"

"Seedy cap, pukka accent? I wondered about that! Your driver?" T.S.

115

nodded.

"Ex-RAF, multi-lingual, previously assigned to Damascus as an eye for British Intelligence. You'll have much in common as seasoned pilots, which should expedite matters in a technical sense. His code name is 'Bird Watch'…as the gaffs would have it, in terms of Gunnar and Amalia. There's a possibility he'll establish contact when you meet with your group in Athens, Keith. You're booked at the Hotel Grande Bretagne according to my notes."

"Not all together, T.S.! The GB's a funnel point for the scientists until we move on to Kos. Aside from doctors Winner and Edwards, I've yet to meet the lot, inclusive of Sr. Nokomo who didn't show last time around. Gunnar I'd recognize from the photo shots and Forsythe's descript, but more likely he's eavesdropping at Antimahia while Amalia cozies the GB hotel. So, better he hangs loose until we know who's who. Later, we've an update session with Dr. Sigurdesson, the Swedish volcanologist…that he could attend with a beard and oily glasses. Nina and I will be staying at her uncle's villa in Kavouri in the interim. But I'll definitely be at hand when we break for coffee, T.S."

"I'll pass it along; bearded or otherwise, you'll spot one another," T.S. commented, bridging his nose with a pair of unlikely sunglasses. "I'd also like to extend my best wishes to Nina, despite her acid tongue. She's a remarkable lady, Keith! So look after her as best you can…foremost, boy! I mean that sincerely, despite my ornery ways!"

Naturally, I gave thought to his comments while he descended the stairs to the lobby. Classmate of my dad, driven by his forceful nature, T.S. was also a warm-hearted and caring individual. And I tended to believe he regarded me as the son he never had.

The general flew on to Riyadh the next morning. Gunnar's 'tweedy bird' apparently long gone when we boarded Olympic for Athens shortly thereafter.

CHAPTER 14

The sky had an unearthly hue while we flanked the coast of France and crossed the boot of Italy. Blood red, the sun lacked its usual luster when lunch was served at high noon.

Her feet on the mend (curled beneath a blanket), Nina was preoccupied with the Sotheby's appraisal, concerned if the proceeds would be sufficient to clear the liens in Piraeus. She was not unobservant, however, viewing the shroud of darkness off our starboard wing.

"It's the ash cloud from Thera – Santorini – Keith. Most times it lingers until the winds take it south. From Kavouri we can see the volcano's glow at night, hear its incessant rumbling, but aside from a sprinkling of ash, Athens is clear and calm. Or was when I attended the funeral," she added thoughtfully.

Not wanting to upset her prematurely, I folded the Herald Tribune carefully beneath my seat. Nina obviously was unaware of the cautionary advice prompted by their correspondent in Greece, of the recent flood of refugees arriving daily from the southern Aegean. Hell's fire, she was looking forward to our arrival in Athens, of our meeting with her elderly Auntie and Uncle; anticipating the celebration they'd planned to introduce me to her many friends and relatives. Why dampen her spirits, whilst the authorities were considering a decree of martial law?

Aside from the interim days in Athens, our sojourn in Kos was high on Nina's agenda. Conditions prevailing, we'd planned to stay aboard the Helena when our schedules coincided. Nina had a maiden aunt in Kos, her Auntie Cleo. A wise old bird who'd looked after Nina while her grandfather was alive, the old man entombed nearby. Acquainted with the events at Arhannes, she'd be privy to Nina's traumatic dreams; as would Captain Stavos, the family retainer vested with the Helena, who'd witnessed the storm that came from the highlands that mysterious night in Crete.

The Boeing lumbered on, but I was aware of our circuitous course while we skirted the pall of Santorini. Hanging in the tropopause, yet far in the distance, the volcano's oily plume was continuously illuminated with streaks of static lightning.

Grim and foreboding...a matter I'd have to reckon with when I circled its molten core. I gave thought to the analysis forwarded by Dr. Sigurdesson. I'd noted her absence from the briefing at the UN, but he faxed comments from Sweden were explicit and sharply worded.

'By all means avoid the column activity' she'd warned. 'The temperature inside the vertical might reach 800 degrees centigrade and create an updraft of 1,200 miles per hour. The column will top off at 20 miles of altitude and cause extreme turbulence within a 200-mile radius. Following this, should you observe a continuation, I predict a Plinian explosion at "moon tide", when the mantle over Santorini is weakened and the sea penetrates its magma chamber, which could happen instantaneously!'

Mitigating thoughts mixed with apprehension regarding Gunnar and his ilk. I shrugged it off for the moment, however, what with Nina's eyes dancing with excitement when we had the Ionian Sea behind us, Kalamai off our port side, the 747 making a long descending turn into Athens International.

"Look off to our right, Keith! she exclaimed. "The Cyclades Islands...Cyclades means 'the wheeling ones' because they whirl like a windmill around Delos. Thera's further south, close to Crete; you can see its smoke bending towards Rhodos and Karpathos. God in heaven!" she gasped, when a spiraling bolt blazed the horizon. Fortunately, the captain made a banking turn to position his final approach, the scene behind us when he leveled off to align the active runway. Nina was nervous, of course, controlling herself as Athens appeared in the distance, emerging from the vestige of a clearing Grecian sky.

Nina was ecstatic, pointing to the cliffs of Kavouri while the Boeing was nose high on its final approach. Smiling while the sea flashed beneath us, she brushed the length of hair aside and tidied her skirt. Her hand gripped mine when we touched down. Bringing her wedding band to my lips whilst she nuzzled my cheek.

"They'll adore you, Keith! Uncle's on the quiet side and Auntie might seem a bit square, but she'll sweep you off your feet when she's had her splash of ouzo! Goodness, their presents! Did I pack them with your shirts?"

I peered at the runway while she ransacked her carry-on bag. The captain had elected to roll its length rather than brake with reverse thrust. Worried for ash ingestion, I assumed, although the runway appeared relatively clear.

* * * * * *

The chauffeur deftly steered the black Mercedes from the divider island where they'd been waiting, and brought it curbside when we emerged from the terminal. Her eyes brimming, Nina skirted our cart of luggage and unlatched their door. The sidewalk reunion at Hellikon would have brought tears to the eyes of the Lion of Amphripolis. Shrieking with delight, she embraced the elderly pair, whirled her tiny aunt about, setting her carefully to the pavement. Roughed her uncle's hair and kissed him soundly as she would her dad. The old man beamed; held her at arm's length for a moment, his eyes moistening. Then he drew her close and buried his head on her shoulder.

Auntie beckoned when she saw me standing in the shadows, reaching out when I came to her side. She looked up to study my face, nodded briefly, and planted a kiss on the ridge of my cheek, smiling when Uncle broke from Nina to clasp my arm. He pumped my hand vigorously, gave it up; spread his arms and hugged me about the waist, welcoming my presence in halting English and beaming when I responded with my travel book Greek. Altogether it was a joyous greeting, and judging from the warmth of their expression, I'd been accepted as Nina's American bridegroom!

Auntie, a small, trim woman for her age, chain-smoked cigarettes from a silver filtering device. She was definitely involved in the business discussion that continued as we drove south along the coast to Kavouri. Nina's uncle, in his late sixties, had thick gray hair, wore glasses and a quiet smile. An older version of the photographs I'd seen of Nick; softer, perhaps. He nodded politely while Auntie had her say, adding a comment when she paused to collect her breath. A mourning band was sewn to the sleeve of his suit; he wore a black tie and wedding band. No frills, aside from a gold Rolex with Nick's initials on the strap. They conversed in Greek, Nina interpreting to English from time to time, while Auntie lofted her cigarette and nodded from across the seat.

"The government is pressing for death taxes, Keith. They normally wait a year for a will to be probated, but they're insisting Papa's residency abroad abrogates the law!"

"Metexas!" Auntie snapped.

"She means the bastard bribed an official to force a disclosure," Nina interjected. Auntie added a dicey comment in Greek, whereupon Uncle pointed to the Alstir Palace Hotel in passing, indicating he wished to change the subject.

The chauffeur searched my face in his mirror when we turned from heavy traffic and entered a suburban street along the sea. I caught his eye briefly, but he quickly looked away. Backside, he reminded me of T.S.'s 'chauffeur' at Heathrow, the ill-fitting hat pulled low on his head. The resemblance stopped there, however. Large of bone (six feet two I judged), his head was clean-, a brownish-gray stubble appearing at the nape of his neck. Fiftyish, perhaps, he seemed strangely out of place with the smaller statured Greeks I'd seen about.

"We're almost there!" Nina shouted when he slowed the Mercedes, interrupting my thoughts. "You can see the villa beyond the cedars and bougainvillea," she added, pointing to a curving wall leading to an imposing set of gates.

The villa was a whitewashed, rambling affair, built on a rocky escarpment facing the sea. Two-storey in part, with a clay tile roof and immaculate inner grounds. The lawn clipped short and freshly watered, a bank of flowers centering the circular drive. A sparkling red jaguar 10 convertible was parked beneath the portico. Nina was ecstatic when she glimpsed the lovely old thing.

"You've had it refurbished!" she cried out, kissing her uncle on the cheek as she leapt from the Mercedes. Delighted, the old man, beaming his pleasure, pointed to the squeaky new leather seats when he slipped her the keys.

"It was grandfather's favorite machine, Keith! God love him; Papa shipped it from the UK on my eighteenth birthday. I pranged it first time around...ruined Papa's hedgerow, I was so excited!" Hiking her skirt, Nina slipped inside and keyed the switch while I helped Auntie from the car and grappled with our luggage. A plume of blue smoke erupted from the double exhaust pipes; the engine coughed and caught, then settled into a continuous roar, spinning gravel when she released the clutch. Grinning, her eyes flashing, she swept her hair aside and sped for the gates.

"Nina, be back soon!" Auntie admonished. "Happy, she have high spirit, hey? Come, my son, allow us to show you your quarters."

A heavy hand met mine when I reached for my overnighter. Startled, I looked up. The chauffeur shook his head, our eyes locked. He continued to stare as if it were a game of sorts. His watery blue eyes were devoid of expression, unyielding, and I sensed he was taking my measure. I knuckled his fingers and he let go. Nodding as he withdrew his hand, he eyed me quietly, as if pondering my credentials. Then, inexplicably, pointed mutely to Nina's luggage and offered a token smile. I was instantly aware of his tobacco-stained teeth and Slavic facial features; stunned by his resemblance to the stranger I'd found sprawled dead in the lobby when I returned with Nina that stormy afternoon in New York.

"Bruno's a deef!" uncle asided. "He's a want to carry your baggage, Keith."

"Bruno's deaf mute," Auntie corrected, inclining her head, indicating he was to precede us when he collected Nina's possessions under his arm. "He's all right, a bit odd," she added. "Cares for our automobile and minds the garden nicely. Came to us a fortnight ago, when our driver joined his son in America." Arm-in-arm, Auntie introduced me to her classic garden patio and Uncle's collection of ancient statuary surrounding the central pool. Their villa bordered the north side, outside stairs leading to a second-storey balcony suite where we'd quarter during our stay in Kavouri. A low wall ranged the cliff side, terminating with a steep hand-hewn stone stairway leading to the rocky shore below. From the cliff they'd carved a seaside alcove with a brightly painted cabana at its southerly end. Low tide at the time, a set of mossy steps ascended to a narrow stretch of pebbly beach.

"I sometimes sun there," Auntie commented, "but the sea is much too chilly for an old lady, Keith." Our conversation was interrupted when we spied the Jaguar rounding the driveway with its top folded down and Nina's scarf trailing behind. It reminded me of a like afternoon at Big Sur and my heart fluttered momentarily while Auntie carried on.

"Time's appropriate for an icy drink," she said, smiling quietly, as if kin to my thoughts. "Come, Nina will show you our villa while Bruno fixes us up. Now, where might he be?" she questioned, shielding her eyes from the sun. Assuming Auntie was nearsighted, I pointed to the balcony. They conversed with sign language while he descended the stairs. Gesturing with a cigarette for her part, Auntie indicated three fingers for a round of ouzo and iced tea.

"Bruno's not illiterate," she asided when he disappeared to the kitchen. "Understands our road signs, reads lips when I speak the English, somewhat."

Uncle was long gone; I assumed he'd retreated for his siesta when we explored the simplistic villa. Like his brother, he was a collector of post impres-sionist art; prudent, in a sense, in that the numerous early sketches by Picasso were apparently acquired when the genius was short of funds. Apart from a lily pond scene by Monet, there was no show of opulence in their home; perhaps maybe he didn't have the green hand his brother had. There was a degree of laid-back intellectualism ingrained in his way of life, however. That and a bound-less love of family, judging from the array of photographs arranged chronologi-cally on Auntie's grand piano. Nina's wedding picture, framed in silver, was foremost on display.

Wary of Auntie's lethal concoction, I settled for a beer and climbed the stairs to explore our suite. She and Nina chatted endlessly in Greek. Her spirits height-ened, the patio echoed with Nina's laughter while they exchanged anecdotes and carried on as old friends are apt to do when they 'splice the mainbrace' in the early afternoon. For my part, sipping a cold beer, the view from the balcony was superb.

To the north, apartment houses and hotels were stacked above the beach at Glyfada. Further north, the mighty super tankers lay at anchor off Piraeus. To the south, the nearby Apollon Palace Hotel overlooked a secluded beach and a yacht basin with fluttering sails. Further south, the coast toward Cape Sounion was clustered with gleaming villas and stands of cedar. The yachts of the 'tanker rich' idled offshore.

The sky seemed equally divided between the haze from Santorini lying ominously to the south, and the brilliant blue to the north, biding time with the prevailing winds; reversing with its southerly shift, judging from the residual ash on the balcony railing. The temperature in the high 80s, the humidity, like summertime in Nassau, getting little relief from the offshore breeze.

My blazer was the first to go, then the shirt and tie, while I considered a soapy shower. The chilly sea was more to my liking, I decided. Lending an ear to the voices echoing from the villa, I stripped and headed for the limestone ledge bordering the murky Aegean.

"Hold your breath and enter slowly!" Nina shouted from the wall, Auntie by her side, shielding her eyes to better her view. Naked to the buff, I looked for a towel, then settled for her sunning pad.

"My, what a sight!" Nina teased mischievously. "So, methinks I'll join you!" she added, abandoning her skirt and blouse to the hand-hewn stairs, naked when we plunged the icy depths. Her eyes sparkled with merriment when Auntie reappeared with a brace of towels.

Later, when we rearranged the twin beds together and had our bit of do, Nina fluffed her hair in the sun and sorted her clutch of mail. Pondering a read-out from Uncle's computer, realizing I had the UN to consider, she suggested I utilize Uncle's telephone in his study to contact the Grande Bretagne.

"He'll be sound asleep, so don't worry it, love. Just don't forget they've planned a party for eight!"

It was after five when I touch-dialed the telephone on Uncle's desk. Curiously, the numbers were self-repeated, as if automatically recorded by a digital answering device. There was, however, no such machine in evidence, although there was an audible click when I was connected with the concierge at the hotel.

"We've a UN seminar scheduled tomorrow at ten," he replied when I inquired of White Dove. "Suite 2B; I've their listing at hand," he added. "May I have your name, please? Are you a guest of the hotel?"

Speaking excellent English, he acknowledged politely when I said I would be staying in Kavouri. Said he'd check with reservations when I inquired of Winner and Edwards, but apparently they'd not yet arrived. They'd received a fax from Dr. Sigurdesson, however, saying her flight from Zurich was delayed until morning and, possibly, they'd be traveling together as a group. As for Dr. Nokomo, no word, although they'd made note of an urgent message from New York requesting his immediate reply.

Winding down, realizing my schedule was doubtful, I helped myself to a tot of brandy from Uncle's decanter and looked about. The villa was turn of the century, utilities added later to the whitewashed walls. Warmed by his superb Metaxa, I traced Uncle's phone line to the pantry and located a junction box above the bar. Observing a wall phone, together with a pad of Auntie's notes, I lifted the receiver, checked for a dial tone and fingered a random set of numbers. Again, the click and digital repeat! Canceling the call, I examined the box to determine its leads. Aside from a line to their private quarters, the main trunk led directly to the adjoining kitchen where, most likely, there was another phone.

The kitchen was a bustle of activity: the clatter of pots and pans, dinner in the making (heady with the aroma of moussaka and dolmadakia), the throaty laughter of Auntie's cook and the caterer's rapid-fire Greek. Not wanting to intrude, I retreated to the patio and scanned the exterior walls.

From my view, the kitchen was attached to a service porch and the nearby garage. Most likely a carriage house in the past, the garage was a two-storey affair with an apartment to house the staff; Bruno of late, I thought, warding the view from his window behind Uncle's hibiscus. The telephone apparently was a late-coming venture. Strung haphazardly beneath the porch, it reappeared as a cable attached to the garage apartment, then to a utility pole beyond the villa" perimeter. If there was a lead to Bruno's quarters, it wasn't observable from beneath the bougainvillea.

* * * * * *

Verging on eight o'clock, while we showered and dressed for Auntie's celebration, there came a mysterious turn of fate, in the form of a brief note of condolence from an acquaintance of Nina's dad. I've pondered it many times since.

"It's a note from Dr. Petrie, Keith. How sweet of him to remember me! God knows I haven't seen him since he lectured at my school in Switzerland. He often visited Papa while they were cataloguing his collection for the British Museum. The doctor's a well-known English archeologist. He has a fellowship at Cambridge and has written several books on the Bronze Age settlements in Crete. Seems he's recently in Athens," she added, puzzling the date on the letterhead. "Goes on to say he's making daily trips with a student group to photograph the frescoes at Akrotiri, but that couldn't be!"

"They're evacuating Santorini with helicopters, Nina. Could it be a couple of weeks back?" Shaking her head, she compared the letterhead with the postmark.

"Day before yesterday, Keith! The envelope's addresses from the British School, and he's penned his numbers on the flyleaf. I can't believe they're tripping to Thera with the volcano breathing fire, especially not with a bunch of college types! Crazy, hey? We must call him tomorrow; he'd be a wealth of information. Something of a nut, if I remember correctly!

Scrawny beard and all that!"

Eight o'clock was another matter, a complete change of venue. The elderly couple's guests arrived en masse, their cars parked the length of Kavouri, it seemed. The older set was genteel in jackets with their smartly dressed wives; the younger set, bachelors with ambitious jeans and their girlfriends in whatever they fancied. Eye-catchers, they sought one another while they sampled the caravides and sipped Uncle's vintage champagne.

Suited for the occasion in a rented tuxedo, seemingly at ease, Bruno tended the bar, mutely accepting orders for drinks while he passed them from a silver tray. Cleft from another time, I thought, his military bearing and clean-shaven head were somewhat apart from the ensemble of party-wise Greeks. Not unobserving, he nodded briefly when I declined a second round, turning his attention to the British Ambassador and his American wife from Brooklyn Heights.

We dined on moussaka - chopped meat with eggplant, cheese and Béchamel sauce; dolmadakia – meat and onions with spice wrapped in vine leaves; koheli – lobster baked in the shell with cognac; cheese puffs filled with feta and yigantes — lima beans in tomato sauce. All served to the candlelit patio tables, replenished with decanters of Santorini wine. Trilling all the while, a bouzouki band emerged from the shadows, stringing the melody from Never on Sunday while they gathered round our table. Then, their violins weeping, they played a haunting love song for Nina, requesting she come forward. As if on cue, a strand of roses was tossed alongside her chair.

Now the party took off! Chairs emptied, tables pushed aside, roses and plates skidding across the floor, followed by Auntie's table flowers and whatever was handy, except for the family silverware. Clapping to the Syrtaki, arm-in-arm, they circled our table, dipping and swirling, beckoning to Nina. Cheering when Auntie and Uncle rose from their chairs to join the mayhem, stepping sprightly to the music, as if the occasion had overcome their mourning and it as Nina's future they beheld.

Suddenly Nina was in their midst, snapping her fingers, spinning on her toes, to do her solo thing! She paused to blow kisses when the crowd was in unison with her long, stringy legs. Green eyes flashing, hair cast aside, she was vibrant and feline, expressing all that she had. Swiveling her hips, touting her breasts, she drew me to my feet, clinging closely while we circled the floor, holding my hand aloft with hers to exhibit our rings for all to see.

The celebration didn't end then. The older set sipped coffee and brandy while the caterers cleared the debris; long-winded conversations, mostly business, continued when we juiced the Jaguar and joined Nina's friends at the Alstir. The Syrtaki not forgotten, we danced until Nina's tortured feet gave out. Close to three, there was a noticeable glow in the south when she waved to her spirited friends and suggested I take the wheel.

"We're off for a swim!" she announced, as we sped the shadowy streets. Slipping her dress over her head, she trailed it alongside, her slippers next. I made it to the driveway where the balance was deposited in my lap. I led my naked bride past the darkened patio and down the stairs; together we swam our cobwebs away in the icy sea.

Nina slept well that night; only once did she stir awake to snuggle close and murmur,

"I love you, Keith."

CHAPTER 15

I am inclined to believe Bruno enjoyed my red-eyed morning when he dropped Nina by her uncle's office and myself at the Grande Bretagne. He lingered, blocking traffic momentarily, watching me pass through the lobby and arrive at the concierge's desk, where I learned the UN meeting had been cancelled and rescheduled for noon the next day. The message, signed by Alan Winner, had been sent that morning from Zurich.

I was annoyed; the concierge apologetic.

"Your group is assigned to the suite for the remainder of the week, Mr. Slater. If you care to rest, I'll have a tray of breakfast sent, a beverage if you wish?" I thanked him but instead placed a call to Nina.

She was definitely in a state. The banks had called a note that morning and she'd have to stand by until their broker credited a sight draft for a ton of edible oil. I suggested we join for lunch at two.

"Make it three, Keith. We'll have to wait the time change before we hear from the office in New York. Goodness, my head's splitting! I can't seem to get myself together. Would it be the champagne you ordered at the Alstir?" She placed me on hold then..."Dr. Petrie, Keith! We had a chat earlier and he said he'd call back. Seems he's flying to Thera at twelve and arranged a seat if you'd care to go along. They'll be back by sunset, love. He's on the line, shall I tell him it's okay?"

I said yes, of course, looking about the monumental lobby while she conversed with Petrie. A square-shouldered, middle-aged man glanced above his newspaper from where he was seated in a cushy chair. Our eyes met for a second; nonchalantly, he flicked ash from his cigar and looked away. The receiver clicked, Nina came on the line again, and I gave the incident little thought.

126

"The doctor's delighted, Keith! He's acquainted with your project, and said it would be an excellent opportunity to see the volcano close up! You're to wait in the lobby; he'll have you paged at 11:30." Still on the line, she asked me to stand by for a moment, then conversed in Greek with a female nearby.

"You had a call from Dr. Winner, darling. Uncle's secretary copied his message. Seems Dr. Gomulaka died of a heart attack while we were in Nassau, Keith! God in heaven, he was such a nice man...'G.G. under intensive care'...Damn it, Keith, were you aware of his problem when we had lunch at the Plaza Hotel?" The answer was caught in my teeth. I passed it off as best I could, said I'd read of the doctor's death in the Times, but hadn't been clued to the fact when I called the UN.

"They weren't sure, Nina. The report apparently came round about when he missed our briefing and his wife inquired later from Warsaw."

An uneasy silence followed; then an abrupt change of subject when she said she would pick me up at sunset, saying I was to call the office if we were delayed. Then, softening somewhat, she said I was to be careful, perhaps Dr. Petrie would join us for leftovers and a bottle of Santorini later on.

Her psychic intuition in mind, I settled in a chair, ordered coffee and scanned the complimentary Herald Tribune, exchanging glances with the gentleman nearby. His newspaper was an Athens daily; he spoke Greek to the waiter and observed me quietly when a bellhop circled the lobby with my name chalked on a chime board. Wadding a bill, I raised an arm, observing a tall, slender man standing nervously at the entrance doors.

"Would you be Keith Slater?" he asked politely, when I crossed over to shake his hand. "Dr. Petrie, here. Sorry for the delay; bloody traffic, you know! Nina said your meeting was rescheduled and you'd be free to come along."

"My pleasure, Doctor. I appreciate the opportunity and hope I haven't taken you out of your way."

"Not at all, not at all! Come, we'll have a chat while we drive to the heliport. That would be my Cortina parked outside, hopefully," he added, peering at the burly doorman standing alongside.

Fiftyish, lean of limb, sharp featured with an elongated nose and chin, the doctor had an uncontrollable shock of curly brown-gray hair and inquisitive brown eyes. Wore a crumpled seersucker suit and soiled sneakers, one untied. His ancient Rolex had lost its elasticity and hung loosely from his wrist, sliding to cuff length when he raised his arm to check the time.

"We're due off at twelve," he said, "but we'll have sufficient time if we hurry. "Have you forgotten something?" he questioned when I glanced warily

127

over my shoulder. My observer had discarded his paper and was lumbering behind. "If not, let's see what we've caught!"

Petrie's Cortina was parked (and locked) directly in front of the Grande Bretagne's impressive entrance, one wheel mounted on a marble step, as if he had attempted to avoid tying up traffic. To that end he'd succeeded, but the doorman was not impressed. He had words for the doctor while the flustered man searched for his keys. I wadded another bill to help matters along, unlocking my door from an open window while my 'bird dog' noted the Cortina's license plate and waddled down the street.

A renowned archeologist, the doctor was an authority on Bronze Age civilizations. By present-day standards, his driving was pure mania. Aggressive-defensive, there was no rationale. I had a blurred impression of Athens passing by...abrupt, seat-lifting stops when as impasse appeared ahead, a pair of buses he was unable to squeeze between, angry gestures from a wrong-way street. Shaken, I called the time at intervals, to avoid a confrontation whenever he raised a hand from the wheel to search his watch. Swerving through a startled petrol station to detour a red light, we made the navy base in twenty-seven minutes. Braked the tortured vehicle, grinning to himself as if he'd fantasized the road race from Mombasa to Malindi!

An uniformed yeoman passed us through with a casual check of our credentials, saluting when we proceeded to the heliport where transportation was awaiting Petrie's arrival. An Alhouette was perched on the pad with its turbine idle, its blades swinging slowly with the breeze while we piled aboard with our safety gear buckled up. Our pilot was a Greek navy officer; his copilot of higher rank...possibly in charge of evacuation from Santorini, judging from the medical supplies and stretchers he'd supervised while they were stowed in the aft compartment.

The winds were offshore when we rotated to cruise altitude and pointed for Santorini. The Alhouette covered the 160 miles to Santorini in less than an hour. Thirty miles from the island, a rich column of smoke rose on the horizon, flattening at 10,000 feet with a drift to the east. Whilst we closed I sighted the immense caldera where the explosion in 1628 BC had blown a chunk the size of Manhattan to the sky. The new volcanic cone had risen off from the center, its sides streaked with incandescent lava. I gauged its height to be a thousand feet and growing.

"That would be Phira," the doctor shouted, pointing to a whitewashed village perched on the cliffside overlooking the caldera. "Akrotiri lies to the south, on the lee side of the island. The small island centering the basin is Nea

Kamene."

I knew Nea Kamene was the residue of a relatively recent upsurge, but it was not the source of the billowing smoke. The new activity, erupting a mile to the north of Kamene, had already shouldered a portion of the inlet. The base, nearly two miles across, was partially obscured by rising steam due to the lava flow spilling to the sea.

"Jesus, Doctor! Has all of this happened in the last two months?" Petrie nodded grimly.

"We're hoping it will taper off, as it did in 1926 and 1950," he said. "As you can see, the cone is already higher than the cliffs surrounding the caldera, and it rose from a basic depth of thirteen hundred feet."

The pilot hovered a few hundred feet above the village while the copilot photographed the spectacle with a telescopic lens. I assumed a part of the mission was a monitoring chore; the doctor concurred.

"The government is keeping a close watch on the situation. Is it Keith or Major Slater, as you identified yourself at the security gate?"

"Keith, doctor! My pass is outdated by a couple of years back."

"Good enough! Now then, the photographs are analyzed every twenty-four hours by the volcanologists in Athens and abroad. The seismographs on the island automatically transmit tremor magnitudes by radio. The latest findings indicate a Plinian eruption may be in the making."

I looked down at the village. A film of ash dulled the rooftops, but activity continued in the winding streets. Cars and donkeys proceeded along the road-ways, and the local population seemed unconcerned.

"A general evacuation has been ordered for the southern and eastern sides of the caldera," the doctor added. "The warning has, however, been largely ignored."

We passed the center of the island, over dust-laden hills of olive groves, fields of early grain, terraced slopes with natives tending their vines, windmills with ghost-like arms of sailcloth slowly spinning and pumping water. The pilot throttled back, then nosed up to descend to the archeological site that had once been the flourishing village of Akrotiri.

We settled on a pad near the sheet metal-covered archeological site. Petrie swung to the ground. The pilot followed, clamping a cover on the turbine intake duct. A group of laborers wearing construction-type helmets gathered around to offload our supplies. An array of crates beneath a canvas covering was to be taken aboard a subsequent flight, or so I assumed from the doctor's gestures and fractured Greek. Our copilot, apparently a flight surgeon with the rank of colonel, took exception, indicating to Petrie (mostly by hand gestures) what he could take and what he couldn't. Then, followed by his cache of supplies, he boarded a waiting Land Rover and disappeared for the remainder of the day.

Pitched nearby were a half-dozen olive drab tents, streaked with ash and recent rain. Their flies were extended to shield the sun and catch the middling breeze. The foremost were assigned to the flight crew and Petrie's field operations. Another, with a mobile kitchen, served as a mess hall for the laborers and a clutch of students. The remainder, most likely their quarters, adjoined a medical tent provided by the Red Cross.

Sprawled in the shade of the tin-roofed buildings, a group of refugees with their belongings waited transport to Athens; some were on litters, together with a tiny wooden coffin and a teddy bear, clasped in a mother's hand.

"They're mostly oldsters from nearby," the pilot commented in fluent English. "We take as many as we can, tend to their needs. Weather permitting, we fly three trips a day, sometimes at night. We've round-the-clock flights from Phira, but transportation is difficult for the aged," he added, pointing to a World War Two-type ambulance and a brace of open trucks. "The youngsters tend to stay put and work their crops, but day to day they're less certain and beginning to move on, slaughtering sheep for the cannery and stripping their groves of ripe olives."

I had a spot of coffee with Petrie at operations while he explained the photographic proceedings he'd sketched for his group of students. Earnest and much to the point, he said he feared an imminent eruption would collapse the sheds and destroy the frescoes for all time.

"We're photographing the murals from all angles, Keith, then removing the catalogued artifacts for shipment to the Institute of Antiquities. You may visit the dig, if you wish," he added, "but you must wear a hard hat. And by all means, if you sense a tremor, exercise your ass for open ground!" With his advice in mind, I exchanged my blazer for a hard hat and followed down slope to the dig.

Overhead, the sky was milky and sparse of cloud, the sun a yellowish disc; eerie, so like a swirling sunflower painted by the agonized hand of Van Gogh. In stark contrast, the easterly horizon was totally black. Most likely the ashy outflow from Santorini had been carried aloft by the westerlies and sledged a warm front over Rhodos and Asia Minor...which could account for the massive build-up of super-saturated clouds we'd observed the previous day. Closer now, caught with the fallout of sulfurous ash, acid rains were observable in the distance, releasing their residue to the pristine Aegean. All came from a recent eruption, judging from the granules under foot and the status of the withering trees. And all too close was the seething monster I'd encounter in the very near future.

With the exception of burping lava now and then, the volcano was strangely quiet, periodically shrieking when it cleared its pipes of debris. How long, I wondered, before a fractured vent would allow entrance of the sea? The result? Most likely a kinetic explosion when the mix encountered the hot spot miles below. Plinian, in terms of latter-day Pompeii, likened to the thermo-nuclear blast that reduced Bikini to an islet with no core. But then Bikini extended to a shallow sea, and Santorini was receptive to the surging Aegean!

Tagging along behind a student with a tripod camera, we passed an abandoned booth where they'd accepted donations a few months back. A cautionary sign, posted in English, Greek and French, advised *No entry without authorization.* With the student yet in the lead, I was admitted by a sleepy guard and explored the shedded dig undeterred.

I'd seen pictures of Professor Martinatos' earlier excavations, but the scope of the recent work was overwhelming. Acre upon acre of ancient Akrotiri had been uncovered and protected by an immense system of steel girders supporting the roofs we'd seen from the air. Electric lights illuminated the narrow streets and crumbled walls of the Minoans. Groundwork from bedrock, a third of the village had been restored to its basic simplicity. Rubble, stone and plaster were added to establish the height of the tumbled villas; doorways with cypress lintels were gauged to the short-statured former occupants.

I was struck by the similarity of the structures I'd seen when we hovered over the countryside. Parapet roofs and second storey rooms were accommodated by exterior stairs; toilets flushed and sewers benefited from water ducts in the hills. A bronze bathtub at one place attested to their habits. Given a whitewash and a motor bike leaning nearby, the villas were twentieth century provincial Greek.

A wreath of freshly cut flowers was placed alongside the wall where Professor Martinatos had fallen, mortally injured, a few years back. And nearby, Petrie's college group were cataloging and crating selected oil vases for the Institute of Antiquities. Chattering in English, their T-shirts identifying the University of Birmingham; faded jeans were from Harrod's rack. A dozen or so locals were ganged in teams of four, propping timbers beneath the supporting girders. The overall activity was both tense and frenzied, as if they were anticipating an accelerated downfall of ash from the ebullient volcano. Curious but apart from their undertaking, I climbed a ladder leading to a catwalk over a recent excavation. Boards creaked underfoot as I threaded semi-darkness to where a light dangled from an overhead girder. Another ladder led down to a series of inter-connected rooms recently cleared of debris. Dropping to my knees, I studied the interior walls. Vividly colored frescoes covered every inch.

The villa was larger than the others and appeared to have once belonged to a wealthy entrepreneur, perhaps a ship owner, judging from the long-prowed vessels depicted in the anteroom. Testing the ladder, I impulsively descended for a better view.

In some areas the frescoes had fallen away and had recently been repaired; the graphic artwork rejoined and re-colored. I could hardly distinguish the old from the new; the reproduction artist had exercised a very talented hand. An unmanned tripod camera faced one of the panels; scenes were being photo-graphed for the record in anticipation of another catastrophe. Plaster thin, they'd be much too delicate to remove intact.

Skirting a section of scaffolding, I entered the adjoining room. The fleet scene continued to the opposite wall. Galley-like vessels raised single masts, with ornamented canopies sheltering figures in repose. Steersmen stood the sterns with a long sweep of rudder; a single row of long oars along the hulls suggest-ing oarsmen of local tenure. The procession approached and came to anchor in a harbor, where an audience waited. There was no indication of hostility, no weapons. They stood on the rooftops, peered from windows, hurried from the fields, ranged the quayside. The mountainous background showed evidence of a volcanic peak in the distance, although the section was blurred and indistinct.

I glanced into the anteroom to glimpse the beginning of the analogue. Antelope bounded the hills; monumental structures bordering the shore were supported by columns. The shoreline and palm trees suggested the coast of Libya, or it may have been Crete. Bodies floated in the sea, indicating a possible storm; dolphins played about as they do today. Was the procession inbound to Akrotiri from Crete...to acquire a sacrificial virgin for the temple at Arhannes...or, more likely, awaiting the triumphant return of an admiral of the fleet?

The third room depicted a bull game. A charging bull confronted a youth wearing a kilt-like loincloth and ankle strap sandals. The boy grasped the bull's horns and somersaulted over its head. The interchanging momentum apparently allowed him to land on his feet behind the bull. A bare-breasted girl in similar costume, wearing bracelets, stood behind the charging bull with her arms out-stretched. Could she be attempting to catch the vaulting boy? Or to applaud? The next sequence illustrated red-painted youths in a boxer's pose; each wore a glove on his right hand. The restoration was incomplete.

Ducking beneath the fresh wooden lintel, I peered into the fourth room. A paint box and crayons lay open on the floor, along with an orange peeling and a twist of bread in a basket. A primitive folding stool faced a fresco the artist was in process of restoring. I reached momentarily for the lintel to steady myself. A generator hammered in the distance. My heart skipped a beat, pumping furiously to catch pace when I realized the emerald eyes staring from the wall were not alive!

Standing tall and slender, dressed in a timeless blouse and multi-colored skirt, she'd been painted life-size beneath an arched motif. Her long raven hair, gathered from the forehead, flowed gently across her shoulders. Circular golden rings dangled from her ears; a gold chain necklace clasped to her throat. Her lips were traced with red, a spot of rouge applied to her cheeks, eyebrows minutely sketched above her expressive green eyes. The familiar slant of her shoulders, her poise, the cleft of her breasts, her classic nose...Nina!

Not wanting to believe the uncanny resemblance, assuming it was a trick of light, I stepped nearer to ponder the likeness. The original brush strokes were somewhat indistinct, as if sandblasted by the hurricane force of the exploding volcano. Fresh plaster filled the missing portions; her hand and shoulders recently restored by the artist, her arms lightly sketched, as if drawn from imagination. The brush strokes were not dissimilar and it was difficult to distinguish the old from the new. I bent closely to examine the necklace circling her long, slender neck, whistling softly in disbelief. The intricate thing was clasped to a miniature gold figurine with slanted emerald eyes! Altogether, a close match to the abominable necklace Nina had pinched from her father's desk!

"Please do not lean against the wall," a voice called from above. I jumped back, looking up. A trim young lady in jeans was kneeling on the catwalk, wagging a finger to turn me away. "You mustn't touch; the paint is not yet dry," she added, evidencing a hearty English accent. She giggled when I backed off and stumbled over the stool.

"The artist," I sputtered, shaken by what I'd seen. "Is he nearby?" I questioned, pointing to the box of paints.

"Strange you should ask," she called down. "We haven't seen him since morning. He works mostly at night. The panel is to be photographed for the Office of Antiquities," she added. "In fact, it was on my agenda when I heard you wandering about!"

"She's incomplete...she has no hands!" I shrilled; my voice high pitched as if I'd lost control of my larynx. Coughing, I repeated, "...she has no hands!" The girl offered a dimpled smile. Smallish, she had an unruly mop of short curly hair, a pudge for a nose.

133

"I heard you," she said. "Deuca was to sketch her hands when we saw him last. The fresco is twenty percent original and eighty percent interpretation. I wonder where he might be?"

Curious, I climbed an adjacent ladder while she looked about. My rubbery legs had steadied somewhat, but when I scanned the fresco close up, an icy chill inched my spine!

"She's the spitting image of my wife," I gasped, groping for a missing rung. "Lifelike; shakes me up!" I mumbled, high stepping to reach the catwalk. Grinning, she extended a hand to help me aboard.

"Deuca is very clever," she said, while I gathered my feet on the spindly walkway. "We sometimes wonder if he's taken license from the frescoes at Knossos, or exercises his genius as a throwback from the past. Deuca came to us from Crete, we think, appearing out of nowhere a few weeks back."

Standing beside me, the young lady reached my shoulder height in her heavy-soled shoes. Lightly freckled, with straightforward, inquisitive blue eyes, she wore a plaid cotton shirt unbuttoned at her throat. Despite the humidity, she emanated a clean scent of soap.

I introduced myself immediately, qualifying my presence as a guest of Dr. Petrie.

"Keith Slater!" I said, apologizing for the inconvenience if I'd disrupted her photography. "I didn't realize you were close by." She dimpled and extended her hand.

"I'm Lesleigh, Keith, Dr. Petrie's assistant, better known by my surname, Butterfield. You needn't apologize," she added warmly. "My work is mostly finished."

Suddenly, an activated siren shrieked nearby.

"My God, another quake!" she gasped, grabbing my waist when the catwalk tipped precariously and brought us to our knees. The sudden tremor rippled the excavation, wrenching our scaffolding like a thing alive. The overhead girders creaked and groaned, sagging in part when a support gave way. A deluge of ash from the fractured roof followed, the lights fading as the generator waned. We were abandoned in total darkness when it coughed and clanged to a full stop.

Sprawled on all fours, I anchored an arm to the planking and held the girl to my side. Clinging desperately, the ungainly platform threatened to topple us into the room below. All the while, the incessantly rumbling, horrendous molar-grinding sound of rock against rock rose ominously from the bowels of the earth. Then suddenly, the tremor ceased as abruptly as it had begun!

There was no fast end to it, however. Pelted with residue from the roof, I shielded Lesleigh's head with my arm until the downfall diminished; helped her upright when the catwalk steadied and she acknowledged a frightened 'okay'.

"Jeepers, that's the second since last week," she murmured, clinging to my belt. Arid dust permeated the sheds as we inched, hand-in-hand, towards a shaft of sunlight from the ruptured roof. My gutsy companion worried mostly for the cameras and film she had left behind. Flashlights bobbed in the distance; students and laborers were searching about, their muffled voices drawing closer, with Petrie commanding a bullhorn while checking names from his roster.

"Lordy, I'll catch it now!" she groaned. "Forgot my fuckin' helmet!"

"Butterfield! Is that you with Slater?" Petrie blared; his lantern beam converging on our grimy faces. The generator chose the moment to catch on and we were rewarded with the overhead lights, much to Butterfield's discomfort when he inquired of her missing hat.

"I've cautioned you time and again!" the doctor gruffed, but not unkindly. His eyes expressed relief when he determined we were disheveled but otherwise okay.

"It's together with my camera," she stammered. "Slides down my nose when I focus; hadn't had time to collect it," she added tearfully. "My camera's worse yet!"

Declining to admonish her further, Petrie pointed to an adjacent ladder, suggesting we head for operations, indicating he'd send a student to fetch the lot. Trembling, but not unwound, Butterfield had other thoughts. Wiping the grime from her eyes with a sleeve, she said she'd bloody well fetch it herself!

"The spool's not yet finished, Doctor. It will take but a few minutes," she pleaded. I righted the ladder, assuming she was standing by. When I looked back, she'd turned foot and disappeared along the walkway.

"Stubborn!" the doctor begrudged, shaking his head when I turned to follow. "Best you join me, Keith. We'll catch up with her later. Lesleigh's a ball of determination," he explained, when I dropped beside him. "Best we have...brilliant, actually...and I find it prudent to let her be. She programs her computer with photographs and site dimensions and screens an extraordinary composite of Akrotiri as it was before the catastrophe."

I stood by while the doctor returned his attention to matters at hand, waiting nearby while he tallied the injuries and the group dispersed outside.

"Bruises and sprains, one broken arm, and six students wanting to go home! Not that I blame them, he remarked. "It's getting a bit too close for comfort, and I fear the worst is yet to come! We have so much to do yet!" he added, casting about for his watch.

I explained the circumstances that had me at ends when I distracted Butterfield from her cameras.

"The frescoes, Doctor...the palace rooms, the boudoir scene, the girl with the green eyes! She's the spitting image of Nina! Same hair, same eyes, same earrings. You talked with Nina this morning," I added, to prod his memory.

"Oh, yes, that would be Pyrrha. Deuca's enamored with the ancient myth of Deucalion and Pyrrha; named her such when he got on with his paints. Legend has it they landed on Mount Parnassus after Poseidon caused the earth to shake and a mountainous wave overwhelmed the shores. Legends are often seeded from realities, however abstract, which is the why of archeology; to explore and determine the facts. Come along," he added. "We'll take a peek for ourselves." I tagged along as best I could; explained my limp when Petrie inquired, and slowed his pace.

"Ah, yes, terrible war! Thought you might have fallen! Now then, Keith, as for the resemblance to Nina, you must remember it's often in the mind's eye we perceive a likeness of someone we know. We've had tourists with similar thoughts," he added, beaming his lantern towards the palace. "Given high heels, she'd pass for a contemporary on the streets of Athens. Her features are not typical of pre-Bronze Age Greece...far from it! Most likely her lifeline stems from Asia Minor, when the Minoans colonized the Aegean. Now what?" he questioned, searching his pockets for the offending beeper clasped to his belt.

Reminded of T.S.'s like reaction, I strolled apart while Petrie scanned the digital display, my attention drawn to Butterfield's flood lamps reflecting the overhead beams.

"Operations, Keith! Seems I have a priority call from Athens. Hopefully it's not an order to evacuate," he added, apparently troubled by the thought. "Best you carry on, satisfy your curiosity. You'll find Miss Butterfield nearby. You might give her hand, but you must return promptly within the hour!"

Saddled with his cameras and the bullhorn strapped to his belt, the doctor made haste for the entrance, pausing to offer his lantern when he realized the overhead lights were mostly blown and inoperative.

"Four-thirty!" he reminded, grappling for his watch. "We'll be short for seats and it's important you be on time!"

Short of breath, given a lesson in history, I traced my earlier routing and beamed the frescoes in sequence until I came to Pyrrha's boudoir. I called out to announce my presence, realizing Butterfield was working the adjacent rooms. Studying the painting closely, I sub-consciously sought a flaw to the resemblance that would alleviate my pounding heart. True, the necklace was dissimilar;

shorter at her neck, the figurine added at some other time appeared to have been recently re-touched. Her facial features as well! A dab of paint looked added to her perky lips.

"Mind's eye? Bullshit!"

"Would that be you, Keith?"

Distracted by a fall of pebbles, I retreated to the shielding catwalk, turning quickly when a shadowy figure flitted through an opening and disappeared. I called out, but there was no answer. Shivering, I beamed the fresco again, eyes drawn to where the stool and paints had been. But they were no longer there, nor was the orange peeling or the basket of bread!

"Satisfied?" Butterfield questioned, appearing at my side, her outsized hat, streaked with grime, like a gamin from the streets of Kuwait.

"Not altogether," I said. "Tell me, is Deuca a little weird?"

"He is a bit odd, come to think. Works mostly at night; stays aboard his boat. Somewhat of a recluse. Why do you ask?"

* * * * * *

The islands of Thera, Anafi and Pachia had, in fact, been ordered to evacuate all souls immediately, a warning broadcast to northern Crete. It was not unexpected, a partial evacuation was well underway, but the jolt we'd experienced apparently had rattled the bureaucrats in Athens. A five-pointer on the Richter scale registered on their seismographs attesting to that! The shock waves expanding from the epicenter, in diminishing force, had been felt as far west as Gibraltar.

The damage seemed minimal: tents steadfast, the recently arrived 'copter unharmed. Its blades spun softly while the pilot, microphone in hand, checked his flight plan with air traffic control. There were anxious faces milling about, nervous conversations in English and Greek, when we deposited Lesleigh's cameras with operations. Word of fatalities in the village of Thira was whispered, of an inn that collapsed and sledded survivors to the sea.

All the while, supreme in the distance, the volcano contentedly smoked its pipe; biding time, having warned the non-believers their day of reckoning would soon come to be!

"It's so peaceful it's scary," Lesleigh commented. "Fills one with a sense of dread, Keith. The eerie quietness, birds in flight, donkeys braying...so like the eve of an horrendous storm!"

Worried for Nina, I tagged the pilot for information when Lesleigh excused herself to wash and change.

"Mostly power failures," he said, cupping an earphone while we talked. "Traffic was bad when we rotated from the base. Hellinikon's on battery power, the heavies circling when a Libyan 707 overshot the active and hit the perimeter fence. Fuckin' camel driver...scared, I think. He barreled in without clearance and caused an Air Italia to abort their final!"

"Athens! Was there damage in the city?"

"Same thing. Transformers blown, stoplights out, traffic messed up, fender benders mostly...hot rods having a ball! Flew Sea Kings with your Navy at Pensacola," he added when I eyed him curiously. "Seen worse when I visited Disneyland! Wish we had your four-laners if three million people have to head for the hills!" The implication remained unsaid when ATC squawked his numbers and he triggered the mike to respond.

Somewhat relieved, I collected my blazer from operations and scrubbed from a tap alongside. I conversed briefly with Petrie when he emerged from the tent with a roll of plans and a package of undeveloped film. Worried for his students, he'd apparently decided to stay on, explaining his reasoning when we walked to the waiting Alhouette.

"Our Embassy's chartered a Dakota DC-3 to take them to Athens this evening. They'll need transport to Thira, of course; I've yet to arrange that. Together with whatever they can take along," he added, glancing wistfully at the crated artifacts that would have to wait another time. "I'm not inclined to panic," he said. "Could be days before they have us out, and we've much to do. But of immediate necessity, I'd appreciate your delivering our site plans and film to the British School in Athens. I've added a furthering address to my compatriots at the university, Keith. God bless!"

Taken by his gutsy manner (reminded of our pre-mission jitters when we leave our wallets for safekeeping, never knowing), I collected the lot and shook his hand. I was looking about for Butterfield when the pilot activated the rotating beacon and the injured student was strapped aboard. There was reason for delay, however.

Siren wailing in the distance, curling dust from the rise, the flight surgeon's jeep rounded the Alhouette with a stretcher case, a flask of plasma attached to the roll bar. An elderly patient clutching her beads. Adaptable to emergencies, the rear seat was removed to facilitate her litter and parcel of belongings. Crammed to capacity by then, I was afforded the copilot's position when the surgeon squeezed aft to attend her needs. The crewman we'd displaced would wait for the heavier Sea King, en route from Iraklion with a team of medics and supplies.

Last aboard, I was adjusting my harness (the pilot graduating the turbine), when we spied Butterfield threading the bystanders with a longish envelope in hand. Waving desperately, her face flushed, she elbowed a restraining guard, skirted the jeep and sprinted alongside, shouting my name.

"No way!" the pilot rasped, reaching across to latch my door. "We haven't space, Slater. Tell her to bug off!"

"Please, it's a letter to my parents!" she pleaded, rapping my window. Grappling with the latch, she fended off the guard, hanging in! Her hair disheveled by the quickening blades, cheeks streaked with tears, she was a picture of determination. I turned to the pilot.

"It's her mail!" I yelled. "She's staying on with Petrie." He throttled back immediately, pointing to the portal window.

"Please," she gasped, thrusting the envelope into my hand, another from her blouse with a tenner attached. "They'll be worried sick, Keith. Please call them! *I sense we'll meet again,*" she added, lowering her eyes as she turned away. Waving from the fringe, a solitary, lonely figure, whilst we rotated to 300 feet and nosed down to gather knots.

I had a momentary glimpse of the cove beneath Akrotiri while we banked to adjust heading, a sidelong view of Deuca's craft lying at anchor nearby. Small, with a sweep of rudder, a red sail furled at its mast. Rigged from ancient times, its lanteen stick had been lowered for shelter with a spread of canvas. These were Deuca's quarters, most likely, judging from the raft beached by a path that led to Akrotiri.

I glanced at Butterfield's envelopes while we were midway to Athens, intending to pocket them in my blazer. The longer was addressed to her parents in Cornwall, their numbers penned on the fly closure. The other was unsealed, hurriedly addressed to 'Keith'.

Two photographs were enclosed, both of the fresco scenes I had reason to remember. One dated from a few weeks back, presumably of the original before it was enhanced by the artist. The second of the scene I'd observed just hours before...the pendant added to Pyrrha's necklace, the greenish tint to her eyes! There was more to be seen, however; quartering the photo, silhouetted by her lights, she'd viewed the artist at work.

Slender, shorter than myself, dressed in homespuns with a sash for a belt, he was kneeling by his stool, his face angled sideways as if surprised by her lights. Fortyish, judging from the gray at his temples, his hair uncut and straggling to his shoulders. His sharply defined profile was more Indo than European.

The pallor of his skin struck me as odd...ashen, as if he seldom ventured the sun. Nearby lay his box of paints...and propped against the box to better his view, a tattered newspaper photo was fastened to a board. The clipping indistinct in the shadowy light, but the pictured likeness indicated his artwork wasn't altogether drawn from fancy!

* * * * * *

We set down at the navy base shortly before seven. The ambulance on target and we dispersed to operations when our full complement was aboard: the elderly patient, the student in need of a surgical arm splice, the jittery girl in a T-shirt who opted for the fastest route home.

The Base switchboard was inoperative when I attempted to call Nina, although they anticipated service momentarily. Worried, I scanned the parking lot for the Mercedes, thinking she'd send Bruno if I hadn't called in. I questioned a yeoman at the gatehouse, identifying a Mercedes in the commander's slot; no luck. He brightened, however, overcoming our language barrier, when I pointed to the cellular phone at his desk and displayed my wallet.

Nina responded immediately, picked up on first ring!

"Thank heavens!" she echoed from the line. "Hello? Is this New York?" she questioned, seemingly confused by my voice. "Nina Slater here. Were you trying our fax?"

"It's your husband, Nina, I'm calling from the base!"

"It's Keith," she said to someone apart. "Sorry, darling, our lines have been out since three o'clock. How did you manage?"

I explained the circumstances, the cellular phone crackling with bips and squeaks, then amplifying suddenly when her service was restored. She placed me on hold then; I waited patiently, subjugated to business matters, until she returned to our line.

As I recall, our one-sided conversation was fraught with silence; Nina was preoccupied with other matters. Lacking interest when I related the happenings at Santorini, her comments were erratic, repetitive -- not given with her usual warmth and sense of humor – complaining of the stifling heat and lack of air conditioning, of the lousy telephone service. In short, the sight draft release from New York had yet to arrive! All things considered, I sensed she was worried of Metexas' shadowy hand.

"Would you mind a taxi to Kavouri? Nina said, when I explained Petrie's delay. "If need be, we'll wait until nine!" Then, softening somewhat, she said,

"Sorry, Keith, stand by me if you will. It's been one hell of a day!"

* * * * * *

The perimeter road was alive with taxis, but they were mostly inbound to Hellinikon with fares. The outbound, hell bent for the city, refused to stop when I flagged from the median. At odds with a mile trek to the terminal, I returned to the gatehouse, hoping to bargain for a ride; I lucked out with a Chevy pick-up equipped with a roll bar and a front-end Pensacola plate.

The 'copter pilot (in civvies) beckoned from the wheel.

"No sweat," he said when I climbed aboard. "Kavouri's long put, but I can drop you off at the Astir. I'd take you all the way," he added, "but my wife's freaked out and I have to haul ass for home!"

"Any damage?"

"Not really, mostly neighbors. She's American and they're jealous of her looks. Spotted her broad ass at a Greek wedding in Tampa," he added, when we joined the dicey traffic. "Got married a month later; bombed me with a son," he asided with a grin. "Three-quarters Greek, he's blue-eyed like her dad who hunts alligators in the sticks!" Not prone to alligators, we spliced the mainbrace with a brandy from the glove compartment, talked shop when I related my assignment with the UN.

"Figured you were a pilot when I saw you reading my check list," he said. "Never seen a U-2. Understand it flies like a glider full of bricks! You'll be pressing your luck, man! Like, you'll have 600 knots broadside if the volcano blows its cool. Reminds me, I've another pick-up at 0900."

I pointed to the Astir when we passed it by. He downshifted immediately, tailgating a gray Opel cruising the avenue ahead; he dropped me, turned about with a brief handshake, and smoked tires on the opposite lane.

I walked the remaining blocks with my blazer over my shoulder, noticing the taillights of the Opel when it drew to full stop yards ahead. There was action of sorts; its right door was ajar, a solitary figure penetrating the hedge? Slack-ening my pace, I stopped short when the figure emerged from the bush and the Opel sped off.

I hadn't realized I was close to the villa until I continued my pace and sighted the corner of the garage apartment. The telephone pole I'd observed earlier lay close inside the intervening hedgerow, roughly thirty yards from Bruno's window. And, looking up, I confirmed the lead to the apartment, the looping line to the pole where it was attached to a junction box below. All in order, or so I thought, until I inspected the tangled hedge where the Opel had stopped.

The leaves at the roots were minutes old, but the innermost branches had been forced before, bent to allow passage. Curious, I scanned the avenue and made my way through. Apart from the manicured lawns protected by high-riding hibiscus, the patch of weeds was unclaimed and partially trampled to the extent of the pole. Its lower regions caught with a mass of thorny vines, the pole appeared inaccessible until I rounded its base and tapped a small metallic box with my shoe.

The street lights were obscured by trees, but there was sufficient glow in the sky to determine a shadowy thin wire leading from the junction box to where it was stapled among the vines. Mostly by feel, I discovered it was a two-parter at knee height, attached with opposing leads to the box. The oblong apparatus, warm to my fingers, was battery powered and padlocked, safe-tied with a wire to the ground. Very professional indeed!

Stunned, I gave immediate thought to Metexas. Who else would have reason to bug the line? Months old, it obviously was installed before Bruno arrived from wherever. Obscure from his window, he'd hardly take note when the cartridge was exchanged from the street. Nor was there indication of his passage; I was certain of that when a car approached and I squirmed through the bush on all fours. The leafy soil was undisturbed, although nearby grass had recently been clipped.

Reeking of sweat and ridden with ash and assorted filth, I crouched inside the perimeter wall until the car had passed. The gates were closed, however, operated by radio signal. So as not to frighten the cook, I reached through the bars and sounded the house bell. The gates opened immediately, closing behind me when she appeared at the door, skillet in hand. Recognizing my face, startled by my condition, the cook was betwixt fright and a giggle. She gave in to the latter, slapping her thighs with the skillet and laughing uproariously. Shaking her head, she clutched her boobs when they came untethered from her blouse.

"My, what a sight!" she exhorted in halting English. "Might you tumble from a lorry? Have accident with a trolley? Best take garden hose, Mr. Slater. Nina come soon and Mrs. Maris fast asleep. Maybe better first have a drink," she added, pointing to the pantry. "We've electricity now; vino in the fridge."

I settled for ouzo straight up, added ice when it threatened my wobbly knees. In her fifties, the cook was a family staple. Round and small, her English seasoned with a Yorkshire accent she'd apparently acquired from Auntie. Beaming when I complimented her cooking, she curled a moussaka from a steaming pan. I inquired of Bruno then, realizing he had access to her kitchen and she'd have a close-up point of view.

"Bruno nice man," she readily replied. "Circumspect, old school, not Greek. *Not deef,* Mr. Slater. Sometimes I hear wireless when old folk gone to bed. Watch telly, seldom go out; tend garden on weekend. Walk to Astir when Maris drive to church."

"Has he a phone in his apartment?" I questioned casually, not to set her off. Nodding, she pointed to the intercom button on the pantry phone. "Watch for light when Mrs. call, never pick up. Comes to pantry where she wait or write message. Has many picture, I notice when I clean flat," she added, sensing my curiosity. "Mostly children, one maybe his wife. Some he keep in envelope and take along, I never see. And something else, Mr. Slater. Not to frighten old folk, I decide not to tell!"

"Okay," I said, realizing she was confiding full bore.

"Bruno keep gun in ditty bag he take with sandwich when he drive Mercedes; also when he walk to Astir Hotel. See when he leave bag in pantry for fresh caravides. Pistol wrapped with towel, small tube wrap same. Not mention when Bruno come to kitchen, think maybe for family protection. They have many problem, Mr. Slater."

"Metexas?" The cook nodded, seemingly relieved we could converse.

"Metexas unholy man, Mr. Slater. You must be very careful. He want Nina and family business. Have bad reputation, friends in low politic. Came to funeral to bow head, have nasty word with Nina. She very angry; threaten with shoe. Never hear such fuss on sacred ground. Came by next day with flowers; Nina came to kitchen for big knife, but George not open gate. Like many folk in Athens, Nina suspect parents' death!"

"George? Was Bruno employed before he went to America?"

"Near same time, come to recollect. Bring Bruno to villa and old lady impress. Maris frightened, not want Greek handyman and Bruno have paper from consulate in Athens." I grounded my glass, completely unwound.

"Consulate...from what country? Czech? German? Polish?"

"Maris not say, Mr. Slater. Maybe Bruno need work permit and family want to keep private," she added nervously.

"Was Nina here at the time?" The cook shook her head.

"Nina gone to New York. Talk often with old lady, so maybe Bruno discussed; not hear what say. All time, many picture in newspaper," she added. "Nina very popular and paper make note, mention party to honor wedding and old lady have many call. You also mention," she added hastily. "Say you fly aeroplane over volcano. You leave Nina with old folk, Mr. Slater? Have plenty worry if she not with you!"

"We'll be together at Kos," I said. "We plan to stay aboard the Helena."

"So maybe okay. Captain Stavos old family, keep watchful eye. Fear for Metexas," she added thoughtfully. "Come from funeral; Nina stare at sea most the night. Have strange eye when I bring tea and tiropites. Vengeance strong word, Mr. Slater. Come now as Nina's husband, I see happy smile while you dance to bouzouki; like Nina old times when she snap finger to Syrtaki. Blessed be, you make fine mate, but you must beware of her mysterious soul and protect her day and night!" Cautionary advice from the household, no less! I bussed the cook's cheek and hugged her closely, sensing her warmth and sincerity.

At a loss for words, I proceeded silently to the patio, at odds with what I'd heard and seen. A plate of sweets was gathering flies when I passed the seaside table. A half-mast bottle of brandy and Auntie's rouged coffee cup sat nearby. The old girl had probably slugged the bottle when the aftershock jarred the villa. Left her beads behind and countless cigarettes crumpled nervously in a tray.

Judging from cook's comments, Bruno apparently arrived after Nina returned to New York, post Gomulaka's disappearance; a quick connection, but whom? Was he on his own, in contact with parties or apart, or just he needed a job?

I gave further thought to Gomulaka while I dusted my blazer and dropped my duds to the floor, recalling T.S.'s comments while I showered full-length with Nina's shampoo. 'The doctor had many friends, he'd said, some with connections to the former Polish underground.' My thoughts were interrupted when the Mercedes' headlights reflected from the bathroom window. I toweled myself on the porch, hoping Nina was up for a splash in the pool.

She passed me with a peck on the cheek, however, while Uncle made straight away to the bar. Squirming from her dress, she went immediately to the shower, commenting of her day, gasping (as I had) when she discovered there was no hot water.

"Same thing all day," she shouted from behind the curtain. "First, our emergency power won't do the air conditioning. Then, the phones gave up and we had problems with the fax! There's a resident genius in the law office next door, so I called him. So now it's a fuss!" Nina continued, reaching blindly for the shampoo. The connection's in a corridor closet and the door's locked. Okay, he springs the lock with my nail file, and what do we find? Damn recording device spliced to our fax machine, Keith! Can you believe that? Like, maybe it's been there for months, all the while we've had the problems calling options! Bloody bastard!"

"Metexas, hey?"

"Who else would be so low? 'Genius' said it's a criminal offense, provided you catch 'em! Would you hand me a towel, please? Not the one you're wearing, Keith!"

"Did he disconnect the thing?"

"Sort of. He's a junior lawyer and had a better idea, like he wants our business. Hooked it up to his office fax, the spare they use for legal descriptions. Said we can't arrest the device, but we'd have a joint case when they trace the line to his office!

"That was the downswing," Nina continued, fluffing her hair. "The upswing, a draft release, when he fixed the bloody fax! Frankly, I was worried sick. What next? Uncle's in a state of shock, blames himself. Next, the tax thing, and God help us if the auction doesn't pay off! So how did your day go?" she added, squirming into a pair of shorts. "The newscast said there were fatalities in Thira. Did you feel the jot in Akrotiri?"

I capsulated as best I could, omitting my recent discovery and conversation with the cook. Despite her lighthearted banter, I sensed Nina was onto a feathered edge; why add to her anxiety? How much could she bear? How deep was her loathing for the source, the suspicious she'd harbored since her parents' death? Was her psychic mind bent for revenge? I'd witnessed the danger signs when she went after Metexas with the candelabrum; noticed the unnerving glint in her eyes when I re-buttoned the blouse she'd slipped into.

We supped in semi-silence, conversations mostly in Greek. Uncle appeared downcast, sipping readily from his brandy. Auntie carried the ball for my part, inquiring of the happenings at Santorini, nodding when I mentioned the old lady we'd transported from Akrotiri.

"Injury, hey? Most part, that's the only way they'll leave, Keith. Old folks cling to what's nearest, not believing the wiles of nature like their ancestors. Like myself," she added. "Sometimes I wonder if we shouldn't take for the hills."

Nina ate sparingly, waving off the cook when she brought tea and tiropites to her side. Preoccupied with business, she had little to say to me. For the first time since Palo Alto, since our wedding and arrival in Athens, I felt an outsider.

Alone in our room, I suffered Nina's silence while we opened windows to avail the listless breeze, sharing a few necessary words when she complained of the heat and questioned the overhead fan. I drew a negative response when I suggested we try the pool. Realizing she was mentally whipped, I turned off the lamp when she pillowed her head and stared at the window, her eyes seemingly drawn to the glow of Santorini. I realized her thoughts were elsewhere, confined to a singular thing she was unwilling to discuss. I spoke to her quietly then, stroking her shoulders when she rolled receptively to my side. Her fingers touching my lips, she murmured,

"Sorry, my love; it's been a terrible day."

Wide awake when Nina drifted off in a nervous sleep, I considered the sequence of events that had kept her mind in turmoil since the fateful morning in the Great Divide...the smoldering suspicions that aroused her psychic being whenever thunderous lightning brought visions of the flailing jet, or the unholy artifacts she identified with her Papa.

Churning my pillow, I thought of the paralleling circumstances that had me at odds and ends...the scenario at the Carlyle and the cable from ITT; T.S.'s continued presence and his unwanted schemes; Gomulaka's disappearance and Gunnar's sleight of hand; Amalia's determined surveillance, and her mentor's doings at Ramenskoye. All seemingly related to the U-2's projected turn over Iran. As for Metexas, there was no apparent connection, aside from the coincidence of my stay with the Maris family while he exercised his dirty tricks. He had reason to have me elsewhere, dead or alive, however. Threatened me in Nassau and, according to cook, had 'low friends in politic', who may have practiced the state-of-the-art in the past.

Fleeting thoughts to consider and combine with an eerie flash of lightning illuminating the hills beyond Hellinikon, together with Nina's tightening hand when a peal of thunder rattled the screens. At three in the morning, the wiles of nature responded to Auntie's warning and quickened my ongoing dreams. A heavy tectonic quake battered Athens and Kavouri whilst I was yet asleep.

CHAPTER 16

icking hard left rudder and hauling back on the stick, the F-15's nose swept the horizon from a near vertical bank. G-force slammed my chin guard into my breastbone, driving my helmet display apart from my line of vision. I had a fleeting glimpse of the SAM arching beyond us, another streaking from the SCUD pad. Leveling off, I chopped the Pratt-Whitneys, calling back to 'weapons' to salvo our hardware. The second SAM, seeking our jettisoned rockets, exploded in the distance while I juiced the afterburners to hump the terrain. But it was all too late; the battery had us ringed, the third missile detonated a tailpipe and the eagle came apart. Wallowing briefly with its rudder section gone, tumbling while we blew the canopy and ejected into the cold desert night.

I came awake, struggling to contain the billowing chute, and Nina clinging to my back amidst a tangle of shrouds and twisted sheets. A deep rumble agonized from below...the insidious grinding of subterranean rock as the over-burdened earth convulsed and jellied the house. The overhead rafters groaned and loosened shreds of plaster, roof tiles slithered and crashed onto the patio. Spasmodic explosions sounded from all quarters, streaking the walls with a glow from distant fires.

The floor heaved like a thing alive, while I collected my wits and crawled towards the doorway with Nina underarm. I had a brief glimpse of an ivy pot skidding across the balcony; then a careening chest of drawers tripped my legs, striking my temple with a loosened drawer and the night dissolved in a blaze of flashing stars!

The quake had subsided when I regained consciousness. My head throbbed from a gash above my ear and I was at a loss for vestige of time. I struggled to dislodge the heavy chest, the acrid dust of plaster engulfing my lungs as I squirmed beneath it and staggered to my feet. Pain shot from my lacerated leg wound as I looked about for Nina. The doorway, strew with toppled drawers, lingerie and personal items, evoked no evidence of her presence...aside from the jewelry pouch abandoned nearby.

Wary of Nina's psychic wanderings, I traced her dusty footprints to the stairway, to a blotch where she'd slipped and assed the lower rise, but apparently landed on her feet. Grabbing a towel from the railing, I wiped the blood from my ear and called out. No response, although I noticed a glimmer of light from Auntie's window.

Sirens wailed in the distance; headlights beamed the boulevard from a garbage truck astride the median. An electric line sizzled snake-like to a nearby utility pole, exploding the transformer and firing the pole. I spotted Nina then, silhouetted by the raining sparks, standing naked on the seawall. The abominable necklace in hand, arms flung to the sky, she was shrilling incoherently to the quartering moon.

I bolted the stairs and raced across the patio, clipped a fallen statue and sprawled amongst the flowers. She'd lowered her arms by the time I climbed to my feet, her eyes riveted to a geyser of flame on a distant hill. I walked slowly towards her, calling softly that she not be afraid, realizing she'd awakened from her trance and was on to something apart. A second explosion echoed from the slope and flames shot skyward like a blowtorch gone berserk. She raised a hand, pointing. As if mesmerized by the compounding fires, she lost her footing and tumbled, screaming, to the ledge below!

Heart pounding, I managed the slippery steps and found her dazed amidst the clutter of chaises and cushioning pads. Not seriously injured, she was crawling on her hands and knees, screaming hysterically in Greek, pointing to the fiery glow reflecting from the cabana. Again I called to her, but she was clawing at the hasp of the metal door, unmindful of my presence until I grabbed her about the waist.

"Pa-ra-ka-lo!" she shrieked, fighting back, knifing my shoulder with bloodied nails, hammering the door as she wrenched away. I caught her arms and spun her about, holding her rigidly against the wall. Setting her hard to the ledge, I backhanded her cheek when she bit my wrist and kneed my groin. Visibly shaken, Nina blinked her eyes, as if suddenly awake but not comprehending.

"Why do you do this?" she gasped, seemingly recognizing my face. "Mama's screaming for help; she's trapped inside! Her dress is on fire; she's still alive! God help me, please. She mustn't die!" Nina's voice faltered then. Distracted by the sirens, she glanced wildly about. Confused by the surroundings, she burst into tears. I thought she was out of it and released her arms, but her eyes were drawn again to the cabana.

Determined to have an end to it, I ripped the rusted lock from its hasp and pried the door, helping Nina to her feet. Hesitant, uncertain, wary of my reaction, she stared at the structure with mixed emotions, then darted inside the inky aperture. I heard her stumbling amongst the folded furniture, her muffled cursing when she banged her head on the sloping ceiling.

There was action of sorts on the patio...Auntie's questioning voice, a flashlight beaming here and there. The pole continued to burn, casting its flickering glow to the ledge and lapping sea. Then, ever so quietly, Nina emerged from the cabana with a clutch of dolls embraced in her arms. Pathetic, heartrending, forlorn...like a little girl snarled in brambles...she was streaked with blood from breasts to knees, her hair hanging damply in disarray. Cobwebs clinging to her cheeks from where she'd encountered them inside. Her eyes were steady, however, shadowed by the half-light, glistening with tears as she toed the watery ledge and came readily into my arms with her gaggle of dolls.

"Don't tell me I freaked out again," she sobbed, pressing her head to my heart. "What happened, Keith? Why are we here? Why do I hurt? Did I walk in my sleep, fall on my ass?"

"Earthquake, honey! You took off like a bird and tried to handle it all by yourself!" She fingered the soggy teddy bear, wincing at the sight of her bloodied nails. Staring blankly at her handprints on the cabana door, wondering aloud.

"I...I had a terrible nightmare, Keith. Papa's plane was upside down on a hill, burning fiercely. I was there; could feel the heat. Papa was inside, all shriveled and black; Mama was screaming; she was still alive. I tried to open the door, but someone pulled me away. My God, how they suffered! It was so bloody real!"

I laid it to the monumental quake and the explosion in the hills. Attempting to ease her mind of the dream, I suggested she'd reacted from mind's eye when the transformer flared, identifying the cabana with the jet when she tumbled from the wall. It served no purpose to mention her trance-like chanting.

"You were disoriented," I allowed. "Barely awake!"

"Had myself a hissy fit and kicked you in the balls, I think. Sorry!" she murmured, pouting for a kiss while I teased a hank of hair aside and wiped the cobwebs from her chin. Oblivious of the billowing fires and Auntie's voice echoing the cliffside, we embraced for a long moment, like two naked lovers on the edge of an abyss, unmindful of the fretting sea.

149

It happened so slowly that neither of us was aware, until Nina reached to catch a floating doll from the surge. It started as an ominous gurgle...flooding the ledge, thrusting from the depths, testing our legs with its icy tongue, rising to our knees while we splashed for the stairs.

"Quickly, you must hurry!" Auntie called from the wall, beaming the steps with a flashlight to hurry us along. I had a brief glimpse of her nightdress, of Uncle's striped pajamas.

"I mean beezness!" the old lady shouted. "Is seismic wave! Make haste before it carry you away." The beam faltered for a moment, focusing Nina's hand on the railing.

"God in heaven!" Auntie shrieked. "Is my Nina badly hurt?"

"I'm alright!" Nina shouted, clinging to my waist while I struggled for a foothold with the surge mounting our backs.

The ascent was treacherous; the steps were deeply cut and ill defined. Precipitous by daylight, they were now a living nightmare with the murky water edging ahead. Unable to reach the railing with the weight of Nina on my shoulders, I stretched desperately for the gutter at the head of the rise. Suddenly, a tightening hand grabbed my wrist. I glimpsed Bruno's chalky face as he pulled us bodily to the patio and stood quickly aside while we found our feet.

The sea continued to rise, frothing the patio with a spread of brine. Uncle headed for the house, I eyed the balcony stairs, and Bruno disappeared, trousers rolled to his knees. But Auntie stood fast, eyed us reproachfully and calmly handed us blankets.

"It go now," she said, as if totally in command. And, inexplicably, it did. Subtly at first, there was a hoarse gurgle as it retreated and flowed through the scuppers in the wall. Cascading from the ledge in a raging torrent, whirlpooling as it was sucked offshore. The rocky bottom glistened in the eerie light; grounded fish flapped helplessly in its wake. Eels slithered to the remaining pools. It hadn't come as a curling comber on the horizon; the sea had simply risen...swiftly, soundlessly, without warning.

"It come again, but not so much," Auntie remarked. "Much trouble for fishing boats, lose plenty good men. Come, dear," she said softly to Nina. "I fix a sedative and put you to bed. You've taken a terrible tumble, I think."

I helped Nina to Auntie's suite, stood by while she sipped the sedative and drifted off to sleep; helped myself to a brandy from the bar while the old lady cleaned and bandaged Nina's hands. Uncle, completely out of it, slumped in a chair. Groaning in his sleep, there was evidence of his having nipped heavily from the decanter of ouzo beside his chair.

"Come now, Keith!" Auntie called from her doorway, shrugging open-handed when she spied the old man in his chair. "I fix your wound with ointment and we talk a little, now Nina asleep."

I redid my blanket and trailed after her to the suite, wincing when she swabbed my gash with alcohol and applied her medicinal ointment. All the while, seemingly searching for words; disturbed, apparently, by Nina's condition.

"Now then, take plenty aspirin and rest on good side," she said, glancing to the patio, then warmly studying my face. "You make fine husband for Nina, my son. Save her from serious injury in the past, I think." I realized what Auntie meant when she drew the sheet from Nina's legs and exposed the livid scars on her feet.

"Nina badly burn, Keith! Recent, I think. Not this night; maybe same thing?" Auntie eyed me curiously while I partially explained the circumstances; that she'd 'visited' a cookout on the beach and burned her toes in the coals. The old lady nodded to herself.

"So, maybe come storm and she walk in her sleep…like maybe this night, when she tumble from the wall?" I attempted to play it down, but Auntie shook her head.

"You must be honest, my son. Was she chanting strange language, wearing that cursed necklace?" Auntie nodded to herself again, anticipating my answer. "Come morning, we have long talk," she said as we stepped outside. "We must be patient, Keith. Nina have mysterious dreams when child, and now they associated with Nicholas' recent death, I think. She idolized the dear man, and now must come to grip with business. She need strength and understanding."

And definitely in need of psychological help, or a psychiatrist, I thought, while I collected a residue of dolls from the patio and piled them on a chair to dry. Nina readily admitted to her psychic reams, defining the beginnings when she dreamed of the princess whilst aboard the Helena. She had no financial pressures then…no deep-seated suspicions to trigger her dreams. Was there something else that keyed her relapses and sent her astray?

I spied the necklace snared in a scupper while I was midway to the balcony stairs. The chain curled defiantly around Nina's cast-off sandal, as if loathe to let go. The figurine icy to my hand, its emerald eyes glaring fiercely when I returned the thing to Nina's jewelry pouch and righted the chest of drawers.

I bathed my head with a dribble from the gravity tank, drew our pillows from the floor, and stretched on the bed to regain my equilibrium. Stars blinked softly through the open window, distantly aloof from the chaotic world. My thoughts returned to Nina's tortured chanting while the waning fires cast dervish shadows on the walls. I gave thought to that afternoon at the Met, the tempestuous night on the beach, the necklace dangling from Nina's throat. Was there an alien presence in her soul, a dominance when she was frightened, a voice that drew her to another dimension in time?

* * * * * *

I joined Auntie at a patio table come morning, when the sun bridged the headland and cast its light on the tranquil sea. Squinting from lack of sleep, she poured a brace of coffee, lit a cigarette, and gazed thoughtfully at the sodden dolls I'd collected from the debris.

"You must dispose of the necklace," she said. "The bloody thing is evil, Keith! Nicholas never intended it for Nina. Many times he say that, say it belong with his donation to the Museum of Antiquities."

"So he kept it apart, locked in his drawer for twenty-odd years? Think back, Aunt Maris. Was Nick superstitious? He gave Nina the earrings when she was eighteen, donated the rings and bracelets to the museum, but not the figurine. Might he have thought it was conceivably linked with a source of Greek mythology…became frightened when he realized it was an object of fixation? He'd told her the story of Deucalion and Pyrrha, most likely associated the artifacts in general terms, never thinking she'd identify with the legend when they visited the dig."

"Give cause for plenty thought," the old lady remarked. "Like all Greeks, Nicholas superstitious. Maybe, like Nina, he find necklace eyes hypnotic. Stir trouble with ancestral past?"

"Aside from that, the circumstances were unusual," I countered. "Consider the time and place, Auntie…the reaction of a child when they uncovered the skeletons; the storm and lightning; Nina's state of mind when they hurried to the yacht; her walking nightmare when she found the necklace and dreamed of the princess. Nick was upset, like 'never more'! So, where's the logic, Auntie? Superstition, a lousy piece of gold? Or the reaction of an eight year old, frightened by what she should never have seen?"

"Nina told you of this, hey?"

"Bits and pieces locked in her mind…subject to instant recall when she recall when she reverts to her dreams. There's a link with her father's death, of course. Nina idolized Nick and he was close to her at the time, so she identifies with the stories he told. Could be the necklace, in her subconscious mind, keys an avenue of escape to an imaginary world, especially when she's emotionally upset; suspicious of Tony Metexas of late? I'm worried, Auntie, scared of a crossover. If she finds reason for revenge, Nina might slip from reality and never return...at least, as we know her now!"

The old lady nodded, drew her shawl closely to her shoulders, and stared wordlessly at the sea. Offshore, a police launch prodded an overturned fishing smack amidst the floating debris. The ruptured gas line flamed spasmodically in the distance, although it appeared to be under control. The nearby utility pole smoldered unattended, its power lines draped uselessly in the trees. There was a measure of electricity, however, at least in the villa, courtesy of a 'make do' generator Bruno had discovered in the garage. Sufficient to brew coffee and pump water from the cistern, but there would be no gas for the kitchen for a long time to come.

The villa had a stress crack alongside the chimney, I noticed while helping Auntie light a cigarette. The complex had lost sections of roof tiles, but otherwise was remarkably intact, as were the coastal villas...aside from their docks and a burnt-out shell on the point. A gruesome scene of reality appeared seaward, however. Caught with a pole from the launch, a limp corpse was added to the body bags astern.

"Amnesia strong word," the old lady murmured, groping for the brandy, hands shaking as she splashed a tot in her coffee. "Stems from Greek language," she added, glancing fretfully over her shoulder as the launch disappeared in the east. "Comes loss of memory when one's in shock, or have mental fatigue. See distance in Nina's eyes when she comes from Arhannes, Keith, never before. Same after funeral when she stay long by the wall; not fright, something more. Again last night, when you fetch Nina from tide, see unbalance when she fight door of cabana; visualize family death in hills, I think? Come next what we fear! Best I tell of Nina's childhood, Keith, her brush with the supernatural when the storm came to be. Then, maybe you'll agree we should toss the bloody necklace to the sea!"

I helped myself to a brandy, listening carefully while Auntie reminisced, thankful of a first-hand view of Nina's early years, despite the old lady's inherent superstition. It was after eight by then, the sun eye level with the Cape. A bevy of tow trucks were clearing wreckage from the boulevard, but there was no way to contact the Grande Bretagne, not until there was minimal passage between Kavouri and the city. Over Hellinikon, however, the heavy jets were active, strung on a long approach; thundering at touchdown, the runways cleared for international arrivals, possibly Swissair and the contingent from Geneva. Perhaps there would be news of Dr. Gomulaka's replacement, Gunnar's appearance with-

153

standing.

"Long ago, family have two villas in Kavouri," Auntie continued, when we'd roundtripped the pantry for a plate of bourekias. "Nicholas' house have same plan, four blocks north. Nina young child when they move to Bahamas; keep dolls in cabana, playhouse when here from school. Say dolls her family; teddy bear her Papa. Happy child then, smile much, have plenty friends. Come now from Arhannes, see difference; seem far away, very serious! Minoan princess, then; dolls ancient people, not be afraid when priest take them away! Show friends letter knife in Uncle's drawer, speak strange language...no longer have friends!" the old lady declared.

"Come later, have long talk with Helena. She tall like Nina, educated, not superstitious. Help Nicholas with society; write important letters when he lack terminology. Not so close to Nina as Nicholas, I think; hadn't spirit for family and Greek easy ways. Keen for Nina's education, however. Place child in private school like English prone to do. Say she note difference in Nina when they return from Arhannes, have reason to worry when she recite strange language in her sleep."

"Same thing?" Auntie nodded.

"Helena matter of fact person. Say scene at Arhannes macabre, not to her liking; too much for a child of eight. Nicholas insisting she bring Nina from yacht when they uncover the skeletons. Same time, Helena see terrible storm in the highland; came quickly with plenty lightning, she say. Workmen frightened, put down tools...say storm bad omen, temple sacred ground. Students not superstitious, so they continue to press with brush and blade, discover bronze knife and sacrificial stone, urn with ancient blood. Nicholas excited, archeologist say date from Minoan times; first known evidence of human sacrifice! All the time, the storm come ever closer!"

"Nina told me the story, Auntie. Said they discovered the princess's jewelry in a crevice by her hand."

"True, and Helena have sharp eyes, Keith. Notice young man watching all the while, attracted to Nina when she came in braids; sketch with paints. Sketch Nicholas and Helena also, I think."

"Deuca?" I wondered aloud.

"Helena not know his name, Keith. Workmen say he artist from valley near Kaphri. Brings often oranges and honey, never ask for money. Archeologist tell Helena he seem familiar with temple ruins, maybe from folklore; speak with strange Cretan accent. Come always near sunset, not like sun."

"...long hair, sash for a belt?"

"You mumble, my son, seem disturbed?"

"The artist, Auntie...the time and place, his fixation with the ruins; Nina in braids, Helena nearby...the likeness of their features? So, twenty years later, he's restoring frescoes at Akrotiri, adds a figurine to a necklace worn by a girl in the mural, identifies her as Pyrrha, calling himself Deuca!"

"Same necklace Nina have?"

"Possibly sketched from memory. The girl's likeness to Nina was uncanny; same eyes, same chin. Shook me up! I've the photos upstairs." Auntie nodded thoughtfully, sipped her coffee and added a splash of brandy to mine.

"Same artist, same necklace? Brings thought to strange story, Keith! Nicholas say different, but Helena not prone to exaggerate. Come later, when workmen flee the storm and the students work with skeletons. Helena notice young man watching all the while. Not afraid, she say...stand apart, not intruding, not interfering with the students' work. Come plenty thunder then, hear warning bell from yacht. Nina frighten and Helena press to leave, when suddenly the sun break free of clouds.

"Helena not believe supernatural," Auntie continued, "but come to think, she frighten, too! Say the scene was both beautiful and awesome...prehistoric, the temple awash with golden light. Remind Helena of Stonehenge; the pillars of stone. Strange silence all the while, students and archeologists immobilized, she say, like ancient statues fixed in time, forgetting their tools to stare at the sun. Same time, she notice young man move amongst them, noticeable because of his clothes! Say he shouting gibberish to bring attention, pointing to the wall nearest skeleton's hand, beckoning students to come with trowel!

"Helena say the students confused, but archeologist come quickly and clear the stone of dirt and ash. Necklace come first, then the bracelets and earrings, all of gold; not corroded, glitter in sun like long ago! Rings she not see; say much excitement and lost from view. All time she stay with Nina and watch from tent. Nina fascinated, Helena say, close to tears when Nicholas think best to return family to yacht. Also decide to take jewelry for safekeeping."

"The artist?"

"Strange thing, Keith! Helena say he all but ignored; archeologists preoccupied, Nicholas remark he 'Billy from the hills', not important! Helena have difference, I think. Say poor man not seem to care; help students fold tent, give oranges to Nina, disappear in rains. Say he younger than thought, pale of complexion with luminous brown eyes. Smell of goats, she say. Maybe why English raise sheep, because odor not so repugnant, hey?" I smiled at her attempt at humor.

"Sounds...biblical, Auntie. The parting of the clouds, the seer with his stick..."

"Premonition, Helena think! Maybe he seed from ancient Minoan long before Abraham; have logical intuition where ancestors entombed. See skeleton huddle near wall, think girl alive when temple collapse. See she not wear jewelry, possibly a maid of high culture. Like, maybe he see what others not believe!"

"Ties with Nina's fantasy, Auntie. Her escape to a dream world when she identifies with the princess."

"Brings thought to the mysterious chanting, my son. Helena questioned anthropologist when Nina visit Athens from school. Brilliant man, also have doctorate in language. Nina frighten at first, but when he offer words from Anatolia, she seem to understand. The language not Greek. Stem from ancient dialects; Minoan language not known. So they play a game of words. Nina delighted, doctor baffled. Say he recognize certain words, but sequence like rote...have no beginning or ending!

"Conjures up the family heritage," the old lady continued, staring again at the sea. "My husband, Nicholas and sister Cleo have bloodline from Anatolia. Seafarers like Phoenicians, they came to the Aegean when Greeks were barbarians...and remain so," Auntie added wryly, "judging from Tony Metexas and our political instability! So, maybe Nina gifted and pick up words seldom used; dialect from Crete when she sail with her Papa. Close to Nicholas, she copy his ways when he decide her brother no good. Laugh much, tell dirty joke. Very funny sometimes, make me smile when she mimic old movie and dance like a whore on the streets of Piraeus. But, deep inside, I know her soul is as pure as the snow of Mount Olympus!"

We clinked cups to that. And for want of words to express my feelings, I hugged the gracious old lady as I would my own, bussing her cheek when she gripped my hand. Selfless, from old stock, she'd offered a candid view of Nina's formative years with love and understanding. As for Nina's psychic nature, Auntie had no ready answer, although I had my thoughts when I considered what she'd said. As a child, Nina apparently possessed a depth of extraordinary perception, not unlike the geniuses that seemingly appear from another fold. Her heritage was thousands of years in the making. Perhaps she was a genetic clone from a like personality from her ancestral past...inherited a characteristic similarity to the girl at Akrotiri, together with latent memories not altogether erased by time.

Church bells were clanging, somewhat out of kilter. Uncle snored peacefully in his chair, an empty glass in hand. Near awake, stirring from her sleep when Auntie eased the blinds, Nina – her fingers swathed in bandages – was clutching a brace of pillows, as would a child in the throes of pain. Pitiful, drowsy from sedatives, she was still incredibly beautiful. The sight of her long black hair strewn on the saffron sheets stunned me into silence when I knelt by her side.

She was aware of our presence; of my shadow shielding her eyes from the sun, of Auntie's sympathetic clucking as she examined her toes. Struggling to an elbow, she raised a bloodied finger to my lips and murmured,

"I love you, Keith...but damn it to hell, you'll have to help me to the loo!" It was a quick, unsteady trip. A further request to fetch her toothbrush and comb, and a testy, "So, what's with the hot water?" then groggy, she slumped once more to Auntie's bed. Accepting a double aspirin when the old lady insisted she rest until noon. We let her be when her eyes closed and she fell softly asleep.

Come next morning, she'd be her ready self again, restless and on to business. For my part, I was worried for the future. Together at Kos, I'd be close at hand, but Nina's commuting to Athens was another matter; risky, if she confronted the abominable Greek! I had no less concern when I'd be airborne with the U-2, or if we were caught betwixt should Santorini explode and consign the Aegean to oblivion. In retrospect, Fate had us by the Achilles heel, and I hadn't the earthly means to change the odds!

* * * * * *

Refreshed after a shave and shower of sorts, I joined the old couple in the pantry while they listened to the late morning newscast, Auntie remarking on the highlights in English. There were numerous fatalities in Athens. Looting had occurred and martial law was in force, with militia patrolling the streets, together with a contingent from the Navy base commanding the intersections.

Auntie referred briefly to the devastation along the coastal regions, expressing concern for friends and relatives. The seismic wave had raced a quarter mile inland, temporarily flooding low-lying streets and docks at Piraeus; it had been of sufficient magnitude for the authorities to consider a general evacuation!

"Better they think in terms of hills and mountains," the newscaster furthered, raising the possibility of a Plinian eruption. "Judging from history, we've reason to worry about a hundred meter crest that might inundate the coast to the rise of the Acropolis!" He was cut off then...censored, most likely, for voicing an opinion. He was right, of course. The Swedish volcanologist had predicted no less, especially if the mantle was weakened by the pull of the moon!

"Fifty meter take villa from Kavouri!" the old lady commented, puzzling the music interrupting the newscast. "Maybe time to visit sister at Mount Parnassus, I think. Come now, have news again, Keith. Not same man?"

Correcting an *unauthorized statement from questionable sources*, a spokesman said there was no immediate emergency pending word from the deputy in charge of internal affairs, although banks and government offices would remain closed until further notice. Hellinikon was mentioned in terms of overcrowding and the scarcity of outgoing flights. An advisory, translated into English twice over, cautioned tourists to remain in their hotels until late in the day and not to drink water unless bottled or boiled.

"Bring hefty price for beer and wine!" Auntie commented when Uncle eyeballed his provisions. "Athens worry now for old folk and pensioner. Same thing; no gas to boil water. Say Red Cross make plan transport needy to Lycabettus and Philopappos; set up tents until utilities restore! Want weather report?" she asked. "Come next, after commodities."

The weather was typically summertime Greece; hot and humid, the oppressive smog smarting my eyes while I helped Uncle to upright his patio statuary. In the distance, a singular stratospheric cloud identified Santorini, and I was reminded of a need for transportation to join my group at the Grande Bretagne. Taxis were out of the question; Nina's Jaguar a bit flashy when I considered the mood in the streets. Auntie's bicycle a possibility, although it was a cumbersome three-wheeler with a basket fore and aft.

"Best to ride with Bruno in the Mercedes," she suggested, remarking on the humidity and the lack of pathways along that *bloody awful Marine Drive!*

"Bruno good driver," she added. "Know the streets, stand by till you finish up."

* * * * * *

Communication? Lacking this on a local level, it was questionable whether my group had arrived, but I assumed it was my 'horseback' responsibility to see if they had. Short-shrifted in New York, our seminar at the Grande Bretagne was a matter of relevant necessity! We'd yet to establish our guidelines, or discuss our operational requirements at Kos. Aside from Winner and myself, we'd yet to acquaint on a first-hand basis, inclusive of the administrator, Dr. Nokomo, the elusive Horst Gunnar and Dr. Gomulaka's replacement whom, as far as I knew, had yet to be named.

As a scientific venture, the project was, in a sense, long past due. Sparked by the group in Geneva and funded by the UN, White Dove was designed to determine the status of the monster on the horizon; long-term, to analyze the stratospheric fallout on the agricultural scene. Judging from recent events, the volcano's tempo had quickened and was threatening the immediate Aegean! I hoped we would act together without interference.

Once at Kos, we'd have a plethora of gifted minds, as well as the capacity to monitor and react to the instruments implanted on Santorini, together with a scan from the U-2 to determine the heat and velocity of the core emissions. Given this, the group would have the means to predict (or quiet) the threat of an imminent explosion. At the moment, unfortunately, the project was seemingly besot with bureaucracy, de facto leadership, and intrigue.

Needless worries, perhaps, but a 3,000 mile flight above 70,000 feet with super pods and an unknown observer, was a tedious thing at best. We also might have problems with the U-2's brand new GE F-101 turbo jet engine, which had yet to be tried under volcanic conditions. All of which, together with long-range communications, was subject to Murphy's Law!

As for the general's project, I had continued mixed feelings. There was mounting concern over the imbroglio in southern Turkmenistan and the border of Iran. Judging from his comments in London, there was no slackening of interest, or intent. The underlying circumstances...the hard-liners and their secretive fleet of tanks...was difficult to believe. I wondered if the security agency was altogether knowledgeable, as Keenan aptly phrased it, of a *festering ideology waiting the torch!* To that end, I had his softly spoken reasoning to consider; his analytical prediction of a crisis in the making. Top drawer, he'd been acquainted with the hard facts and, obviously, realized a need for immediate reaction! Perhaps with Moscow's tacit approval, there would be a decision to have an end to it...by means undisclosed.

I could dwell with misgiving or rationalize my duplicity and carry on. Most likely the agency had contingency plans, apart from the means proposed at the Carlyle, although my hasty briefings indicated the U-2 was a priority which the general continued to press! There also was Gunnar's questionable status with the ex-KGB; their deadly interest in Gomulaka's chair. In the back of T.S.'s mind, might there be a progressive plan to draw them in, then step aside for an outsider to do the trick?

Something to consider, hey? Then came the unexpected while I lingered with my thoughts.

"Come now, Keith! Bruno ready with Mercedes," Auntie shouted from the kitchen, evaporating all else!

CHAPTER

Devoid of expression, erect in his seat wearing sunglasses and a white guayabera shirt, Bruno followed slowly with the Mercedes while I manually operated the gates. Apparently worried about the old folks' security, he nodded affirmatively from the curbside when I re-fastened the inner locks; nodded again when he offered the right seat. A minimal gesture, perhaps, but considering the mayhem along the boulevard, I realized his sense of responsibility was not altogether token and he'd accepted my presence with no misgivings.

Stolid, taciturn while we maneuvered the littered streets, Bruno replied with a knowing nod when I pointed to my pad and pencilled 'Grand Bretagne. Have meeting with UN. OK?' Curious by then, reminded of his response when he pulled us from the flood, I gave it a try.

"One o'clock, or thereabouts, do you comprehend?" His reaction was studied, not immediate, but when he scanned his watch, we had mutual understanding.

Thereafter, I dispensed with the pad and communicated in English, clarifying any Americanisms that he questioned with a frown. If he could talk, it required an effort he was reluctant to make. Stroking his throat, he indicated a physical problem and replied as best he could – mostly by gestures and an agonized grunt – when I expressed concern over the mind-bending traffic.

Recently shaven to the nape of his cap, there nevertheless was indication Bruno could sprout a full head of hair. With a beard or a mustache, there'd be a vast difference in his appearance; without his cap he could pass as a skinhead, or Genghis Khan on vacation. His military posture he couldn't shake. As a pilot, I recognized the impression of earphones on his cheeks, and knew where he'd been when the quake jolted Kavouri. True to cook's comments, he quartered a brown paper bag between his knees. I assumed, from its heft, it was not altogether his lunch!

Conjecture, perhaps, but I was mindful of the cook's description of the contents of his drawer. If armed for security reasons (given the old folks' concern over Metexas, and looters of late), he'd keep the weapon readily at hand, most likely bag it when he had sufficed their transportation needs, with them never knowing what he was doing. The silencer she described was illegal and deadly; was he on to something? If so, there apparently was a long standing, premeditated purpose for his mysterious presence in Kavouri. He offered a clue of sorts when he downshifted the Mercedes to thread Marine Drive.

Snarled at the intersection, Bruno had cancelled the air conditioning to conserve fuel. The heat was stifling, rank with diesel fumes from the slow-paced trucks. Sweating profusely, he shed his cap. When traffic came to a full stop, he looked about and reached inside the paper bag. Instantly wary, my thoughts raced and I instinctively readied a 'chop'. Continuing my motion, I wiped the sweat from my chin when he produced a furled copy of the Herald Tribune!

If he was aware of my reaction, he kept it to himself as I relaxed in my seat, somewhat unwound. He watched furtively as I opened the newspaper and spread it on my knees. Thinking it was a sop for our lack of conversation, I turned the pages slowly, noting the issue was dated before our arrival in Athens. When he spread five fingers and added two from the wheel, I turned immediately to page seven and read on.

The three-column spread was complete with a picture of Dr. Nokomo, inclusive of his Nigerian cap and lengthy credentials; presumably his press release from New York when we were abandoned at the UN. The columnist was factual: White Dove's conception was credited to the scientists' hasty meeting in Geneva, together with their names and comments regarding the super-active volcano. I was quick to note that Dr. George Gomulaka's name was underlined with a pencil; I turned to question Bruno, but a horn blared behind us and he geared the Mercedes, indicating I should read on.

My name was mentioned in a secondary paragraph, together with Horst Gunnar and the Canadian representation. Lastly, a description of the U-2, which was described as a former American spy plane, recently modified to determine the drift of the volcanic haze. Bruno had underlined all of this, as well as an update by the columnist pertaining to our meeting at the Grande Bretagne, *where the distinguished Swedish geophysicist, Dr. Ingrid Sigurdesson, would outline her prediction of a Plinian explosion and later meet with members of the press.*

As for Bruno's point of interest, my thoughts were inconclusive. The volcano was prime topic and, possibly, had to do with Auntie's passing comments regarding my duties with White Dove. He obviously was well read, presumably a northern European, fluent in English, who most likely listened to the nightly newscast from the BBC. His need of earphones was unlikely, however, unless he was pressed for instant communication. With a transceiver radio concealed in his apartment, he could respond by Morse code if he was altogether mute. I was still considering the possibility that Bruno might be allied with ongoing interest of the project's personnel when we encountered the aftermath of terror in the streets of central Athens.

Marine Drive was understandably slow paced, mostly service trucks and venturesome commuters, but the outgoing streets were clogged with vehicles strapped with mattresses and household belongings. Pushcarts of all descriptions were attended predominantly by the elderly. Shawled in black, clutching her possessions, a pathetic soul was astride a donkey...tethered to another with an old-fashioned sewing machine strapped precariously to its rump. They momentarily halted traffic while they trotted bravely through an intersection. Otherwise, courtesies were forgotten and, with stoplights malfunctioning, it was a vehicular game of Russian roulette. The military police, gesticulating helplessly, were generally ignored.

Bruno was visibly shaken, expressing his agony with gestures; nodding or shaking his head when I pointed to a street urchin with a looted TV underarm. No way could I fear this man, although he was quick to resume his posture when we drew abreast of the stately Grande Bretagne. He donned his cap when he reached to unlatch my door. Declining valet service, he indicated he'd prefer to personally park the Mercedes.

The hotel and its adjoining structure seemed unaffected by the tremor, although there were rumblings of an in-house generator straining to supply its needs. Short of air-conditioning, I noted when the doorman ushered me through the heavy glass doors. Circulating fans inside provided business as usual for the palatial hotel. Outgoing crowds awaited transport, eyeing their luggage, drinks in hand (hopefully mixed with boiled water). The regulars were seated in the cushy chairs, including the heavyset man with his newspaper, who returned my impulsive wink with a shrug when I passed him by to confer with the concierge.

Referring to the roster attached to his clipboard, the bilingual attendant checked me off with the project's arrivals, including Edwards, Fraser and Dr. Sigurdesson, who'd arrived as a group from Geneva. Notably absent were Dr. Nokomo and his entourage, which was not surprising, given the conditions on hand. Nor had Gunnar appeared, but there was an explanation by way of a fax from the UN; Gunnar was delayed and would proceed directly to Kos. Dr. Gomulaka's reservation had also been cancelled. There was no lack of attendance, however, although mostly of an administrative nature. A half dozen or so had apparently arrived the day before. Also attached to the clipboard, addressed to my attention, was a sealed envelope containing a match folder from Zonar's Restaurant? Puzzled, I put the lot in my pocket, checked my watch when the concierge drew my attention to the brass-framed bulletin board on the wall behind his desk. Contrary to my notes, the seminar was posted from 12 to 1:30, followed by a coffee break to meet the press. It appeared the meeting was already in progress and I was definitely a latecomer.

The corridor was sparsely lit with emergency lights, dank with cigarette smoke, and echoing feedback from a high-pitched voice and faulty loudspeaker; Dr. Sigurdesson, I assumed, judging from the Scandinavian accent. Following the sound to the suite entrance, I found tall, slim, dishwater blonde in her forties, casually dressed in a powder blue slacks suit which matched her eyes. She nodded briefly when I presented my credentials at the door and gathered a chair alongside Dr. Winner. He acknowledged me with a wink and whispered,

"She's in somewhat of a snot, Keithy! Like, Nokomo skipped the stopover and they detained her computers at customs!"

"So who's in charge?"

"Would you please be quiet!" Sigurdesson interjected from the microphone, providing a partial answer.

Dr. Edwards, the project's geologist was identified by his beard and scruffy khakis; Fraser, the historian, by the Scottish wit he expressed with members of the press, who'd obviously arrived as a group from the bar. The others, aside from administration, were mostly from the university or members of the government, several in uniform.

Referring to an illuminated viewing screen, Sigurdesson was well into her theories of tidal influence upon the tectonic plates beneath Santorini; empathizing the draw of the quartering moon which, she reasoned, was a source of the recent upheavals. Favoring thin cigars, gesturing with one in hand (occasionally replaced with a pen light), she drew attention to the explanatory diagrams she'd prepared in advance.

"Come full moon I'd anticipate a compounding weakening...or a fracture...of the plates above the hot spot, exposing the magma chamber to the creviced limestone and an onslaught from the sea. From there on, it's a matter of minutes before a violent reaction triggers a paroxysmal explosion of unbelievable magnitude! My tidal theory is open to dispute, of course, but judging from the growth of the volcano, we should make note of a similar occurrence from history.

"Lately," she continued," it has been determined by sulfate ash strata found in glacier Greenland that the paroxysmal explosion that destroyed the island of Thera occurred within twenty years of 1628 BC. Consider the magnitude of the explosion! Fifteen cubic miles of the island's center was ejected to a height of 130,000 feet, followed by a tsunami tidal wave of no less than 165 feet!

"Now then," the doctor added, "the nearby islands and northern Crete would share the devastating impact, the gaseous fireball preceding all! What of the lowlands, of the Nile and its marshlands, and the low-lying valley of present day Athens? We've evidence of an eighty-foot crest in the Straits of Gibraltar, some 1,800 miles to the west! Piraeus was a Stone Age fishing village at the time! Survivors, most likely, were fishermen in their skiffs far at sea and shepherds in the hills. Of present day, can you visualize the sea rising to yonder window, and continuing to the floors above? It's not my purpose to frighten anyone," she added somberly. "There is no such thing as a scientific prediction that can't be flawed and, hopefully, none of this will come to pass!"

With that, she wrapped it up, introducing Doctors Winner, Fraser and Edwards…and myself, when prompted by Alan Winner. Then, microphone in hand, she answered questions from members of the press. Multi-lingual, Sigurdesson parried in French with the science editor of Le Monde, and spoke Italian with a corresponding physicist from the University of Milan. She responded politely in German to an inebriated chap whose knowledge was kin to the National Enquirer. Never flinching, although visibly tired and needing rest, she handled the questioning like a trooper until, expressing fatigue, she switched off the microphone and blew her audience a kiss. Pausing to gather her gear, she acknowledged the warm-hearted applause with a ladylike Scandinavian bow.

High marks for her spirit, I thought, gathering enthusiasm for the project now that it was evident we'd have a basic core of scientists. Their initial intent was to analyze the volume and extent of volcanic haze in the atmosphere, together with the implanted instrumentation to determine its volatile nature. She'd deftly handled the escalating interest and need for a prediction with a mixture of fact and history. Assuming the press would judiciously disseminate the information, a possible panic could be averted. To that end, there were no strobe lights, network cameras, or the like. This had been arranged at Sigurdesson's request, with tacit consent of the authorities.

Standing apart from the crowded coffee carts, charts underarm, conversing with Dr. Winner (noting my continued presence with a puzzled frown), she turned politely to greet me when Winner took it upon himself to introduce us. Warming, recognizing my name when he mentioned the U-2, she offered a long thin hand, studying my face momentarily, as if we'd met before.

Close up, she seemed older than I first thought. Her facial features were drawn by fatigue or possibly a lingering illness, judging from the Kleenex she kept in her hand. She had been pretty once, her Nordic features highlighted by a strong chin and teeth, the latter stained by the Dutch cigars she constantly smoked.

"Yes, of course!" she said. "I'd hoped to meet with you earlier, Keith. I've read of your research over Colombia and Mexico; I compared your thermo readings with my analysis of Santorini. Come to think I've your picture in my file at Stockholm, together with Dr. Gomulaka in California, I believe. Poor chap; we were closest of friends, worked together in Indonesia while researching Anak Kratatau. Did you know him well?" I nodded, and furthering my thoughts, asked if she'd been advised by the UN of his replacement.

"Screw the UN! Would you believe the proceedings of yesterday? Latvia, tiny Latvia, out of the blue proposed an ex-Soviet pilot with no confirmable credentials in meteorology! Fortunately, the Russian ambassador voted *nyet*, inciting a squabble with Azerbaijan and Armenia, who apparently were in concurrence. Fiddle faddle, mostly...arguing amongst themselves, ignoring our immediate needs! Typical bureaucracy...overpaid, overstaffed, aside from the workhorses in the field. Nokomo, for instance! With due respect for his OBE, never once did he return my calls to New York! And where was His Excellency when they impounded my computers at customs? Do you know where he was? He'd flown directly to Kos by chartered jet! Furthermore, aside from the birdies with their typewriters, no funding was arranged for our transport beyond Athens!"

"We're working on that," Winner interjected, allowing a breather. "Our consulate contacted the American Embassy and, hopefully, they'll requisition a 'copter from an offshore carrier. Their main concern is the weight of our equipment, Keithy...close to a half-ton. They can accommodate if there's an HH-3-E available. Would that be a Chinook?"

"Same horse! Navy-wise, an updated Sea King," I explained, my attention drawn to a remote corner of the suite.

"When are we to know?" Sigurdesson questioned, expressing anxiety for her computers.

"The Consul said he'd come by with his car at 1600. Said he hoped we could load up at noon tomorrow, depending on availability. Nice chap...Canadian, of course!"

"My computers, Alan?" Winner grinned.

"Should be downstairs by now, compliments of the concierge, my dear! I contacted him earlier and he contacted customs with his cellular." Given a moment while she impulsively bussed Winner's cheek, I stepped aside to better my view of a matronly figure I'd observed while we were discussing the situation.

A latecomer, I assumed, conversing with Fraser and the journalist from Le Monde. Occasionally glancing about, she was dressed in a stylish business suit and a broad-brimmed hat, a press card on her lapel, sunglasses perched owlishly on her nose. Although her ample backside predominated my view, I wondered...might she possibly be Amalia?

"Haven't the vaguest," Winner asided, catching my eye with a smile. "She was standing bar with the German chap when we first arrived.

Sigurdesson, unobserving, produced a pack of cigarillos after a search through her purse.

"Would either of you have a match?" she inquired, frowning at her depleted lighter. I reacted instinctively, remembering the folder in my pocket. Detaching the match, I stared blankly at the sketch penned artistically on the underleaf.

"Zonar's, hey? Try the scratch side, Keithy," Winner commented, noting my bewilderment. "Now you have it...careful!" he warned, when I flamed a match just short of Sigurdesson's nose.

The group had dispersed to the bar (or other venues) when I looked about, noting the departure of my ongoing point of interest with the affable Dr. Fraser and the gentleman from France.

Retreating to the nearest emergency light, I examined the match folder closely, noting the Thurber-like drawing of a gooney bird wearing aviator goggles and a leg watch on the inner fold, the numerals set to three o'clock. 'Bird watch?'...Willitts' code name? The advertisement on the cover indicating his availability at a given time and place! Aviator goggles...ex-RAF! I smiled at the portrayal while I quickly checked my watch. It was on to 2:30 when I located the hotel's emergency stairs and exited to an adjacent street.

I was immediately confronted by the Mercedes, heading a long line of limos, commanding an unobstructed view of the hotel's marble entranceway. Bruno was sprawled in the rear seat with a newspaper and a straw fedora to shade his eyes. Not wanting to disclose my presence to all parties, yet needful to unburden my brief case and blazer, I approached the Mercedes from the street and Lightly tapped on its rear fender. Bruno reacted instantaneously; spinning sideways...reaching beneath his seat, allowing a sheepish nod when he determined it was I.

"Can you hold until four?" I said when he shed the unlikely fedora, noticeably unnerved by my sidelong approach. "I've a quickie appointment up the street and it's better you hang in and keep an eye on the doors, if you know what I mean?"

Bruno nodded quickly, indicating I should pass on whilst I tossed my blazer and brief case rear seat. And, from that moment on, we had an 'understanding'! Bruno grateful when I included my read-out of the seminar's roster...inclusive of the attending members of the press!

The cafes on Syntagma Square were loosely packed with tourists and Athenians when I circled behind the hotel and emerged apparently unnoticed. The conversational topic was universal; gestures surmounted the language barrier. They appeared tired, haggard, and frightened by the upending volcano. A street urchin with a bouquet of roses tagged beside me when I crossed over to the Royal Palace and idled time on the palace grounds. Waiting behind me while I window-shopped the battened stores along Zola Costa. I flushed loose change from my pocket; he grinned. Hardly ten, he looked as if he'd washed his face with his tongue that day; had no shoes, insisted I accept his flowers. I unfolded a bill and sent him on his way. It was 2:45 when I checked my watch.

There was no mistaking Zonar's bright red awning on Panepistimion Avenue. The huge café enveloped a block side with its red tables and chairs, heaping pastry displays, and darting waiters. Business was brisk. Tables fringing the sidewalk were taken, but there were vacancies along the inner aisles. I draped my tie over a chair, place the roses on the adjoining table, ordered coffee and stepped inside the restaurant to see if I had someone waiting.

A stereo blared *Vale Ki'allo piato sto trapezi* to the nearly empty parlor. The locals apparently preferred to stay at home that infamous day following the deluge, aside from a table of four busy with yellow pad and calculator, estimating their damage. A brush-browed pensioner was scrutinizing a day-old copy of the London Times; a blue-jawed heavy was relishing a plate of galaktobourek. A waiter approached and I pointed for the men's room; washed the humidity from my face and returned to my chair to scan the street.

I was on to my second coffee when a dusty Rover dropped Willitts off at the corner. Brown suede shoes, baggy trousers, a blue striped shirt sodden with sweat. He'd shaved his mustache and carried a newspaper furled underarm, his red face glistening with sweat. Aside from his dark glasses, there was no hint of disguise. I shrugged my shoulders and looked away. He eyed the tables at length, nodded briefly, and then plumped himself into a chair by the table where I'd deposited my bouquet of roses.

167

"Bloody hot, hey! Kept you waiting, Slater?"

"You could have borrowed an air-conditioned Rolls from the British Embassy," I replied. He fanned himself with the newspaper.

"Received my message, I see. How nice of you to bring me flowers!"

"You might have called," I replied with a coquettish frown.

"Your phones were tripped, Slater...or were until early this morning."

"By a business rival of Nina's family, I think! A banker known as Tony Metexas?" Willitts nodded.

"My counterpart checked him out, also his affiliates...criminal element with political clout and eyes for the green. We also intercepted low frequency radio transmission from you villa, but I'll get to that."

"Bruno?"

"All right, have it your way! Better known to Interpol as Joseph Piludski, the grandson of a Polish nationalist, same name. During the Cold War he infiltrated the KGB, until he was found out and tortured; they severed his tongue, Slater!"

"Jesus Christ!"

"Ghastly, hey? He later joined the Polish underground, which is non-official. Interpol indicated he's strictly hands off, possibly one of theirs."

"Have you information on Stash Obolensky? I questioned with my hair on end. Willitts briefly eyed the nearby tables.

"Gunned down in Vienna; recently identified at a morgue, Slater. He held special status with Intelligence, I believe, but other than that there's nothing on file."

"Goddamn it to hell!"

"Friend of yours?"

"Yes and no! Is T.S. aware of this?" Willitts nodded.

"Said to break it gently, Slater, which leads to a related matter."

"Gunnar?" I asided.

"Exactly! Seems his support has faded with the ex-KGB of late, although he's not short of funds. He apparently bribed a connection to an ambassador at the UN...which is off the record, by the way...but we do know a former Pact pilot was nominated for your project's observer slot! Apparently he had a change of heart, however, and the Russians nixed the deal! Sees they're rattled by conditions along the Caspian and Black Seas, Slater, what with the hard-liners and their lot...Muslim fundamentalists, more to the point!"

"Has Gunnar be seen lately?"

"Last sighting in Romania. From there his movements are sketchy, but we spotted his mistress at Hellinikon days back. Odd sort, not difficult to track, she frequents a bistro up the boulevard where the so-called local element hangs out, mostly at night. Other times, she's at the Grande Bretagne."

"Have you an agent there?" I asked from curiosity. Willitts nodded.

"Local gent, source of our information actually, Interpol, but don't prompt for an introduction, Slater!"

There came an immediate halt to our conversation when a foursome of tourists commandeered the adjoining table. Italian, perspiring profusely, a jovial lot...the ladies in shorts and loose halters, the men wearing longies and faddish shirts, their chests draped with gold chains and amulets. Chain-smoking, quickly into am liter of wine and a double order of spanakopita, apparently a ready item from Zonar's enormous marbled buffet. Judging from their tickets and luggage, they were waiting for the Alitalia jitney, standing empty at curbside with the driver asleep at the wheel?

By then the tables were virtually filled and the waiter nervously in need of ours. Willitts into his second gin and tonic seemingly preoccupied with a match folder and the waiter's ballpoint pen. He'd paid his tab and was waiting for change, realizing (as I had) we'd draw attention if we moved elsewhere to continue our conversation. Quick of wit, no less a gentleman, Willitts drained his glass and gathering my roses from his table, graciously tendered the lot to the grinning Italians! Asiding "See you at Kos" when he jostled my chair, he dropped the match folder in my lap on his way out.

It was after four when I emerged in the lobby of the GB via the underground tunnel from the annex across the street. The rotund gentleman was seated in his favorite chair, seemingly surprised by the direction of my entrance, returning my wink with a defeated shrug when I made straight away for the bar, now jammed to capacity with the air conditioning restored. I located Winner having a beer with the Canadian Consul (judging from his blazer, a miniature maple leaf affixed to its lapel). Thirty-odd, his rosy complexion and brownish hair, neatly clipped and combed, reminded me of Willitts; his accent implied he'd been schooled in the UK.

Bearer of good news, however. Courtesy of the US Sixth Fleet and the American Embassy, we'd have a heavy 'copter available tomorrow noon!

"No later than 1300," the Consul cautioned. "Chap at the American Embassy advised they'll need to refuel and change crews; said they've been flying rescue mission since dawn. I understand they're evacuating Navy personnel from Athens and Crete, presumably to the carriers offshore, Major Alter."

"Mr. Slater," I corrected, noting Winner raising an eye from his beer. "I've no connection with the military," I added, "other than past service in the Gulf." The Consul seemed puzzled.

"Embassy chap said you were listed as such with the priority fax they'd received from the Pentagon. Most likely to expedite an official requisition with the navy department, which is the norm in like circumstances. Matter of fact, the order apparently was in process when Alan came by our office, although we weren't fully apprised until three! Nevertheless, it's all said and done! Cheers," he added, "tout le meilleur pour votre project at Kos!"

I suspected T.S.'s long-reaching hand from his headquarters at Riyadh! Aware of the emergencies in Athens, he'd be anxious to have us established at Kos. Perhaps he'd 'greased wheels' at the Embassy, not knowing the Canadians' efforts were coincidental. Whatever the case, it was gratifying to realize the Pentagon had a handle on the situation when Nokomo had us up for grabs. Their source of information? Most likely Keenan's 'enlightened' chain of command; Willitts most likely!

Ex-RAF, unknown to Gunnar's generation, according to T.S. Not lacking as an artist, his message was vividly clear when I fingered his match folder and chanced a look-see? Expertly sketched, the flailing gooney bird, now burdened with a pencil and pad under wing…goggles as before, indicating we'd be joined at Kos by a member of the press!

"Problems, Keithy?" Winner questioned from his beer. "Try them judiciously, one by one. Practice makes perfect! More to the point," he added seriously, when I crumpled the folder to a cuspidor, "we've an ongoing problem with Ingrid, I believe! Cancer, Keith! Confessed as much when I saw the medication in her room."

"Terminal?" I questioned immediately. Winner nodded.

"Sloan-Kettering gave her six weeks! Her husband's American; died a few years back. Same thing!"

"Holy shit!"

"Won't help! She's a tough bird, Keithy. Intends to carry on; like, it's her last time around and Santorini's a mountain she hasn't climbed. In other words, we have to look after her, treat her lightly. As for the cigars?" Winner shrugged, stroking his beard. "Said they're one of the few remaining pleasures of life, and doesn't intend to give them up!"

"Jackets after five, gentlemen!" the bartender announced. I stared at my face in the mirror, wondering where I'd left my tie. Haggard from the long day, needing a shave, stunned by the disclosure of Sigurdesson's malady, I ordered a pair of boilermakers to help us along with the beer.

170

It was after five, the Consul long departed, and the bar emptied for lack of jackets when I agreed to meet Winner at the Navy base next day at 11:30. Mindful of Nina's needs, I bought a package of bandages at the lobby shop, together with a gift-wrapped bottle of Yardley's Lavender and a day-old issue of the London Times. The lobby was virtually deserted, inclusive of the portly gentleman who'd abandoned his chair. Apparently, with Hellinikon in operation, the tourists had departed *en masse*.

The Mercedes was not in evidence when the concierge followed me out the door. Instead, parked firmly in its place, Nina's Jaguar was in the process of being washed.

"Your wife came at three," the concierge allowed, handing me the keys. "Said she needed your car and driver to help move things from her office. Borrowed my pliers, in fact!"

"Was she okay?"

"Appeared so; limped a little. Said her shoes hurt and it was difficult to drive. Beautiful lady, Mr. Slater. I knew her Papa! Said she'd be home before dark, not to worry. Had my boy clean it up a bit," he added. "Not many 140s around anymore." I thanked him for his courtesy with sufficient tip to accommodate the pliers and the boy. I also noted a pair of garden gloves alongside the Jaguar's shift stick, the lingering scent of Nina's lavender when I keyed the 'straight eight' to a crackling roar.

* * * * * *

The villa was a scene of activity when I pulled in around six and was confronted with a van parked alongside the portico. Auntie had apparently decided to transport her paintings and antiques to Mt. Parnassus for safekeeping, including the grand piano, which was already aboard. How she'd arranged the van, I'll never know. The telephones were useless; possibly she'd exercised her three-wheeler, or requested Nina's assistance when she sped off with the Jaguar. No question, there'd been a family decision to vacate the villa for higher ground. Most likely with Nina's goading, I suspected, when she arrived with Bruno and Nick's collection of memos. Tired but upbeat, she'd retrieved a laptop computer to take along to Kos, together with a modem to communicate with Uncle's office. With Bruno's help, she had rewired the mainstay connections to her lawyer's unlisted line!

"Fortunately, the lawyer was in his office and realized I was upset when I appeared out of nowhere with my bandages and a pair of pliers!" she said.

"Bastard Metexas! And, you'll never guess what Uncle discovered in the brambles, Keith!" I knew exactly what she meant but reasoned it best to let her unwind!

"It was after one and I was yet in bed," Nina explained. "Like, I itched but couldn't scratch, decided to get up when I heard Uncle outside the garden window. Auntie said he'd found a loose wire amongst his hibiscus and, thinking it was hot, was trying to disconnect the thing. You'd left with Bruno and, knowing Uncle's ineptness, I hiked my nightie and traced it to a box that came loose from our utility pole and it fell in the neighbor's trees. Same bloody thing, Keith, hooked to uncle's telephone line! He wouldn't believe me, of course."

"Did you report it to the crew in the street?"

"No way! I borrowed Auntie's camera after I showered and changed. Our lawyer has the lot now. Said he'd file for an immediate investigation but with Athens in a dither, who knows? Like Papa's accident report, the authorities are out to lunch! Quick to assess our estate tax, however! Shady business is one thing, but if they find its sabotage, I'll..."

"We'll invite him for sandwiches and hemlock tea! Change of subject, Nina! We're off tomorrow at twelve, compliments of the Navy."

"Frigate or light cruiser?"

"Two hour hop with a helicopter. Economy, no lunch!"

"Okay, gives me time for a chat with the girls in the office, provided they show up. Change of schedule, Keith? We had reservations with Olympic."

I explained the circumstances in general terms, mentioning my conversation with Winner, that she'd have time to get acquainted with Dr. Sigurdesson and the group before we dispersed at Antimahia. Of this, Nina was delighted; more so looking forward to time aboard the Helena.

"Frankly, I'm bushed, Keith. Need a couple of days in the sun to charge my batteries. As a husband, you've been more than forgiving! The past weeks have been chaotic, such as last night when I was someone else. *Someone else?* That's what bothers me mostly, my love. So maybe with a few days privacy, you can decide if I'm a freak..."

"...or a good cook!"

"I'll buy that, so long as we make love and skip dessert! But, aside from your insatiable appetite, I'm famished! Rain check for your starving bride?"

Despite the confusion of loading the van, there was an unmistakable aroma of moussaka from Auntie's kitchen. Judging from the clatter of pans, the cook was totally in command. Promptly at eight, we were treated to a sit-down dinner of moussaka and roast lamb, and a chilled bottle of Santorini white, followed by feta cheese and Greek coffee, together with a snifter of Metaxa to ease the strain of a very long day.

Despite problems with fork and spoon, Nina was in high spirits...communicative, relaying Uncle's comments in English. In part, they'd agreed the villa was not to be totally abandoned, with Uncle deciding it was best if he stayed on.

"Better he tend to business," Auntie explained, grasping my hand, saddened at the prospect of leaving the old man behind. "Come tomorrow, it's important I fix cottage near sister at Mt. Parnassus," she said. "Not so long drive, two hours with Mercedes. Nina come often to Athens, hey? Need hand at office, need place to sleep, I think? At Kos she have Auntie Cleo and Captain Stavos. Many old friends, Keith, maybe have time to sail the Helena. Nicholas would like that," she whispered, her eyes filling with tears.

"You're not to worry!" Nina said. "I'll be in touch every day and Bruno intends to stay on! He's not deaf to English, Auntie, nor French with which Uncle is better acquainted, for when Bruno needs directions."

I cocked an ear to this. Bruno apparently multi-lingual, and obviously handy with pliers! Whatever his guise or motivation to stay on, in a short span of time he'd nurtured in Nina an element of trust, and I wasn't displeased. Apart from their safety, there'd be a continuing need for transportation. With the conditions in the streets, the elderly couple would need his service with the Mercedes, as would Nina when she commuted to Athens. Considering an exodus from all parts, the airport would become an avenue of convergence, a focal point for interested parties. I held the thought in abeyance when a rumbling after-shock rattled our dishes and brought the cook from Auntie's kitchen.

Nina slept soundly when we'd showered and reassembled our bed. Swathed with bandages and Vaseline, she clung to my back without a murmur. I was grateful for her warmth and femininity, thankful she'd survived her grueling spill by the sea and bounced back with determination. When I stirred awake during the night, my thoughts were given to an endless review of the unbelievable events since we'd met on the beach at Big Sur. All the while, as if reflecting my thoughts, the ghoulish glow from Santorini was steadfast in our window, never ceasing throughout the night until paled by the early dawn.

CHAPTER

ina was up and gone when I stirred at seven o'clock. Her luggage packed and waiting by the door, her towels draped on a chair to dry. The necklace retrieved from where I'd hidden it in my shaving kit, I was quick to note when I made my way to the frigid shower. Outside, the sky was gloomy gray. Judging from her sandal prints on the porch, the prevailing breeze had shifted to the southeast during the night and showered Kavouri with a grimy layer of ash.

"Nina take Jaguar to office," Auntie announced, when I joined her for coffee in the kitchen. "She say she return at eleven; have importance to discuss with staff. Uncle have problem to come awake," she added. "Poor dear, mix ouzo with Metaxa, I think. Worry for tanks at Piraeus if come another deluge. Worry for business, and Nina too, but not of you, my son. Say you have steady eye like Nicholas; depressed you not stay."

Bruno was also up and gone, as was Auntie's three-wheeler, I noticed when I carried our luggage to the Mercedes, which was thoughtfully covered with a tarp in the garage. With petrol in short supply, he'd most likely taken the bike to market, possibly to pick up the morning Herald Tribune at the nearby Astir. Hadn't Auntie remarked of his habitual morning stroll? I gave thought to this when I spotted my blazer on the rear seat...carefully folded, unnoticed, together with my brief case and program from White Dove, all of which I'd totally forgotten in the process of sharing a beer with Winner at the GB.

My brief case was unlocked, but it contained little of interest, other than a study manual of the hybrid U-2, which was strictly off the shelf. The roster had been thumbed, however, absentees underlined with a pencil, inclusive of Dr. Nokomo, a member of his staff, and Horst Gunnar – the latter two followed by a question mark in the margin...conceivably for my attention?

Aside from Obturi and the winsome English lass at the UN, I wasn't familiar with Nokomo's staff, nor did *H. Schumann* ring a bell. Presumably he was a latecomer, or a tagalong from New York. Bruno's relationship with the Astir more interesting at the moment. The chic hotel was a gathering spot for the international set; lately with executive types and entrepreneurs of sorts, such as Amalia during her rounds. In Bruno's instance, if he had a contact on the premises, or was on his own, he'd pass as a middling handyman-chauffeur from down the street...apart from the brown paper bag he often carried, possibly as a lethal reminder of three dead Poles waiting their revenge!

According to Willitts, Bruno's presence was known to Interpol and, presumably, military intelligence. They'd apparently developed an alliance for ferreting information...possibly leads from underworld sources, interconnected with the likes of Amalia...or an ongoing investigation of murder and sabotage, linked with suspicion of bribery to conceal the facts! This would explain the why of Interpol at a local level, and Bruno's furthering interest, judging from the rapport he'd established with the family. If so, he'd most likely play it cool at Kavouri and wait his turn. Better left for Willitts, I thought. At Kos, I'd need a clear head!

Of immediate concern was Auntie's curio cabinet, a priceless piece of art nouveau she insisted be sandwiched with mattresses at the rear of the van, requiring reshuffling when she discovered it had been loaded previously with her grand piano. All of this with the temperature in the high 90s! A baker's oven inside the van! Stripping to my shorts, I lent a hand when the crew threatened the old lady with overtime. And about 10:30, the van labored from the portico, the driver puzzling Auntie's directions to her sister's home at Mt. Parnassus.

The utility crew arrived shortly thereafter and Auntie made productive use of a line they jerry-rigged from the pole, which was of keen interest to Uncle when they detached the illegal recorder and tossed it, without comment, to the trash inside their truck.

In the interim, Bruno had appeared with Auntie's three-wheeler and victuals from the market, mostly in high-standing paper bags, which I eyed reproachfully while he sorted the lot between the pantry and the Mercedes. His floppy fedora, of which he'd apparently grown fond, sufficed our lack of eye contact when he proceeded to his flat.

Sweating profusely from my turn in the van, wanting a dip in the sea but short of time, I located a brace of towels and skimmed a film of ash from the pool. Waiting for Nina, assuming she'd have like thoughts, I heard the 140 parting traffic along the avenue. The gates were ajar when she thundered the portico; the Jaguar with its top down was grimy with ash, as was my bride when she braked full stop short of our luggage! Smiling gleefully when I pointed to the pool, she stripped to whatever, abandoning her sandals en route, unmindful of her wounds. We plunged the cooling depths, neither of us realizing we were sharing the last minutes of our last day together at the family home in Kavouri.

* * * * * *

The drive from Kavouri to the Navy base was a nightmarish experience. What with the sun a dull red apple in the murky sky, and headlights bobbing like jack o' lanterns when we turned on to the expressway; tail lights flashed repeatedly when we queued with the stop-and-go traffic. The outbound lanes were congested with vehicles of all descriptions, laden with household possession, presumably fleeing to the highlands of Greece. Along the walkways, spirits were obviously at low ebb; the pedestrians masked with gauze or holding handkerchiefs to their mouths. The ashy grit was everywhere, together with the oppressive summer heat and lack of a freshing breeze.

We observed all of this from behind tinted windows in the air-conditioned Mercedes. The Mercedes was knee-high with cartons from Auntie's larder; sweets for relatives at Kos, canned goods for the Helena, a fresh bougatsa pie for Captain Stavos; our luggage secured in the trunk with goodies from the market. I shared the front seat with Bruno; Nina back seat with Auntie, her cigarette smoke curling while they discussed business in rapid-fire Greek.

Bruno, proper in his uniform cap, slowed for the security gate when we entered the base, lowering his window to allow me to tender my pass. His attention seemingly elsewhere; eyes narrowed, his expression indicated he was immersed in a time span…reflective, introspective…perhaps viewing a flashback; the tethered aircraft, the military presence from another time? Instinctively returning the yeoman's salute when he returned my pass.

The Sixth Fleet helicopter was idling its turbines on the ramp when we drew close to unload. Sigurdesson and Winner were waiting at operations with their luggage and Ingrid's computers; Edwards and Fraser just checking the equipment they'd retrieved from Swissair. Our copilot tallied the lot with his weights and balance list, although we were six plus crew and the 'copter would accommodate twenty-five fully loaded troops. Litters, together with medical supplies, were loaded into the rear compartment. The Sea Hawk, apart from the diversion to Kos, was primed for rescue missions at sea.

Logistics done, I hugged the old lay and bussed her cheek, helped Nina from the car. Refreshed by her swim, her dampish hair gathered with a scarf, she wore a lightweight skirt and blouse to fend the humidity, clenched her fingers to conceal her bruises, and smiled gamely when I introduced Winner and Sigurdesson, loosening her impish grin when Edwards complimented her earrings. Happy with new acquaintances, she was immediately taken by Ingrid, having read of her work in the field of volcanology. They arranged to sit side by side, chattering incessantly after she'd waved to Auntie and the crew chief guard strapped the open port.

Winner and Edwards sat in the rear of the cabin astride their equipment to balance the weight in the forward compartments; Fraser rode alongside his laptop PC and reams of notes. A dozen litters were strapped opposing a double tier of bucket seats midway in the cabin, remindful of the Air Force Jolly Green Giants' heroic rescue missions in northern Vietnam. Our pilot, a dusky Navy Lieutenant Commander, motioned me forward to buckle in with the chief, visually checking our belts; he nodded to the fire guard and engaged the rotors. The twin GEs whined as he applied full thrust; we hovered to point the windsock, then rose rapidly over the hangars toward the open sea.

The commander paralleled the active runway at 300 feet until ATC confirmed a heading of 135 degrees at altitude 1,500 and requested a fix from the Sea Hawk's transponder. Noting Kos lay 30 degrees further east, I casually inquired if they'd had a change of plan. The commander leveled off at 1,500 feet before he answered; picked up 180 knots and turned in his seat.

"We've an emergency request to divert to Thera, Major. Came last minute while we were filing at operations. Seems an archeological group's stranded at Akrotiri; their DC-3 charter had to turn back with a blown engine. It's no wonder; the damned grit ain't good for proper flyin', man! Like, I worry for our GE-5s all the while. Place is a seething hellhole, Slater. We did double duty this morning…six from a fishing smack and a dozen litter cases from the village. You have to see it to believe it! Reminds one of Dunkirk when the Brits had the Nazis up their ass!"

The commander turned his attention to the turbine readings, jocked the stick between his legs and discussed an ash ingestion problem with the chief. Sweat coursed from their helmets, the humidity heavy from the greenhouse effect. Visibility was down to three miles in the haze; the lumbering Sea Hawk wallowed and lurched in the unstable air. Contacted by ATC, he reset the transponder and made a note to his copilot, a lieutenant junior grade from Charleston, South Carolina.

"Watch out for an Olympic MD-80 barreling from Mykonos at 4,000, they think! They don't have him on radar, most likely huggin' the deck VFR! It's like flyin' in a beehive, Slater…a couple of days back we had a near miss with a

Libyan 707."

The visibility improved as we closed on Santorini, however. The sun brightened; the pall fell steadily behind us. The immense cloud of ash boiling from the caldera had cast an anvil head in the stratosphere, feathering a 300-mile swath to the northwest, engulfing Athens and the mainland until the winds aloft would readjust to carry it further south.

From twenty miles, I could visualize a pending catastrophe in its accelerating stages. The fallout had increased during the past 48 hours; volcanic mass encompassed a third of the ancient caldera. Nea Kamene had been enjoined to its smoldering flank; tongues of lava veined the slopes and licked the sea. An angry glow rose intermittently from the cone, juggling tons of volcanic debris to the boiling Aegean.

When we closed on the village, Sigurdesson slipped from her seat, unobserved by the crew, but I had a fleeting glimpse of her legs when I looked back to check on Nina. Worried, I nudged the chief when she made her way to the open port with a brace of cameras slung from her shoulders, obviously intent on photographing the village or, at long range, the volcano.

It happened quickly, before we could react...a surging updraft caught the Sea Hawk and lofted it towards the inferno; the helicopter spun on its axis, nose high, verging a stall. Sigurdesson's screams sounded above the turbine as she somersaulted the barrier, clinging desperately for purchase.

Aware of a problem, the commander righted the floundering 'copter and looked back, shouting to the chief when he spied Sigurdesson hanging like a bean bag with her weighty cameras pulling her towards the inescapable abyss. Wherever I gathered the strength — or the courage — I'm not sure. Sensing the chief was indecisive, I snagged the safety line underarm and, sprawling head first, managed to grip Ingrid's thin wrist. From there it was nip and tuck until the chief bolted from his seat and we hauled the unconscious Swede from the port, lengthened a seat belt and strapped her to a bucket seat.

The commander was livid.

"Tell her this ain't no goddamned camera safari," he bellowed. "You, too!" he warned Winner, who was attempting to help. "Get back in your seat, you fucking idiot! Is she okay, Slater? Seems like she passed!"

"*Min foto's...min fotograf apparfi!*" Sigurdesson groaned, semi-conscious, groping blindly for her cameras, a spittle of blood foaming her lips.

"Give her a shot!" the commander shouted from the cockpit, his attention given to the heavy turbulence as he banked over the village towards Akrotiri. The chief reached for the medic kit, but I had other thoughts. Anchoring a foot to a seat, I slapped her gently on the cheek. A sudden down draft sufficed, however, bringing her upright against the restraining straps, her eyes wide with terror when she spied the open port.

"Is unbelievable," she gasped. "So close to Santorini I almost fall!" Excuse please, I think I have bled." Reaching weakly for her purse, she coughed into a tissue and swallowed a pill with a jigger of brandy Nina had thoughtfully brought along.

There were others aside from Petrie's group awaiting our arrival when we rounded a hilltop church and descended on Akrotiri. Forty or fifty, perhaps, with more trailing the Sea Hawk in vehicles or on foot. Black-shawled women, laborers from the dig, their ragtag suitcases and bundles underarm. The commander hovered at 20 feet and inadvertently dusted the lot.

"Break out a shotgun, Chief. You're not to load," he added, "it's just for show, man. Understand?" The chief nodded and unbuckled his belt. The commander motioned the copilot to take over, swiveled in his seat.

"Which one is Dr. Petrie, Slater?" I pointed to a rumpled seersucker suit and the tiny lady by his side. The commander handed me his bullhorn.

"Tell him we'll take twenty as far as Kos, countin' students and children, and no more! If they run for my ship I'm clearin' the deck! Can't risk them kids getting' trampled! So where's a right place to set down?"

I pointed to the area where the Alhouette had landed and blared his instructions to the crowd. A barrel-chested local who understood English faced the lot with a show of authority, motioning them to stand back until they formed an arc alongside the operations tent. Satisfied the chief was in position with the shotgun, the commander nodded and resumed control. A deft pilot, despite the freakish winds he maneuvered the 10-ton Sikorsky to a slow descent, easing the rotors as it settled on its struts with an audible 'whoosh'.

Cautioning the copilot to remain in his seat, the commander unfastened and made his way aft. Warning the group to stay put, he peered closely at Sigurdesson, who'd drowsed asleep on Nina's shoulder, cameras loosely held in her lap. I assumed he had medical experience from rescue missions or past education; he tested her pulse, checked her eyes, and held his hand on her forehead, noting the blood on her blouse and labored breath.

"Did she have a shot?" he asked the chief.

"No, sir! She took herself a pill...painkiller, I think." The commander nodded and turned to Nina.

"You alright, ma'am?"

"Scared silly, but don't worry about me! She had a nasty spill, Commander.

Hemorrhaging…"

"Not from the spill, ma'am. Her lungs need medical attention. Best keep her quiet until we get to Kos, Mrs. Slater. Okay, twenty minutes to stretch your legs! He announced, addressing the group. "Stay close in, like we might have a problem with them folks wantin' your seats!"

The commander dropped to the ground and stayed close by while I had a reassuring word with Nina, noticing her eyes were riveted to the cove beyond the ravine. With the chief standing guard, we proceeded to meet with Petrie, halting briefly when Butterfield broke ranks and darted alongside.

"My goodness, it's you Keith Slater! How nice of you to come!" she said, dimpling her square-toothed smile as she skipped alongside to keep pace.

"My pleasure, fair lady! Miss Butterfield, Commander Whitehead! He's come to take you to Kos until you've means of transportation, my sweet!" She curtsied to acknowledge the commander's gentlemanly bow, and tagged along while I introduced Dr. Petrie and the others in tow. The commander laid it on the line when he observed Petrie's boxes of crated artifacts, however.

"No way!" he said, handing the doctor a tally pad. "We'll be needing your students' names and country of origin, including yourself and the young lady. Navy regulations, Doctor… how many all told?" Petrie blinked, shaking his head, seemingly bewildered by the commander's stern black face. An associate professor stepped forward to tick them off, circulating the pad for names and addresses.

"Eight including Dr. Petrie and myself, Commander. All from the UK."

The commander scrutinized the nervous group, mentally calibrating their weight with his diminishing fuel load, adjusting for our immediate party and equipment, allowing for the 90°-plus temperature and unstable air. Then, scanning the line of wishful faces, he turned to the barrel-chested Greek.

"I'll take twenty of your kinfolk, fella. The youngest and the oldest, no more than thirty pounds of luggage, and I want them strapped under belt! Do you hear me loud and clear?" The Greek nodded, his mouth ajar, however, his fingers clutching the crucifix dangling from his neck. The locals backed away, wide-eyed, as if the Sea Hawk had fetched a creature from outer space. The commander turned quickly, puzzling the open door; I spun on my heel!

Nina stood in the open bay with her golden earrings glistening in the sun, her long black hair flowing to her shoulders, her eyes fixed in the distance, as if she were in a hypnotic trance. Seemingly aware of the surroundings but not of the bystanders, her arm raised towards the ancient ravine, the necklace dangled from her fingers as if intended as an offering to the bellicose volcano.

The crowd hushed to silence, their eyes fixed on her gleaming necklace. The students stumbled upon one another, whispering amongst themselves. A bay whimpered, unattended; a donkey brayed. I sensed Butterfield's hand on my arm. "My God, she's the image of the girl in the fresco, Keith! *Is she your wife?*" Nina slipped to the ground and walked dreamlike towards the cove, as if bidden by the ancient steps leading to the sea. The crowd parted silently to let her pass. An old woman drew a shawl to her face, pointed to the necklace, fingering her beads. An audible gasp came from close by; the pendant's eyes glowered ominously, as if it were alive!

"God in heaven! Catch up with her, Keith, she's likely to fall!" Butterfield shouted, hurrying beside me as I circled the immobilized crowd. I called softly to Nina so as not to frighten her, realizing she was in a deep traumatic trance. Called out again, but she slipped away, her eyes fixed upon the boat in the cove.

Her arms hung loosely at her sides as she majestically descended the steps – her bearing suggesting she'd stepped from the fresco to join a ceremony in the cove. Was the cobbled path before her lined with ancients waving their feathered plumes in rhythm with rumbling drums? Was there a fleet lying at anchor, a fleet of ancient ships awaiting her procession? Waiting to take her to Arhannes, to the sacrificial temple of her recurring dreams?

A muffled explosion rumbled from the caldera; a gaseous vent opened, emitting a piercing shriek in ultrasonic decibels. Gas flamed and writhed upward, reflected from the anvil head in the sky. The ground jellied; we fell to our knees clasping our ears. The volcano belched; the shrieking faded; then, an unearthly silence prevailed.

"Five minutes, Slater!" the commander bellowed. "We've got a mess of trouble coming down the turnpike...shake it! Go git her, man!"

Nina stopped short of the entrance leading to the dig, turning her head slowly to stare into the shadows. I ran to her side and reached for her arm, but she held it rigidly to her side and her eyes were not for me. Her lips moved, voicing words in a strange language. An agonized voice whispered, "Pyrrha!" from the darkness, as if the legendary name had been torn from his soul. An icy shiver descended my spine.

His eyes were like two black holes from the depths of space; reflected no light. His face as white as the homespun tunic he wore; his legs wrapped with leather thongs. Not as tall as I... slightly built, handsome in a strange way, his dark hair bearing ringlets of gray.

"Deuca comes from Praisos," Butterfield intoned, clutching my arm. "He came to is with his boat, which is anchored in the cove."

181

He spoke to Nina softly, in a language that was not Greek; she hesitantly answered with like words that seemed to echo from an ancient tomb. As she moved trance-like towards the voice, a terrible sense of helplessness – a ghastly premonition – drained the blood from my heart!

"Lordy, she's the likeness of the fresco he's drawn in the fourth room," Butterfield whispered. "He's speaking words from the ancient language, asking her, I believe, to come and see the drawing. Strange, she seems to understand! Might they have met before?"

Behind us I was aware of compounding confusion spurred by the tremor; of beeping vehicles approaching the village, the hysterical screaming of women and children, expletives and cursing exchanging vibes with the bullhorn. A warning blast of a shotgun, then the quickening 'flap' of the Sea Hawk's twin rotors!

"Damn it, he's taking off!" Butterfield shrilled as we spun about. "Lordy, the dust and all those people. Will he be able to take us aboard, Keith?"

An enormous shadow provided the answer; the Sea Hawk descended the ravine like a giant condor seeking its prey. Its rotary wings stirred a cyclonic dust in its wake, scattering ladders and debris with its down-thrusting blades, whipping Nina's skirt to her midriff as she turned suddenly about, her eyes widened with terror!

"Heads up, Slater!" the chief shouted from the open bay, the gun cradled in his arm. "We'll take the ladies first. Move it, man! Git the tall skinny one before she loses her skirt!"

The helicopter hovered over the pathway with its turbines laboring from the heavy load, squaring with the breeze as I hoisted Butterfield by the seat of her jeans and turned to collect Nina. A roof section of the dig collapsed from the down wash as I ran to her side. Deuca's cadaverous face receded into the shadows, disappearing from the entrance when I tucked Nina under my arm and scrambled to the thundering Sea Hawk. She came willingly, smiling weakly when I stripped the necklace from her throat and settled her firmly in the open bay.

I wasn't last aboard, however. Shouting from a dead run, clinging desperately to the trailing barrier belt, the barrel-chested Greek eyeballed the wary chief. The chief undecided until a child wailed for his papa and he hauled him in by the seat of his pants. Directing him aft with a heavy shoe. Glowering all the while...juggling his controls, mindful of the mob descending the ravine...the commander rotated the overloaded helicopter. Motioning the chief and me to belt up, he rounded the headland at Enchendra and sped for the open sea.

With his load balanced and the Sea Hawk gathering knots, the commander nodded when I unbuckled to check Nina and Sigurdesson. Strangely, completely out of context with the macabre scene in the ravine, the twosome were sharing comments and the brandy from Nina's flask – as ladies are prone to do when they're party to a misadventure of their making. Nina glancing apprehensively at me, Sigurdesson hard put to believe she'd nearly bought the park when I hauled her aboard with her bloody cameras. The commander glowering all the while, but then that's the way ladies are.

Directly behind us, Winner, Edwards, Fraser, Dr. Petrie, the associate professor and Butterfield were into the six pack from Auntie's larder, comparing notes...happy to be off the 'rock'! And, searching further aft, I located my brief case midst our luggage. The black-shawled elderly ladies nodding their approval when I tossed the damnable necklace inside and snapped the lock!

We flew the 120 miles to Kos in forty-five minutes. Passing the lovely island of Astipalea midway, we raised the mountainous shoreline of Turkey at 2:45. The Dodecanese lay to the right off our course...arid, brown, like pebbles strewn upon the powder blue Aegean. The hazy outline of Rhodos lay sixty miles further south.

From the windscreen view, Kos resembled a swag-tailed fish entering the pincer hold of two jutting peninsulas: mainland Turkey. As we closed in, I was surprised by the proximity of the 40-mile island to Turkish authority. The upper peninsula lay within sculling distance of the northern shore; the southern peninsula at most an hour's sail.

"There's no commerce with the mainland," Nina commented, slipping beside me. "The Turks are uptight and we Greeks have lookout posts along the beaches. At night, however, it's a smuggler's dream."

I gripped her arm closely. Rebounding from her trance-like wanderings, she was on to her usual self again, her spirits aroused, anticipating our arrival at Antimahia. Was she aware of the trauma at Arhannes, I wondered...might she have thought she had fallen from the door, as Dr. Sigurdesson had? Hopefully, until she looked down at her bandaged fingers, smiling apologetically.

"You needn't tell me, I know! I blanked and wandered off again."

"You need a rest, honey."

"I need a psychiatrist! You're being kind. Ingrid just told me I took a stroll in the ravine, and I don't remember a damned thing except for that volcano blowing its nose! And all these people, do they come from Thira?"

"From nearby. The commander's one sweet guy; the Navy would bust his ass if they knew we were overloaded!" She turned to scan the crowded cabin; an elderly woman drew her shawl, a child giggled. Nina frowned. I pointed to the port windscreen for change of venue.

"Is that the city of Kos the east end of the island?" She leaned from my shoulder to see; the scent of her lavender quickened my heart, I loved her so!

"That would be the capital, and there's the harbor between the two jetties. The Helena should be in now. Might you ask the commander to circle, Keith?" I shook my head.

"I wouldn't dare, honey. He's due back at Athens at 1700. How far is the airstrip from town?"

"Thirty kilometers. We could phone the café across from the docks. If Captain Stavos is there, he'll pick us up with the van." She turned to pass a few minutes with Dr. Petrie.

The commander nosed the sea hawk along the coast at 1,200 feet, setting up the tower frequency. The bilingual operator asked the commander to stand by.

"Navy 887! Cleared to land following the Olympic 737 departure," the overhead speaker sounded. "Please use the paved section of the ramp."

"We'll drop off the refugees and students first, major," the commander announced. "Best your party stand by, or remain aboard."

The field complex evidently was two part and divided mid-center by the active runway. Directly below us, the recently constructed commercial terminal abutted a busy ramp; an Olympic 737 was clearing the area where we would be setting down. Beyond the tower, a cargo DC-3 and a Swiss Lear-24 were in process of refueling, an assortment of private aircraft was parked elsewhere.

To the east – across the strip – lay the former terminal buildings...the abandoned tower, a rusty hangar, and several newly painted Quonset huts. The ramp was overgrown with grass and weeds, although there was evidence of mowing in recent weeks. For the most part, the area was consigned to the local militia, subject to a short-term lease to the UN.

Parked on the scrubby tarmac, obstructing our view of the hangar, an Air Force C-141 was offloading an abbreviated fire rescue truck. An outsized fuel tanker, apparently first out, was parked nearby; the flight crew lounged beneath the wing. The C-5 was long gone, but there was evidence of the U-2, a spar of blue and white thrusting beyond! Realizing my interest, the commander made a wide banking turn, pointing across the way as we cleared to land – and there she was!

Glossy white in the slanting sun, the UN's blue insignia was painted on her high-standing tail. Her long needle nose was shaded with tarpaulin. Graceful to the eye, a beauty in the sky, yet a bastard to fly! One hundred and three feet of wingspan and sensor pods, our hump-backed tandem version of the U-2R! The flickering reflection of white and blue was quickly lost from view. Towering in the distance, as if vying for attention and not unseen, the anvil head over Santorini glowered ominously from the horizon like a monstrous cobra rising from a basket of fire.

"Seems you got yourself competition," the chief commented, noticing Nina peering from my shoulder. "Sorry, ma'am," he added when she glared a response. "I ain't never seen a U-2 close up! Excuse me, Major! I was admiring the bird, but didn't say it right, I reckon!"

A bevy of Red Cross ladies greeted the refugees when they descended, hefting their belongings from the bay. Last but not least, the chest Greek with his son underarm blurted his thanks to the weary chief. I jumped to the tarmac to guide Petrie and his students to the transient facility, whilst the commander stood by to count heads; his copilot on the horn with ATC. Butterfield was last out, the chief handing her down until her toes touched the ground. Shouldering her haversack, she came to my side. Her chin smudged with dust, her mop of curly hair awry from the rotor's wash. A tear coursed her cheek as she looked up to study my face with her straightforward blue eyes.

"Is this to be good-bye, Keith?"

"Afraid so, Lesleigh. Space available, they'll most likely book your group to Athens by tonight." She turned to shade her eyes from the sun, wiping her face with the corner of her sleeve.

"Dr. Petrie plans to stay on a few days. There's an early Bronze Age cave at Aspri Petra that hasn't been dug."

"With his students?"

"He hasn't the bloody funds, Keith. I've offered to pay my bed and board, however. Would you be upset if I stayed on?"

"Upset?" Words eluded me as I realized what she meant! Puppy love at my age? Shaking her head, she stirred a pebble with her shoe, her eyes glazed with tears.

"I can't bear to leave you," she murmured. "So, maybe I'm an idiot! I've known you so briefly, but I know your heart, Keith. And some day you'll need me...I know, I just know!" she added tearfully. Slipping away before I could collect my wits and explain the facts of marriage. Nina eyed me curiously when we boarded the Sea Hawk for the short trip across the strip. Nodding to the fire guard, the commander juiced the turbines, engaging the rotors. Hovering short of the runway to await a flashing green light, we quickly passed over to the obsolescent terminal ramp, dusting the C-141 as the Sea Hawk settled alongside

185

the AV tanker to replenish its fuel.

We were met by a militia lieutenant, who shared a Jeep with my crew chief, immediately recognizable from a photograph in my file. Formerly with the 99th at Beale, MacDougal was a ruddy-raced Irishman on the short side of sixty. He'd been loaned by Lockheed to mother the U-2, knowledgeable of its innards – and T.S.'s black box. A warm friendly bear of a man, he wore a Dodgers baseball cap with its visor pointed aft, a pair of rumpled shorts that fell beneath his knees, and an unlikely Berkeley T-shirt stained with grease. Scanning my face, he pumped my hand. Tilting his blues, he clasped Nina to his side as I helped her from the bay.

"You're a sight for Red's rheumy eyes, sweetie! Been waitin' to see your pretty face since we heard you'd be comin' to visit with Keith. I knew his daddy from F-4s in 'Nam; same stringy legs! Have a rough ride in that old Chinook, hey? Looks like she passed a batch of gravel through her blades!"

"Have you JP-8 in the tanker?" the commander hoarsed from his cockpit, spinning MacDougal about.

"Needing fuel, hey? So cut your turbines and we'll load you up, sir. It's fresh from Texas, man...seein' the local JP is testin' piss and water...sir!" Ex-Air Force versus Navy and the commander's ebony face. They warmed immediately when he slid from the cockpit wearing his ribbons from Desert Storm, however.

Aside from MacDougal, MacDougal's crew and the lieutenant, our arrival at Antimahia was apparently unnoticed. Not so much as a staff member from Nokomo's in-town office. Although his entourage had arrived with Olympic the previous day, they'd obviously split for the capital city, seemingly oblivious (or not advised) of the project's counterpart on the opposite side of the commercial terminal. Fortunately, the lieutenant spoke English and, understanding the urgency, herded our group to the abandoned terminal, pointing proudly to the freshly painted interior and up-dated latrines.

The lieutenant also had a basic understanding of the project's primary purpose and requirements at Antimahia. Noting the commander was pressed for time, he conferred briefly with the group regarding their equipment and computers. Gauging Sigurdesson's condition, he motioned an orderly to show her to her quarters, suggesting Nina tag along as an interpreter if there was need to summon a medic. Then, standing by to supervise the unloading, he waited patiently by the Sea Hawk until the commander and his crew returned from a 'fresh up', zipping their flies.

"I have here a list of supplies promised by the UN,' he announced in agonized English. "Also, a facsimile acknowledgement from their offices in New

York, which was initialed by the lady who was recently here."

"Maureen?" Edwards questioned, lending an ear.

"I believe so, Dr. Edwards. She was most pleasant; spoke Greek. But we've had no further word, sir. No bill of lading, and we presently are in short supply."

"We were short-sheeted, or she was fired!" MacDougal commented, aware of the problem. "Figured a much when we unloaded the U-2. I got Texas on the horn and the C-141 brought a couple of pallets. Food for me crew and a batch of blankets. We share, of course, but come another week we'll be passin' the cup!" Concerned, but wanting to be airborne, the commander said he'd contact the embassy to spike the UN: "Follow up with Navy department."

"We need plastic sheeting to cover the bird," MacDougal interrupted. "Also APUs (auxiliary power units) since they already stole one of ours. It's all on the list, sir, including the data-link Slater'll be needing to test hop the bird. Figured it was shipped with the charter over there, but come to find out it was loaded with desks and chairs!"

Pleading with his hands, the commander motioned his crew to board and belt up. Moments later, nodding appreciatively while MacDougal stood fire guard, he rotated the Sea Hawk and lumbered to the west, and the chief waving from the barrier belt as they passed overhead.

"Place was a fuckin' mess when we arrived with the C-5," MacDougal explained as the 'copter vanished into the sun. "If it weren't for the lieutenant, we'd be sleepin' in the tower, Keith. Contractor walked off the job; hasn't been paid. So the lieutenant rounded up his men to finish our rooms, requisitioned mattresses from a store in town, set up a kitchen on his own. He's a beaut, man, like his CO, fella by name of Fotis Krokzohis! How's that for a handle? Okay, so you're lookin' around to see what we have, hey?"

From a bird's-eye view, the project would appear double tiered. Across the way, the new terminal provided a gate to Athens and Rhodos...servicing for international flights and charters, transportation to the capital city, and points such as Aspri Petra. All were necessary, inclusive of Nina's commuting to her business in Kavouri.

In terms of White Dove's requirements, the discarded complex provided housing and offices for the scientific enclave; the renovated tower a sanctuary for their sensitive instrumentation and mainstay computers; its upper region a space for communications and a data-link with the U-2. All told, it enabled the project's findings to be combined for analysis and transmitted by satellite to the interested world.

Despite the ramshackle buildings and need of logistics, the missing communications package and, apparently, Horst Gunnar, the setup was sufficient for the field-wise group of scientists. For my part, thanks to Lockheed, T.S. and, indirectly, the Air Force, the U-2 was comfortably nested with knowledgeable hands. Although my lodgings aboard the Helena might raise an envious eye!

The project's administrative infrastructure was stationed thirty kilometers away, with nearby hotel and office accommodations. Noticeably missing, however, was an apparent spirit of cooperation. The personnel, apparently, was on a par with the field group, on a basis of five to one – maybe more, judging from the arrival of the Lear-24.

"We see'd that Nigerian struttin' around with his swagger stick," MacDougal commented as we walked to the cordoned U-2. "He has his wives and children along, so maybe that's his problem. They took off in a pair of stretch limousines and never came by. Shit, man, maybe he was jealous of your big white bird!"

"Horst Gunnar?" I questioned when the guard cradled his AK-47 to let us in.

"Nary a word, boy, an' we're needin' the equipment! Fella came by yesterday noon, Keith. Thought it might be him; was starin' at the bird and wantin' to come in. Skinny type, wearin' loose suspenders; looked like a beanpole in a pair of shoes. Said his name was Schumann; came with Olympic, but all he had was a satchel, so the lieutenant sent him on."

"Schumann? Was he alone?"

"Came by with a broad in a taxi, Keith. Man, she was all tarted up an' wearin' a hat! Like she was wantin' to flesh the militia, but she weren't no chicken. Like I said, the lieutenant chased them off!"

Close up, not unlike a tethered albatross waiting release from its cage, the U-2 was balanced precariously on its mid gear. Her long tapered wings were supported by pogo wheels in process of assembly (the struts fall away at takeoff, reattached by a ground crew immediately upon landing). Amid a beehive of activity, a team of mechanics was running a cockpit check on the GE 5-29 engine; a spare, capsulized in the hangar. With her inspection plates open and test lines coiling from her electronics bay, the U-2 wasn't a thing of beauty.

"Come tomorrow we'll have her buttoned up," MacDougal commented, "including the slipper tanks, once we test the system for leaks. Come next, we'll clear the deck to wheel her out; figure she'll need a 300-foot radius to turn about. Worst part, I'll be short a pair of top hands when that C-141 takes off. Leaves me with four from Hughes, plus a half-dozen locals. Includin' the smartass what stole me APU. That your wife shoutin', boy? Seems I heard a horn blarin' a while back. Appears she's rounded up your transportation, man!"

Nina confronted the amused gate guard with a mixed bag of expletives and dockside Greek, verging a hissy fit. She rose to her toes when I hurried to the gate, pointing wildly to a sprightly white Fiat fronting the weedy drive.

"It's captain Stavos, Keith. The Helena's off charter; reached him with the Lieutenant's cellular," she said, casting a contemptuous frown at the guard. "Come now, I've our luggage and Auntie's hampers out front, but we couldn't find your brief case, my love. Might you have left it aboard the 'copter? My God, I hope not!" she added reflectively, fingering her earrings.

We located my brief case amidst Sigurdesson's cameras and ditty bag in a remote corner of the terminal. Following Winner's suggestion, we tried the door to her room. Rested from a quickie nap, fresh from a shower and clad only in a hasty towel, her hair was clinging damply to her face. The Swede apparently on the upside, smiling quietly when we presented her cameras, and ditty bag of cosmetics and tinned cigars.

"She has that 'time to get to work' glint in her eye," Winner commented while we manhandled Auntie's hampers to the outside portico. "Be up most the night, I think...studying the moon, tallying her notes, hell bent when we connect her computers. She's running scared, Keith; knows she's short of time. Needs someone to cozy up with, girl-to-girl talk," he suggested, turning to Nina.

"Ingrid has no family, honey...she's just hanging on a string, needing companionship. Her chest must hurt like hell!" he added, shaking his head. "Okay, so I'll bug off and see you in the morning," he decided. "Appears you've muscle to load your belongings," Winner furthered, peering at the burly figure alighting from the driver's seat.

* * * * * *

Captain Stavos was a short, broad-shouldered man of olive complexion, with a burr of white hair and caviar eyes. He spread his gait with a seaman's roll when he swung from the Fiat to greet us; embraced Nina, and gripped my hand with fingers of steel. In his seventies, I guessed, although he would easily pass for fifty if he'd shave the stubble from his jaw. Slim-waisted and muscular, he wore a pair of faded jeans and a spotless white shirt knotted beneath his chest. His feet were callused...stained with pitch, strangers to shoes. He appraised me briefly while we loaded our luggage into the rear of the van. Nodding silently while he helped Nina to a seat, he waited patiently until I'd slipped beside her and slammed the door.

We passed the startled guard in second gear and turned onto the perimeter road without waiting our stop. He drove casually with one hand, as if he were conning the helm from the steersman" chair, gesturing with the other while he chatted to Nina. He held a steady 80- kilometers, treating the road as if it were his personal lake. A flock of nimble-footed sheep gave way; a laboring truck pulled to the side. If the van had brakes, he was loath to use them. He was, however, an expert with the stick shift. We quartered the village square at Zinari with a 10° yaw, recovered, and accelerated to cruise speed before the village was behind us.

The eastern shore was lovely...whitewashed homes, walled gardens, orange trees, flowering hibiscus, and bright-eyed children playing soccer in the fields. If there was poverty, it was in the narrow streets leading to the sea or within the hovels clustered above the olive groves in the arid hills: poverty, perhaps, but not hunger.

To the west, the dark brown mountain ridges rose, zigzagged with access roads and dotted with sparkling villas; some reconstructed from early Grecian ruins. Water glazed the cliff sides, seeping through porous rock to feed medicinal springs Hippocrates had used to mend the sick.

Kos was an ancient island, steeped with history since Neolithic times. The capital city was founded by Greeks as a trading center, long after the catastrophic explosion decimated the Aegean. It fell to Alexander in 336 BC, then to the Ptolemies and the Romans. Ravaged by Saracen pirates in the eleventh century, then given by the Genoese to the Knights of St. John in 1315 AD, it was they who built the fortress observable in the distance as we topped the final rise to enter the city. Facing the straits separating the island from mainland Turkey, the fortress was constructed of limestone hewn from the harbor, together with the splendid marble colonnades and edifices the Crusaders had savaged from the ancient temples for the sake of the Holy Grail.

"They went on to sack Constantinople," Nina commented, as we circled the square and descended a street leading to the harbor. "The fort fell to the Turks in 1522 and we were ruled by the sultans until the island was surrendered to the Italians in 1912; to the Greeks with the Dodecanese in 1947. The Turks built the prayer tower by the square and the mosque you see at the edge of town. It's a bloody shame to realize Christians and Moslems are still fighting to this day!"

The parallel breakwaters projected from Mandraki harbor. The Crusaders' fort towered over the eastern side; a cruise liner moored in its shadow, fishing trawlers tied to the narrow docks. A dozen or more yachts were hawsered stern first to the long concrete pier fronting a busy street called Akati Kountourigtou (the harbor street), comprised of tavernas, sidewalk cafés, umbrellas and tables, darting waiters and a waning residue of tourists sipping coffee and ouzo, observing the yachts and action across the way.

The Helena was not the largest...an enormous English double-decker was tied alongside her; a 12-meter sloop with a French tricolor flag flanked her starboard side. She was, however, the prettiest; steel hulled, painted hunter green, her superstructure mahogany and teak, gleaming with polished brass...a classic beauty likened to the 50s; I could readily understand why Nick had named her for his bride.

More motor vessel than sail, she carried a raised salon aft to a raised cockpit, continuing with a sheltered promenade to her stern. An 80-footer, she supported the masts of a ketch, sufficient sail to weather the mid-Atlantic should her diesels give out. A seaman in shorts was arranging flowers at a table on her fantail, waving to Nina, beaming when she alighted and raced the length of the pier. She was barefoot, I realized, when I discovered her slippers in my lap.

The sun had slipped to the horizon while we showered and changed in the master cabin. Dusk was upon us when her friends and relatives descended the pier. Much the same as our first night in Kavouri...Domestica white from Roditis, supplemented with Mayrodaphine Patras, while gifts were exchanged. Nina was beside herself with excitement, flashing her smile, embracing them as they boarded, guiding the lot to the galley to heap their plates with Auntie's moussaka. There were introductions and names I would never remember except for one...a tiny old lady with a gathered shawl: Auntie Cleo.

Her piercing eyes examined me from the depths of antiquity, finally accepting me. Offering her hand, she requested I come and sit beside her.

"You have a strong, kindly face," she said, her accent evidencing English tutoring or acquired from years abroad. "You will be good for my Nina, I believe. She's in need of understanding and I am happy you have come to us from America, despite the uncertain times," she added, clearing her throat with a sip of wine, smiling when I squeezed her hand. Beautiful once, Nina resembled her in a way: her quirky smile and subtle intelligence.

"Since Nicholas and Helena die, she's come upon tortured times beyond her callings, Keith. This I realized when I attended their funeral in Athens," she added, frowning at an oldster devouring a napkin with his moussaka. "And now I see lines in her face beyond her years. Answer me truthfully! Has our Nina been ill?"

I studied the café across the street, seeking words. Cleo's probing sobriety contrasted with the laughter and tinkling glasses in the salon. A tourist couple rose from a table, *a tall man wearing suspenders waiting for his check*, his rotund companion busy with her purse.

"Not exactly," I answered, my attention straying. "Nina's caught with business problems, Auntie Cleo…Nick's estate, death taxes, and the lot."

"'Not exactly' is not an answer!" she responded. "You are being evasive, I see it in your eyes! I've known Nina since she was a child and I'm aware of her dreams, of her wanderings when she's asleep. Have you experienced this in recent weeks? I thought so," she added quietly, gathering the shawl to her shoulders. "You've answered my question with noble silence, my American nephew! We will talk again. And now, I must return to my cottage where I live alone with my cats and dogs."

Prompted by a nod from Nina, I helped Cleo from the stern to the pier, where she steadied her footing. Noticed when she grasped my arm she wore a large garnet ring on her maiden finger, but no wedding band or its like. Possibly the garnet a lingering memento of her long ago past, remembrance of a lover who'd since passed away?

Peering into my eyes, she questioned the necklace. Had Nina worn it in my presence? Was I aware of its source? I allowed that Nina had found the necklace in Nick's desk the day we were married. Seemed surprised to find it; said she hadn't seen it since she was a child; told me of its history. Later, she wore it in Nassau when we were entertaining Tony Metexas.

"Since then?"

"Keeps it in her purse out of sight," I responded, declining to elaborate.

Cleo shook her head, pondered the fading twilight.

"We've wondered how she came upon it. Nicholas intended the necklace for the Museum of Antiquities. I wonder why he kept it so many years. Superstitious, my brother; often said the necklace was bad omen, the hideous pendant not for Nina's eyes. Nicholas conceivably regarded the necklace as a catalytic key to Nina's 'escape world' when she's emotionally upset," she said. "Likened to the night at Arhannes, or years later when she suspicioned the cause of her parents' untimely death!"

My thoughts raced to the scene at the Met, the explosive storm and spurious artifacts? The evening in Nassau, of Nina wielding the deadly candelabra, and her wanderings during the storm.

"Nevertheless," Cleo continued, noting my reaction with a knowing smile, "as Nina's husband, you must insist she oblige her Papa's wishes and dispose of it immediately! Else I foresee a dreadful happening, knowing Nina's reactive mind!" With that, not waiting for an answer, Cleo released my arm and disappeared in a darkened alleyway with her cane. Easier said than done, I thought, although I agreed with the intelligent old sage who'd apparently conversed with Auntie by phone earlier in the day.

The couple at the café had disappeared. The party aboard the Helena in process of waning when, caught with my thoughts, I ventured to explore the nearby streets. Intrigued by the island's history, I studied the fluted columns embedded in the fortress; Roman columns, scrounged by the Crusaders from the ancient ruins, carved by master craftsmen from marble a thousand years before the Knights of St. John descended with their armor and swords.

The street turned to circle the fortress, to widen into a boulevard bordering the harbor. The resort hotels beyond...the Xenia, the Atlantis...were a bustle of activity with late-departing tourists, mostly German and Scandinavian, ion abbreviated skirts and shorts. Palm trees lined the boulevard; botanical gardens were filled with bougainvillea and hibiscus blooms folding for want of sleep.

The Government House, an extensive whitewashed building of Moorish design, displayed a residue of the Turkish occupation. A newly arrived Hummer with UN insignia was parked in the courtyard; a white Opel and a pair of nondescript military Jeeps were nearby. The UN insignia alerted me to the possibility that Dr. Nokomo's office was in the immediate vicinity. The Opel pulled away before I could determine the alignment of the offices, but I had a fleeting glimpse of the driver...of a stern black face wearing glasses, and starched khakis, a Rolex on his arm when he waved politely and turned towards the Xenia hotel.

Curious, I located the UN office by the dove-wreathed placard suspended from the archway on the ground floor. A newly typed letter pasted on its door read: *The United Nations Environmental Studies Group, Dr. Jomo Nokomo, Administrator.* The door was locked, the darkened interior a maze of desks and chairs, none aligned. There was activity in the adjoining offices, brightly lit despite the hour. The headquarters of the local militia, I assumed, judging from a corporal standing guard. Best to check it out in the morning, I decided, turning heel to help Nina disperse her remaining guests.

CHAPTER 19

The morning brought a bright new day. I slipped from our double berth, leaving Nina asleep with her clutch of pillows and climbed the stairs to the upper deck. Captain Stavos was seated in the sheltered cockpit, a thermos of coffee at hand; the steward and deckhand were clearing the promenade deck of napkins and debris. Forward, in the galley, a temporary local was busy washing dishes; the Fiat was parked dockside awaiting the collective garbage. Overhead, true to Winner's prediction, the stratospheric winds were southwesterly bent, shielding Athens and the northern Aegean from Santorini's oily plume, hopefully allowing the U-2 a span of clear weather to test the volcano close up.

"Have a some coffee," the old man grunted, offering a cup from his thermos. I made a fruitless try at small talk while sipping the sugary brew liberally laced with brandy, nut he lent his ear to the morning broadcast, eyeing me quietly from his perch, not sure he'd accept my presence as Nina's American spouse.

Shrugging, I decided it was best to let it be. With the project in mind, I showered and changed to my faded khakis. Pausing midway in the companionway, I remembered my brief case tucked in the locker and, peeking at my sleeping bride, retrieved the necklace before she could come upon it, knowing she was too adept with combination locks!

The sidewalk café was a scene of activity when I stepped from the sternway, drawn by the aroma of breakfast pastries and pitchers of fresh orange juice on the café buffet. The early morning clientele were mostly pensioners. Knotted at their tables in rapt conversation, the singular souls were enveloped with their newspapers and coffee. A scattering of tourists, waiting for Olympic's bus to Antimahia, were watchful of their luggage piled nearby. None had little more than casual interest in the yachts hawsered to the pier, aside from a perimeter table with a view of the Helena.

Sheltered partially by the table's umbrella, a matronly lady in a floppy hat turned ever so slightly when an urchin offered a day-old Tribune and I searched my pockets for change. From the corner of my eye, I could see she wore glasses and loosely held a shoulder bag. Her back glistened with perspiration. Amalia, of course!

For what plausible reason was she so obviously nearby? Was she keeping tabs on visitors? Casing the project for information, reporting to Gunnar by cellular - could be? But would she be so naive not to realize I was aware of her presence? Or was she testing my reaction? Assuming the latter, I skipped the pastries, nodded politely to the pensioners, and proceeded to the government house to present my credentials. A chapel bell sounding in the distance clanged eight bells to announce the hour.

Nokomo's offices were dark and locked; a pair of office types in tight skirts waited nearby, apparently lacking a key. Seated on a concrete bench, satchel at his feet, was the lanky chap who'd arrived the previous day. Apprising my face, he climbed quickly to his feet and pointed to the wreath and dove insignia above the door.

"Schumann?" I questioned, venturing an introduction in my very best NATO German.

"Dr. Henric Schumann," he corrected in flawless English. "Might you be Keith Slater? He added, nodding as if he knew. "I've come from Jakarta by way of Amsterdam to assist Dr. Sigurdesson," he added, extending his hand.

"Ingrid's at Antimahia, Doctor."

"Yes; I knew she was expected, but my appointment was last minute and I've yet to receive notification from New York. Which is somewhat disturbing," he added. "She would know of my research in seismology, identify me, once I locate a source of authority."

"Seismology?"

"Apart from volcanology and meteorology, I'm a geophysicist," Schumann announced, noting my puzzled expression. "I volunteered my services when I heard Dr. Sigurdesson was ill, knowing many of her theories coincide with mine. I also have a valid Dutch passport," he added with a toothy grin whilst I gripped his hand.

Relieved he wasn't another loose cannon, and pleased we'd have a helping hand, I unlocked my brief case. His name was listed on the tally sheet from the Grande Bretagne, underscored by Bruno's pencil. Also the clammy necklace which I quickly dispatched to the snap lid, spinning the combination when I had my file.

He was taller than I was but near the same age, with brownish hair, a long jaw and shirt pockets stuffed with notes and worried pencils. A toothbrush completing the inventory, apart from the canvas satchel he'd brought along from Jakarta. Schumann obviously was anxious to be afield again and, assuming the roster would warrant a pass, I suggested we check with the militia instead of the UN which, judging from the state of affairs might take a few days.

"We were here yesterday when the lorry brought their desks and chairs," he commented. "Fortunately, the soldiers had a key."

"We?"

"Lady on holiday. Odd sort; kept me up most the night," he added. I let it go at that.

A gray-uniformed sergeant nodded when we entered the ready room. Unsure of our purpose due to my labored Greek, he presented a registry pad, indicated we should take a chair, and disappeared in a hallway. The room was freshly painted, décor sparse aside from a vase of flowers and Greek periodicals on a nearby table. Noncoms wandered in and out; none wore sidearms, I noticed. Their belts were spit and polish, indicative of care and discipline in the otherwise casual community. All the while, the desk phone buzzed unattended, until the sergeant returned with a young lady wearing a blouse and jeans.

"Mr. Slater?" she inquired, puzzling Schumann's suspenders when I rose from my chair. "Major Krokzohis will see you now," she added with a pretty smile, obliging Schumann with the same, seemingly amused by the toothbrush and smudge of lipstick on his collar.

"The Major's English is a bit loose and I'm filling in as his interpreter," she continued, "what with the UN next door and the balls up with their desks. Matter of fact we expected you to come by...it's Keith, isn't it? Cleo called yesterday afternoon, said you'd be staying aboard the Helena. Invited Fotis but he had too much on his plate."

"Cleo called?" She nodded.

"It's a small island; we're all more or less related. I've a degree from NYU, teach English at the University of Hippocrates. Fotis is my cousin. You'll like him; he's a helluva nice guy. Takes his job too seriously, I think. Worried sick by that thing at Thera. He's off the phone now," she abruptly added. "Speak slowly, he's not so good with English." We followed her down the hallway. I noticed she had wide-sprung hips like Nina's and the same crackling raven hair.

Fotis was a tall lean man, slope shouldered, more Anatolian than Greek. Possibly in his early thirties, he had short, curly blond hair, the blue eyes of his heritage and a serious demeanor. Wore his uniform shirt casually open at the throat (acknowledging the climate), although his bearing was strictly military, authoritative. He'd be excellent in the field...a cool number, analytical, not given to reacting from emotion, I thought.

We hit it off immediately. He was pleased to meet Dr. Schumann and deeply interested in the U-2's high altitude program, listening carefully while I described the purpose of the multiple missions. He made a surprising request...would I copy him with the velocity and infrared readings when we circled Santorini?

"He's concerned for the people if the sea should rise," the girl explained. "His men have installed sirens in the fishing villages to warn them to higher ground." The major interrupted in Greek; she nodded, turned to me.

"He said to tell you the old people would have to be forcibly removed if the volcano explodes. He anticipates a crest of 200 feet and is afraid there wouldn't be time. Two hundred feet! My God!" She blanched, spun in her chair to question him further.

"It's true, Mr. Slater. Katrina does not comprehend the past!" Fotis said in halting English, then speaking to Katrina in Greek. She nodded nervously.

"The Major tells me they've found pottery shards on the hillsides near Kefalos that date from the Minoans, that they came from a village that lies beneath the sea at Kamari. Sea level was much lower in 1600 BC," she added. "When Thera exploded, the sea receded to fill the cavity; when it returned, villages were inundated by a wall of water. Whatever floated was cast upon the hills. Sounds like words from Exodus, hey?"

The major rose from his desk and led us to an adjoining room. He pointed to a seismograph and a seismoscope he'd obtained from lord knows where, and explained that he'd been able to predict the whiplash, the rising sea resulting from the tectonic quake that had rippled the Aegean nights before. They had successfully cleared the docks and warned the yachts to ride it out beyond the harbor.

He was either a closet volcanologist or frustrated by lack of information to the point of desperation. His worktable was cluttered with books by Bullard, Rittman and G. S. MacDonald. An article by Tuzo Wilson was overlaid with a graph he'd compiled. Wanting a temperature study from Santorini's fast-rising cone, he was evidently comparing centigrade readings with Wilson's theories of St. Helens. Pressed for time, Fotis pointed to an active radar screen he could monitor from his desk. Explained its workings to Katrina, who interpreted as best she could.

"It's slaved to a radar scan located on top of Mount Simetros," she said.

"The dome was constructed by the military years ago, to watch the straits between Kos and Turkey, but aside from smugglers, it's had little use and he's raised the scan to accommodate Santorini. You are not to let Athens know!" she confided. "Fotis is prepared to assume full responsibility, but should the Defense Department find out, they'll have his ass!"

I complimented his resourcefulness; the scan would provide an instant reading if the volcano came apart. Communications from Athens would only echo the blast.

"Uncanny," Schumann mused. "Primitive but workable, although his seismograph is in need of adjustment. Might I obtain a pass to the field office, miss? I've need to communicate with Dr. Sigurdesson but have no papers from the United Nations." I produced the memo roster, Schumann his Dutch passport. Katrina questioned the major, but apparently he had other thoughts.

"Fotis will be driving to Antimahia in a few minutes, Dr. Schumann. He has an urgent matter to discuss with Lieutenant Tseretopoulos and would accommodate your pass if you'd care to go along. He also would like to meet Dr. Sigurdesson and inspect the U-2, Mr. Slater. Frankly, he has the hots to see it up close, Katrina asided. "Said he'd have you back by 1600, if you're agreeable."

I was thankful for the opportunity, of course. Knowing the Fiat was hauling litter, I'd have to wait my turn or catch a bus. I anticipated a flap with Nina, however, remembering she'd planned a luncheon aboard the Helena.

"Wouldn't worry about it," Katrina confided. "According to Cleo, she's invited the ladies for sandwiches and tea. Are you ready for that?"

Promptly at nine, in unison with the clanging ells, the major reappeared with his braided hat underarm, and pointed to a flag-bearing Jeep. I noticed action of sorts in the UN offices as we passed. The secretarial types had arranged their desks with a midway aisle...no chairs or telephones, however. Nor was Dr. Nokomo in evidence, although his Mercedes was parked by the Xenia, which Fotis noticed and, displaying his smattering of English chose to comment when he geared the hill.

"Is much confusing," he commented. "Come nice girl from New York. Make arrangement for office and accommodation at Xenia, but leave no drachma for deposit. Come now with Dr. Nokomo, we think. Cause plenty worry," he added with a shrug. "Contractor have no fund to roll asphalt at Antimahia." Which would present a problem for an extended takeoff, I thought. The U-2's engine wasn't designed to ingest loose gravel and sand.

Pleased we could communicate in fractured English and my kindergarten Greek, I was reminded the island was under partial military law when the major stopped to chat with the villagers along the way, mostly dispensing useful information should Santorini blow its spike. Authoritative in his braided hat, but not overbearing and obviously respected, Fotis was a welcome relief from the indecisive bureaucracy I'd sensed in Athens. Which accounted for the lieutenant" snappy salute when we drew abreast of our office at Antimahia.

The lieutenant recognized Schumann from the previous day, although unsure of his status until I produced the memo and Fotis indicated he'd be quartered with the group. Pointing proudly to the newly painted entrance, he sent an orderly to fetch Dr. Winner, interpreting for the major when Winner appeared in raggedy-ass shorts, an apron of tools strapped to his belt.

Winner, a can of beer in hand, seemingly bewildered by Fotis' braid; acknowledged the formality as best he could, flashing a left-handed salute! Peering at Schumann's beanpole features, he grasped his arm with startled recognition. "Henric! Of all faces...you've come at the right time!" Winner chortled, leading Schumann to the lobby, introducing Edwards and Fraser, then Major Krokzohis in turn. "Henric was an associate professor when I was first in Indonesia," he added, introducing Sigurdesson when she was drawn from her work by the incessant chatter.

Sigurdesson was delighted! Although they'd never met, they'd communicated by fax when she requested post specifics of Galunggung in Java. She also was pleased to converse briefly with Fotis, pleased by his layman's grasp of her theories (should the tides weaken Santorini's magma chamber on the eve of the full moon).

"God knows where you found him, Keithy," Winner asided. "Like, you've come up with the best set of brains we've encountered since Geneva. Seismology, volcanology, meteorology... name it! For our part, a mechanical genius! Ingrid's seismograph hasn't been right since it was impounded in Athens."

Schumann was much too tall to squeeze inside the U-2's rear cockpit, much less fit Gomulaka's pressure suit...obviously not intended for the chore...but I was thankful of his presence. Together with Fotis, he offered the project a degree of stability, which was sorely needed in terms of morale.

None of this was lost on the major whilst he looked about, observing the Internet computers, their linkage with the sensors implanted on Santorini. Nodding when Sigurdesson explained the need of a particle count from the U-2's collecting pods, he seemingly understood the necessity of an altitude probe to determine the cone's thermo velocity; the close-up radar and infrared scan needed to update her analysis, which the U-2 was equipped to transmit electronically. But lacking a ground base data-link, she'd have to wait for my screenings and interpret the readings from our onboard computers.

"Short term, I can call in what I see or read visually," I commented, with the lieutenant's bilingual help. "But long-range at altitude, we'll need a qualified observer to relay information. To that end, our VHF transceiver is short-range; our HF suspect if we encounter a spate of weather. The U-2 is equipped with space-age technology: GPS for navigation, a digital satellite link for communication. Until our base link is established, however, we haven't the means to communicate with the project's mainstay computer."

Nodding his understanding, Fotis said he'd send a technician to couple a VHF frequency with the tower across the way. We could then communicate with the project indirectly with ATC via satellite. The tower hadn't the means to relay the transcript, other than by voice, which would be helpful to the group until the data-link was installed. *Although unbeknownst, except to MacDougal and myself, I'd have Riyadh at fingertip at all times!*

The major suggested we maintain contact with his office on a CB channel. He'd monitor with an open ear and equip Nokomo's office with the same. Pointing to the U-2's jutting white tail, I asked if he'd care to see the bird close-up?

Supremely poised on her bicycle-like undergear - wings balanced on her pogo struts – the U-2 was waiting a hand on her stick and willing to fly! Drawn from her stall by a ground tug, she'd been turned about to face the active runway. The open cockpits were sheltered by an awning suspended between a pair of mobile A-frames; an APU energizing unit chattered alongside, indicating a progressive test of her sensor probes was underway. Peering from the rear cockpit, a red-capped MacDougal was testing the infrared scan with a brush fire on a distant hill.

His cap fixed Bronx-wise, sweating profusely from the heat, he nodded when we climbed the ladder to see what we had, offered a two fingered salute to the major, who had apparently been on hand when they offloaded the C-5.

"So far the systems check okay," he said, waving to a mechanic to disengage the APU. "Likewise the avionics," he added, climbing from the rear seat to afford the major a view. "In fact, I was talkin' with the tower on 119.1 while we checked the transponder.

"We haven't turned the F-29 as yet," MacDougal reported, "but she's fueled for an hour at the blast fence, an' come morning we'll juice them seagulls with 19,000 pounds of thrust! It's the same series they hung on the B-2, Keithy. Main thing, you gotta keep her hauled back or you'll leave her wings on the strip when you take off with that firecracker up your ass!"

The lieutenant's interpretation notwithstanding, Fotis was visibly taken by the instrumentation when I slipped into the front cockpit to scan the checklist and familiarize myself with the avionics. Adjusting the rudder travel to my legs, I unlocked the controls and checked the rudder swing with the cockpit mirror, traveled the stick to activate the elevators and ailerons, rolled the elevator trim – intending to visually check the tabs from the ground.

We briefly ran basic procedures: power settings, temperature gauges, flap control, gear handle, flight instruments, NAV-aids, GPS, oxygen supply. And lastly, the ejection toggle!

"You've a zero/zero envelope," MacDougal commented. "She's not like the old U-2s when you had to hold 200 knots in level flight to eject. Don't worry it if you enter a spin. The charge will blast you free of the tail. Same system we used with the SR-71s." I nodded numbly. At 60,000 feet the outside temperature would be -56° Centigrade; we'd have fifteen seconds of free-fall before our pressure suits gave out...60,000 feet over Iran another matter! Reminded of our flight gear, I inquired of the lot when we dropped to the ramp; had it arrived on the C-5 together with the thermal underwear and my trunk of equipment from Mountain View?

"Affirmative, Keithy! First off, unpacked the first day around. Figured the suits needed a good airing," MacDougal added, pointing to the air-conditioned office adjoining the hangar. "What with sticky hands hereabouts, I keep them locked with me supply of 'Bud'." Double locked with a pair of hammer-proof padlocks, I noticed when he searched his wire of keys.

An old hand from the 99th, familiar with our needs, he'd rigged the office as a change room...pegged the pressure suits upright to afford a flow of air, our boots and gloves alongside; the faceless helmets staring grotesquely like aliens from outer space. The smaller of the two was sadly identified 'Dr. George Gomulaka' with a stenciled patch on its breast. On a nearby shelf were his pad of notes, together with the helmets and oxygen masks he'd worn during our low altitude flights from Moffet Field; mine a battered relic of Desert Storm.

"Figured you might give the volcano a close-up when you test-hop the bird," MacDougal commented. "Maybe take Dr. Winner along, seein' you won't be needin' them pressure suits below 40,000. Heard tell he flew with Miami Hurricane Watch while back. Ain't likely to git sick!"

He had more to add in private, however, when he locked the door behind us.

"Not to worry, but I'm having problems with a pair of mechanics I inherited from Olympic," he aside, inclining his head towards the hangar. "Like that greaseball wearin' a pony tail stole my APU. His buddy's been duckin' Major Fotis, I think. Backtracked to the engineering shed when you first came in." I had a fleeting view of a swarthy type with the stomach of a chronic boozer.

"Like yesterday, when you came with the Sea Hawk, I see'd Pony Tail sittin' in the cockpit where he shouldn't have been; his buddy foolin' with the elevator tabs. I'm busy with the AV truck, so they don't think I've come to notice! Sorry, fellas," MacDougal added apologetically, offering the six-pack he'd brought from his larder. "Was discussin' a problem with Keithy an' near forgot we was thirsty!"

Fotis was aware of the abrupt change of conversation, however, and queried the lieutenant while we returned to the terminal.

"Major Krokzohis would like to know if you've a problem with your mechanics, Mr. MacDougal. He's concerned about workmanship and security, sir. Questioned if they've presented certified identification?"

MacDougal popped his beer and gave it thought.

"Shit, man! Tell him they were here when we offloaded the C-5. We needed muscle an' I never thought to ask. Okay, so we put them to work as ground crew, and they done a good job, 'cept them two with Olympic credentials that came from Athens."

Fotis listened carefully to the interpretation, curiously without comment, although he was in rapt conversation with the lieutenant when they passed security to the terminal. I lingered with MacDougal for a moment.

"Couldn't rightly say what I meant," the Irishman fumed. "I was afraid to put the lieutenant in a bind, but once Jomo makes payroll I'll fire the bastards, seein' they're up to no good."

"Meaning?" MacDougal inclined his head to the U-2.

"See'd you wheel the trim all the way forward while back. The elevator tabs are set for fast descent. Meaning to do that?" I nodded.

"Ground check, Red. I wanted to see the alignment."

"Figured as much, but it got me thinkin' about what I said. Them greaseballs was doin' the same thing, Keithy. So now this bird ain't no F-15; them trims date back to cables and spools. Supposin' they come to be reversed, or maybe the spool is reset to zero, but you don't know it ain't right? So now you're loaded with 40,000 pounds of fuel and you roll back trim to take off, but the nose doesn't come up and you're wonderin' what the shit? Meantime, the bird's gatherin' knots and you're runnin' short of strip, so maybe you have time to abort; least eject before the U-2 bombs the park!

"Now, we ain't about to let that happen," MacDougal continued while we walked to the gate. "I've been crewin'"U-2s for thirty odd years, and it'd take some doin' to catch me blind with hanky panky. Like yourself, Keithy; no way would you take off on a combat mission less'n you gave your bird a strong pre-flight. Comes with long habit, man! I see'd you were given to similar thought when you spun the tabs."

"Could be," I admitted; he had eyes in the back of his head!

"Figured as much! Like, maybe you were thinkin' about that corporate jet that bought the park a short time back. Same problem, like the pilot muscles the trim tab and stalls on takeoff, not knowing the tabs are reversed and he doesn't know which from what!"

"Recently, you say?"

"Yeah, man! Was readin' an FAA Notam the Captain had aboard the C-5. Like they suspect a balls up with a Lear 21 they's investigatin'. Same thing...trim set for takeoff, throttles full thrust! Like the pilot was fightin' the tabs when he clipped a hill and stalled upside down: no survivors, man!"

"A Lear 21?"

"Lear 21 series, Keithy. The wreck was burned out 'cept for the console and tail sections. The FAA's working from that but haven't completed their investigation. Like there was no precedent with the series until they was called in. Brought to mind 'cause the Lear was in a hangar waitin' a charter and had no history of mechanical problems. In fact it was fresh in at Hellinikon the day before!"

"*Hellinikon!*" I sputtered.

"You gotta pull the key before you sip the beer, old buddy! Like the Notam ain't for sayin' it were sabotage, but it left plenty questions...indicatin' the series be inspected immediately for trim malfunction. Interesting, hey? Seeing you have like thoughts when you were checking the U-2's trim tabs from the cockpit while back."

An icy premonition coursed my spine. The coincidence of MacDougal's keen-eyed observation whilst I tested a theory I'd held to myself! The FAA's analysis of 'cause of accident' my concern, should it come to Nina's hand! Not the U-2, although it was also subject to strange doings, if so planned?

* * * * * *

A distant church bell was sounding the half hour, 11:30 by my watch, when we returned to the ramp and I proceeded to the complex to see if Winner was agreeable to a romp with the U-2. Allowing for an early morning takeoff with four hours of fuel, subject to weather, I reasoned we would circle the volcano at minimum altitude, then climb to 40,000 and penetrate the ash plume to activate the collecting pods; return via Rhodos and screen the findings for Sigurdesson's analysis. As a meteorologist, Winner'd be an apt substitute for Gomulaka's chore – short term, although he hadn't volunteered. High altitude another matter, and at the moment I preferred to go it alone.

Fotis and the lieutenant were conversing in the entrance hall all the while. Fotis apparently wanting to be off, he carried a yellow tally pad underarm, his brief case together with mine. Fraser was busy at his typewriter; Sigurdesson and Edwards engrossed with their computers; a jug of coffee sat next to a tray of spent cigars. Winner and Schumann were upstairs in the former tower, Fraser allowed when I inquired. Heeding the major, I said I'd come by in the morning to discuss our test flight with Dr. Winner, letting it be known I intended to be airborne the following day.

Our return to the capital city was stop and go, hell bent until Fotis pulled aside to accept a strand of roses from a gnarled hand. He reassured the old lady, who was worried of her goats that had split for the hills.

"Animals are weather wise," he said, pointing to the pall on the horizon. "Is instinct, Major Slater."

"Mister," I corrected automatically.

"So, all right, but I believe we share mutual worry. For me, is my people. For you is important your aeroplane not in hand of greedy mechanic!" he allowed, nodding silently to himself when I stared wordlessly at the road. Then, pointing to the yellow pad by his seat, he slowed to further his thoughts.

"It was beneficial you came to office this morning," he said. "We've recent advice from Interpol...cannot confide, but it suit purpose to visit Antimahia in your presence. I was impressed with your scientists and Sergeant MacDougal...also with your aeroplane...having cause to be remind of a report included with file.

"Comes to point," he added. "I have obtained names of UN employees and insist they be fingerprinted and identified with security badges by tomorrow noon! We have reason to request such," Fotis furthered when he geared the rise to the city. "We've recently recovered an auxiliary power unit; from which we have fingerprints we wish to compare!"

MacDougal's missing APU, I surmised...but suddenly we had an immediate problem with Fotis' Jeep – a sidelong skid when the road rippled and came apart midway the rise! Spinning gravel to right the careening vehicle, Fotis activated his siren when a wail sounded from the hills. His expletives not for repeating, when he topped the rise clutching his hat, shouting to a lorry to stay put, slowing to accommodate a gaggle of hysterical geese.

We entered the city with the siren full blast, spurring the indecisive to flee for higher streets. The waiters at the sidewalk café were lofting tables and chairs to the parapet roof when Fotis dropped me dockside. A rumbling aftershock momentarily rattled the vehicle.

"Come low water and high sea!" he shouted. "Best take Helena deep water; have only few minutes, Major Slater!" I knew exactly what he meant, but aside from the frightened steward and deckhand, there was no evidence of Captain Stavos, the van or Nina when I raced alongside and leapt aboard.

The sea was relatively calm, but its surface appeared to be dancing, as were Nina's party balloons drifting astern, bouncing lifelike from the agitated waters. Realizing the Helena was equipped with diesels, I keyed the glow plugs and waited until the cylinders warmed; I engaged the starters, advancing the throttles when the engines responded with a throaty roar! With power at hand, I shouted to the steward to cast off the stern lines, motioning the deckhand to slip the bow lines while I steered cautiously towards the open sea.

Unrestrained, the Helena leapt through the parallel breakwaters like a raft shooting the Yellowstone, swerving with the outgoing tide while I countered with the throttles. We grounded briefly, but I gained steerage when we had green water astern. In a clod sweat, I applied full power to keep abreast of the tide, chancing a look back before it turned about.

The shoreline was exposed as far as we could see. The sea had fallen eight or ten feet in a matter of minutes and continued to flow from the narrow harbor as if the bottom had fallen from the depths of the Aegean. The emptied basin, quivering with stranded fish and eels, was strewn with mossy wreckage that hadn't seen light for countless years. All the while the sirens continued to wail, the streets thronged with young and old moving quickly to the nearest hill. Offshore, the cruise liner and a gaggle of fishing trawlers had barely made it. Not so lucky the French sloop, heeled on its side; the English yacht hopelessly grounded next to the pier. Owners and crew scaled the docks, knowing what to expect in their lee.

"It come now," the steward muttered, pointing to the west.

It came, subtly at first; the Helena seemingly tensed while we buckled in. Then, a rising mound of water on the horizon approaching quickly as I maneuvered to bring our bow to bear, clinging to my chair. There was no cresting wave as we mounted the rise of thirty feet or more. The shoreline of Turkey was clearly visible in the distance...until we cascaded downside, twisting and heeling while we fought for control. A successive wave hurled the Helena skyward, and we smacked the ongoing roller with a massive thud...wracking her frame, flooding the aft deck...while we continued our hair-raising ride. The Helena was game; heavily built, she finally stabilized, shedding brine from her scuppers as we rode the diminishing swells.

Off to our starboard, the liner had also ridden it out; her screws chewed the sky on the downside of the trough; her bow buried in the green, rising like a careening whale as she shook herself free. In the distance, bobbing like corks in the quieting sea, were the trawlers - aside from one with her decks awash, her crew atop the deckhouse waiting a pump or tow, all had survived. The worst was over, apparently, but there was havoc ashore!

The fast-moving swell crested when it struck the subterranean shelf, tumbling upon itself as it swept the harbor with a torrent of angry brine. Breakwaters and docks were submerged as the comber mounted the rise, spuming the fortress to its parapets, flooding streets into Venetian-like canals, until it spent itself in the village square. We watched silently as it ebbed and returned. Slowly at first, it then resonated, as a cataract of milky foam, dragging with it whatever would float. We braced ourselves to meet the onslaught, throttling for steerage.

A tangled mass of wreckage emerged street-side. The French sloop lay atop the hapless yacht; a sports-fishing cruiser rested mid-street; abandoned cars were strewn about like forgotten toys in an emptied tub. The scene was much the same coast-side, with fatalities among the flotsam, judging from the ambulances bleating from all quarters. I was worried for Nina and Stavos, of course, but assumed they and Cleo would be safe.

We steered towards the draining pier at near idling speed, the deckhand prodding the wreckage aside with a gaff pole until we had sufficient clearance to turn about and, when the tide level stabilized, I reversed the props to ease us in. Our dockside lines remained secure to their cleats, but were trailing out of reach. Unsure of my docking ability, I held off to scan the pier for a helping hand. We hadn't long to wait. Focusing Stavos' binoculars, I spied Nina racing down the street from Auntie Cleo's house on the hill, the streets much too cluttered to oblige the view. Her hair bound with a scarf, she reminded me of the Goddess Hera, ruler of the waves. Then, Captain Stavos on aged legs, racing to our depleted moorings, trilling his Bosun's whistle like a seaman gone berserk. No less alerted, the deckhand coiled a line astern and waited until I positioned the motor-sailer abreast of the pier.

Like Hercules with a spear, he hurled the weighted line to Stavos, who caught it and tauted the cleat. We had it together then! With the stern line secured, I eased the Helena forward until the steward cast our bowline and

Stavos drew it in! Captain Stavos then scrambled aboard to attach his bumper pads, beaming but noncommittal when I slumped at the wheel, completely spent! Nina's cheeks were smeared with tears and mascara when she slipped aboard. She sat quietly beside me for a while. Not unlike returning from a combat mission, there's no fright until one brakes at the ramp and finds one's legs have dissolved to willow wands. Post reaction or whatever, I savored and shared the ouzo and ice the steward brought from the pantry. Stavos stroking his chin for lack of words, visibly shaken by the carnage. He caught my eye momentarily, however, lofted his glass to mine!

"We felt the shock when we dropped Auntie Cleo at her cottage," Nina said. "It was unbelievable, happened so quickly we hadn't time to start the van. Then a balcony fell and the alley was blocked. Thank God you came along when you did, Keith! Katrina sent word you weren't due back until after five. Then the cruise ship took off, and when Captain Stavos saw you aboard the Helena, I said my prayers!"

Likened to Kavouri, the quay was a scene of somber activity. Fotis' men had come upon a very old man floating face down amidst a hundred oranges, his shattered vendor's cart a few yards from his hand; then an elderly pensioner who'd strolled the streets, unmindful of the wailing sirens. Nina turned her head aside, crying softly when they were placed in body bags and a waiting ambulance. There were tears in Stavos' eyes as well, the vendor someone he knew.

We had power and water aboard the Helena, but there was total blackness in the city until the streetlights blinked mid-hill, easing worry of Auntie Cleo. Street-side, a portable generator came to life while we watched the sun set on the horizon and Stavos produced a supplement of ouzo, the steward and deckhand long gone by then.

True to their nature, the waiters began arriving at the devastated café, mostly on bicycles, assessing the damage and chattering among themselves, whilst they lofted a charcoal bier and hampers of supplies from a caterer's van. A hardy lot, they had the street-side café in operation when the timid reappeared from the streets.

Somewhat unsteady by then Stavos called it quits for the night. Hitching his legs to accommodate the stairs, he went forward to sleep it off, not unhappy with a bottle of ouzo clutched in his hand. Nina and I supped from a plate of moussaka and watched the waiters mop the sidewalk across the way. By eight o'clock it was business as usual. Townspeople wandered from the hill to assess the quayside. Tourists came from their sodden hotels to settle into chairs and talk quietly among themselves, mostly a frightened and nervous lot. The northern

Europeans had come from an environment where nature's awesome strength was seldom felt.

"They'll be queuing the Olympic counters in the morning," Nina observed. "It's terrible to think they've come all this way for a few days of sun."

When we turned in for the night, Nina came softly to my arms. We shed our clothes in the darkness and clung naked together upon the bed, our bodies pressing, our tongues exploring hotly, until our sensual pleasures were raised to frenzy. A private moment apart from the traumatic day, a moment of wild release, a superb moment of love that throbbed from our souls until we lay exhausted, clinging, caressing, and expressing our love!

CHAPTER

awn came late that morning, a blood red in the east as it raised from the Turkish hills and cast its eerie light upon the town. Church bells had yet to chime, although there was an audible chant from the Muslim Lotzia Mosque; sparrows chirped from the tree of Hippocrates above the spring. A lorry rumbled by, its lights beaming the deserted café, silhouetting the morning fisherman righting their splintered boats. Leeside, a trawler chugged past the muted fortress with its nets in tow, returning from a night in the Straits. The somber crew, faces gray, reflected the volatile sea that apparently had dispersed their evening catch to depths beyond their nets.

In addition to the tectonic undercut, the volcano had left its calling card during the night – a film of ash lay underfoot when I stepped on deck, slippery to my fingers when I grasped the rail. Carried aloft by the winds, powdery and light, the opalescent haze had drifted seaward, nevertheless drawing one's thoughts to whence it came.

An early riser, Captain Stavos was seated in the salon, chewing a cucumber from the blade of his knife, when I joined him there. He wore the spent T-shirt from Berkeley (a gift from Nina, I assumed), together with a pair of greasy khakis belted with a rope. Not unfriendly, he climbed to his feet and poured a mug of coffee, indicating it was for me.

"Have some cucumber," he said, offering a slice from his blade. "Is good for the gut to start the day!" I thanked him and declined. The cucumber was the last thing my stomach needed at 40,000 feet. I explained to him why.

"So you fly tomorrow, hey? Maybe cucumber is not so good. I get some yogurt and fresh peach!" He disappeared in the galley without waiting for an answer, returning with a bowl of peaches swimming in yogurt. Producing a spoon from his hip pocket, he sat down at the table until I'd had my bowl of peaches;

then, leaning forward on his elbows to study my face, he furrowed his aged brow, struggling for words.

"So maybe aeroplane fly like ship in nervous sea," he furthered. "Take plenty experience fly bad storm, I think. Mind helm and engines, not for neophyte...take gut and steady hand! Have some more peach," he added, pointing to the galley with his knife.

"Pilots are kin to sailors," I said, drawing an analogy he'd comprehend. "We share an understanding of winds and freaks of nature, Captain. Updrafts are like riptides; they pull you in and shake you up! At altitude we can handle it," I added, "but ships are not so lucky if they're hard against a rocky bottom!"

"Give cause for plenty worry," Stavos muttered. "Full moon bring floodtide and Kos not safe harbor." With Sigurdesson's prediction in mind, I inquired if he'd considered an alternative, which he apparently had.

"Sail once with Nicholas to Astypalaia," he said. "Astypalaia lee side of island, protected by Cape Loannis. Find deep anchorage there, not so much surge. Nicholas have interest," he added. "Say long ago ancient people find shelter in caves near by."

"Have you mentioned this to Nina?"

"Nina busy with friends and kinfolk, but maybe now she have reason to discuss. Worry for Helena, I think...come maybe when she wake and listen to old man. Near village of Astypalaia be Kefalos," Stavos added. "Long reach from capital city, not much for party time, but nice beach at Kamari and plenty bottom for ship."

"How far from Antimahia?"

"Fetch close to fifteen kilometers," Stavos reckoned. "Half again closer to aerodrome than capital city. Not so much vehicle, but plenty goat on mountain road."

Advantageous in the event of an emergency, I thought, assuming a catastrophic floodtide would inundate Kos and dismember its highways. An imminent move conjecture, however, not for me to decide, and Nina not quick to concur. In days to come I'd have reason to focus on the mountainous reaches of Astypalaia, however.

At the moment, I was anxious to get on to Antimahia, my pending test flight and the project's operational status much in mind. With an eye to my sleeping wife, I showered and shaved, remembering to collect my brief case away from her nimble hands. The van was available for the day, once retrieved from up the hill. I was caught with my questionable values and Stavos' honest integrity when he offered the keys and slipped a St. Christopher medal into my hand.

"Is for good luck," he said. "You have come to Kos with good intention, my son. Old man not soon forget!"

* * * * * *

The Fiat was not so quick to oblige my presence, however. Damp and missing a couple of cylinders, we leapt and jerked until we were abreast of the government house. Fotis' office had been sandbagged anticipating the tide, but not successfully. The militia was wielding buckets and mops, as were Nokomo's mainstays, barefoot in the residue, lamenting the lack of electricity to brew their morning tea. Nokomo had located to the Alexandris Hotel; seemingly his Mercedes flooded to the glove compartment when the wave swept the low-lying Xenia. The Hummer their mode of transport while they collected his soggy files.

"Dr. Nokomo intended to meet with you this morning, Mr. Slater," a young lady advised, "but due to the circumstances, he's extremely busy. Sends word he'll contact you later," she added with a dazzling smile.

"Tell the doctor I'm en route to Antimahia, my sweet. Should be back by one, however, my wife needing the van."

"It's Sabina," she corrected. "Have you a cellular?"

"At the base we do."

"Better we call you there. And would you bring along our invoices, please? I understand they've yet to be paid." I nodded to this. Like Schumann, she brought a breath of fresh air and hope for the beleaguered.

Fotis was elsewhere, I thought, noting the absence of his jeep. As for Amalia, she was missing from her morning stand. Lurking about for new fodder, most likely, figuring Schumann was no longer useful, aside from his services the previous night. She might also be on the lookout for, or wary of adverse criminal types she may have contacted in Athens; possibly privy to information leaks linked with sabotage (and names in high places). She'd be frightened by their presence if she sensed they intended to tamper with the U-2. The upshot...guarding Gunnar's flanks would inadvertently cover mine!

All this was conjecture, of course, although the shady lady obviously was at Gunnar's disposal. Skeptical of recruiting help, she'd be playing a lone hand, treading a dangerous avenue with time closing in! My thoughts flitted to Willitts and T.S. while I maneuvered the cluttered streets.

With the newscast concentrating on Santorini's rumblings, I was unsure of the international scene. Needed an update of the situation in southern Turkmenistan and a possible change of venue. My primary questions...the status of my unnamed observer and Gunnar's mysterious delay. Might Gunnar have spooked the UN and made himself available to fill the rear seat? An altogether shitty thought!

However illogical, the thought wasn't new. The doctored charts were a tip off, prior to our meeting at the Carlyle. Clumsy as it was, there was an obvious attempt to disorient the U-2 to where it shouldn't be...a remote corner of the Caspian Sea! Seemingly coinciding with T.S.'s scheme to recon a like area, paralleling interest of the de facto KGB, a residue of hard-liners who'd have reason to be delighted should the U-2 be downed in their yard!

With thoughts such as these, I found myself tailgating an Olympic bus, and found another ahead when I attempted to pass. Both crowded with tourists wanting to be elsewhere, presumably a northern clime. Considering the traffic, I laid back to avoid the diesel fumes, giving my thoughts time to unwind. Again came repetitious flashbacks of the events at Mountain View; the bearded scientist celebrating his wings at Hennessey's Bar, his life linked to an assassin he never knew?

And what was the purpose of eliminating this kindly man? And why the cover-up murder at the curbside of my apartment; the mitigating photos of Gunnar at Ramenskoye? What sort of a monster was this? A rank egomaniac on the edge of insanity; a self-appointed messiah attempting to revive a dead ideology? Why else would he familiarize himself with a duplicate of the U-2, unless he envisioned himself in control, remotely or directly, perhaps planning a heralded forced landing to embarrass the UN? Giving the militants a moment of spite to loosen their funky tanks beyond the shores of the Caspian? Meanwhile, and I gave thought to the possibility, General O'Brien playing it cool and laid back, possibly waiting the opportunity to unleash his stealth B-2s and proximity fused bombs!

Missing parts of the equation began to sort themselves when I drew abreast of the terminal. Word from the lieutenant that Gunnar was due the following afternoon on a round about charter from Cairo. Nearby in the lobby, Willitts was discussing our venture with Schumann and Winner. Not to be ignored, the magical sight of grading machines in process of supplementing the U-2's needs!

Willitts, with no disguising mustache or oily glasses, wore an identification badge that disclosed he was a correspondent from the London Times, his surname unchanged. He played it cool, suggesting we'd met briefly following the symposium at the Grande Bretagne, although he neglected to mention the flowers! All things considered, he looked the part of a journalist on per diem. Clad in rumpled khakis, his ruddy English face unshaven, questioning names, recorder in hand.

"Reckoned the project would rate our Sunday feature section," he explained. "Possibly front page, allowing our readers' apathy towards phenomena...apart from royalty, of course! Had a bloody time of it in Athens," he added. "What with martial law and conditions at Hellinikon degenerating to bartering for flights to London and the like!"

"So how was the weather en route?" I inquired, realizing he was needing an out. He expressed his observations in layman's terms, although his terminology was tongue in cheek.

"Zero visibility until we were west of Astipalea, Slater! The milk bottle effect; all sweat! In fact, Olympic had a problem with heavy turbulence and I've yet to inspect my drawers!"

"Did you encounter static lightning?" Winner questioned. "Vertical or otherwise...spontaneous bursts, Mr. Willitts?"

"Vertical, like myself when we penetrated the cell, Doctor. Otherwise, the clouds were constantly lit with eerie bursts of luminosity, swirling off our wing tips until we were clear of the overcast."

"St. Elmo's Fire!" Winner interjected. "Harmless in most instances, although it's a portent of bad weather." Willitts nodded to this.

"Caused a squabble in the cockpit...tripped the auto-pilot, I believe; had the stewardess on her knees!" Winner passed it off without comment, although I sensed a trace of anxiety I hadn't foreseen. Perhaps there was an inherent fear in his casual make-up, a fear of the unpredictable elements whilst strapped rear seat!

Come morning, the embedded cold front would have moved to the south and, aside from the shroud over Santorini, we'd have excellent visibility for our short-term flight. Moreover, we'd have an easy shot back to Antimahia, should Winner experience a problem. With a stable platform, I doubted it would come to that; it was a matter of wait and see.

The time was ripe to reiterate our operational guidelines for the oncoming mission to test the U-2. Specifically, the responsibilities of the individuals involved, including MacDougal and his ground crew. The lieutenant would serve as interpreter with a bullhorn during the takeoff phase, wherein he'd parallel MacDougal's chase Jeep with his own. Also for consideration was our subsequent landing and the U-2's unaccountable float, its tendency to ground loop unless pogo wheels were immediately attached. Not to be forgotten, the need of communication with the tower across the way, the means to divert traffic from the runway should we have reason to abort takeoff, or stretch our approach from miles away.

Schumann filled the communications slot, and I was happy with that, together with Edwards monitoring Winner's meteorological data from the U-2. The infrared readings they'd hand off to Dr. Sigurdesson who, at the moment, was eyeballing her computers out of hearing and detached. As was Fraser, busily updating our mainstay computer which had arrived with Olympic's morning flight.

Myself late arriving, MacDougal was on hand when I diagramed the U-2's flight plan on a chalkboard. The lieutenant nearby in starched khakis was discussing logistics with ex-Group Commander Willitts, our aspiring journalist from the London Times.

"Once in place, our takeoff roll will be less than 1,000 feet," I said. "With a light load the U-2's quick to climb, more so with her new engine and extended wings, although she droops like a gooney bird unsure of its feet. At 8,500 feet we'll level off and throttle back to cruise -- monitor our engine readings, try a few turns. No stalls," I added for Winner's benefit.

"Will you be testing Thera?" Willitts none too wisely inquired.

"We'll fly a direct course to Cyprus," I answered obliquely. "Roughly 430 nautical miles before we turn west on the 35th parallel. There's a RAP U-2 base at Cyprus if we encounter a problem, Mr. Willitts. Most likely they've dispersed their aircraft, although they'll have service facilities if need be. If all's well, we'll climb to the west and top off at 20,000 feet. We'll be on oxygen, of course, entering the downwind haze area, which we'll screen with the collectors at plus 2,000 foot levels until we turn north at $26°$ longitude over Crete.

"From there on, our $26°$ bearing will return us directly to Kos," I continued, neglecting to mention we'd be IFR until we topped the plume or leveled off at 40,000 feet (our maximum altitude without a pressure suit). "When we close on Santorini, we'll activate the sensor probes and record the readings until we're clear of the envelope," I added. "We'll also image the cone with a radar scan at automatic intervals, but Sigurdesson will have to wait for the cartridge until we taxi in."

"How long will you be airborne?" Willitts inquired. I shot Willitts a quick eye, hoping he'd shut up before Winner went off the wall!

"Close to four hours, plus an hour of fuel in reserve," I replied.

"Topped you off with six," MacDougal corrected. "Figured you might need it, Keithy." I nodded to this. The old fashioned gauges were suspect with the fuel sloshing from wing to wing.

For Winner's sake, I'd simplified the procedures as best I could. The U-2 was cumbersome to fly. Its controls and gauges dated from the '50s, and I'd be flying mostly by the seat of my pants. Fortunately, our electronics package was space age; the GPS encoding our flight course at all times. Luckily, Schumann was familiar with the U-2's electronics and communication needs; suspect, in a sense, as if he'd been previously apprised by parties unnamed? Lacking our ground-based data-link and HF transceiver, his makeshift relay via the tower would allow Winner to transmit our readings from 200 miles or so. Doubly important, the means to communicate with Air Traffic Control. Otherwise we'd be restricted to VFR and untenable delays when we penetrated the haze.

Hopefully, Willitts had further information, but MacDougal was nudging my elbow when the group dispersed and we'd have to wait a moment of privacy. MacDougal was hell bent, however, lowering his voice when he drew me aside.

"Problems, Keithy! Been wantin' your ear since you came in!"

"The U-2?"

"Negative, man; she's ready to go! But come this morning, we had a high priority shipment from Berlin. Came prepaid with Olympic," he added. "The militia picked it up and we have it in the hangar. Three hundred pounds of electronics, man!"

"The data-link?"

"Probably, but the instructions were in German and we didn't know which from what!"

"Did you notify Schumann of Dr. Winner?" I questioned.

"Schumann first off; he seems to have a handle on things. Said to let it be until Gunnar shows up. Odd sort, like he came out of nowhere, but I cotton to his ways, man. Like he was wise to the instructions, but didn't say!"

"Other than that?"

"For my part, he's strictly no fuss, old buddy! No interference on the line; helped us tune the VHF, in fact! He's also spent time with Fraser; our mainstay computer was programmed in German and they were at odds with that!" I gave prickly thought to Maureen's comments at the UN. Horst Gunnar's sleight of hand!

"Likewise, we have problems with the Swedish gal," MacDougal furthered. "Like she was coughin' blood when I brought her a beer. We gotta look after her, Keith! She has fever in her eyes, but won't let go! I'm also short me two Olympic mechanics," he added brightly. "Most likely Fotis scared them off, Keithy! Last seen, they was boozin' with the fat lady, sportin' the car they bought when they stole me APU, I think." I considered the likelihood of mutual elimination, and let it go with the thought.

My immediate priority had to do with familiarizing Dr. Winner with the U-2's high-riding rear cockpit and means of control, however. And knowing Willitts was keen to observe the hybrid U-2 close up (allowing for his journalist credentials), I motioned him to tag along whilst we proceeded to the change room to size the Doctor with an off-shelf flying suit and a pair of boots he'd require in the frigid air above 20,000 feet.

The sun was at 10 o'clock by then, the humidity insufferable, but I insisted Winner wear a helmet and oxygen mask whilst he adjusted his length rear seat, and MacDougal explained the emergency procedures we might encounter at altitude. The Chief, supplementing a breather from the portable AC when Winner's visor became glazed with sweat and he raised a glove in desperation.

Winner was gutsy, however, and mutely hung in whilst I traveled the stick front seat to make certain it didn't interfere with his lengthy legs. He was also adept to his electronic chores (the multiple readings he'd monitor at altitude), despite his cumbersome gloves. I was reasonably sure he'd make it short term. Long range at high altitude was another matter! It would take time consuming days to adapt as Gomulaka had at Mountain View; a certain kind of nerve to endure nine hours or more at 80,000 feet. True, Winner had flown the Miami hurricane watch, but there was a difference of confinement betwixt a U-2 and the commodious Navy P-3.

We spent an hour or so in the rank humidity...Winner stripped to his shorts whilst I reiterated procedures, not wanting a clumsy boot on the controls when we encountered turbulence or IFR conditions in the hazy ash! Willitts, besotted with his first sight of the hybrid bird and endless procedures, fortunately contained his comments until the Doctor sped for the shower and change of clothes.

"Hardy type for a neophyte," he commented dryly. "But definitely not for Iran or whatever your plans, Keithy man!"

"So why didn't you lay off? The doctor's bloody scared, you stupid ass!"

"Takes a pilot to know a pilot, Keith. Call it the way you like, but there's concern in high places should you have need to abort midway with a problem."

"Stressing a time slot, hey?" Willitts nodded to this.

"'Sooner the better', to quote General O'Brien. I'm not sure of his objective — or yours for that matter — but apparently NATO has common interests with Russia and Turkmenistan regarding a hot spot they'd like to resolve. More to the point, a toehold of ex-Soviet generals with tanks and atomics playing a fundamentalist card in the region! Like General Dudayev in Chechnya, Keith"

"Did T.S. alert you to anything else, preferably specifics?"

"I was to advise you of a fleet of wide base transport craft detected in the southeastern Caspian. No specifics, although I assume a photo recon when you corner Iran?" I laid back with that, realizing Willitts' knowledge was short tether and I was essentially on my own.

"Gunnar's also bloody well frightened," Willitts commented, seemingly aware of my thoughts while we walked to the terminal. "What with retribution in New York and Vienna, he's fearful of his hide and definitely on the run! Arrived in Cairo by way of Damascus! Seems his support's eroded with the de facto KGB, and he went underground when Stash's assassins spilled their brains. Same macabre scene in Warsaw, we understand. Two dead blokes with Gomulaka's obituary tagged to their shirts! Poles have long memories, it seems!"

"Bruno?"

"Relentless, Keith! Word has it he stalked Amalia until she wised for Kos; in process cancelled her companion near the Alstir Palace. Presumably a long-wanted assassin type from Lebanon, quietly put to rest with a silencer equipped 9mm."

I gave instant thought of Bruno waiting patiently in the Mercedes, his eyes glued to the BG's palatial doors. Obviously Horst Gunnar was high on his list from years back. Of which Gunnar was seemingly aware, when he cancelled at the BG. Leaving Amalia as an unwitting accessory whilst she recruited willing hands from the Athens' underworld to guard Gunnar's stance. One of which Bruno put down...not realizing there might be others with no de facto history, such as a pair of mercenary Olympic mechanics strangely on scene at Antimahia when she solicited their help?

"Change of venue, Willitts! Like all of a sudden I'm reading between the lines and figure Amalia's had second thoughts!"

"Spell it out, Keithy!"

"Okay, so first off she tailed us to London, thinking I'd contact T.S., which would immediately alert Gunnar's suspicions, let's say. Failing this, she tagged us to Athens where things went astray; subsequently arriving at Kos where she enlists covert help and plies her trade with an ear to the ground."

"Schumann?"

"Schumann's too smart for her likes! But let's say she kowtows with the two Olympic mechanics Fotis recently fired. Like they're pissed off and she learns they've nasty plans for the U-2, which would be counterproductive to Gunnar's thing!"

"Sabotage!"

"Inclined to believe so, man! I got to thinking about this when I was flexing the U-2's trim tabs and MacDougal mentioned an FAA Notam dealing with a chartered Lear 21 that blazed a hill near Athens with its tabs reversed! Laid a heavy on my mind, man! I'd played a pilot's hunch and inquired the FAA's synopsis a while back. The Lear 21 one and the same that killed Nina's parents and crew." Obviously stunned, Willitts reached for his brief case.

"You had a call from Dr. Nokomo," someone said. I spun about.

"Dr. Nokomo?"

"Hot as a kettle!" Fraser allowed. "Seems he wasn't apprised of your test flight, Keithy boy!"

"Did he ask for Winner – or Dr. Schumann?"

"Seemed to be unacquainted with our roster, Keith. Made a point to demand your presence at 3 o'clock sharp! Also Mr. Gunnar. Had himself a fit when I said he wasn't due until tomorrow. Cut me off!"

"Did he call back?"

"Young lassie did; polite, apologetic. Requested you bring along your flight plan and our payroll stats. Couldn't rightly place her accent...melodious, Caribbean? Not Nigerian."

I checked my watch. Allowing for traffic and hopefully lunch with Nina, I had less than an hour to finalize matters with Schumann, Edwards and Dr. Sigurdesson. Sigurdesson resting in her quarters when I inquired, however.

"She's plain tuckered out," Edwards explained. "Been up since dawn and needing help with her computers. No secretary, although she was promised as much in Geneva! Perked up a while back, though. Seems your wife contacted the Institute of Hippocrates and they've pledged a half-dozen science majors to help out. Starting this afternoon, in fact. Nice gesture. Time's appropriate for them to be involved in their own future!"

"Nina arranged all of this?"

"Sponsored a nurse to look in at night time, we understand! Lovely lady, Keith ...unselfish, pretty as a lark. Bless your luck, old chap!" I nodded to that, blessed thing! How best could I protect her should the world come apart while I was fitfully half asleep at 80,000 feet?

* * * * * *

It takes a while to bleed knots and bring a U-2 down. A spirited glider with engine at idle, she'd prone to loft with the rising thermals, requiring sweat and muscle with her stick and rudder...a time-consuming process following lengthy hours at the helm. Needless concern at the moment perhaps. Our morning test flight was short-term and we'd have ATC on the horn. The long haul was another matter, however, and I was wary of Gunnar's interference once our data-link was installed. Might there be a potential flap betwixt Schumann and Gunnar when the latter arrived?

"Moot question," Schumann countered, when we had a minute together. "Our immediate concern is Santorini's accelerating activity, Keith...our least Horst Gunnar's appearance, if you anticipate a problem with that."

"Not by comparison since you put it that way."

"Then note the erratic readings from the seismograph implanted at Thera," Schumann continued, pointing to Ingrid's charts pinned to the wall. "Specifically, the highs and lows, and the hourly timing between. Allowing for error, compare the time elapse with the rise and fall of the tides," he added. "When the tides are at their fullest reach immeasurable pressure is exerted upon the crustal plates verging Santorini's hot spot; followed by an upheaval or contraction when the sea recedes. The severity of its flow will result in an undercut and the toppling waves we've experienced of late. All of which is not unusual when tectonic plates overlap one another, but the adjacency of a venting volcano, together with the pressures of a full moon tide, is indeed a matter of concern."

"Sigurdesson's theory full circle, hey?"

"Frankly, Keith, we fear a disaster in the making should a fracture occur in the volcano's venting pipe and allow an intrusion of the sea. Minute amounts are all that's needed to enhance a super venting to a height of fifteen miles or more. Massive energy! Which in turn would deplete the magma chamber, allowing its wall to collapse and admit the sea to its molten core...likened to the Niagara plunging undeterred into the cavity on all sides. The cavity at this point would be enormous, encompassing a third of the island with incalculable depth. The end result: within minutes a Plinian explosion of a magnitude unknown to mankind! In its wake, at supersonic speed, a massive outflow of incandescent gas that would vaporize life forms for hundreds of miles. Not to mention the resulting juxtapose when sea compounds upon itself to flood the Aegean!"

"Take it easy, Schumann! I need a breather before I split for Antarctica!"

"I'm not amused by your sense of humor, Keith!"

"So don't relate to it. I've a wife and family to consider, but we don't intend to leave momentarily."

"Okay, but in the interim we're in desperate need of the cone velocity and screen readings for Ingrid's analysis! Perhaps I've elaborated to express our concern, but there were like occurrences at Tambro and Krakatoa...similar adjacency of the sea and converging crustal plates, such as the belt beneath Santorini stretching from Europe to Asia Minor. In essence, it's the presence of immense quantities of water that precipitates a paroxysmal explosion, as described by Pliny the Younger following the eruption of Mt. Vesuvius."

"Following the death of his uncle, Pliny the Elder, who was asphyxiated by its fumes! And so we learn from history, Doctor; but I've a brand new engine to test before we penetrate the plume. This could damage the blades or cause a compressor stall, which is not a nice thought. Our sensor and radar readings amount to an easy show, so long as we're beneath the cloud cover and make a visual approach."

"Which is important, Keith! But dare I persist or repeat myself? We're in need of the pod screenings to further Ingrid's analysis...the possibility of salinity in the mix."

"You're a tough apple, Schumann! Let's see how the weather checks at dawn. If it's clear, we'll give the feather edge a shot, provided the systems check out...and Winner hangs in!"

Close as possible, Keith. We need a taste of the prime ingredients. Make certain to avoid the rain areas when Winner activates the pods, however."

"Loud and clear, man! I intend to follow our flight plan until we turn west from Cyprus. Which reminds me of my 3 o'clock with Dr. Nokomo," I added, checking my watch. "Seems he's upset in regard to our test flight, but I'll call collect if he pulls the rug."

"Counter to our objectives? I doubt that, Keith. Best to reckon with him wisely, however. Most likely he's defensive of White Dove's shortcomings in New York of late!"

"You're pulling my leg!"

"I beg your pardon?"

"The project's shortcomings, Schumann? So fill me in."

"I assumed your group was advised, and thought it best to let it be!"

"Negative, man! In terms of Nokomo, he didn't show at the Grande Bretagne and we wondered about that. Odd, what? Presumably he was elsewhere when a house cleaning was requested by the Greek ambassador to the UN?"

"Don't rightly recall the circumstances, Keith. My information came about when I was contacted in Amsterdam, although there's coverage in the herald Tribune, of which Willitts would have knowledge."

"The bottom line, Doctor? We share the same rock!"

"The investigation has to do with administrative matters, Keith. Mismanagement, over-staffing, unrelated expenditures, and lack of consideration for needs in the field. Indicated his infrastructure's savaging the project for wants of its own. In short, if I may utilize your vernacular, the ambassador pulled the rug and they've dispatched an economist from Jamaica to check accounts!"

"Sabina?"

"Don't recall the name, but apart from that, the UN questioned the project's absentee components and capability to disseminate critical information from the field! Couched in diplomatic terminology, of course!"

"Meaning they have the picture, but haven't a clue as to who's in charge?"

Schumann nodded.

"Needing Dr. Sigurdesson's findings, primarily! The volcano's no longer an object of curiosity, Keith. They also expressed the need of a seasoned volcanologist to lend a hand with Ingrid. Second opinion, possibly! And to that end, I was solicited by your State Department while en route from Jakarta; caught as I was with my valise and the shirt on my back! Had time to respond to a call from America, however. A mutual acquaintance I believe expedited my appointment to White Dove."

"Rex Keenan?"

"I was pressed not to mention names, Keith, but let's say he's concerned of the U-2's current status. He was also knowledgeable of Nokomo's problems; suggested we treat him diplomatically. From all accounts, the doctor's a dedicated man, Keith. An educated agriculturist, but not a geophysicist...nor an apt administrator, apparently! Insecure, perhaps. So best to play it by ear and hear him out. He'll come to reason, I believe."

"Is he aware of your appointment, or let's say your presence, if the shit hits the fan?"

"Depends on the status of his fax machine, Keith! It presumably needs fixing since it was immersed in high water."

"So, maybe you should come along and lend a hand with that!"

In diplomatic terms it's better I not, Keith. Most likely he's received word by pouch or cellular. Frankly, at the moment, I'm in need of clothes, of which Willitts has my list, if you'd care to take him along? Knickers and shirts I have, thanks to MacDougal and Dr. Winner; I'm mostly in need of trousers...extra long, no cuffs!"

"Perhaps Willitts needs a shopping companion, Henric? Should I drop him off at the café and let him try his luck?" Schumann's Adam's apple convulsed, but he covered up with an affable grin.

"No comment, Keith! Let's say I've advised him accordingly, presuming you're pulling my leg!"

* * * * * *

It was after 12 when I ran a copy of my flight plan and collected our payroll stats from the lieutenant per Sabina's request. The long hours I'd spent with Dr. Winner were beneficial, however, and I'd gained straightforward information I damn well needed, thanks to Willitts and Schumann. But I had further questions to inquire of ex-Group Commander Willitts, regarding Schumann.

Intellectually bent, handy with electronics, fluent in German, the Dutchman appeared an excellent choice to counter Horst Gunnar. But that, obviously, wasn't the UN's intent although he was sorely needed. But what was his status with Rex Keenan and T.S.? Was he knowledgeable of the circumstances following the U-2's turn over Iran or was Willitts himself likewise so informed?

"Second question first," I intoned when we piled into the van and cleared the bypass to Olympia's terminal. "Schumann: is he kin to Air Force Intelligence or otherwise for real?"

"No connections whatsoever! We suspect Keenan had a handle on his appointment to keep the project on track. In fact, I was informed to wise up and 'play it cool' as you say. I've a feeling he recognized my face from somewhere, although he didn't needle my credentials."

"Or lack of a typewriter or laptop computer?"

"First question next, Keithy! I've an envelope in my brief case addressed from the FAA, certified mail, to your name at the UN, which T.S. countersigned and forwarded to our drop in Athens."

"So now you're telling me this? Anything else, Willitts, like my billing from American Express?"

"Not to make light of it, Keithy! T.S. obviously inspected the contents, as I did! But I thought it best to hold back, until you mentioned a possible fiddle faddle with the U-2's controls!"

"More so than that, man! If the FAA suspects sabotage, it's Nina's reaction that blows my mind! So come up with it, Willitts, I'm not the child I used to be!"

"So calm it, Keith! I've also had my licks in Desert Storm; Bosnia and Kosovo of late!"

I pulled off the road and came full stop. The envelope contained photocopies of the jet's surviving components. The elevator trim tab section circled and noted, as was the cockpit trim control...which were mangled but diagrammed to their position at the point of impact. In essence, the tabs were downswept for rapid descent whereas the control was set for maximum climb, indicating the spool was reversed, as I'd suspected!

'Contradictory maintenance procedures and lack of visual inspection' the synopsis noted. 'Also, the aircraft had returned from charter eight hours prior and no malfunctions were reported by the pilot in command. Nor did the Company have record of a request for realignment while the aircraft was hangared and later serviced from the charter to Heathrow and JFK.' The time in the hangar also was noted; approximately eight hours followed by a question mark, indicating the FAA was doubtful of security.

"How else to phrase it?" I vented under breath. "Picture yourself full throttle with the yoke set back for lift off, and you're wondering what the hell?"

"Wouldn't like it, Keith! T.S. indicated Interpol has a slice of fingerprints they're comparing at the moment. Better to keep a closed mouth, the report's confidential and they're wary of a leak to the media." Worse yet...should a trail of green lead to the perpetrator and its source be named! But that could be weeks away, or politically intervened. I gave furthering thought to Nina's psychic instinct; her seething mind set for vengeance!

"You're pale, Keith!"

"Scared, man!"

"Meaning your wife?"

"Greek fire when she's lit! I'm curious if Fotis has a copy? It's a small island, fella, and word gets around."

"Pause for thought, hey? His leads likely stem from the stolen APU, but I doubt if he were copied with the FAA's photos and letter."

"Makes sense," I admitted, "but it's not nice to have around, and I'm worried about your haversack should it end up in odd places." *Nor would I trust it to my brief case,* I added thoughtfully to myself.

"Think it best we destroy it, Keith?"

"I'd like that, fella. I'll shred, you drive, okay?" Paper waste, bits and pieces, spiraled in our wake, better left to memory and the due process of law. The insidious cobra head on the horizon was a grim reminder of nature's devious ways, however.

Wary of Amalia's whereabouts, we exchanged seats near the edge of town and I dropped Willitts at the bus stop with directions to the Xenia. If need be, we agreed to make contact following the U-2's flight from Antimahia, which would allow for his interest as a journalist when our pod screenings were analyzed by Sigurdesson and Schumann.

The sidewalk café was not as busy as usual when I parked alongside the Helena. Attendance mostly locals with their newspapers and whatnot. The majority of tourists had long since gone; the remainder awaited Olympic or LTV charters. Amalia was not in evidence, her usual table at the café unoccupied. Nor was Nina aboard the Helena when I called from the pier.

"Nina have-a lunch with Cleo," Stavos allowed, beckoning I should join him for a plate of pastitsio and a glass of Santorini wine. The wine I declined, but I had my fill of the pastitsio whilst he brought me up to date.

"She make a plan for nice supper," he continued. "Veal Avesnoise with cheese, fresh tomato and mustard sauce: no cucumber in salad! She plenty busy, Keith. Have long telephone call with London, I think." Veal Avesnoise? Shades of our first evening together in Palo Alto! I gave heavy thought to that while the church bells chimed the half-hour before three.

* * * * *

"A one percent decrease in solar radiation would cause our world's surface temperature to decrease about one degree centigrade. A decrease of 10 or 15 percent would cause an ice age. We might possibly be entering a decade of transition. The potato famine in Ireland was the result of a cold sunless summer, when a permanent veil of volcanic dust prevailed. We cannot, of course, prevent this from happening, but we can predict its tenure in time. The world's population is dependent on the fruits of agriculture; with a diminished sun their crops will fail and we shall starve. Our concern is the density of ash in the very high altitude, to determine its spread with the winds that span the continents...we are not here to investigate its source!"

I was being scolded. The Nigerian was reprimanding me, the graphite face before me was stern and sour. *It was he who would determine the scope of our mission, not me!* I reminded the doctor the missions were dependent upon the U-2's performance. As the pilot in command, the routing of the test flight in the morning was my responsibility, not his! He wide-eyed me, puffing his cheeks. He wore his cloak of authority with a crown of righteousness. I played it down, appealed to his rationale.

"The wing pods require a flight check, Doctor. The infrared sensors and sulfuric acid collectors haven't been tested since they were assembled. The field team will need an appraisal of our feedback to the computers, an electronic count of the particles we encounter. Santorini is an easy shot."

He nodded reluctantly, toyed with a ballpoint made notes on a pad. I believe he might have suggested the test flight had I not broached the matter myself. When our eyes leveled, Nokomo smiled and reached for my hand, motioning me to take a chair. We discussed the missions in sequence, with provisions for the winds aloft. Mission One was programmed for the Nile to the Sudan, continuing along the Rift Valley bisecting Kenya, then a turnabout over Afar's Triangle for an infrared reading of the tectonic plates.

"If fuel is sufficient, I request the U-2 climb above Djibouti and sample the dust until you reach the topmost layer," he said, tapping his ballpoint pen. "Thence to follow the easterlies over the sub-Sahara. It is here where we anticipate an imbalance in the seasonal rains!" he added, pointing to his wall map indicating countries along the equatorial belt: Ghana and Nigeria!

"Subsequent flights over the mid-Atlantic will give us the particle count we need to predict the fallout over the Caribbean and North America, Mr. Slater."

"Time allowing," I said. "The Arab countries were scheduled for Mission Two," I reminded and stressed the point.

"Yes, of course, Mr. Slater. You are to overfly Israel and Jordan, Saudi Arabia and Oman, until you sight the Persian Gulf, then make a sweeping turn to the northeast over Iran." He hesitated...the remainder of the flight would be ticklish, and he knew it!

"We have obtained permission from Iran to overfly their boundaries to the Caspian Sea, but the Republic of Turkmenistan demands strict observance of its boundaries with Iran. Apparently there is unrest in the Ashkhabad area and there's no guarantee of safety."

I studied the wall behind him where he'd displayed his doctorate from King's College, an honorary degree from Harvard, another from the University of Edinburgh, a fellowship from Corpus Christi College, Cambridge; pride of place he'd given to a commendation from the Department of Agriculture Research Center in Maryland. Photographs of his wives and children were arranged on his desk: he'd spent considerable time decorating his office. He had the complacent look of a college administrator – if he'd smoked a pipe and worn a dark blazer instead of a sweat-stained bush jacket.

"We have much paperwork to attend to," he said, his voice echoing faintly from miles away. "Procedures to follow, raw data to analyze. I sometimes wish I was young again and could follow the work I originally intended, but I'm old now and hopelessly outdated. It's better I do what I do. You have an outstanding group to work with in the field, however. Dr. Schumann is expected tomorrow, as is Dr. Gunnar – from Cairo, I'm so informed." I hadn't the heart to tell him Schumann was at hand. The doctor allowed he'd been out of touch...'pursuant to a business trip to Nigeria'.

"I was in Lagos when I was informed of a problem in New York," he continued. "Accounting irregularities according to the press, of which I share the responsibility, although due to my lecture schedule I'm dependent on my staff. I've found means to fund the difference and we've – ah – replaced the prime offenders. You'll take a liking to Sabina, my valued aide de camp from Jamaica.

At the moment she's repairing the fax machine, I believe!"

"We met this morning," I said.

"Yes, she mentioned that. Now then, may I address you as Keith? Now that we have a basic understanding, I feel obliged to offer my transport to our base complex. I've yet to greet your group, Keith. Say eight o'clock sharp tomorrow morning?"

"Six or earlier, Doctor. Takes a while to suit up!" In the end we agreed to share coffee at his office at six. Which was helpful, knowing Nina's waking hours, if he geared the Hummer dock side the Helena at dawn! Likeable, well intentioned, as Schumann had said, the doctor was politically savvy, but somewhat of a dodo, I thought. His long-term views as an agriculturist ill suited to the inferno that would lay it all to waste.

Fotis' office was a scene of activity when I passed it by with the van; what with a tow truck and a bevy of military Jeeps fronting his door! Nina was foremost in my mind, however, with the sight of her scarf trailing from the Helena when she greeted me dockside.

We had a lovely sunset dinner, just the two of us: a lovable night I shall never forget. Small talk, lovers' talk whilst the band played the bittersweet Greek melodies across the way: then Nina's joyous laughter when we joined the troupe and danced to the bouzoukis until we were spent. Then, naked aside from our wedding bands, we embraced in the shower and sprawled together upon our bed. Thoroughly aroused, Nina shrieked her delight of our splendid orgasm, and then she slumped in my arms and trailed off to sleep.

"I love you, Keith," softly said, an expression of love I shall always remember.

CHAPTER

inner and I sat in our cockpits breathing pure oxygen whilst MacDougal completed the remainder of our pre-flight list. Our fuel quantity at engine start was 890 gallons, sufficient for a flight of four hours with reserves. Our gross take off weight, inclusive of the sensor pods, was slightly over 21,000 pounds. We wore flying suits, not pressure suits...heated for altitude, not cooled. Perspiring profusely, I contacted Winner on the intercom to cross check our oxygen pressure systems. When he acknowledged, I gave the Chief a thumbs up and we were ready to spool the GE F-29.

The engine start was relatively uncomplicated: when we had idling, the chief disconnected the mobile air compressor and stood by while I checked the engine instruments. I signaled when they were in the green, the ground crew drew the cart away and we were ready to roll. I called in to ground control for clearance to the active. The Chief piled into a Jeep to lead us along the taxiway; a pair of militiamen ran alongside our wingtips – the U-2 has a tendency to totter when she taxies: the wing tips a tendency to gather runway lights and sprinkler heads. I had a moment to remember the night behind me, a moment, while the unwieldy bird lumbered to the intersection, to reflect that I had not seen the suspect mechanics since they were last seen with Amalia; our ground check assuring the trim tabs were A O.K.!

The U-2 was more sail plane than jet; a delicate thing to maneuver on the taxiway, handling like a truck on a slippery highway until we had the strip aligned with the needle-like nose. I checked with the tower when we were firmly in position. Athens Air Control Center had cleared us to flight level 40,000, advising commercial traffic to remain at 38,000 until 1200 hours. The tower cautioning local traffic to stand clear of the outbound active until we passed through 6,000. A green light flashed from the tower, I switched to intercom and checked Winner's canopy latch. The Chief pulled the Jeep off into the grass; the two militiamen climbed in beside him. He waved his red cap. I rolled the trim tab to a 6° nose down setting and advanced the throttle to maximum thrust.

The F-29 took about six seconds to spool up; the initial takeoff roll was slow until the engine reached full thrust and we catapulted from the runway in less than 800 feet. The pogos fell away; I lifted the nose to approximately 60° climb and held at 160 knots. The island faded behind us in the brownish haze. With the sun on our backs and an indistinct horizon, I flew the gauges to maintain a climb profile and we leveled off at 20,000 four minutes later, our rate of climb averaging 5,000 a minute.

I looked down and back; the island was the size of an almond chip scissored between the two slender peninsulas protruding from the Turkish mainland. I reset the throttle to hold a 400-knot ground speed, adjusted the trim, engaged the autopilot and turned the transponder code to 4460. Athens Control acknowledged our ident and released us for a frequency change. I immediately contacted Schumann to verify our position, handed off our altitude reading. He spoke briefly to Winner, and the doctor toggled the electronic relay systems. We were ready for business.

The U-2 was equipped with an internal guidance system for navigating the primary missions, but there was no immediate use that morning. The dirty plume rising from Santorini would be visible for the extent of the flight, and we utilized our ADF to correct our drift, our lookdown radar for time lapse.

Continuing our flight plan, we had Rhodos beneath us in a matter of minutes; drew a bead on Cyprus a half-hour later and contacted the UK base to confirm our systems were okay. In fact, the F-29 engine performed superbly, wanting to climb when we turned west to vector Crete. All the while, Schumann on the horn whilst I called off our readings. Judging from his belated responses, I suspicioned he was on his cellular with T.S. in Riyadh, confirming our GPS readings and altitude.

Comforted by the thought, eyeing the dust strata on course, I decided to climb to 40,000, advising Winner accordingly, allowing that at various levels we'd be flying IFR. Game, he indicated thumbs up to my mirror; he confirmed his oxygen was in green and engaged the pods, making note of the variable strata colors until we topped out at 40,000 where the U-2 reigned supreme. At 40,000 and above the outside air was stable, requiring only minor corrections to the autopilot, its lateral displacement calculating to an uncanny 1/6°.

Over Crete, the stratospheric dust cloud was southwesterly; our line of sight visibility unrestricted, the curvature of the earth quite evident along the horizon.

The sky ranged from light blue where it met the deserts of Libya to varying shades of deep blue and indigo, then the black of outer space directly overhead. The outside temperature read -48°F, but the warming element in our flight suits had us relatively comfortable in the close-confining cockpits, and the sun would melt the frost from our masks when we came about to the east.

At 9:40 we bisected the 26° longitude, then banked north to follow the 26° bearing which would lead us to Santorini. The worst was to come, however. I contacted Winner on the intercom to make certain of his harness as we closed on the island. His tome was suspect, but he didn't beg off, adding thumbs up when I viewed him in the mirror. The tilt of his helmet suggestive of St. George challenging a dragon of fire.

An ungodly plume of ash and smoke writhed skyward like a giant cobra minding his master's future. At high noon its ominous shadow would fall upon the Nile and blot out the sun from the beach-goers at Tel Aviv. Its ugly throat was needled with lightning, an unimaginable thing to behold from our proximity. I throttled back to Mach 0.75 to avoid a buffet from our increasing speed as our fuel load lightened, tightening my harness.

We called in to Schumann when we were 40 miles from Santorini's perimeter. A pair of minute-sized liners was anchored off its northern shore; the waters crisscrossed with the wakes of small craft transporting evacuees to Athens and beyond. The caldera and volcano's rise were hidden by dense, oily smoke; the town of Thera no longer glistened its whitewashed walls. I switched on our synthetic aperture radar scan, studied the scope, and shivered from what I saw.

"My God! Do you see what I see?" Winner was shouting over the intercom. I nodded numbly. The volcano's shank had formed a new shoreline to the northeast, enveloping Manoia. Nea Kamene lay within the growing mass to the south; the small crescent of water lying to the north of Akrotiri was all that remained of the ancient caldera.

I toggled the videocassette to record the unbelievable scene, calling in to Athens Control to alter our clearance. We would circle the perimeter from 20 miles, descending from 40,000 to 10,000 and continue on to Kos. Their answer was delayed. I banked to the south and disengaged the autopilot while we waited ATC's response, adjusted the starboard aileron trim and triggered the transfer pump to balance our remaining fuel.

Athens Control Okayed the maneuver a few minutes later. I opened the bleed air vents in the engine intakes, dropped the landing gear and opened the speed brake for drag. We turned toward the boiling smoke holding 170 knots. Athens Control relayed a request from the Department of Meteorology, then. Would we make our readings available? I referred the call to Schumann and asked him to contact the tower, advising Athens when he acknowledged. We hit the smoke a minute later. I hand flew the bird, monitoring the pressure ratio to avoid a compressor stall, hauling back to 140 knots to flatten our glide.

The brownish ash struck the windscreen as if we had entered a heavy rain; sifted into the cockpit, clinging to my gloves as I bent forward with my eyes glued to the flight instruments. I monitored the radarscope to hold a 10-mile radius and switched on the gust-dampening system. The U-2 bucked as it encountered a thermal, rose, then fell a thousand feet. I lowered the EPC setting to 1.90 and hung in. The panel lights glowed weakly through the dust as we flew into the heaviest portion; the outside conditions were deep brown, as if we were immersed in a world of chocolate milk. The altimeter spun through 20,000 to 16,000 as we spiraled to the north, the deep rosy glow off our port wing signifying the volcano's hoary being.

The brown turned to a dirty gray as we struck a composite of pumice and steam. The sky lightened and we had a few seconds of snow-white translucency, then the blue as we broke through. I checked our bearings and continued to bank around the upwind side of the volcano. We were down to 12,000; the U-2 was coated with ash and sulfuric acid droplets, the windscreen crazed and almost unreadable.

"That's it!" I called back to Winner. "If we ingest any more we'll lose the F-29. How's it feel to fly through an ash storm? Got cinders up your ass?"

Lighthearted, I was happy to be out of it, but Winner wasn't amused. His helmet was bent to his radarscope when I made our turn to the north and set up our approach to Kos. I switched off the gust-dampening system, computed our fuel load, and called in to the tower. The surface winds had shifted around to the east, as Stavos had predicted; we were cleared for a straight approach to the runway. The surface winds gusting to 12 knots, the tower advised. I canceled with Athens Control and dropped flaps for a long final, holding 120 knots, leaving our gear in its down position. Winner's voice crackled the intercom when we were 20 miles out. Totally shaken, he mumbled he was having problems with his mask. When I looked back, his oxygen mask was askew and he was fumbling with its straps. He obviously was ill, shades of pale green.

I dumped full flaps and reduced throttle when we crossed the coast, calling in to MacDougal on the tower frequency. He replied immediately, said he was waiting at the end of the strip with the Jeep. I canceled our thrust as we passed the threshold at 80 knots, hauled back on the yoke, pressured the heavy rudder to maintain center line of the runway. MacDougal monitored our altitude as he

raced alongside…"Six, five, four, three, two…hold her steady, Keith!"
I had the yoke in my stomach, the fuel-light U-2 wanting to climb.
"You cotta tail wheel!" MacDougal shouted from my earphones. I heard the
tail wheel crunch; the bicycle gear touched. I held the yoke full right to offset
the crosswind. The U-2 stabilized until she had no lift, then the port wing grazed
the runway and we spun softly to a full stop. The militiamen sprang from the
lieutenant's Jeep to attach the pogos. MacDougal drew alongside while we
exercised our canopies. The panel clock read 10:58. Winner was first out, scram-
bling down his ladder to bless the leafy grass.

We rode to the terminal and went directly to the locker room to shower while
a ground tug pulled the U-2 to her ramp. She was due a heavy hosing to wash
away the ash and corrosive acid; the windshields would be replaced, air intakes
cleansed, turbine blades examined. The canopies were badly grazed, but there
were no spares available until the C-141 returned from Beale. They'd make do
for the long-term mission, however. Mainly, I was delighted with the hybrid's
performance, and reasoned the chief would cope with the fan blades if they were
pitted from further use.

We tossed our suits in a bin for cleaning and showered down immediately.
The sulfurous ash had penetrated our gear and etched a rosy necklace where
the helmet joined, again at our wrists, and our legs at the calves as a result of
our loose fitting boots.

"Was doing okay until you hit the thermal and had me hanging on my
straps," Winner allowed. "Thought I'd upped my coffee, Keithy…my God, what
a ride! And the brown ash? I've rounded St. Helens in a 'copter, but never seen
anything as bad. Our sensors were reading 800 Centigrade from the cone, *and
that's a gnat's ass from a Plinian*, old buddy!"

"Prediction?" He shrugged his shoulders, slipped into his trousers.

"She's growing, Keith, spreading her ass pretty fancy, but not venting
magma as yet. Calculated three hundred mph in her tube! If it winds up to twelve
hundred, we'd better fetch the far side of them hills!"

We waited until MacDougal removed the screenings, tagging them in sequence while Winner checked the lot with his notes, an altogether tedious
process; then they were carted to the hangar for analysis, Schumann quickly at
hand, observing the granules, sampling for salinity. I left it to Dr. Winner to brief
the group of our sightings, needing a walk around with MacDougal to inspect
the bird first hand.

Outwardly, the U-2 was a mess, but her innards were in good order. The F-
29 engine would require minute inspection; rule of thumb, if there was no

observable damage, four hours airborne would require twelve in the shop.

"We've a brand new 29 in the hangar, Keithy, but I hope it doesn't come to that. So how was the ride, rough and tough? Looks like you're needin' a beer, man!" MacDougal was obviously concerned of our primary mission, hopefully within the next 48 hours.

"I'm worried for me hide, seein' that volcano's feather edge, Keithy. Like, we gotta pull it off before T.S. climbs the wall, or we evac with the C-141. Short order! I plan to be outta here which way or what!" No way I could disagree, and all the while I was eyeing the terminal drive. Nina had promised to be on hand when we landed, but there was no evidence of the van. Miscued the time, I thought, glancing at my watch.

A bus from the Institute was parked alongside the portico. A cheerful group of students peered at the U-2 from the security fence. A tidy lot of teenagers with Fraser in attendance, bilingual, judging from their comments. They'd apparently viewed Sigurdesson's seismograph charts and were anxious to meet Ingrid, who'd address them shortly, according to Fraser's walk along commentary.

Dr. Nokomo was also present, conversing with Willitts and a photographer from the local media. Nokomo, replete in a starched bush jacket and trousers, indicated he'd round-tripped to the Xenia while we were tasting Santorini. His interest in our test flight seemingly heightened by Athens' request for statistics, which apparently were aired on the 11 o'clock newscast.

Fotis and the lieutenant were in rapt conversation in the background, certainly not for media purposes! The twosome declined to be photographed alongside my battered U-2. Nor were Winner and I invited to stand in, most likely due to our cut-off shorts and my skivvy shirt from L.L. Bean. My comments regarding the U-2's performance were seemingly irrelevant, although Sabina copied our debriefing when I rejoined Winner and Schumann. Across the way, a glistening Olympic Airbus was poised for takeoff, turbines whining as the centered the active. It was most likely the 12 o'clock to Athens and I'll long remember the eerie feeling I experienced while it thundered to the northwest!

The feeling prevailed while I cast about for sight of the van. Was Nina having problems with Sotheby's? Had she blown a tire? I joined the students gathering in the lobby, intending to call Stavos on the cellular when Fotis came off the line.

Edwards had set up a wide-angle screen to view our radar imaging of the volcano from 20 miles; Fraser was snapping Polaroid shots to fax to Athens. Ingrid had superimposed a recent satellite picture of the island, adjusting the lens until we had a vivid picture of past and present. The difference?

"Thirty cubic miles," Ingrid said, addressing the students. "Approximately twenty percent more volume than the ancient volcano. I'm calculating from the 1,200 foot depth of the caldera, of course," she added. "The cone has risen only 2,200 feet as opposed to 3,000 feet in ancient times, but you will note the ejected matter has a radius of six miles and nearly enveloped the village of Thera." She switched off the viewer and turned wearily in her chair.

"Our infrared sensors do not indicate the extreme high temperatures which precede a Plinian venting, although the bulge you see below the cone in the northeast quadrant would cause us to believe a weakness has occurred within the volcano's structure, a weakness the underlying pressure is likely to exploit. In other words, a paroxysmal explosion is conceivable...imminently if the chimney aperture ruptures and further widens. You already have noted the accelerating tremor sequence I described yesterday," she continued.

"There have been thirty-six minor tremors and three approaching a magnitude of five on the Richter scale during the past twenty-four hours. Each of the larger quakes results from a drop in the crater's floor of approximately thirteen feet. I am sure you understand, as the pressure cavity increases in volume, the magma and gases will continue to expand!"

"Until?"

Sigurdesson shrugged her shoulders; she'd made her point. She informed the students that Fotis had been fully apprised, and was in contact hourly with the base. If the volcano's venting increased its intensity, there would be two – possibly three – days to evacuate Kos' western exposure.

"Are you willing to predict a time for the occurrence?" a brown-eyed girl in pigtails asked. Sigurdesson's eyes narrowed. There was a scraping of chairs, a twitter of whispers. It was a loaded question. The fiery object pluming the horizon was not to be ignored. Ingrid coughed; wheezing for breath, she turned to Fraser. The Scot stood in, pointing again to the charts.

"Speaking for our group, we're deeply concerned," he said. "Dr. Sigurdesson's theories coincide at the moment with Dr. Schumann's. If there's a detectable trace of salinity in our screenings, it's a matter of days, not weeks!"

A sticky silence followed a nervous giggle from one of the students. Fraser continued, ignoring the interruption.

"As the doctor stated, we've detected a series of accelerating tremors since we set up our equipment. The latest you've experienced, and we anticipate a heavier shock within the next twenty-four hours. If this pattern continues, the shocks will increase in intensity. Dr. Sigurdesson theorizes the floodtide at full moon will set the ball rolling, if you will pardon the analogy. Better she explain the circumstances herself. I'd appreciate it if you'd not scrape your chairs."

He stepped aside; Sigurdesson pulled herself upright. Obviously weary, she clung to my arm momentarily, smiled gamely when she addressed the group. I wasn't beyond noticing, however, the scars on her arm, as if she'd recently undergone a series of injections.

"The rise and fall of billions of tons of water affects the tectonic plates," she explained. "Theoretically, the shifting tides might undo the delicate balance we've seen to date. The venting so far has been relatively harmless; an escape valve for the underlying pressures so to speak. If a secondary force infiltrates the hot spot beneath Santorini and releases the magma from the bowels of the earth, we shall be witness to the floodgates of hell!"

The lieutenant arrived quietly and took a seat. The doors opened and closed several times. I observed Nokomo's ashen face and sensed the presence of other parties. Together we listened while Sigurdesson explained the making of a Plinian blast - the horrendous venting that emptied the volcano in the past – until it literally collapsed upon itself. There followed the incalculable explosion that occurred when the sea poured into the abyss, the cannonade heard worldwide, the largest explosion known to mankind.

"As if one poured a glass of water into an overheated saucepan," she added. "The sea flowed into the emptied caldera after a massive fireball devastated the Aegean; then the caldera overflowed and formed a mountain of water that spewed outward at four hundred miles per hour to flood the shanks of the Mediterranean."

"And Exodus speaks of 'a pillar of cloud by day, a pillar of fire by night' that guided the fleeing Israelites on their journey," a voice behind us said. Heads turned, but I knew who it was. Butterfield had obviously stayed on at Aspri Patra with Dr. Petrie. "And so the Israelites detoured to avoid a large desert directly to the north," Butterfield continued. "Then, to shake the pursuing Egyptians, they abandoned the road to Palestine and headed for higher ground, southeast of Lake Manzala. It was there that the miracle occurred...not the Red Sea, but in a 'sea of reeds" And as the two forces faced off in the morning, a huge flood swept away the Egyptian chariotry. Their enemies vanquished, the Israelites turned south because the flood had made the northern route impassable. I quote in part from the work of Hans Goedicke, an Egyptologist, who suggests the exodus occurred during the time of a volcanic explosion that flooded the Nile." Lesleigh gathered her voice and continued.

"We have evidence of a royal decree from the female Pharaoh Hatshepsut, who reigned from 1490 to 1468BC. She boasts when she allowed 'the abomination of the gods to depart, the earth swallowing their footsteps. That this was the directive of the primeval father, the god of water, who came one day unexpectedly...' And there we have it! Two comparable stories ingrained in the sands of time...'the parting of the waves and the deluge that followed'. And mind you, there is less than forty years betwixt the legendary accounting and *the factual timing* of the explosion, determined from a carbon dated analysis of ash deposits discovered in the glaciers of Greenland, give or take a number of years!"

The air conditioner rattled away in the windowsill; Sigurdesson coughed; Butterfield blushed, as if she'd spoken out of turn. Fraser got to his feet and broke the silence.

"Bravo, little miss! Those were words for sore ears. Investigate a legend and you'll find a grain of truth; the Biblical stories were not drawn from fiction. Elaborated, perhaps, most likely distorted by the Greek scholars and medieval monks, to coincide with their interpretation of time!"

"Time is fraught with conjecture," Sigurdesson interjected. "I'm a volcanologist not an archeologist or a student of divinity, Mr. Fraser. The events the young lady describes are possibly resultant from an earlier explosion, although the magnitude coincides with the carbon date from the strata discovered in Greenland. But we must understand there was no written language between the ancients at the time; no factual dates aside from our gleanings, which were primarily derived from rote! The explosion occurred in the Bronze Age. The format was much the same, however; the adjacency of the sea and continuing hot spot beneath the converging plates. These, in turn, are affected by the moon tides, which will crest within the next few days. History appears to be in the making, but we can continue to hope that it won't happen again!

"Now, if you'll excuse me, I must rest," Sigurdesson announced, casting a baleful eye towards Butterfield; softening somewhat when she observed Lesleigh was in tears. "Dr. Winner has just returned from the flight circumnavigating Santorini and would be most pleased to brief you further. Again, I would like to thank you for your undivided attention and continued cooperation."

She clung to my arm when I accompanied her to the door. I offered to see her to her room, but she shook her head.

"I'll be alright, Keith. I would, however, appreciate a beer! It helps me sleep. I have been so tired of late; only recently have I been released from my hospital bed! You've determined my physical condition, have you not?"

"Chemotherapy?"

"Painkillers in recent weeks! I haven't long to go," she added when I appropriated a beer from MacDougal's cache. "Curious, isn't it? To dedicate one's life to science as a comparative unknown, thinking all the while as I lay there on my bed of how little I have accomplished; praying for one more opportunity to redeem those many years. Seeking, if you will, a particle of recognition."

Her blonde hair clung damply to her forehead; her facial features were etched with pain and creased by time. I felt a lump in my throat when I scanned her thin wrists, the scars on her arms, her wedding band from another time.

"I was intrigued by the story of Santorini as a child," she said. "Fantasized I lived there long ago and perished in its flames. I had only my imagination to dwell on then to brighten my days. Sweden is so dark and somber. When I received my cap and entered university, I decided I'd major in geophysics. My father was horrified! A female volcanologist!

"And I discovered it was a man's world! Since the days of Pliny the Elder, women have been subordinated to men in volcanology. I was never really accepted. My theories? Never! Although I was often called upon as an assistant to join the observers in the field. Mind you, I had my doctorate, but I was mainly confined to copying their notes – although overtures were often made, after hours," she added wryly.

Sigurdesson drained her beer, tossed the can in a trash container.

"We've come from our corners of the world to research the sky, Keith. We did not suspect this ungodly thing that is about to unfold, although I must admit, of late I've had a premonition that I shall die here and be consumed by the onslaught I have fantasized since I was a child!"

I saw Ingrid to her quarters – a simple, spartan room. A photograph of her late husband from younger days stood on her dresser; beside it, a recent photograph of her children. They'd be in their twenties, both with cap and gown.

A dark-eyed teenager skipped to my side as I was returning from the barracks. She handed me a note and walked beside me to the terminal building, seemingly puzzling her thoughts.

"The orderly said your wife called at eleven, Mr. Slater. I was listening to Dr. Sigurdesson and near forgot. I believe she phoned from Cleo's house. Is she all right? Dr. Sigurdesson, that is! She's so thin and pale, feverish, obviously on medication."

"Dr. Sigurdesson's bushed from her long trip, sweetie! What with jet lag, she needs rest for a day or so." The young lady shook her head.

"She's terminally ill, Mr. Slater...cancer of her lungs, I believe. I'm a fourth-term medic; I know the signs. She's in terrible pain and sedatives won't help."

"That's not for me to say, young lady! But I'd be pleased if you would look in on her now and then. She needs laid back support; she's playing it from sheer guts."

"It's Sophia, Mr. Slater, and I'm not alone with my thoughts. We recognized the symptoms and we're fascinated by her intelligence. We don't see it very often...her analytical approach is similar to our ancient patron's teachings."

"The apply Hippocrates' methods to help her last days, Sophia! At the moment it's spiritual; her body is shot to hell and she senses she's short of time!"

* * * * * *

Cleo's phone was busy, off the hook perhaps. I reached the Helena on the lieutenant's cellular, only to be greeted with Nina's clipped response on her answering machine, referring to Cleo's numbers, which I tried again with negative response whilst I looked about for means of transportation. Dr. Nokomo was long gone, as was Butterfield, who'd apparently split for Aspri Patra.

"African hasten to greet Mr. Gunnar," the orderly informed me, pointing to the terminal across the way. "Little miss leave in big hurry, Major Slater. Come often at night; take shower in barracks. Say she investigate cave with English gentleman who came from Akrotiri."

Fortunately, Fotis offered a ride while I was considering MacDougal's un-licensed Jeep. He seemed overly pleased to have me along, indicating we had an urgent matter to discuss. Whatever it was, he held it in abeyance when he spied Nokomo's Hummer, flying the blue UN pennant from its fender, when he rounded the bypass from the commercial terminal.

"Drive wrong side of highway," Fotis grunted, narrowly avoiding a head-on collision. I had a fleeting glimpse of Horst Gunnar then, recognizing his face from Colonel Forsythe's photographs in New Jersey; his tight-lipped countenance and high-bridged nose! Clad in khakis buttoned to his lengthy neck, at the moment pointing a bony finger towards my beloved U-2, his teeth glinting metalically in the midday sun.

"Important person?" Fotis chided, gaining control of his Jeep. "Have inter-esting past. Came by way of Baghdad," he added, grooving the macadam to the capital city. I held a tight lip, realizing Fotis was awaiting or seeking my com-ments. Fotis containing his thoughts, however, until he slowed to draw off the highway, coming to full stop near a narrow stretch of beach.

"Confide now a matter of mutual interest," he allowed, unlatching his brief case. "Come last night, have news of bad accident, major. Plenty folk around, call tow truck when they see what happen." Fotis pointed to the heavy ruts leading from the beach, extracting a recent photo from his case for me to see.

The photo was a grainy image of the suspect mechanics' blue BMW submerged within a foot of its roof top, the driver's window wide open. An outstretched arm was seemingly fixed in time; the driver's head semi-immersed, as was the rear seat occupant, floating face down.

"Rigor mortis," Fotis commented, pointing to the grotesque arm. "The vehicle was under water for several hours before they came upon it, Keith. Apparently drifting seaward from the beach with the tide. Not its tire tracks short of the beach, the bottles scattered about! They'd obviously been socializing, possibly watching the sunset, when the gears were neutralized, allowing the vehicle to roll to the sea."

"Could be they passed out and drowned when the BMW hit the water, Major?" Fotis shook his head.

"There was no evidence of water in their lungs. Our coroner said they died of coronary seizure, a seemingly unlikely deduction since they were observed in a social nature near sunset at the Xenia Hotel."

"Recin?" I muttered, thinking back to the macabre scene in New York. Fotis' ears perked.

"Odd you would say that, Keith! A physician at the Institute is of like opinion. When I researched further, I found the drug is a lethal ingredient for prompt assassination!"

"Homicide?"

"Exactly, but near impossible to prove. The drug is difficult to obtain, more so the means to inject! It's a small island, Keith; none so clever here. Which lends to outside connections, and possibly a suspect. Shall we say a recent arrival?"

"You're calling the shots, man! Should I hazard a guess?" Fotis shrugged, returned the photos to his case.

"I'm an attorney in civilian life, Keith. As such, I was naturally intrigued by the mysterious factors when the physician allowed of the drugs used by the KGB in recent years. And with the *Madam* much in mind, I researched Interpol's files, thinking there was a possible link with their ongoing investigation of the incident at Hellinikon, and the lady in question. Which proved negative. She was, however, well known to Interpol as a de facto KGB operative, has many aliases it seems. They also indicated she has affiliations with Dr. Horst Gunnar, which I found interesting, although Interpol played it down. Point at hand, we have insufficient evidence to hold her for questioning, the motivation being unclear!

"So now, I'm confronted with the elimination of witnesses, or parties I believe were involved with the tragedy at Hellinikon," Fotis furthered. "Factually, I'd anticipated gainful information from the pair, intending to question their working hours at Hellinikon prior to the tragedy. Also, possible leads to their source of funds...when they arrived post haste at Antimahia, whilst the U-2 was in process of re-assembly, Keith."

"So let's back track to Interpol, Major. At which point did they become involved with the balls up at Hellinikon? Not that I'm negative, but I wasn't aware of this until you popped the cork!"

"Moot question, Keith! Possibly when they were forwarded a copy of the FAA's analysis of the wreckage, which I presumed you also received! As to the source of their inquiry, they wouldn't divulge, nor have I seen a copy of the report, but I was informed the aircraft's trim controls were deliberately reversed prior to its chartered flight to New York!"

"Interpol suspicioning a pair of Olympic's off duty mechanics, I take it?"

"Affirmative, Keith! In fact, they requested a copy of their fingerprints...that fortunately we'd screened from the stolen APU! And, to make doubly sure, I faxed the cadavers' fingerprints as well!"

"So what's the feedback? I'm hearing you loud and clear, man!"

"All together, an exact match with the prints on the tools available to the mechanics when they serviced the jet!"

"Jesus, Major! When did they tell you this?"

"Early this morning, Keith. But realizing you'd be considerably upset, I thought it best to wait until you returned from circling Santorini. The information is *extremely* confidential, of course! Fearing political interference, Interpol has yet to apprise the authorities in Athens of the investigation, I was told. They also indicated they had a viable lead on the perpetrator, who conceivably had reason to sabotage your abominable U-2!"

"Has to be Tony Metexas," I muttered, recalling the asshole's venomous threats. "Man, I'm not worried for myself! But should Nina catch word...she'll be on to the bastard with whatever comes off the wall!" Fotis wiped his brow and stared mutely at the ever-moving sea.

"Goes without saying, knowing Nina as we do! But hopefully we can contain the matter in abeyance until we have indubitable evidence that can't be challenged or coerced in court!"

I glanced at my watch, wondering where Nina might be? An icy premonition coursing my spine when I gave further thought to the time frame of her call to the base. The U-2 all the while in process of being towed to the ramp whilst my rear cockpit observer expressed his relief on the newly cut grass. Myself noting Olympic's 12 o'clock flight to Athens waiting its passengers across the way…the flight boarded and long gone when I was advised of her call. Guesswork, possibly…she may have responded to an urgency in Athens whilst we were probing the bloody volcano.

"Past time to worry whatever you're on to!" Fotis chided, seemingly aware of my thunderous thoughts. "Mind you, Keith…I'll drop you off at the Helena in good time," he added, observing I was eyeing an oncoming bus to the capital city. "But first we have a tiddling matter we must discuss!"

"Okay, so let's get on with it, man!" The Major smiled benignly and drew a faxed newspaper clipping from his brief case. The clipping dating near about the time I was flying for NASA at Moffet Field. The photographic spread obviously faxed by Interpol to Fotis' attention, with a question mark on the side. And there he was, Group Commander Willitts in full uniform, standing with Air Marshal Lord Branall, and General T.S. O'Brien conspicuously in view!

"Had reason to suspect Mr. Willitts was more than a journalist, Keith! And despite your apolitical stature with the UN, I have reason to suspect there's more than greets the eye? But whatever the circumstances, knowing your state of mind at the moment…I wish you luck, whatever your endeavor!"

A giant of a man with multiple problems, Fotis had apparently decided to let it go at that. Pleading ignorance from the offset, his command of English understated, he'd voiced his views, as might a lawyer testing a court case. Illustrating fluency when the chips were on the table, he twisted my arm in the process, to let it be known he was aware of the facts. Alternating from friendly terms to address me formally as 'Major', he indicated he was suspicious of my role with the UN, but not necessarily oppose!

* * * * * *

I realized there was something terribly wrong when Fotis dropped me pier-side. Nina conspicuously absent when I spied Cleo and Stavos peering from the Helena's fantail, apparently waiting my arrival.

"Where's Nina?" I shouted, quickening my pace, not knowing what to think when I noted the van was missing.

"Come quickly; we must talk!" Cleo called from the railing, adding to my fears.

"Has Nina had an accident?" I gasped, racing the gangway.

"No accident, but cause plenty worry!" Stavos muttered while he helped me aboard.

"So lay it on the line?" I retorted, noticing the expression on his face. "Is Nina hurt? Did she fall, freak out?" Stavos shook his head, guided me aft. "Same problem, maybe! Come morning, Neenie have long talk with London. Say plenty bad word, all mix up; have strange eye when party disconnect! Seem all confuse, call base but they say you not reach back. Think call Uncle's office, run see Cleo with plenty long face. Short time, maybe hour, hear Neenie in master cabin – not confide in old man. Fetch bag, take Fiat and leave in big hurry. Catch Olympic to Athens, Cleo say!"

"When was this?"

"Near eleven," Cleo interjected, gripping my arm. "I hasten from cottage, but she not listen to old lady, Keith. Say you know what she must do, important catch noon flight!"

"My God, I was across the field!"

"Nina try and reach you, worry you not return; leave message on machine." I stared numbly at the pair. She'd obviously been hell bent for Antimahia while we were towed to the ramp!

"Nina had bad news from London," Cleo furthered, apparently aware of my thoughts. "Sotheby say auction postpone. Receive notice from Paris gallery, say Nicholas' paintings fraudulent copies, have little value!"

"Copies? Hell's fire…the Picasso she shipped from Nassau was signed when he was a pup!"

"Is nonsense, of course. Nicholas no fool! Purchase paintings over years. Keep documents in office safe. Nina hasten there now, intend fax copy London. Is very unfortunate," Cleo added. "Same time banks call storage notes, say estate not worthy!"

"Metexas?" Cleo nodded.

"Who else tell banks same story, same day paintings display for auction? Nina very angry, Keith. Have not seen such face since she a child; worry for what she do! She try phone office from Helena, but lines busy. Kavouri not answer, think old folks at Mt. Parnassus, but not wish to cause them worry."

I went immediately to the deckhouse to give the cellular a try. I had the same problem, however. The office lines were busy, as were their fax numbers when I prompted the machine. Given an hour en route, possibly another in city traffic, she'd have reached the office by 2:30. Possibly unable to contact Bruno, she'd have a problem hailing a taxi. Better to try later, I thought, mindful of the congestion at Hellinikon.

I went below to check our stateroom, thinking Nina might have scrawled a note. The stateroom was a shambles, the bed strewn with airline tickets, together with her passport. Obviously, she hadn't planned to continue to London! Packed what she needed in a single overnighter and left her jewelry purse in a drawer.

My brief case was another matter! She'd apparently clued the combination and sprung the lock. The lingering scent of her lavender filled the space left by the missing necklace. And curiously, she'd thumbed the U-2's flight manual; the control cables of obvious interest as she'd ripped the section from the manual and taken it along. Her analytical mind added to my fears; the auction a lesser evil!

I had Auntie Cleo to contend with when I joined her topside. Her command of English faltered when she helped herself to the brandy, indicating she was worried for Nina, knowing her ways and hatred of Metexas! I grasped her aged hand when she insisted we walk the crooked alley to her cottage, realizing she had more to say. Captain Stavos remaining by his phone, his attention given to the sea.

Cleo's cottage was spacious, uncluttered, colorfully furnished, and contemporary. A red grand piano and a pair of seascapes spaced a whitewashed wall. Watercolors from Nice, signed by herself, kept company with photos of Nina and her brother when they were children; Nina, pert and beautiful, her eyes glinting their familiar green. There was another photo of a young man in uniform, a rose lying beside it, obviously a memorial.

"My fiancé," Cleo said. "He was shot by the communists in 1949. We had tough times then, as you Americans say; but thanks to your General Van Fleet, we endured, and brother Nicholas was enabled to fund his tankers. Also to revive the olive groves that out ancestors had tilled since ancient times. The seedlings had gone to rust, the vines savaged by the barbarians to place their guns. Stone age creatures in modern times, such as the likes of Tony Metexas, who would blaspheme Nicholas' paintings to seek his own ends!"

Suddenly, as if replying to Cleo's vehemence, the piano skittered sideways and the photos toppled in a domino effect, followed within seconds by the sound of wailing sirens from the hills. The clang of church bells pealed in unison. Fotis' warnings of a repetitive floodtide, apparently detected with his radar array, had become reality!

Reasoning Cleo was relatively safe, once the dust had settled, I split for the alley and managed to reach the pier as the deckhand was casting the Helena's stern lines, the bow lines furthering as I leapt aboard. The Helena lurched forward, gathering knots while I climbed to the bridge. Stavos throttled his engines to position the yacht between a pair of trawlers, cursing, fingering his beads. The fleet spread in a ragged line from north to south, pointing generally to the west at crawl speed. A half-dozen fishing smacks had emerged from the Turkish mainland and swung about to join us. The CB alive with bilingual chatter, crew members scurrying to bring booms to center, lengthening lines to the trailing dories.

Stavos grunted to acknowledge my presence when I buckled in, lowering the volume of the portable radio. Aponi Zoi fading immediately, the music somewhat at odds with the mood of the day.

"To-ra!" Stavos shouted. The deckhand ran aft and climbed the bridge. Stavos studied the water and spun the wheel, called a warning to the trawler alongside.

"Ef-ko-lo, you stupid shit!" He husked a clod of spittle to the lee side and spread his feet. "It come now," he said.

It came, gently at first, as it had before. The fleet rose with the mountainous swell until the fast-draining harbor came to view. Stavos pointed astern. I turned in my seat and shuddered. The fortress' outer wall had crumbled onto the quay; apparently the quake had stabbed the coast. Its black dungeons peered like rat holes from the decimated ruins; its brittle bones gleamed in the yellow light like a carcass torn from the grave. Marble columns, lintels, bits and pieces of statuary, gut material sledged from the ancient temples. The Helena knifed the sky and descended with a monstrous thud. The fleet swirled at beam ends; the awesome sight was lost to the rolling green.

Stavos levered his clutches to reverse to fight the downswell. The trawler on our starboard lost steerage and broached, came upright shedding the sea. A lesser wave rose beneath us and we watched helplessly while the first engulfed the town. It rose swiftly over the jetties, spuming the streets to the village square, geysering the fortress, roaring into its stony heart.

When it receded, the café was gone; the French sloop was where the sidewalk had been. The government building had given its splendid esplanade to the sea; water spilled from the Xenia" windows. I gave thought to Nokomo" inconvenience, to the intuitive major" shattered offices, and prayed for Cleo's safety.

"She be okay, the sea not tickle her hill," Stavos allowed. "But come next time?" he added, leaving his comment unsaid.

The wave crested twenty feet and swept the low-lying shore for a quarter of a mile. The entire Aegean would have felt it…Athens, the cliffs of Kavouri, no doubt!

"Cleo be alright," Stavos reiterated, handing me his binoculars, "but Kos not safe harbor for Helena, Keith. Waste plenty diesel, come to seek anchor at Astypalaia, I think. Next time not so lucky, not want to lose ship!"

Next time? I'd witnessed the beginnings hours before, a voluminous volcano verging an explosion. Bone tired, I agreed immediately. Astypalaia offered a safe haven, close to the roadway to Antimahia, but what of Nina?

* * * * * *

Throttling back to minimum cruise, Stavos spread a chart on the console table, weighting it down with a brace of beer. He'd had the foresight to previously plot our course, I noticed, when he had the headland on our starboard helm, steering a southeasterly heading while Fotis' sirens sounded an all clear. We had others in our wake, a pair of trawlers with a hitch of skiffs, staccato voices on the marine radio comparing notes in Turkish and Greek. It was nearly 1700 when we rounded the easterly head of the island and set course for Cape Loannis, hoping to reach Astypalaia by nightfall, or stand off until dawn.

I gave Nina's office another try at 5:30. First came the usual static, the connection tone, then a replying Greek voice placed me on hold when she had identified the source of the call. Seconds later, Nina's secretary, who was fluent in English!

"Is it Keith?" she questioned, and I agreed to that.

"Thank God!" she replied. "We tried to reach you at Cleo's but her lines were out of order. Nina came by at 3:30," she added quickly. "She was hysterical, Keith, not her usual self; in tears when her call to London encountered the time difference. Demanded we open the safe, which we did, and she took along documents from Nicholas' portfolio!"

"Took them where?" I rasped.

"Our attorney's chambers down the corridor. She also acquired your mail, which we assumed was all right."

"My mail?"

"An express envelope from Washington, I believe. Came certified to your attention a few days back. Apparently a copy addressed to yourself at the UN."

"Holy shit!"

"I beg your pardon?"

"Sorry, miss! Do you have the attorney's numbers?"

"Nina's no longer there! She returned an hour or so later. I tried to reach you privately, but she had the office in a tizzy; her eyes dilated, staring from the window, mumbling incoherently. Had me at wits' end! I let the staff go, thinking I could reason with her, but she didn't seem to know who I was! Kept staring at the window, pounding on the safe!"

"You're holding back!" The reply was a long silence, although I could hear the fax machine, the sounds of traffic, a siren in the distance.

"Yes, Keith, but it's out of my hands now! Nina opened the safe on her own, God knows how, and seized Mr. Maris' revolver from a drawer; dropped it into her purse and disappeared! I called after her, ran to the elevator, but she was down the stairs and onto the street. Should I call the police? I fear for her safety, Keith!" I gave it rapid thought, my heart pounding. Stavos, lending an ear, nodded grimly to himself.

"Better to warn Tony Metexas," I blurted.

"His phones are off the hook. Can you hear the sirens? I believe it's too late!" The sirens were distinct in the background, converging blocks away. My attention turned to Nina's state of mind...murderous or not, she obviously was on to a trauma. Where might she go?

"Would you try the villa?" I said. "Could be she's with Bruno. Did he pick her up at Hellinikon?"

"Bruno's at Mt. Parnassus, Keith. I phoned a while back, caught the answering machine. He's not deaf, you know. I'm worried sick! I think she shot the bastard! Should I call the police?"

Miles offshore, there was no way I could handle it. The morning Olympic was my best chance. I asked if she had a car and she said her boyfriend did; normally came by the office at seven when they closed. I checked my watch. It was on to six and she obviously was in tears.

"Would it be possible to check the villa?" I asked in desperation, not wanting to clue the police.

"Yes, but allowing for traffic, it'll take a while. Athens is under martial law. If Nina's there, what should we do, what with the revolver and all?" I reasoned with her briefly. Nina was not otherwise a violent person, I said, suggesting they scan the villa for lights or recent activity.

"Meanwhile, I'll stand by on the cellular," I added. "You have the Helena's numbers and I'd appreciate it if you'd call me back at eight, or leave a message for Bruno on Uncle's answering machine. Say I'll hopefully arrive on Olympic at nine tomorrow morning and it's urgent he pick me up."

"And what if the police are there?"

"Cruise by and let me know! Same sequence, however. Call in a message to the machine. I'll get there otherwise. Have you a phone at your house?" I asked, scribbling down her numbers, not wanting to call the office in the morning.

"I'll try my best, Keith. Nina was my classmate in Switzerland and I know her ways!"

We signed off with that. Hopefully, she'd find Nina at the house or possibly Bruno by the gate. Bone tired and hungry, I went below to savage the fridge, calling the villa methodically, raising the answering machine but no pick-up. Alternatively, I call the base, reaching Schumann in the lieutenant's office the first try.

I explained I was aboard the Helena; that we planned to anchor off Astypalaia towards evening, and come dawn I'd be in desperate need of wheels; that I'd come ashore with the inflatable and trek the highway leading to Kefalos.

"Six-thirty or thereabouts," I added, indicating the yacht should be visible from the road. I filled him in to the emergency that had me at ends, of course. Schumann quick to allow he'd contact Olympic's reservations on my behalf, which was helpful. The lanky Dutchman confirming he'd meet me along the highway, most likely with MacDougal's Jeep.

"Now then, Keith! We've encountered a problem with Dr Gunnar in your absence. Typical of his sort...the asshole announced he'd oversee our communications systems from here on in, and I quote Dr Winner's comments verbatim! He also had a brush with Sergeant MacDougal when he insisted he inspect the U-2's guidance systems. Surly chap; they had words of sorts until the lieutenant intervened. Apropos to this, he'd apparently sent along an updated 'Data Link Module' from Berlin, which he plans to install in the U-2! Which you can deny, of course, as the pilot in command!"

"Blatant, hey?"

"Frankly, I fear he's lost his noodles, Keith! His facial expressions not from my world, his authoritative mannerisms mindful of the Gestapo my parents endured before I was born! But nevertheless, as a confirmed representative of the UN, I intend to see he toes the wire!"

"Anything else while I have you on the cellular?" Schumann placed me on hold. Apparently there were mitigating problems in his office, possibly a call relating to Nina? Moments later he cleared his mouthpiece, however.

"Dr Nokomo, Keith! Apropos to your absence, he spilled his marbles when the aftershock rattled the base this afternoon! Bloody well frightened, I must say...totally incoherent until we calmed him down. 'Lost his starch and hauled ass like a scalded cat!' as Dr Edwards aptly put it!"

"Has he called back?"

"Just now, Keith! What with his offices and quarters flooded, he intends to evacuate his personnel and equipment to Antimahia; might the lieutenant have a lorry available? He also needs a nearby villa to suffice his *personal* needs."

"Meaning he intends to hang in?"

"Pursuant to obtaining a charter from Antimahia, I believe! But in the meantime, we're faced with an onslaught of clerks and secretaries needing quarters...fraught as we are at the moment, Keith. Fortunately we can cordon our work area in the terminal, but not Ingrid's privacy...need she be put to this?" I reluctantly signed off, realizing Schumann had a full plate. The needless confusion resulting from Nokomo's ignoring Maureen's earlier advice! All of this with the project into its critical phase, needing the scientists uninterrupted concentration. The U-2 hopefully ready to fly before the volcano leveled Santorini and the group's evacuation to the hills became a necessity! Myself gambling a risky measure of time, if I was unable to return from Athens before it came to be!

What then? Neglect of duty was not my thing, but where does one separate his heartstrings from the group's ongoing dependency? And suffering thoughts such as these, I once again tried to reach the villa at Kavouri, to no avail. My heart biding time with the chattering diesels when I fell asleep at Stavos' elbow. The old salt casually steering the Helena's wheel with his foot, his eyes glued to the compass.

* * * * * *

Midnight, possibly. The overhead black sky cast with a rosy hue from the west, when I was awakened by a blast from the console radio, the volume full tilt. Captain Stavos beside me, cupping an ear whilst he translated the Athens newscast into English.

"Tony Metexas shot dead, Keith! Find behind desk with plenty of blood. Appears put up fight; have pistol in hand, but kill dead before use!" I sat upright in my chair, wide-awake.

"When did it happen?" I blurted. "Have they mentioned Nina?"

"No say, Keith. Assailant unknown. Maybe tall lady with sunglasses and scarf, long hair? She disappear in hallway, not take elevator to street." My heart sank. I listened carefully while Stavos translated the jargon; the commentator was apparently on site. Seemingly, the assailant entered Metexas' office without a word and proceeded directly to his chambers. His secretary, elsewhere at the time, thought she heard him shouting, or pleading, then a muffled explosion. The staff ran to a window, thinking it came from the street. In the interim, the

247

assailant disappeared.

"Have much say about Metexas. Say have plenty enemy, keep pistol in belt. Say police question mistress, but she not look alike; wife in France, long time divorce."

"No mention of Nina?" Stavos shook his head.

"No say, but bring plenty worry. Neenie family have high respect, but come time they investigate problem with Metexas, maybe house at Kavouri!" I reached for my cellular and tried Nina's secretary. It was after twelve and I had a pick-up first try. Yes, they'd heard the newscast.

"But the murder doesn't tally with Nina's disappearance, Keith. Could be she wandered the streets in a daze. She's been here, however. The gate's locked, but it appears she climbed the wall!"

"Did you get inside?"

"Same way! Found her sandal prints in the ash. The patio's a flooded mess, but we tracked her to Auntie's suite. Found her clothes where the bed should have been. No sign of her."

"Did you check the apartment?"

"First off, Keith. It was dark and gloomy, no sandal prints on the steps. So we checked the seawall, and she'd been there! Barefoot, her sandals along the wall, her dress nearby, Keith! We couldn't find her purse, nor any sign of her on the ledge. Doesn't appear she was suicidal, how-ever, like she just up and disappeared!"

"Any evidence of Bruno?"

"No tire tracks in the gateway," she said. "Appears he was off to Mt. Parnassus before the ash fell this morning. I'm leaving a message in the garage, however; he was supposed to help evacuate the office at noon. We're out of here, now," she furthered. "Same way, over the wall! There's nothing else we can do at the moment, Keith!"

I settled the cellular on the console, my spirits low ebb. All things consid-ered, might Nina have slipped into her traumatic dream world when she fled to Kavouri? Dazed and unnerved, seeking the sanctuary of Auntie's quarters...out of touch with reality, confused by the shuttered premises and locked gates? If so, I wondered where she might wander in her trance-like sleep; picturing Nina standing by the wall, her eyes fixed to the fiery thrust from Santorini in the evening sky. Grievous thoughts, considering the abandoned sandals, the possi-bility she may have slipped or fallen to the ledge below!

Thoughts such as these fueled my dreams when I fell fitfully asleep along-side the Helena's wheel. First, visions of Nina beside me whilst we climbed the hill from Big Sur; fleeting glimpses of her trailing scarf whilst she wandered the marbled halls of the Metropolitan Museum. Then suddenly, she was no longer in view, although the scent of her lavender drew me to the grove by the beach when I discovered our bedroom door ajar...found her standing in coals of hot embers, her arms out flung, here eyes fixed to the abominable necklace while she chanted to the glowering sky!

Thence came a mismatch of fleeting scenes: T.S. steadfast by his gleaming Bentley; Auntie's admonishing voice; Uncle staring at his fallen statuary; Bruno's helping arm when he assisted us from the slippery ledge. *The ledge*, seemingly paramount to my dreams whilst Nina wandered trance-like towards the dig at Akrotiri. The sequence seemingly drawn to Deuca's graven face whilst he stared wordlessly at Nina, with his box of paints underarm. Strangely then, Butterfield's voice echoed from the depths of my nightmarish dream. 'Deuca came to us from the highlands of Crete', she said. 'His boat has a red sail, a sweep for a rudder. You might see it anchored in the cove leading to the sea.' Deuca's double-ender appeared to be a relic from the Bronze Age. His unblinking eyes seemingly wrought from a pair of black holes in outer space!

Suddenly wide-awake, Deuca was a lesser evil when my thoughts returned quickly to Kavouri and the ledge by the sea. The cabana...Nina's soggy dolls and the chaise pads we'd left to dry? Might she have sought refuge in the cabana, possibly fallen asleep with her childhood dolls under arm?

* * * * * *

CHAPTER 22

D awn came silently, sullen and gray, when I raised an eye to determine where I was. I glanced at my watch: it was on to 5:30. The aroma of fresh coffee activated my physical being, although my mind was at odds while I showered and shaved with the tepid water from the Helena's tanks. Gathering a change of clothes and my brief case, I was met midway to the bridge with a mug of steaming brew and Captain Stavos' crown of gray. His olive face was expressive when he pointed to the raft he'd dropped astern.

"Helena find good anchor here," he said. "Plenty shelter, close to beach. Test outboard this morning, have plenty guts when I take you ashore."

I stared at the graying clouds; a cold front was passing through with a light rain in its wake. I also was aware of a powdering of ash on the Helena's decks.

"Fall last night," Stavos said. "Also have tremor in Athens, Keith. Plane evacuate city, radio say!"

"Word of Nina?"

"Say suspect lady maybe catch bus to Hellinikon late afternoon, but driver not see. Stop many times with traffic, not tally passenger."

Kavouri was relatively close. If it was Nina, she'd possibly hoofed it from the bus, joining the mainstream evacuees.

"Say police search aeroport," Stavos added when he had the inflatable underfoot. "Think suspect maybe flee Athens...so maybe not Neenie, see passport on bed!"

We made it to the beach in a matter of minutes, Stavos steering towards a tumbled cottage midst a grove of ancient cedars. He'd spotted it earlier with his binoculars, noting the remnants of a timber pier and proximity to the highway.

There was evidence of recent picnicking when we beached the

inflatable...papers strewn about, graffiti on the cottage walls. Most likely lovers' rendezvous, judging from the rutted cartway and tire tracks in the weedy turn-about.

"Good place anchor van," Stavos allowed. "Not far from Kefalos; maybe 10 kilometers Antimahia. Come time, fix pier for long boat."

Standing tall and supreme, the Helena's masts were an excellent guide, readable day or night; secure offshore, accessible from Antimahia. "Blink lights when come from Athens," Stavos requested. "Keep raft off stern, skiff on davit...ready all times, stand by telephone. Old man pray for Neenie, Keith. Say plenty bead she okay. Best take path now, road not far."

The old salt shook my hand and turned quickly about, his eyes glistening with tears when he touched his cap from the raft. Neither of us realized the torturous days that would lie ahead.

* * * * * *

A lorry rumbled by, stirring a plume of ash in its wake as I emerged from the grove of cedars. Another, not far behind, its headlights aglow, precariously loaded with crates of bewildered chickens, apparently destined for the morning market at Kefalos. The driver slowed momentarily, seemingly puzzled by my appearance on the lonely stretch of road. I waved him on, assuming the Jeep was close behind.

My watch was on to seven while I waited by the roadside, stirring the ash with my shoe, listening, watching fretfully for the Jeep; a donkey brayed in the distance, the bells of a herd of goats tinkling nearby. I hadn't long to wait, however. The roar of a blown muffler resounded from the east, fetching to a screeching stop when I ventured midway the highway. MacDougal was at the wheel, Dr Schumann alongside and, surprisingly, Willitts rear seat! Grimy with ash from trailing the lorries, welcome faces nevertheless!

"You've a seat on Olympic," MacDougal shouted, belting the macadam towards Antimahia. "But you have to be back tomorrow noon, Keith! Like, we've got problems with Gunnar, man! Fuckin' Kraut was wantin' to pull the U-2's inspection plates! I told him to bug off, so he pulls rank, shoutin' in German, like I'm some low class mechanic! Ain't no way I'll take that kinda shit! Like I was about to lay him out when along comes the lieutenant before I had him with me wrench!"

"We reasoned it out later," Schumann interjected. "I speak German and Horst allowed a misunderstanding. Said it was his right as out communications officer to establish the connections with the data-link."

"Had no right to pull the inspection plates!" MacDougal shouted. "Communications officer? I haven't heard such shit since 'Nam!"

"Okay, okay!" Schumann countered. "That wasn't my war! We've a mind bender to contend with, Keith. Gunnar brought along a pressure suit, vintage Russian I believe. Said it was adapted to fit the U-2, connections and all."

"Sized to himself?"

"Apparently, but he was evasive, Keith. Said it was strictly a standby; hangs short of Winner, however. I think he's unsure of what he's about, as if he had someone else in mind, but it hasn't come to be."

"Did he bring along a set of charts?" I asked obliquely, mindful of the forged addendum I'd encountered at Moffet! "Long-range navigational charts, Doctor; radio frequencies, similar to the sets we have on file?"

"He came well prepared," Schumann gasped, gripping the windshield when MacDougal rounded a herd of goats without braking! "Brought a kit of charts and the like, including notes clipped to a knee pad, which I came upon while he was haranguing Sergeant MacDougal. Also a satchel of electronic parts I hadn't time to inspect; a sidearm in the pocket!"

"Did you have a chance to read the notes?" I shot back, the sidearm the least of my worries.

"Yes, indeed! Was about to come to that. The notations were jotted in German, numbered in sequence. ADF and GPS fixes, commencing from the RAF base at Cyprus. Seemed to parallel your projected flight plan to Iran, but not your return. Interesting, eh? The presence of a clip pad with binder straps to accommodate a flight suit?" I shook my head, numbed to the bone.

"Has Gunnar been into our chart drawer?" Had he been copying or altering the notes I had compiled?

"Not to my knowledge, Keith, but he was prowling around before he journeyed to the city, and I thought it wise to remove your data during his absence. In fact, I secured the lot with Winner for safekeeping. Presumptuous, perhaps, but it's best they be elsewhere until you exercise your prerogatives!"

I allowed my eyebrows a double take, glancing at Willitts, but he shrugged and examined his fingernails.

"Was Gunnar on hand this morning?" I asked, assuming he'd establish contact with Amalia. Schumann smiled and shook his head, but he knew what I meant; as did Willitts, who continued to examine his nails.

"Wouldn't deny his pleasure, Keith. Perhaps he had a problem with transportation, but we expect him momentarily."

"Took off in a taxi about the time you called in," MacDougal remarked. "Like he had the hots for the broad at the Xenia." Schumann motioned him to slow down. We had reached Antimahia, and the doctor obviously had more to say. "I believe this man has become *mentally unbalanced,* Keith. Paranoid, such as his rantings when he discovered we'd converted our computer language from German to English! As if he'd envisioned a profile that's no longer viable!"

"I'm not keen for a rear seat mental case, if that's what you mean! I'll handle it when I get back. If it comes to a showdown, I'll go it alone!"

"You have given up on Dr Winner?"

"At 70,000 feet? No way!"

"That's not what I meant, Keith. Winner's acquainted with our data-link and we've a serious problem! Our instruments on Santorini have either toppled or were consumed with lava. Aside from Ingrid's seismograph and Fotis' radar, we've no input from the volcano!"

"Meaning you need another close-up? Jesus, Schumann! Aside from chancing the engine, I'd have to drop Winner at Kos or Cyprus, refuel and climb out; otherwise cancel the long stretch. That's calling it close, fella...ten hours at the stick, if I make it back!"

"I hear you, Keith, but at the moment we have a catastrophe in the making! We have come from all quarters to lend our expertise to a prediction...we do not intend to abandon what we've set forth! Ingrid needs updated infrared and cone velocity readings; the closer the better, and timing is bloody important! Your turn over Iran, the long stretch you refer to, is totally irrelevant, obligations apart. These are the options I speak of, Keith; you choose!"

Confused by Schumann's rhetoric, MacDougal had slowed to a crawl. Equally surprised, I stared at the doctor, who sank wearily in his seat, mumbling an apology of sorts. Honest to the core, fed up with the inauspicious by-play, he'd meant exactly what he said, and he'd triggered my conscience.

"Forty-eight hours!" MacDougal announced from his wheel, pointing to the U-2 across the field. "She'll be topped off and ready, Keithy. 'Spect you back come hell or high water, if'n you know what I mean!"

My thoughts came full turn...from Nina and Schumann to T.S.'s cigar! Guardian of the wizard's black box, MacDougal was aware of its intent; he knew of the long-range requirement, but not the target! What about Willitts? Of Schumann, I hazarded a guess, although it was unlikely Keenan would divulge the bottom line, again lending credence to the deputy's remarks:

Intelligence is segmented for security reasons. No one person, aside from those present, is totally versed in the subject we've discussed tonight. Leaving the ball in my court!

Fotis' Jeep was parked alongside Olympic's terminal, I was quick to notice! It appeared unattended, but I spied his braided cap on the console when MacDougal drew astern. Assuming he was inside, I searched for my gear, my mind in turmoil. Would have news of Nina? Might she be under arrest? Why else would he be here? I had a partial answer when MacDougal turned in his seat and pointed to Amalia! The madam was paying off a taxi pulled curbside a few lengths ahead, seemingly intent with her luggage; seemingly unaware of our roadside-stained Jeep.

"Same broad came by a few days back," MacDougal commented, when she extended the wheels of her suitcase and towed it inside. "Like she made a buck or two at the Xenia and splittin' with the loot!"

With Nina and Fotis in mind, I hadn't realized Willitts intended to catch the flight, until he tagged along behind me when I pressed the lobby doors. Curious, I turned about, but he diverted immediately to the men's room, seemingly to avoid Amalia's eye. The lady, preoccupied with her tickets, had caught the lot of us by surprise.

"Come quickly," a voice behind me said. I spun on my heel. Fotis looked every inch the cultured, professional lawyer; at the moment, however, a major with the Greek militia, motioning me to follow. Stopping short of the security office, he directed me inside and quickly closed the door.

"I'll not detain you unnecessarily," he said. "I have information at hand, however, which I deemed you should know!" I gripped my chair, not knowing what he meant.

"Nina?" Fotis shook his head.

"Relating to Interpol's ongoing investigation, lately joined my authorities in Athens when we came upon a matter that required their expertise! Now then, Keith...pursuant of our conversation concerning the murdered mechanics, we searched their quarters at length. And subsequently discovered a mechanical diagram of the U-2's flight controls, when we pried open a foot locker belonging to the two! The diagram apparently photocopied from a Lockheed maintenance manual, Keith! As to when and how, remains a moot question."

"Meaning they had the U-2 targeted for certain, hey?" Fotis nodded.

"Would appear so, Keith! All of which lends credence to the motivation leading to their demise. The motive no longer unclear when I gave thought to the recent addition to your staff at Antimahia. Who presumably had the foresight to maintain a listening ear on the island; shall we say in his behalf?" I stared numbly at the wall, vaguely aware of Olympic's first call. Aside from keeping a running tab of my contacts, Amalia apparently knew from the offset that Gunnar, or his option, intended to occupy the U-2's rear seat!

"The madam is boarding the flight to Athens at the moment!" I stammered. Fotis shrugged.

"Yes, I'm aware of that, Keith. We gave her 24 hours to remove herself from Greece, or face charges. Not necessarily in her behalf! So now, listen to me attentively, Keith. I've requested Olympic to hold the flight until you board from the gate...and I want you steady on your feet!"

"I caught the evening newscast, if that's what you mean!" Fotis shook his head.

"Allow me to continue, Keith! In process of searching the locker, we discovered an envelope containing an unused bank draft and the copy of another – both made payable to a third party! The unused draft curiously post-dated, the date coinciding with your flight yesterday morning! The copy of the preceding draft – which apparently was honored – was dated for the day following the fatal crash in the hills beyond Hellinikon, Keith!"

"Jesus Christ, man!"

"Amen! Now that you've said that, I'll take it from there! First off, we faxed the draft copies to Interpol, at which point they contacted the Athens police, requesting information of the third party, if they had such? Interpol wary of political interference. But it so happened the police had his name prominently on file...a local mobster type, known to arrange certain matters for a percentage, his signature on a bail release.

"Mind you," Fotis continued, "the drafts were of sizeable amounts, indicating the perpetrator was gambling high stakes, in your instance a hefty price for your head! All of which may have gone unnoticed had it not been for Sergeant MacDougal...and the cross purpose of yon dowager I've allowed to proceed to Damascus."

"Bank drafts require the name or signature of the purchaser, I believe?"

"Yes indeed, Keith! It also so happened the issuing bank was affiliated with a subsidiary controlled by an Athenian business tycoon! And, what with Interpol apt with computers, the withdrawals were quickly traced to a director of the subsidiary...and I'll hazard a guess as to whom I mean! And consequently, in short order, an indictment was processed charging an 'undisclosed party' as an accessory to commit first degree homicide! The indictment under seal when it was delivered to the Department of justice, although it appears it will never be served...at least not in this world!" Fotis added grimly. "As for the mobster who cashed the draft and orchestrated the slaughter, he's apparently 'on the lam' as

255

you Americans say. Word passes quickly in the underworld, Keith...what with the police broadcasting his description for immediate arrest, he might also be a 'seeker', or conversely a 'target' for revenge!

"Damnable circumstance," Fotis added, glancing at his watch. "A matter of hours before we had chance to avert what came to be! As it is, I'm deeply ashamed for the unaccountable delay...knowing how you must feel, judging from the expression on your face!"

"Did the police mention Nina at any time?" I was quick to ask, realizing Fotis was equally upset, possibly holding back?

"Nary a word, Keith! In fact, I doubt if they've resolved a connection with..um, Metexas' assailant. At least not yet!" he added, rising to his feet when Olympic sounded last call. "At the moment, Athens is on to other matters, looters and the like, refugees fleeing the city...not likely searching for an unknown! As for your quest, a stewardess will be standing by at the Boeing's rear stair, for your convenience. I wish you well from the bottom of my heart, Keith...God bless!"

'A matter of hours?' I mulled to myself whilst I threaded the ground equipment drawing from the vintage 727. Less so, 'a matter of minutes' had I shortened our spiral over Santorini... the possibility I might have been available when Nina phoned Antimahia from somewhere nearby.

"Please hasten aboard!" the stewardess prompted with an unlikely Scottish accent. "We are running a tad late, and need to get on to Rome from Hellinikon. I've reserved your seat last row forward of the loo," she added, climbing the stairs behind me. "The aisle seat directly across from an English chap, sir!"

I slung my satchel in the overhead bin, fastening my seat belt whilst she retracted the stern stairs and latched the door. The 'English chap' so happened to be ex-Group Commander Willitts, smiling coyly from across the aisle...a pair of Heinekens in hand, which he'd obviously pinched from the stewardess' trolley while she awaited me at the ramp.

"How nice of you to come along!" I said, eyeing the overnighter stashed beneath his seat. Willitts smiled sweetly, offering a beer from the pair he had.

"Wasn't altogether my idea, Keithy old friend! Appears the general knows of your wife's journey to Athens yesterday noon...and reasoned you would join her later today. And, what with Gunnar near off his rocker, he bent my ear from Riyadh at 0500 this morning...advising me to 'make bloody certain' you made it back, come hell or high water!

"Problems a-plenty, Keith...Nokomo wanting to pullout, Sigurdesson insisting we hang in, Schumann playing it cool until they have the analysis of the cone's 'temp and velocity', T.S. pressing to get on with whatever he has in mind! Myself wondering why I ventured from Duxford, where I'd have my wife's company while we watched the fireworks on the telly with the kids!"

* * * * * *

Amalia sat first row, in what normally would be the first class compartment. The 727 apparently on loan from a British regional, judging from the placard in my seat pocket and the stewardess' north country accent; Olympic, apparently utilizing their heavy jets to evacuate refugees from the mainland. Our inbound flight was lightly loaded with tourists and pensioners; the locals seemingly preferring the hills of Kos to the turmoil in Athens. I gave judicious thought to that, wondering if I'd find transport to Kavouri if Bruno miscued or had yet to return from Mt. Parnassus.

"Lordy!" I muttered to myself, picturing Bruno's reaction if he were waiting with the Mercedes and recognized Amalia; noting she'd be first out and most likely armed! Then again, would she be so foolish as to venture from the waiting lounge until her flight to Cairo-Damascus was called, realizing the deceased mechanics' contact might have interest in her arrival from Kos? And conceivably, Fotis had paralleling thoughts, knowing the underworld also had a code of justice that would serve double purpose!

My thoughts were contained to the uncertainties that lay ahead, however; least of Amalia, when the captain juiced his power package and we rotated from the strip, the Boeing's gear clanging under belly while we climbed for altitude and banked to the northeast.

The yacht was a speck of green on the morning sea, her masts momentarily catching the sun as she passed from view. Sturdy, she'd shown her capabilities and, protected by the headlands, was capable of riding out a heavy swell. Not altogether safe haven, but apparently there were others sharing Stavos' point of view; notably the numerous white wakes crossing the straits towards his anchorage. Large and small seafaring types and I sensed their urgency when we had the volcano off our port wing.

Rising high and mighty to the west, topping 70,000 feet or more, the immense cloud over Santorini was awesome from a distance of a hundred miles. Caught by the sun, the anvil head was bent to the southeast, indicating stratospheric steering winds would have Athens clear of the haze; Egypt and the Middle East would be sharing the brunt of the fallout. The volcano's mushroom-like stem observable when we leveled off at cruise altitude; glowing spasmodically, furnace-like, from the proximity of the cone, seemingly multi-fold from what I'd observed the day before!

"God, what a beast!" Willitts rasped when I unbuckled to peer from his shoulder. "Shades of Krakatoa and Galuggung, hey? Appears to have grown overnight," he added, pointing to a rise of steam from the volcano's northerly shoulder. "She's spreading her ass like a fat lady on the loo! Still plan to give it a go, Keithy?"

We were too far out to sight the coastal reach of the island, but its northerly exposure seemed relatively clear of the plume, affording the best approach for a close-in probe, provided the stratospheric winds contained the fallout to the southeast for the next 48 hours.

"If the winds hold, I figure we can deck it from Kos at daybreak, " I allowed. "At 0700 we can ride the calm and, with the sun behind us, have a clear shot with the sensors close up! So we'll sweat a couple of minutes at float knots, but Sigurdesson will have her readings when we climb out! From there it's up for grabs, but I'll have Cyprus under wing if I have a problem rear seat!"

"First problem first, if I hear you rightly, Keith! I admire your spunk, but the U-2 wasn't designed for a deck job at 100 knots. She's likely to kite and stall a wing if you hit a thermal close up! Case for soiling one's knickers, to put it mildly! You'll also burn off a half ton of fuel, if you plan to carry on from there?"

"Come off it, man! Yes, of course I intend to carry on...once I rest the volcano close up so as not to let Ingrid and Schumann down! So I'll be light an hour of fuel and worry my turn over Iran, but the bird has a long stretch from 70,000 feet and I've reason to make it back to Kos, come hell or high water!"

"I read you, Keithy, but 48 hours is a mite tight to sled back from Athens if Olympic cancels their morning flight, which also lends to the old man's concern! And, what with the conditions at the base in a state of flux, he's worried Dr Nokomo or the UN might intercede last minute, and insist you fly the U-2 to safe haven whilst they evacuate the project's personnel!"

"Could be, but don't press the envelope with conjecture!" I commented, picturing Ingrid being forcefully bound and dragged from her computers -- whilst I flew the U-2 to safe haven? No way!

"More to fact, I intend to be out of there and long gone before Nokomo has a chance to brew his morning tea! So give or take an hour to feed back the volcano's temps and cone velocity to Ingrid and Schumann, Winner and AWAC's will have the U-2's data-link and GPS position when we climb out for Iran, if that's what's bugging the old man!"

As would the General's command station at Riyadh, giving him time to marshal and advise the MD-11 recons circling Iraq! From there on, they'd acquire my data-link and plot the U-2's GPS position with their on-board computers. Neither of us in radio contact, however! Although a channel was available if we came to a problem!

All of which I was loath to mention to Willitts, realizing he hadn't been apprised of the U-2's multi-purpose flight over the Caspian, at least not in total. It was also highly unlikely he knew of the wizard's black box encased in the U-2's portside wing: the name of the game! Same token, I doubted if Willitts was aware of the Athens newscast that had me uptight, although aware of my comments regarding the FAA's report, of course. Although, here again, I doubted he'd link the significance with Nina's trip to Athens and Metexas' assassination. Not so T.S., however – knowing his double tiered mind! As a matter of routine, he'd most likely scanned the FAA report, near about the time I received my copy. And, what with Intelligence screening the Athens newscast for an update of the evacuation, he'd conceivably caught word of the assassination. And knowing Nina's ongoing suspicions and contempt of the bastard, T.S. would be quick to piece it together when he called Willitts at 0700, and learned she'd flown to Athens to 'attend family business'! Which was a gross understatement, once T.S. gathered his wits!

At least, these were my assumptions when the Captain flashed the seat belt lights; the Scottish lass eyeing Willitts balefully while she flounced the aisle, collecting the depleted cans of Heineken he'd stashed in a seat pocket apart from his.

* * * * * *

The scene at Hellinikon was, as expected, chaotic. The gates were completely booked; a dozen heavy jets waited their turn. Off the ramp where we shut down, twenty medium transports were in process of loading a straggling line of obviously worried refugees clutching whatever they could take aboard. Our 727, like the others, was chartered or on loan from Europe's regional airlines. In the distance, adjacent to the Navy base, sat an Air Force C-17, presumably evacuating the embassy's personnel. Next to it were a RAF 130 and a Canadian MD-11; altogether a sense of urgency prevailed, despite the blue Athenian sky and a startlingly bright sun!

To the southeast there was reason for worry. No longer a thunderhead on the horizon, Santorini's volcanic plume was a dominant feature. A good half of the observable sky was cast with an unearthly shadow of gloom. From a distance of 200 miles, the static lightning effect, not unlike an aurora borealis in the northern clime, was an eerie thing for an Athenian to behold!

We were met by an Olympic van, another behind it waiting its turn. Amalia was already aboard when we exited the stern stairs. The events that followed were not entirely by chance. Amalia was not in view when we traversed the baggage claim area. Willitts headed for the loo and out of view when I walked to the curbside, scanning for sight of Bruno. There was no evidence of the Mercedes amongst the cars parked alongside the domestic terminal, however. Thinking the worst, I broached the passing traffic to hail a taxi, my thoughts drawn to Nina's anguished wanderings along the cliffside at Glyfada, her primordial fears, her transcendental reaction. Was I already too late?

A taxi slowed when I whistled, the driver turning in his seat. I fanned a wad of drachmas and waited for passing traffic. It was then that I spied Amalia with her suitcase in tow, walking beneath the portico to the International terminal yards ahead; the gray Opel I recognized from Kavouri glided behind her from the secondary lane. Realizing something lethal was in the making, I bolted for the cab. The door was locked! The cabby smiled and asked where I was going.

"Kavouri!" I pleaded. "Open the damn door!"

"Fifty dollar to Kavouri, Mister!" I handed him my drachmas which he counted carefully whilst I eyed the Opel. It pulled curbside, apparently intent of intercepting Amalia.

"Is only twenty dollar!" the cabby complained.

"Hang in, I'm coming around to the other side!" I searched my pockets, came up with a twenty-pound note; he wouldn't accept it.

"This is ludicrous! Will you take an American Express traveler's check?" His eyes narrowed.

"Corfiotes here, first name Napolion." I thumbed my brief case; he handed me his ballpoint pen. "Pay now!" he said. "You make a me nervous!"

"I scrawled my signature on a fifty and handed it to the driver. Amalia had stopped short of a portico column, her eyes on the Opel while she fumbled with her purse. Fronting the International terminal, a car length away, I spied the Mercedes!

"Looks okay," the cabby said, reaching back to unlock the door. I collected my brief case and motioned him to hold, looking about for Willitts.

It happened quickly then! A blast from a 9-millimeter erupted from the Opel, raking the column, shattering the lobby windows! Amalia was a cool number! She raised her Beretta from behind the column, tossing her hat aside! The feint drew an immediate response from the 9-millimeter; she aimed and fired. The pistol clattered to the pavement. A rifle appeared from the Opel's rear window, but Amalia was quicker. Standing erect, she emptied the Beretta and the Opel burst into flames, its exploding gas tank adding to the mayhem!

Screaming with pain, the rear seat occupant rolled to the pavement. His clothes were ablaze, blood gushing from his mouth; the front seat was engulfed in flames. I watched helplessly as the flames spread and licked the heels of a fleeing bystander. A hideous scream lofted from the Opel.

The cabby's foot slipped from the clutch; the vehicle lurched forward and I found myself with the Express check in one hand, my brief case in the other. All the while, Amalia was crouched behind a trash bin, calmly reloading her Beretta! With traffic at a standstill, I scrambled for the Mercedes, wanting desperately to be long gone. Fortunately, the Mercedes was unlocked, key in the ignition, Bruno's cap on the seat. The glove compartment unlatched, his paper bag lying crumpled on the floor.

I spied Bruno then. A solitary figure striding towards Amalia, seemingly oblivious to the awesome carnage. Shoulders erect, revolver in hand, he appeared to be stalking a demented animal with obvious intent! Amalia recognized him immediately and, shouting an obscenity in German, she fired the Beretta close range and ducked for cover.

Bruno staggered from the impact, but he continued his pace, his shoulder torn to the bone. Cowering behind the trash bin, eyes wide with terror, Amalia fired again, emptying the clip. The fusillade was wild, and then Bruno was onto her. Unmindful of her pleading, he kicked the bin aside and, with no show of mercy, dispatched Amalia with a single shot to her head! And, having accomplished his intent, he collapsed to his knees.

Although I'd strafed and killed, suffering close encounters in wartime, the scene before me was a stunning reality! Call it self-defense, whatever, the stench of burning flesh and the sight of Amalia's bloodied forehead raked my soul to its depths.

I reacted automatically, my impulses kicking in. Bruno was in need of help, and definitely not the police! Tossing my brief case in the Mercedes, I ran forward and managed to raise him to his feet. Semi-conscious, his shoulder bleeding profusely, he looped his arm around my neck, and together we staggered to the car. The revolver dangled from his fingers whilst I fumbled with the rear latch. Fortunately, help materialized when Willitts' brawny arm appeared to assist Bruno rear seat!

"We'd bloody well better get out of here!" Willitts shouted, retrieving his bag while I secured Bruno's door. "Navy base is the best shot, Keithy! I'll bind him up; you drive!"

I slid front seat and keyed the ignition, studying our options while Willitts rounded the Mercedes and slipped alongside Bruno; wadding a shirt from his overnighter to stem the blood oozing from Bruno's lacerated shoulder. Forward of the Mercedes we were faced with a gridlock of stalled vehicles and throngs of bystanders drawn to the flaming Opel and gruesome scene in its wake. The scattered trash bins yielding yet another victim sprawled face down midst the debris; the bleating horns and shrilling police whistles adding to the confusion.

The mayhem was compounded when the taxi I'd abandoned was struck sideways whilst the driver attempted to merge with the outer lanes of traffic, effectively blocking the incoming vehicles to a standstill. The pile up offering a moment of opportunity, however, when I spied an interim lead to the short-term parking area directly across the way. And, assessing my chances from the rear view mirror, I juiced the Mercedes and made a quick right turn from curbside, shifting to second gear as we roared diagonally across the median, braking momentarily to collect a ticket from the automatic dispenser as we sped inside!

"Crawl it, or you'll draw attention," Willitts pleaded, his eyes riveted to the Mercedes rear window. I threaded the maze of parked cars, located the outgoing tollbooth midst the drift of oily smoke. The attendant was obviously among the gawkers when we drew abreast his gate, the spiked barrier presenting a problem to the boxy Mercedes. Idling neutral gear, I leapt to the open booth and, so not to be a sneak, rewarded our ticket with my wad of drachmas, and activated the gate!

"Good show!" Willitts shouted.

"Collect his Webley. It's somewhere on the floor!"

An ambulance passed us, heading in! But there was no hint of pursuit behind us while we circumnavigated Hellinikon's two-mile outer perimeter and pulled short the Greek Navy's blue and white gates. Heavily guarded by the militia with AK-47s underarm, I feared another impasse when a yeoman peered inside our tinted windows, curious of the rear seat.

"VIP!" I shouted, producing my UN pass for the noncom in charge.

"Americano...he bleeds from the mouth?"

"Plenty sick," I acknowledged. "Would you direct us to a medic?"

"Americanos depart with big plane," he said, pointing to the looming C-17. "You may pass," he added. "Find accommodation near helicopter pad."

Bruno was hacking incoherently in Polish when we drew abreast of a medical tent processing a line of multi-national refugees. The response was immediate when his condition was observed. A wheeled stretcher from a standby ambulance was rushed to the Mercedes, an American Chief Petty Officer in attendance. "Lordy, what a mess!" he said, applying a stop gap compress while a medic prepared a plasma drip. "We'll need to fly him to a flat-top; he's in need of surgery and we haven't the facilities here. Appears he's been shot," he added, snipping Bruno's shirt away. "Shattered collarbone, lacerated shoulder, extensive hemorrhaging," he noted, applying a stethoscope to Bruno's chest. "We'll need his particulars before I can authorize the transfer," he added, extracting a form from his valise.

I filled out the form as best I could, Willitts correcting my spelling. The chief puzzled the boxy Mercedes, an ear to the wailing ambulances.

"Reckon I've seen you before," he said, noting my signature on the bottom line. "UN, hey? Same party Commander Whitehead flew to Kos a few days back! Same Mercedes! Seems like you caught a stray bullet from the street," he added, peering at the bloody rear seat.

"You might say that," Willitts interjected, struggling with the folds of his overnighter. "Best to park it and move on," he cautioned me aside. "I'll take it from here!"

"And who might you be, sir? Seein' you're talking over shoulder and all splattered with blood. What with all that commotion at the terminal, the commander will wanna know!" Willitts grimaced, produced his credentials, and asked if they might talk in private. They conferred in the shadow of the ambulance, the chief red of face, sputtering,

"Yes, sir! I'll see he's aboard at once! Ain't got no spat with British Intelligence!"

The presence of the bloodied Mercedes was an ongoing problem, however, its descript likely to be broadcast once the police obtained on site information! Driving it on to Kavouri an asinine venture! I had a hopeful concept as to where I might fetch an alternate set of wheels, however, knowing the owner would care less if I borrowed them overnight.

Speaking briefly to Willitts, I described the family villa at Kavouri, the telephone numbers by rote. Then, keying the Mercedes, I drove onto the base parking area and found a likely spot to abandon the vehicle; beyond a dozen or so cars that had obviously been there for days on end, judging from the residue of ash which gave them the appearance of a mummified twentieth century garage!

Shrouded with ash of varying degrees, it was near impossible to determine one from another. But knowing Dr Petrie habitually parked his Cortina with its windows down, I quickly discovered there was one such, his key ring in the ashtray, naturally! And giving a thoughtful turn of its engine, the Cortina wheezed and sputtered to life, seemingly relieved for a helping hand. Its petrol on the lean side, but sufficient for my journey to Kavouri and return. And utilizing the doctor's sodden tweed jacket, I cleansed the windscreens fore and aft, deposited my brief case front seat - ready to roll, once I'd checked the valiant Mercedes!

It was after eleven by then, and sweating profusely from the midday sun, I retrieved Bruno's Webley from beneath the seat, including the silencer he'd fixed last minute. The Webley full round, with one spent cartridge. And giving Bruno's intentions further thought, I popped the boot, discovering his tote bag with a change of clothes and a close-cropped, dark-haired wig! Plain clothes Greek in fashion, together with an open ticket to Kos!

'Jesus! Given a day or so, he'd have had Gunnar on his knees, if I hadn't come along when I did!' I thought, picturing Gunnar's expression when he sighted the Frankenstein's apparition staring from the door!

I was quick to gather all told in Bruno's tote bag, however, aside from his keys to the villa, when I sped the Cortina to the gate. The yeoman offered a quick salute, Willitts smiling benignly when I laid rubber for Kavouri!

* * * * * *

The boulevard from Kavouri had been augmented with an additional lane across the median and was jammed to capacity; traffic was at a standstill awaiting instructions from the militia. Luxury cars were topped with bulging suitcases; others were bumper-to-bumper in the feeding streets, desperate to make their turn. Drivers waved frantically, the oddball cutting across the sidewalks. The resultant collisions compounded the confusion! The remaining ingoing lane was virtually deserted, however, and once allowed passage from a checkpoint; I had the lane much to myself.

How different it was from when I'd first seen Kavouri…the beauty of the flowering trees and tended lawns, complacent villas with tiled roofs, youngsters cycling the shady sidewalks. But now, the Apollon was shuttered. Weeds sprouted from its circling driveway; trees were mummified with ash. The villas abandoned; the youngsters long gone; sidewalks cluttered with uncollected trash; the aged wondering where to go.

Judging from the tire tracks that lay beyond, Bruno had visited the villa not so long ago. The gates, firmly locked, yielded to his key. Clasping his tote bag, my brief case underarm, I single-footed the tire track so as not to leave an imprint observable from the street; calling vainly for Nina when I gained the patio.

Multiple shoe prints varied with the settlement of ash; Bruno's most recent, judging from his heavy-soled shoes; the spiked heels underlayer evidenced the presence of Nina's secretary the previous night. Relieved the police had not yet been to visit, I crossed the patio in search of more, absently uprighting a statue alongside the algae-laden pool. Bruno had collected the messages and circled about, most likely searching for Nina. His shoe marks lead to Auntie's suite. Nina's skirt and blouse lay on a stool, a scattering of towels on the bathroom floor.

I found her sandals and a trace of bare feet along the wall, leading indirectly to the stairs of our apartment. I stared blankly at the balcony, noting the windows were shuttered like the rest, the door barred with an iron strap. If she'd tried the door, she'd have trodden the powdery ash on the sheltered rise...which she had! My heart quickened at the sorrowful sight.

She'd torn a batten strip from the shutters, attempting to lever the bar from the door; bloodied her fingers on a nail, her palm prints mute evidence of her trying again and again! I steadied myself against the railing, looking down to determine if she'd tripped or fallen below.

Spotting a towel on the lower ledge, I vaulted the stairs and raced to the ledge, discovering Nina's footprints by the bloodied, seemingly abandoned, towel. Eyeing the cabana, I tried the door, hoping to find Nina asleep inside with her bevy of dolls; but it wasn't to be! She'd been there, obviously. Dolls were scattered about, her teddy bear missing, but she hadn't lingered long. The chaise cushions were neatly stacked and undisturbed.

Thinking the worst, I stripped and dove into the icy sea, swimming south with the current beneath the cliffs, searching the rocks, calling her name. Apparently in response, a gardener appeared from the neighboring villa with an unlikely pair of hedge shears. Allowing he hadn't seen Nina for days, when I questioned him from the mooring dock. I considered the long rugged coast and turned back. Nina was a strong swimmer, and many hours had passed. She might be anywhere, possibly cowering half-naked in a deserted house, wondering why she was there, if she hadn't been caught by the outgoing tide and swept to sea.

Frightened of this, I searched the murky bottoms until my lungs gave out, realizing I'd panicked when I surfaced again by the ledge. *The ledge* was seemingly entangled with my past and present thoughts, whilst I grasped the coping to roll topside, eyeing its length when I noticed something odd? An icy premonition coursed my spine when I observed the coping was freshly scarred with black paint at the water's edge! The flakes of oily paint lightly dusted with the pre-dawn fall of ash!

Rising quickly to my feet, I traced the soft yielding ash for evidence of a boat recently tied in? But there was no imprint of a line cast to the mooring post, much less withdrawn. Although I instantly recognized Nina's footprints paralleling mine whilst I scanned the coping to where a craft had obviously laid in. Her footprints crossing before me to the water's edge, but not returning or progressing further on. The prints also lightly dusted with ash, not so fresh as mine. Scuffled somewhat at the water's edge, as if she'd made certain of her footing before she leapt or was helped to the waiting craft!

Shaken, heart in mouth, I explored the ledge's length to where it joined the rocky cliff, but there were no other footprints. None leading to a sodden shoulder bag I spied on the outcropping where it had been lofted by the high tide. Recognizing it was Nina's, I toed the bag to the ledge, peering upwards to the wall, noting her sandals topside...realizing she'd deliberately tossed the bag to the sea when she first arrived! The bag conspicuously open, her scarf entwined on the strap.

Worried the police might arrive momentarily, I searched the contents and found Uncle's vintage Smith-Wesson revolver wrapped in a damp handkerchief! I spun the cylinder; there were six rounds, one spent, and the handkerchief reeked of cordite! Examining the bag closely, I discovered a blackened hole in the leather front. The.38 had been fired from inside the bag...obviously by Nina when she cornered Metexas behind his desk!

The evidence could hang her once analyzed with her fingerprints in the lab! The courts not prone to forgive homicidal revenge, despite the mitigating circumstances that set her off! The deed forever done when she came to her rational senses, moreover. And I pictured Nina's anxiety when she fled for Kavouri, her lovely face pale and drawn whilst she hurled the bag desperately to sea!

Rational but increasing bewildered by nightfall, I thought, recollecting the secretary's comments and my observations of Nina's ceaseless searching for familiarities in the shuttered premises. Her sandals, perched on the wall facing the sea, indicating she stood there when she returned from the cabana. Most likely in the full light of the rising moon, her eyes focused upon the fiery plume towering the southerly sky. The volcano's incessant rumblings possibly keying her trance-like dreams.

Of this I had reason to wonder, while I searched her bag for the abominable necklace and figurine! The remaining contents were the usual, however...compact and mirror, drachma notes and loose change, but not her driver's license or Olympic ticket to Kos; nor the damnable letter from the FAA she'd intercepted! All of which she'd conceivably shredded along the way. The jewelry pocket was conspicuously open, however, the zipper snarled as if opened in haste. The pocket empty aside from a pair of shell earrings she'd purchased in Nassau. Nassau? Lordy, I thought, recalling the unholy scene in the grove; the pitiful sight of Nina standing barefoot in the embers, the necklace dangling from her fingers whilst she chanted words from another time, seemingly by rote, as if she were bidden to offer herself to the ominous thunderhead that was near upon us! Wondering why and how she'd gotten there when I slapped her to reality and she came quickly to my arms.

The necklace was an innocuous relic from the past, of course, not a supernatural object — aside from the eyes of its beholder. Such as Nina's when it apparently linked her childhood memories of the sacrificial scene at Arhannes with her troubled dreams of the young girl entombed beneath the temple, the necklace discovered close by. Conceivably worn by the 'princess' while she waited the sacrificial knife, in Nina's mind's eye.

How else to explain her walking nightmare when a cyclonic storm tossed the Helena during the night, arousing Nina to pinch the necklace from her father's desk in throes of a traumatic dream? Nina identifying with the 'princess', the necklace in hand whilst she chanted singsong words from another time, until Nicholas came upon her. As I had when she freaked out midst a thunderous tropical storm in the grove. The peal of thunder seemingly stirring her childhood remembrances in motion; as it had when I found her wandering trance-like in the halls of the Metropolitan Museum.

There was no way I could explain the workings of Nina's psychic intuition, of course. Her genetic ties to the family's ancestral past another matter; which her father seemingly fostered with his archeological quest at Arhannes when she was but a child, to his subsequent regret. Obviously wise of Nina's psychic nature in later years, realizing the necklace had become an opportune conduit to Nina's 'netherworld' during her traumatic dreams, Nicholas had apparently seen fit to secure the necklace from her hands and eyes. Most likely fearing she might favor her 'netherworld' in throes of her dreams and become a permanent victim of walking amnesia! However farfetched, but cause for concern, once observing her trance-like behavior when she was stressed and had the bloody thing in her hands!

Unfortunately, like sticky gum on a shoe, the necklace seemed destined to reappear time and again. As it had when she filched it from Nick's desk in New York, following the trauma of the 'accident' at Hellinikon that did in her parents! Her contempt and suspicions of Tony Metexas obviously a clue to Nina's behavior when we found her chanting on the ledge below! Auntie's voice resounding in my ears, when she commented later that day. 'You must dispose of the loathsome thing, Keith! Nicholas said it's not for Nina to have or wear, lest she come to no good end!' Like Nina's state of mind when Metexas pulled the rug on the auction in Paris, I thought. Her psychic intuition of the sabotaged Lear 21 most likely guiding her hand when she slipped the necklace from my brief case and hauled ass to confront the SOB in Athens.

All of this in my screwed up thoughts whilst I stared at the outgoing tide, the flotsam drifting silently towards the sea, Santorini's incessant rumblings drawing my eyes to the misty horizon, whilst I wondered where Nina might be. The fate of the necklace unresolved…until I sensed Nick's fatherly hand on my shoulder and bent to examine the sandals she'd abandoned topside the wall, knowing she'd discard the glittering thing once relieved of its gasp, as she had in the past!

And there it was! Coiled like a golden snake betwixt her sandals, the figurine's emerald eyes glowering its contempt, seemingly admonishing me for letting Nina go! Conjecture, of course, but how else to deal with her footprints fading to the ledge below?

* * * * * *

Her ways and means of departure, wherever she may have gone, I'd agonize when I collected my wits. Stunned as I was, her safety and wellbeing were foremost in my heart! And fearing the police might arrive momentarily, I realized it was grievously important to dispose of the leather bag that bobbed to the surface in her wake. Also the bloodied towel that would shed evidence of her presence, once her DNA was established in a lab.

Likened to a Chinese fire drill, my mind wasn't altogether whilst I collected the towel and Nina" scant belongings from Auntie" suite. Her shoulder bag bulging at its seams when a pair of F-15s thundered overhead, apparently inbound to the base at Hellinikon, quick to remind me of my duties at Antimahia, once the U-2 was serviced and ready to roll! I was also increasing aware of an ongoing problem, should the police find Bruno's tote bag, realizing I'd be hard put to explain his silencer-equipped Webley and my presence in the villa. Hastily retrieving the satchel, I advantaged its capacity with Nina's overstuffed shoulder bag, the necklace last in, nesting with Bruno's Webley. Glaring ominously when I added a weighty stone from Uncle's garden to make certain it wouldn't return with an ebbing tide. That done, glancing furtively over shoulder, I tossed the bag from the ledge and dove the icy waters to follow it down, dragging it along the stony bottom until I came upon a fallen column and wedged the bag beneath if for a future archeologist to find!

In time, the damnable evidence would rust and wither away, but gold doesn't erode. The necklace, in my mind's view, seemingly following me to the surface when my lungs gave out and I entered an eerie dream. Swirling sparks of green and gold, then chest pains and the taste of salt as I slipped into a rapture-like dream and sense of peace. Opening my eyes when I heard Nina's voice as she swam towards me; wearing a long white gown to the tips of her toes, arms outstretched, her long black hair trailing from her shoulders, beckoning me to follow as she turned to hover in the haze of golden light, fetching her winsome smile, her eyes softening when she said, "I love you dearly, Keith...you mustn't give in!" Then suddenly she frowned, shaking her head, kicking her long legs elusively, gesturing I wasn't to follow whilst I reached desperately for her hand, her flowing white gown disappearing in the iridescent light. Then a surging force seemed to lift me from the depths and I surfaced by the ledge, gasping for air, calling her name!

* * * * * *

"Good heavens, you'll catch your death of cold!" a voice called from the wall. I spun about, thinking it was Auntie, to be greeted by the cook's beaming round face.

"I have come to pack canned goods for Bruno to fetch to Mt. Parnassus, Mr. Slater. Might Nina be with you? Not see the Mercedes."

Bare-ass, I collected my shorts, zipping up in the shadow of the wall.

"They're...not here at the moment," I gasped, toeing my shirt within reach.

"Oh my...best I brew a pot of tea, then, you appear a mite chilled," she added. "Did you have a nice swim?"

I don't recall what I said, nor can I describe my wretched state of mind when the cook hurried to the kitchen and I climbed to the patio, staring numbly at the sea. For one part, I was thankful Nina was alive when she disappeared from the ledge, as opposed to my sinking heart. Wherever she was, I'd compulsively hidden the death-dealing revolvers, hopefully for all time, with no feeling of remorse! There would be questions, of course, once the authorities pieced the puzzle together but, as Fotis had said, they were preoccupied with other matters. For how long was unanswerable but, at the moment, she was beyond their reach.

"Come, I have tea and a sandwich," the cook said, calling from the pantry door.

"Did you come by yesterday?" I asked when she dusted off the patio table and added a splash of brandy to my tea.

"Come by every morning," she responded, pointing to Auntie's three-wheeler. "Fetch things for Mrs. Maris. Bruno leave mostly before noon, come from Parnassus with big list. Spend night sometime, never much see."

Boats...was there a boat nearby at any one time?" The cook gave it thought.

"Fishing craft, maybe. Plenty yacht pass in big hurry, but see strange craft two days back. Come from south, I think, not from Kavouri; no catch fish hereabouts."

"Small, a double-ender?"

"Not so large, have long sweep off stern. Come to anchor with big stone," She added, pointing to a shoal fronting the burned-out villa. "Think maybe looter, but not come ashore." I deliberated my next question, knowing the answer.

"Black hull, red sail?"

"Old-time boat, have mast like this," she said, crossing her fingers to indicate a lateen rig. "Red sail, hang to dry, but now I see...same boat disappear?" My eyes flooded; I was dead inside.

"Have bug in eye, Mr. Slater? Come, I fetch handkerchief, plenty water on stove!" she added, hurrying to the pantry. I begged off, took a sip of brandy. Turning to stare at the sea again, I thought of Butterfield's words at Akrotiri: *Deuca came to us from Crete,* she'd said. Auntie's comments relating to Arhannes when Nina was a child: *The lad came from a valley near Kaphri, Helena said he speaks a language that's not altogether Greek, and often brings oranges for the workmen at the dig.*

"You not hear telephone?" the cook shrilled from her pantry. "Maybe news of Nina, Mr. Slater!"

News of Nina? I repeated to myself, wondering if the cook had pieced it together, when I picked up Uncle's phone.

"Might that be you, Keith?" Willitts questioned.

"More or less," I said, studying the map on the wall where Uncle's desk had been. *Given a 12-hour lead, with winds full sail, they'd be west of Milos,* I thought. *Santorini 60 miles to the east by nightfall, given a southerly bearing to northern Crete.*

"Speak up, Keith! Did you locate your - er - 'luggage'?"

"Not exactly," I replied, "but I know where it might be."

"Safe?"

"Depends," I said, gathering my wits. "I've a case of the jitters and a bug

270

in my eye! So what's the drill?"

"First off, we've 'no name' aboard the sixth fleet and he's likely to survive! I've also been in touch with T.S. on the Navy's 'Z' channel at Commander Whitehead's office by the 'copter pad, but he didn't say where he was at the time."

"Did you tell him what I said?"

"No way, Keith! He's bloody worried Nokomo will fuck things up before you make it back, and what with Olympic scrubbing most of their inter island flights, he's near off the wall!"

"Meaning the morning flight to Kos might be up for grabs?"

"Could be. So I'm waiting for Commander Whitehead to fetch back from Cyprus, to see what he can do. T.S. saying it's 'critically important' you fly the U-2 out of Antimahia and hammer the turn over Iran, no matter what! Likened to the BBC morning newscast, methinks; apart from Santorini, it appears there's a military build up along the eastern Caspian. Hard-line loose cannons and fundamentalist types, eyeing the oil regions in Baku. BBC speculating they're armed with 'experimental tanks' the Russians abandoned in Turkmenistan (intending to use them in Afghanistan) years ago.

"Same bloody area marked on your charts," Willitts added under breath. "Could be Gunnar has the hots for the same yard before the Kremlin or NATO intervenes. Altogether excellent timing, Keith! What with the media sot with Santorini, the world could care less!"

"Did T.S. clue you any further?" I questioned, wondering if he'd divulged the bottom line.

"Negative, old buddy! Methinks it's top secret, but I've flown recon over Iraq and I'd be an idiot to say I wasn't aware the U-2's equipped with means to analyze and fix the targets, so that the old man's stealth 'eager beavers' could arm their precision guided bananas and trash the lot!"

"Sorry to interrupt your video game," a female voice cut in from the PBX. "Commander Whitehead called in to say he will land at the top of the hour, Mr. Willitts. We also have a message from General O'Brien, requesting you stand by until he confers with the Commander. The message two part," she added quickly. "I wasn't on duty at the time, but it appears he requested information of a Major Slater's whereabouts since you arrived from Antimahia!"

My heart skipped a beat, but fortunately Willitts played it cool.

"Did the General say or indicate where he was at the time?"

"Lieutenant Matthews here, Mr. Willitts! I'm in charge of our evacuation team, at the moment subbing for the yeoman who's out for lunch. But judging from his notes, the messages were relayed from the tower at 15:30, local time," she added, "so best you check with Operations, Mr. Willitts. I've another call to attend." I stared warily at the four o'clock sun; clicked the receiver repeatedly to draw Willitts' attention, his thoughts apparently coinciding with mine.

"You might gander the ramp for a pair of F-15s fresh in from Riyadh, old buddy!" The line went silent whilst I pictured Willitts staring from the office window.

"Yeah, man!" he said, when he picked up the line. "Like a pair of 'Strike Eagle 15-Es', desert tan, under heavy guard?"

"Now you have it! Has to be T.S. checking things out on his own! So bear with me, and don't hand my numbers or allow to where I might be, damnit to hell! At the moment I'm stressed out until I get my act together and flush my brain with a night's sleep. God knows where, but not here!" I added, wary of an unsolicited visitation during the night.

"You're overreacting, me thinks!"

"Could be! But at the moment I'm up to my ears with family matters I can't rightly discuss, assuming you know what I mean. But I'm not about to flake out, if that's what's bugging T.S.!"

"The old man has yet to show face, Keithy, but he knows that's not your style! More likely holding back until he cuts a deal with Commander Whitehead to fetch you to Kos, what with Olympic threatening to cancel out! If so, how do we get in touch once you haul ass and leave your phone off the hook?"

"At the moment, I don't know! So let's say I'll definitely show up at the crack of dawn, or call the base if I have a problem with the Cortina and have to go it by foot."

"Fair enough, Keithy, no questions asked. In fact, once I see this through I'm out of here to Mildenhall with the evacs from the Consulate, T.S. granting his okay!"

"Don't tell me you're fading, man?"

"Call it what you like, Keith! Bosnia and Kosovo were a blast, but I've had my share of kicks. And, what with the bloody scene at Hellinikon this morning, enough is enough!"

"We're not out of this yet, Willitts!"

"That I know! But with the 'witch' out of the picture, there's little else I can do aside from holding Ingrid's hand! And with doomsday hanging on the horizon, it's better I join my wife and kids; fly a desk and enjoy life at Mildenhall with RAF senior staff!"

"So why pull the rug when you can fly a kite from high places, command a Group in the field?"

"Moot question, Keith! But like you and T.S., it takes a certain breed of cats! Despite the circumstances, it's been a pleasure to know you since we met at Heathrow, Keith. It also goes without saying, I admire your spunk, God bless!"

That said, Willitts clicked off while I juggled the phone, not knowing what to say, not anticipating his farewell address. Although fearing he might be identified with Amalia's assassin when we helped Bruno aboard the Mercedes, he had reason to be elsewhere, especially once the police questioned the witnesses. My game leg and blond hair compounding a double feature, should they screen the video cameras monitoring the terminal.

Supposition, of course, what with the police preoccupied with the ongoing evacuation from the low-lying city. Sufficient reason to jar my quirky nerves, however, when a siren sounded in the distance, coinciding with the phone ringing in the pantry. The siren subsiding elsewhere, while the cook shouted from the door,

"You have another call, Mr. Slater. Nina's secretary, I think!" I picked up the extension, staring warily at the gates.

"I'm calling from Paris," she said. "Bruno didn't show at the office, but we took along what we could. Have you found Nina or know where she's gone?" she added, obviously close to tears. I answered as best I could, saying Nina had left the villa voluntarily during the night, seemingly in good health, but I was at odds to where she may have gone.

"Thank God she's safe, Keith! But I thought it best to warn you, the police came by while we were clearing uncle's desk, inquiring if we'd seen her lately."

"So what did you say?"

"Said she'd most likely tripped to Paris, what with the auction at loose ends. And hopefully she has, Keith! Might you have found her shoulder bag and things she took along?"

"Whatever she had is definitely not here or in the villa!" I answered truthfully, realizing what she meant. "So what say with Paris, did they pick up the scent?"

"Strangely, they didn't seem to be concerned, Keith! But judging from their comments, I believe they intend to check the villa and question whoever might be there." I glanced at my watch and quickly signed off, allowing I'd send word to Auntie once I had a lead to Nina's whereabouts; the cook my immediate concern!

Dedicated to the family, I realized she had the situation pretty much together, and wasn't to be taken lightly. Knowing Nina since she was a child, most likely she was aware of her presence during the night, of her mysterious habits. So how would she handle it, should she be questioned by the police, Loving Nina as she did? My sodden appearance on the ledge adding to her quandary, when she spied me from the pantry. But fortunately, I realized her thoughts were attuned with mine when she made point to collect my loafers and sat down beside me whilst I tried to fit them to my mangled feet.

"Fear Nina flee to Kavouri when morning news say Metexas shot dead, Mr. Slater! Not care smidgen for him; worry police jump conclusion and search for Nina, knowing family have spite for likes of him! Come then hasty quick to fetch her to safety; scent her perfume in pantry, see you have rightful cause to fetch her satchel to the sea! Know then you love Nina, not care for yourself! So now, best take heed and leave matters to me, before police catch sight of your wretched face!

"Come night, I visit relatives in Pendlikon with son-in-law," she added, suggesting I button my shirt and not forget my brief case. "When holocaust pass, maybe sun shine again at Kavouri! Maybe then judgement say Nina have right to honor decent family with just cause!"

I hugged the old gal closely, thankful of her warm heart and depth of understanding. Realizing her intentions were kin to mine when she appeared out of the blue, fearing Nina's wellbeing should the police find trace of her in the villa, as I had? Our thoughts fortunately in accordance when I allowed to discovering her sandals and shoulder bag nearby, and thought it best to dispatch the lot to the sea, hopefully not to be found! Loath to mention Uncle's rusty Smith-Wesson contained in the bag, nor Bruno's lethal Webley I'd added last moment.

The Webley quick in mind when I realized the cook was also concerned for Bruno, expecting him to come with the Mercedes to collect the provisions she'd purchased for Auntie; where might he be? To this I had no ready answer, but again thought it best to set matters straight, assuming she wasn't aware of the 'incident' at Hellinikon when he came to fetch me with the Mercedes. Knowing she'd be at wits' end once she caught word!

Apologizing for my forgetfulness, and capsulizing as best I could, but not factually, I said Bruno had had a 'close scrape in traffic' at the airport, but I'd heard he was okay, the Mercedes parked nearby the Navy base last seen. The cook nodded thoughtfully, eyeing my means of transport to the villa when she saw me to the gates.

"So best I phone Maris not to expect Bruno tonight, maybe tomorrow? Maybe," she added when I bent to buss her cheek. "So come now I also have big worry for yourself, Keith! Family knowing you have decent obligation to brave fire in sky with your airy plane, Nina not beside you same time! So take heed our hearts are with you and we care matters here!"

That said, she scanned the boulevard and pressed the gates, but I realized she had more to say when she touched my hand and added obliquely,

"You must also heed confidence of captain Stavos and Auntie Cleo, Keith! Often theenk Cleo like Nina have magical ways, maybe know where she come to be, bless her soul!"

* * * * * *

Numb to the bone from my tumultuous day, noting the Cortina's petrol was low edge when I was repeatedly stalled by the heavily laden outgoing traffic, I eventually found myself at Varkoza, desperate for a beer and a hot meal! Nearing sunset by then, the sprightly village appeared nearly abandoned, the remaining villagers seemingly resigned to come what may, or straggling on foot pushing their belongings in supermarket carts. I could have sold Petrie's Cortina on the spot!

Fortunately there was activity of sorts in the village square, and I located an open-for-business taverna opposite ends of the Orthodox church. The sallow faced proprietor acknowledging he had a room available for the night, offering the key when I displayed my American Express checks on the bar. Inquiring if I had need of a lady friend for the evening when I counter-signed the checks and he spied the remaining fifty dollar note in the folder. Which, fortunately, sufficed a plate of warmed over moussaka, a curl of bread and a jug of fairly decent wine. Surprising, what with things as they were in Varkoza.

Key in hand, wary I'd find myself without transport come morning, I removed the rotor arm from the Cortina's distributor. Noted the rusty Volvo parked alongside with jugs of much the same wine; leading to believe the proprietor and his lady friend intended to set up elsewhere should the deluge come.

The room was appropriate for a quick turnover from the streets...a single bed plus a fiberglass shower stall, lacking soap. There were towels aplenty, however, and I made do with my shampoo. The door wisely chained from the inside, I stretched out on the bed, desperate for sleep. Nonetheless aware of the 747s thundering overhead, the adjacency to Hellinikon's low approach, and the hills that lay beyond...where the Lear 21 had bought the park!

My dreams were fitful at first, mostly repetitive images of the day: Amalia's pleading eyes and Bruno's deadly stance; Nina's sandals and the bloodied towel;

the ghastly figurine glowering defiantly when I lodged her shoulder bag in the crevice beyond the ledge. Suddenly, the dreams became peaceful.

I was a youngster, flying rear seat in my dad's restored Stearman PT-17. We were wearing goggles; his blondish hair protruded from his leather helmet, while his gloved hand steadied the stick. Below lay the neatly furrowed fields and greenery of summertime Tennessee. *'Easy does it,'* he shouted from the gosport. *'Keep your eye on the needle and ball, and don't lose altitude when you make your next turn!'*

And then, I was home from the academy in my starched Air Force blues. We were seated side by side in a vintage Beech D-128 he'd rented to teach me loss of engine and instrument procedures. He was older then, recently home from Vietnam, a single star on his collar (he never wore ribbons). *'Okay, Keith, you're at 2,000 feet IFR on a straight-in approach, and you lose number one,'* he instructed, pulling back the mix control. *'Now you have it, opposite rudder and be quick to check the panel. Okay, so feather it and maintain your flight path. Call in to approach and say you've a mayday -- dead engine. They'd have you on radar, so don't panic and maintain a controlled descent. One thing to remember, son; never turn on a bad engine, or you'll be on to a Dutch roll.'*

Once again, years later, we were in a T-37. He had his second star by then, his hair speckled with traces of gray, his voice not so sprightly. My mother had died recently and I was on leave from the 17th Air Force. We were tracking the muddy Mississippi, reminiscing as old friends -- when suddenly we were IFR in a volcanic haze over the limpid Aegean! *'Eyes front, bring her back to 135 knots,'* he said, scrutinizing a chart when we emerged in the brightening sunlight.

I dropped quarter flaps, advanced the twin turbo jets to hold what he said. He brought a pair of binoculars from behind his seat and scanned the horizon to the south. I knuckled the wheel and strained my eyes; a cruise liner passed to the west on a long sweeping turn, the horizon was silhouetted with fleeing ships, now with sail.

Milos fell rapidly to the east; Nissi Ananes appeared below us, a splinter of limestone, hedgerows, and cottages. The Greek flag flew at half-mast, indicating distress. The sun, low in the west, cast streaks of orange and shadows on the sea when he focused his glasses and indicated thumbs up. I leaned forward in my seat, wiping a curl of sweat from my brow. *'Red sail?'* *'Red sail!'* he replied. *'Black hull?'* *'One and the same,'* he agreed. As I peered from the canopy, a diminutive speck appeared on the horizon, its red sail bent to the gusting breeze. I advanced the throttles, holding short of a power-on stall. The double-ender loomed a few points off the Cessna's nose.

276

Deuca stood motionless at the tiller, facing the bow; my eyes were not for him...it was Nina! It was she! She sat closely by his side with an arm resting the gunwale, a white shawl draped about her shoulders. Shielding her eyes as our shadow passed, she frowned, as if mystified by our wing spread. She brought a hand to her ear, bewildered by our throbbing jets, but seemingly not afraid!

I gathered air speed and wheeled the Cessna into a 360° turn for another pass. The general cautioned my hand when I leveled off and firewalled the engines. We skimmed the swell; hanging a stall, I banked to avoid the sailboat's stays, braced to stare from the canopy. My heart thumped wildly; had she recognized us? Or was she beholding an enormous bird!

Deuca shouldered the tiller without looking about, his hat tilted to the sun. His ruby eyes scanned the horizon, his chalky face devoid of expression. I craned my neck as we passed. Nina was cowering wide-eyed by his side, her golden earrings glistening in the sun. Naked to the waist, the shawl had fallen to her feet.

I waved and shouted from the canopy, but her eyes were not for me. She'd turned her head, buried her face to Deuca's chest. I advanced the throttles as they faded behind us, climbing to the east, my heart a bag of sand.

'Beautiful girl.' I nodded; what else could he say?

'I'm too late. She's slipped into another world!'

'And that would be Deuca?'

'He calls her Pyrrha, damnit to hell!'

'It would appear he has taken her for his wife.' I turned in my seat to sort him out.

'I didn't need that!'

'Of course not, but better face up to it. There's nothing you can do about it now!'

'I'm dead, for Christ's sake...buzz off!' He cuffed the wheel and fixed me with his eyes. I looked back from the canopy; the craft was miles behind us.

'She's alive, you suffering ass! Thank your bloody stars! She'll be safe in the mountains when Santorini unloads; there'll be another day! The world isn't finished!'

'You don't understand! Deuca's a throwback from another time. The frescoes at Akrotiri would rattle your mind!'

'Don't you think I ached inside when the Reaper selected you mother, son?'

'That was different.'

'Was it now? For you there's hope; Nina is alive! For me, it will never be.

Jenny's gone forever.' I eased off. He was wanting to talk and there was so little time.

'*I dragged ass for a while, feeling sorry for myself, wondering what my years in the service had brought...a burned-out general, too little time at home, a hand-carved desk in the Pentagon.'* He reached down to switch tanks, engaged the aux pumps until the pressure held.

'*I was holed up with a House committee one day, you mother a year in her grave, when I realized I was more dead than alive. Decided I had to fly again, start from scratch before I was too old to swing a prop, feel the wind bite my face in an open cockpit, tease the corn tassels with a set of wheels. Do you know what I mean?'* I nodded, begging to understand.

'*Sometimes, when I'm sitting up there all alone, with an old engine beating my ears, I hear the sound of ethereal music, your mother's voice rising above the chorus. Like it did years ago, when we stood together in her little church.'* His shoulders sagged. He brushed a hank of hair from his forehead, and brightened when I said I'd heard the 'music' before.

'*We haven't had much talk since the day we pinned your wings,'* he added. '*Been wanting to say, you're never far from my heart. Deep love is a spiritual thing, like flying, son. A God-given gift to behold. Giving in to yourself is selfish and cruel. Grab yourself and hang in. Express your love in other ways!'*

CHAPTER 23

I was awakened by the whine of a C-130's turbine engines rattling my window on a low approach to Hellinikon. Thinking I'd overslept a long ago mission over Iraq, I parted the blinds and peered outside. Realizing I'd experienced a long, heavy dream, when I was greeted by early dawn and a view of the Greek Orthodox church. The dream so realistic, I sensed my dad's presence in the room.

My haggard face in the mirror told me I was in need of a shave and had minimal time to check with Olympic and round robin the base to determine if T.S. was factually on hand. Knowing he'd pull rank with Commander Whitehead to get me on to Antimahia, Olympic failing!

The icy shower was cruel when I soaped down; the vivid dream etched my mind while I toweled and shaved the face I assumed was mine. My dad's words a salve to my soul, despite my subconscious fears of Nina fleeing with Deuca, I'd gained a measure of resolve. As if the old man had sensed my anxiety across oceans of time and hastened to reassure me I was never far from his mind. Far reaching, when he expressed his sorrow for my mother in words he'd never admitted before; although I had seen it in his face when we stood by her grave.

Sight of the depleted Cortina brought my thoughts back to reality, however, noting the petrol tank had been tried and given up, a suction hose abandoned nearby. The Volvo seemingly not tampered, adding to my suspicions when I replaced the Cortina's rotor; gasping my relief when she responded with a throaty roar and we made haste to track the back roads to Vari and Glyfada, the fuel gauge reading 'empty' when we slow-paced it through Glyfada and had sight of the Marine Drive!

I'd taken the circuitous route to Hellinikon to avoid the congestion and find a place to rest my weary bones, but from here on I had no choice but to enter the highway and chance it out. Knowing the approach lanes would be relatively sparse of traffic, and I could make it by foot once the Cortina gave up.

But fortunately, we had a providential kick in the ass and managed to turn off to the base with the Cortina sneezing its last; chugging the remaining mile until I saw fit to ease her gears to neutral and coast to the gates. Here again, fortunately, the militia guard recognized the Cortina, my thatch of hair and the UN credentials I flashed from the open window. He quickly raised the gate, allowing the Cortina to coast on through. The turn to the parking lot somewhat of a bugger, the power steering failing when I eased the faithful thing to where I'd found her, high gear sufficing for lack of brakes!

Thanking my luck, hopefully the start of a decent day, I rolled up the windows and dropped the keys to the floor, noting the boxy Mercedes was yet in place when I gathered my brief case and closed my door. A light film of ash obscured the license plate from inquisitive eyes. Next in mind, the pair of F-15-Es I spied on the ramp, the flight crew assembled nearby, seemingly waiting to be airborne momentarily.

Thinking it best to check with Commander Whitehead, I made haste to his office, noting his Sea Hawk was posed and ready on its pad. Not expecting to be greeted by a blast from T.S., when he opened the door and I stumbled inside!

"Damn it to hell, Keith! You said you would call in if you had a problem with transportation, which you didn't! So we've been waiting since 0700, and suddenly you come whizzing by, not looking right or left, like you're out of your fucking mind!" Noting the Commander was also present – the twosome on to their morning coffee – I explained the circumstances as best I could. Allowing I hadn't the loose change to call in, thinking I'd give Olympic first shot until the Cortina conked out.

The old man softened somewhat, collecting a fresh Panatella from his flight suit; he fixed it habitually in the corner of is mouth.

"Was worried for you, son! Figured it was time we had a quiet chat when I caught word of 'Metexas' and reasoned you would split to Athens. Sent Willitts along when you did! And hearing Olympic was about to close shop, I made from Riyadh *in two hours flat!*" he added proudly. "How's that for an old fart who bussed you to school when your mom and daddy were down with the flu?"

"I'm impressed, T.S.! In fact, I spotted your pair of 15s from the villa and figured they belonged to you! So where do we go on from here?"

"First off, it's prudent you not show face at Olympic or hereabouts until we get you off to Kos, Keith! What with the regional newscast indicating a partici-pant in the massacre at Hellinikon was last seen aboard a fleeing limousine! The driver, a tall chap with a noticeable limp and head of blond hair, possibly American, judging from his knee-length shorts! And I quote verbatim, my hair on end when you breezed the gates togged as you are!"

"Willitts filled you in?" The general nodded.

"Hauled ass for Mildenhall last night, bleeding from the nose!"

"Can't knock him for taking off, T.S.! Willitts had the guts to lug Bruno aboard, mind his wounds and get him on with the evac to the Sixth Fleet, no questions asked! Like he didn't know Bruno by sight, until I clued him in! So let's get on with what has me uptight...did the newscast mention Nina in any way?"

"Nary a word, Keith! But knowing your state of mid, I contacted Interpol regarding an AWOL matter and inquired what they knew of the Metexas flap while I had them on the line. Yes indeedy, they had Tony Metexas on file! Saying he'd been identified as a prime suspect in a 'sabotage incident at Hellinikon', weeks back! They were also aware of his assassination, but declined to comment further. No mention of Nina, however!

"Frankly, boy, since the Maris family is well known and highly respected, the facts of the Lear 21 'incident' seemingly common knowledge, I tend to believe Metexas' homicide is bottom drawer at the moment, despite your fears! Like the Greeks are traditionally known to accept rightful revenge as a family affair and tend to let matters be. If, in fact, they regard Nina as a suspect, less said the better!

"So you bit the bullet to protect your wife, and I respect you for that!" T.S. continued, nodding to Whitehead when he produced a visored cap and Navy flying suit from his locker in my behalf. "I also have a back ass hunch you might know where Nina's likely to be, and intend to search things out once you round trip Iran, Keithy lad!"

"What makes you think that?"

"Your tenacity, and love for your wife, no matter what! Like your daddy, you take it on the chin and get on to matters at hand! As he did in 'Nam when he lost your mom, God bless her soul! You also inherited his unconventional ways, Keith! Likened to his love of flying when he split the Service to fly bush for the Peace Corps, with Jenny heavy in his mind. Like yourself, when you nearly lost your leg and had the guts to hack it with NASA, flying U-2s. Adds up to a plus, Keithy. What with your experience flying combat in Iraq!"

"Is that why I'm here?"

"Why else would I put up with your behavior, with the Security Council riding my ass!"

"Change of subject, T.S.! In regards of my dad, when did you hear from him last? We invited him to the wedding, but lost contact when he didn't call back."

"Well now, Keith...since you obviously don't know, he had a forced landing in the Sudan and had to make it back on foot!"

"Jesus, man! Is he okay?"

"Sprightly as ever, boy! In fact, we so happened to have a C-130 in the vicinity and he's most likely in Riyadh near about now!"

"So why didn't you tell me first off! Jesus, man...I dreamed of my dad last night! Mostly years back when I soloed the Stearman he restored when I was a kid. Then suddenly we were flying buddy in a T-37 searching for Nina!" I stopped short, the scene vivid in my mind; opting to fit my length into Whitehead's flying suit, the Commander fortunately same size.

"Provident dream, hey? I'm not up to spiritual things, but appears you're on the same wave length, knowing he's been worrying for you, what with the volcano spitting fire."

"Is he aware of the 'action', T.S.?"

"I...uh, I believe so, Keith. He also seems knowledgeable of Nina's disappearance, or at least of the problem. In fact, I didn't intend to mention this until I heard of the scene at the terminal, and thought you needed a deserving vibe! Appears you're also in need of a haircut," T.S. asided when I topped myself with the cap.

A van with embassy plates passed by the commander's window while I paid heed to my ungainly reflection...wondering of the last time I'd been sheared. My thatch of hair definitely at odds with the tight fitting cap! New York, the barber upstreet from Clarkes...that long ago day when I'd stood with Nina at the Greek Orthodox Church.

"Evacuees from the Consulate!" the Commander commented, tidying his desk, as if he doubted he'd make it back to Athens. "Once we load up we're out of here, General! First off, to drop Slater at Antimahia and top our tanks provided MacDougal has spare. If not, we'll tap the auxiliaries and skirt the coast to Incirlik (Air Force Base in Turkey). Like we'd have a problem making it to a flat top, what with the fleet heading points west!"

"Critical move, hey?" Whitehead nodded.

"Flank speed, General! Not wanting to test the clock, Admiral Curts thought it wise to disperse the ships to where they can ride it out, should Santorini pull its plug and surge the Aegean! Basic problem, if and when? Like at the moment, Athens is waiting for Dr. Schumann's analysis of the volcano's pulse and vapor salinity, once he has feedback from the U-2. Like he's predicting an imminent pyrotechnical explosion, should the sea penetrate the magma chamber, which has the authorities on edge!"

"If, and when?"

"Yes, of course, General! The 'if' pending trace of salt water intrusion, the 'when' up for grabs! So we're on to an 'if and when' situation, but at the moment we're paying close heed to Dr. Sigurdesson's 'moon tide' theory, which I understand is controversial, but appears to hit the nail on the head! Quoting Admiral Curts, when he advised us to evacuate our base and Consulate personnel by sunset today, which is presently under way."

"Now you're telling me this! Hell's fire, I thought we were discussing 'ifs and whens', not a predictable time elapse! So clue me further, Commander. Last heard, it was up to Dr. Schumann to call the shots!"

"Rightfully so, General...so let's call it a Navy decision! Like it appears I fetched the cart before the horse, thinking you had the update when you flew in from Riyadh."

"No way! In fact, Schumann made no mention of this when I contacted him yesterday morning, pursuant to Keithy's return, which you've since confirmed!"

"Explains matters! Apparently, Schumann and Sigurdesson got their heads together later day and made a 'joint statement'; near about when you set down. Myself en route from Cyprus at the time, but I caught the recap on telly while you were seeing the English chap off to the UK."

"Cross purpose for my part, damn it to hell! So what did they have to say?"

"Like I said, General, Schumann's waiting for feedback from the U-2, but the lady doctor made a flat out prediction while he was standing by! Saying she agrees with his format, but fears the magma chamber is so weakened it will 'collapse with the weight of the flood tide within the next forty-eight hours'! Schumann not all that certain, but, man...she was insistent she had it right, pleading to be heard out! Close to tears, feverish, down to skin and bones since I saw her last!"

"Forty-eight hours, you say?"

"As of last night, pursuant to the ebb tide, General! So it's an 'iffy' prediction, not yet official, but fortunately Athens is paying close heed. And once the authorities sound the sirens, comes next the stampede!"

"Were you aware of this, Keithy?" T.S. thundered, obviously at odds with his homework, not wanting to be put down by the ebony faced Commander. So, how to deal with it, so as not to disgrace the old fart in the Commander's presence? Ingrid's prediction least in mind whilst I was exploring the deep six.

"Sigurdesson's been on to her 'full moon tide prediction' since she met with our group at the Bretagne Grand, T.S.! No change of equation when we set up at Antimahia...in fact, she had the 'time of the month' underlined on her calendar when I saw her last, insisting her calculations were factually correct when we round-tripped the volcano and she had the feedback in her computer, inclusive of our photo scan when we viewed the volcano close up."

"Indicating what?" I gave thought to the unwieldy U-2 at low altitude, Winner's green face, our canopies brazed from the searing ash!

"Judging from what we could see, it appears the outer shank is deeply creviced short of the high water mark, T.S.! Which is tidal, of course, but lends to her fear of a 'Plinian rupture'...should the fissures erode with the tides and allow seepage to the magma chamber from the sea!"

"Schumann's theory...we've discussed this at length, Keithy!"

"So hear me out, T.S.! Ingrid buys that, but fears acceleration is in process and takes it on steps further! Predicting the full moon ebb tide will decompress and weaken, or uplift the mantle to where the sea can juice an explosion! Comes next a 'double whammy' when the oncoming flood tide caps the lot! So now what do we have if her prognosis comes to be?"

"A forty megaton bomb, to put it mildly!" Whitehead interjected. "The likes of which the world ain't never seen since Moses led his flock across the 'sea of reeds'! Appears we're out of touch with the lady's almanac, General! For my part, I'm out of here once we load up and fetch Slater to his eye in the sky!"

T.S. nodded silently and strode to the window to stare at the specter hanging the horizon. The bright blue overhead sky seemingly mocking the oily plume...until a responsive tremor reached out and jellied the ramp. T.S. amongst the believers when he gained his feet and played it tongue in cheek.

"Well now, Commander, since you put it that way! Comes next the moot question for my part: just when does the full moon occur in the central Aegean?" I had chance to take T.S. off the hook, realizing he was hard put to equate the celestial difference betwixt Athens and Riyadh, if in fact he was aware of the status of the moon.

"Locally, tomorrow night between sunset and dawn, T.S.! Near about the time I make my turn over Iran! So we're dealing with an 'iffy' prediction, but I've a gut feeling we'll see the last of Santorini when Schumann has my feedback and I haul ass for Iran, while Sigurdesson calls the odds!"

"Meaning you *intend* to turn the volcano first off, contrary to my dissuasions, hey? Come to your senses, boy! You'll bleed two hours from your tanks and jeopardize the long stretch! Needlessly, I think!"

"Terms of my contract, T.S.! Athens needs the group's feedback...and I'm not about to flake out, come what may!"

We met eye to eye then, words unsaid in the Commander's presence. The U-2's fuel consumption not the issue, what with Lockheed strengthening and extending the hybrid's wings to accommodate auxiliary fuel should we encounter matters undisclosed! The wizard's top secret 'black box' T.S.'s primary concern! Specifically, the need to pace the time slot allotted to the U-2's penetration of the inviolate air space over Ashkhabad before dawn! The 'critical timing' his obvious worry, should we encounter problems en route...and fault his long laid plans!

Fortunately, T.S. edged off, realizing his comments were ill put with the emergency at hand. Insisting to be heard out, however, he expressed concern of the U-2's fragility, should I venture the volcano close in; the possibility of the GE turbo-jet ingesting ash and calling it quits, aborting the flight altogether!

"First part's no sweat, T.S.! Our flight plan filed with ATC, calls for a quick climb out for 50,000 feet, to top commercial traffic, give or take fifteen minutes. And, with the ash plume drifting east-southeast, we'll have a peripheral view of the spike and can gauge its height! So we'll needle it from the lee and climb to top it off if need be...at least to where Schumann will have our feedback of the cone velocity and vapor salinity. Hopefully the turbulence below and behind us while we turn east and track the drift, according to plan. Which should have us over Jordan in two hours flat, considering the hundred knot tail winds Edwards predicts tomorrow noon!

"Okay, let's say we're level wing at ready altitude, our fuel consumption low ebb, our data link with Antimahia in the green. But comes the second part," I added quickly, realizing the Commander was anxious to be airborne and I'd yet to discuss, much less resolve, an 'upcoming problem' that would have the General off the wall!

"As of yesterday morning, our satellite scan indicates the ash drift is curving to the south with the winds aloft, T.S.! Which will have us at odds with our projected flight plan when we bend off course to screen the tailings with our pods. Needlessly, most likely...what with the volcano on edge. But nevertheless, an integral part of my contract with the UN. Which we can accommodate in terms of fuel...so's not to jeopardize our continuation over Iran, if you read me rightly! Basic problem, the loss of time...which could add up to 'two hours' once we climb to max altitude and converge our flight plan, calling for the dog leg to horse it east of Tehran!"

"I, uh...understand what you mean, Keithy! So what do you propose?"

"Pilot's prerogative, T.S.! With Santorini about to blow its lid, I'd have reason to track our projected course, no sweat! But with Dr. Nokomo on to our data link, he'd have cause to abort the 'long stretch' unless I can persuade him otherwise, since he's calling the shots for the UN! So I'm at 70,000 feet with beggar-man's choice if I can't bring him to heel, knowing he has a long nose!" T.S.'s reaction was true to form, knowing his double-tiered mind. His thoughts obviously elsewhere while he fished a fresh panatelá from his flight suit, forgetting the stogie habitually clamped in his jaw. Until I had chance to set his right...realizing he was churning my pre-rogatives should Nokomo challenge or abort the turn over Iran. The savvy Commander affording a measure of privacy when he glanced at him watch and pointed to the ramp!

"What with time running short, I'll be needing to board me ground crew and APU...once you fire up yon F-15s, General! Like I said, we plan to be out of here when the Lieutenant counts heads. Say, round about 9:20...figurin' you need time to breeze it with Slater for reasons I can't rightly say! But off record, I reckon it has to do with the situation brewing in Turkmenistan...and I wish you God speed, knowing the U-2 has eyes for such things. Main thing, to get 'Keithy' here on to Antimahia quick as possible, observin' he'll be up to his ass with double duty near about the time when the volcano blows its guts!" T.S. nodded grimly, but played it laid back. Seemingly relieved by the Commander's understatement, the U-2's salient features something else again!

Returning the panatelá to pocket, he expressed his gratitude for the Commander's perseverance and lent hand to board his luggage to a waiting ground tug. The driver presumably intending to retrieve the APU alongside the F-15s once they were airborne. Near forgotten, the General's overnighter, which I quickly shouldered whilst he returned the Commander's snappy salute, offering his 'fives' to the Commander's obvious delight. T.S.'s indefatigable style, in terms of things well done! Not so for my part, noting his bag was conspicuously laden with artifacts he'd purchased in Athens, presumably for his wife of recent years.

Light of hand, I collected my brief case and strode for the ramp, feasting my eyes on the sight of the pair of 'Strike Eagles' close up, noting the comparative obsolescence of the F-15s I'd flown over Iraq, whilst T.S. labored to keep pace with my ungainly limp. His wingtip pilot cautioning me to hold back, obviously puzzled by my Navy flying suit and the Commander's cap perched atop my shock of hair.

We had a good natured, instructive talk, however, when T.S. caught up and allowed I was ex-Air Force with combat time in F-15s. The Captain, near my age when I'd last flown the series, offering a peek of the forward cockpit. The array of updated electronics foreign to my eyes, not so the familiar ejection seat that had me at odds over the desert when I delayed my chute, fearing the raking AK-47's blazing from below. Remembrance of things past...with my 'savior' standing by while I dropped from the ladder and he pointed to the shadow of the tactical fighter's wing.

"Now that you've had your lick, comes time to face up with the long stretch," T.S. asided, motioning his rear seat armament officer to retrieve and stow the shoulder bag aboard.

"So what do you propose, T.S.? With Nokomo monitoring our data link, there's no way I can cancel the turn, least I pull the plug and haul ass with egg on my face!"

"Could be, dependent on his availability, so hear me out, Keithy! According to Keenan, the UN"S insisting Horst Gunnar's to ride your rear seat and monitor the data link! Which is not yet official, but leads to believe Nokomo pulled the string, what with Nigeria funding the Project in heavy terms!"

"Jesus, T.S.! Now you're telling me this!"

"Easy goes it, boy! Given the turn of the morning, we had no chance! Frankly, I've loathed Gunnar since Viet Nam, but I have no choice in the matter, and it's up to you to decide, should it come to be. And could be you're stuck with the bastard...but there's no way he can jockey the controls, if you follow me rightly!"

I stared silently at the forward strut, thinking back to the Colonel's briefing: 'Gunnar's also prone to airsickness, judging from what was observed at Ramenskoye. Most likely subject to vertigo should he become unturned!' That I also didn't need with the complexities of 'juicing' the corridor above 70,000 feet, not knowing what he had in mind?

"Rest assured, we'll have your exact GPS position on our data link with the E-2-C monitoring the area from our 'no fly zone' over Iraq," T.S. continued, his voice seemingly echoing from other parts. "No way do we intend to abandon you, Keithy. We'll have a pair of Pave Hawk helicopters loitering nearby, but it's all important the U-2 penetrates the target area by 0400 GMT, give or take a half hour spread!"

I cupped my ear and listened carefully, aware of the allotted time spread from past briefing, but not of the peripheral scope of T.S.'s planning, until he laid it on the line.

"We'll have the area projected on or cyberscreen at all times," T.S. continued. "A three-dimensional, computerized picture of the terrain and building features as you would see it in broad daylight, inclusive of their SAM sites. Once entering the threshold, we'll simulate your position in motion, provided there's no interference with your data link!"

"Meaning I'll be flying in cyberspace and you'll have me painted on video screens while you're passing the popcorn balls around?"

"Multiple screens, Keithy, constantly updated to Intelink from our satellite photos and emissions from their command posts. The clincher comes at nighttime when we're unable to detect field forces in motion, specifically the robot tanks, since they offer no infrared emissions detectable by satellite. Hence the 'analyzer', boy! Once Intelink deciphers their signals, we can track their positions minutely."

"And all the while a covey of B-2s at terrain level will be matching my ground speed, a few lengths behind?"

"I didn't say that, Keith! In all fairness, however, we've evidence of activity in the mountains of northern Iran. Also, the presence of shrouded motor barges in the vicinity of Cheleken - 200 miles across the Caspian from Baku – of which the Russians also have interest, fearing a land and sea pincer movement will threaten their boundary with Azerbaijan non-stop!"

I had no chance to comment further, my attention given to the mournful wail of a siren sounding from the hills. In open field, there's but one way to respond to an aftershock's unsettling movements...sprawl on all fours and pray it soon be over! Fortunately, the F-15s' struts were stressed for hard landing while they pirouetted momentarily, stabilizing while we regained our feet.

Anticipating a 're-visit', the General gripped my hand, voicing,

"See you later, Keithy, boy! I'll tell your Dad you're lean and healthy, like he was when we teamed together in Nam."

I stood by while he climbed to the forward cockpit, his armament officer already aboard, adjusting his harness when T.S. gave thumbs up to the ground crew and turned the PW220s until they gave throat to a low rumbling roar. The pair of Strike Eagles taxiing quickly to the business end of the 'heavies' strip, traffic obviously at low ebb when they immediately took off in close formation, igniting their after burners whilst they climbed out and spiraled to the west, most likely intent to observe the source of my worries close up!

The pair of eagles out of sight when I caught a ride on the ground tug drawing the APU to the waiting Sea Hawk. The Commander already aboard, waiting turn to juice its twin GE turbo shafts and collect the APU aboard. The ebony faced gentleman offering me the co-pilot's seat, realizing I had need of an unobstructed view of the coast whilst I gathered my wits.

288

CHAPTER

studied the waters beneath us while we rounded the coast of Greece at 500 feet to avoid commercial traffic. Noting the remains of the Greco-Roman stone piers immersed by the melting glaciers of the late Ice Age. The rise, accounting for the separation of present day Britain from the continent when the inhabitants were 'hunter-gatherers'. Near about the time the Bronze Age Minoans arrived and developed a cultured civilization in the islands of the Aegean. Peaceful people, their commerce flourishing with trade to Egypt, Libya and Anatolia...until the volcano on the island of Thera (Santorini) blew its cap and the barbarians descended from the north. The later day Greeks absorbing their culture in terms of mythology; Plato describing the lost civilization as 'Atlantis' a thousand years later.

All of this ancient history, of course. But I pictured the seafaring Minoans fleeing the islands with their sleek lanteen sailing craft as we crossed over the Aegean. Their craft not all that different from the scores of fishing boats, fleeing for sanctuary in the highlands of Turkey, lying portside our windscreen. The Commander edging cautiously offshore, whilst I gave thought to my dream of Nina and Deuca fleeing the self-same thing!

Contacting ATC, the Commander climbed to traffic altitude (1200 feet) and called in to the tower at Antimahia when we had the island on the Sea Hawk's nose. My earphones noting the lack of response, my eyes given to the north shore where captain Stavos had laid in with the Helena, which had apparently moved on! Dead ahead, the commercial terminal appeared to be shorn of transit aircraft, aside from a Swissair 10-11 charter boarding passengers for wherever. The tower's make do attendant beamed a green light from the ground while we flared our approach, however. The Commander muttering to himself whilst he maneuvered the heavy 'copter and set down across the way!

MacDougal's jeep was first out to greet us while we spilled from the cockpit, observing the hybrid U-2 was poised and ready on the ramp, our lone APU conspicuously guarded by a pair of Fotis' militia. Electing to idle the twin turbo jets, the Commander cautioned his passengers to 'stay put' whilst he shouted to MacDougal, inquiring if he had sufficient AV fuel to top the Sea Hawk's tanks?

"No way!" the sergeant replied above the din, obviously relieved by my presence when I shed my Navy togs and he spied my blaze of hair. "Last heard, they've spare at Cyprus, Commander! Best hasten, however, hearin' they plan to evacuate the base by 1300!"

The Commander cupped his ear and nodded politely, reaching from his seat to grasp my hand when I returned his togs and retrieved my brief case.

"Like I said, God speed, Keithy! Could be sportin' for a lookout when you make it back, God bless!" he added, motioning me to stand back when he revved the twin GEs...the Sea Hawk quick to climb out, swirling dust and debris in its wake as it sped to the west.

"Wasn't wantin' to say, but fact is I'm holdin' close to a ton and a half of spare fuel (approximately 400 gallons)," MacDougal asided, offering a beer from his cooler while we piled aboard the jeep. "Figurin' you'll need the lot to top your tanks, includin' the extra fuel cells, if'n you plans to turn Santorini before you hikes it to Iran!"

So here we go again, I thought...realizing what he meant. My attention drawn to the U-2 in process of being towed to the blast fence, presumably to test the turbo-fan's replacement blades.

"Like it'll take all we have, an' there ain't more across the way, Keithy. Fact, Fotis closed up the terminal to save diesel, the Tower makin' do with solar panels to keep touch with ATC."

I popped my beer and sipped it slowly, my watch on to high noon when we drew abreast the hybrid U-2. Fotis' security guards containing themselves in the shadows of the maintenance shed to offset the oppressive humidity. The twosome nodding politely, recognizing my face when I stepped from the jeep to gander the 'Dragon Lady' close up! Better said, aside from her needle like black nose, she resembled a stretched out white swan in mid flight! Her glossy paint tediously scrubbed to erase the battle scars from the volcano we'd explored with Dr. Winner glassy eyed rear seat. The forepart of the ash-pitted canopies had also been replaced, I noted. The remaining issue, the F-118 turbo engine I'd faulted from flying close in! Noting the replacement blades were spinning freely when I tested them by hand.

"Like she's ready to roll, once we run her up!" MacDougal allowed. "But you has me worryin' for a compressor stall, what with Santorini spittin' bricks and pumice, if'n you plans to try it again!"

MacDougal's well-meaning deterrence I understood, giving thought to what lay ahead. Venturing the volcano would be a definite 'bruiser', although I intended to probe the spike from a distance, relaying the cone velocity and temperature to Sigurdesson and Schumann via our data link. Depending the reach of the U-2's multi-sensor photo-electric optic, which I could monitor from the cockpit; the canister collecting particle count and salinity analysis up for grabs, of course. But at least they'd have sufficient readings to alert Athens...if and when to sound their sirens. My projected turn over Turkmenistan not the last of my worries, knowing the depth of my heart!

All things considered, I had thirty hours to touch base with the group, deal with Dr. Nokomo (and most likely Horst Gunnar), catch a few hours sleep, breakfast a liquid diet, pre-flight the U-2, suit up, check my space suit for leaks whilst I pre-breathed pure oxygen, belt in to the cockpit, contact ATC for clearance above 50,000 feet, taxi to the business end of the strip and take off by 1800 so as to time an 'intrusion' over Turkmenistan at the stroke of midnight, 0400 GMT!

"So best top the tanks in the cool of the morning and we'll take it from there!" I said, knowing MacDougal was knowledgeable of the routine from his days with the 99th.

"Well now, Keithy, I'm pleased you made it back when you said you would, not knowing if you has a change of mind. But 4500 miles is a long stretch, man! Close to fourteen hours or more, once you dog leg Santorini and maintain minimum cruise. I'm also sayin' there's no way you can trust the fuel gauge...since it's calibrated in gallons an' you has to transfer the weight from tank to tank, short of draggin' a heavy wing. Like the bird ain't stressed for aerobatics comes a SAM homin' your infrared at 70,000 feet, like you knows what I mean!"

"Could be," I allowed, reflecting a 'flame out' I'd experienced when the system was drawing from an empty tank. "But if things work out, I'll have the sun on my back at the break of dawn and Kos is an easy glide!"

"Understand what you mean, Keithy. Figurin' you has personal reason to make it back, seein' Nina's van parked over yonder gatherin' dust! But I'm also sayin' you'll be strictly on your own if you decides to give it a go, Keithy man! What with the UN expectin' the U-2 to terminate at Incirlik (Turkey), they's chartered a C-130 to stand by and evacuate the Group to Incirlik once we sees you off! Meself included Keithy! Like we has option to stay on an' hit for the hills if an' when Santorini blows its lid, but meself, I has no 'option', what with T.S. wantin' to make certain the bird's 'clean slate' before NASA takes over and she comes off lease...like you knows what I mean!"

I nodded, knowing precisely what he meant! Once the analyzer served its purpose, it needed to be retrieved...'if or wherever' I made it back! The recording disc a moot question and I wondered of that? Its usefulness past history once the General's targets were resolved! Like the U-2 and myself, conceivably 'redundant'? Perish the thought...but never the less!

"Meanwhile, we has another problem to load on your back!" MacDougal asided, pointing to an unlikely space suit hanging to air on the change room's door. "Like, all a sudden 'Frankenstein' arrives out of the blue, sayin' he's your 'duly appointed observer', Keithy man! Nary a word from Nokomo, mind you...but appears he fetched him from Olympic near about the time you split for town with Willitts! Most likely passed them comin' or goin' methinks. Schumann believin' they circled close by before they hit for the city. Like they wasn't wantin' to show face till the weirdo's appointment became official. Which the UN confirmed later day."

I gave thought of the scenario, Gunnar's sense of timing! With Dr. Gomulaka out of the picture and Nigeria funding the long turn, Gunnar obviously played it laid back until the UN tallied their votes and he had the observer slot in hand. Nokomo a conceivable factor...unwitting most likely, not knowing of Gunnar's past. Near certain, however, the Nigerian's dislike of Dr. Schumann for usurping his 'voice of authority' when Keenan dispatched the savvy Dutchman to get the fundamentals on track!

"So when did Gunnar factually show face?" I questioned, assuming he'd spent the night with Amelia whilst I was rounding the coast aboard the Helena.

"Not till yesterday morning, Keithy! Appears Nokomo fetched him from madam's hotel and introduced him to the group 'round about the time we returns from seein' you off to Athens. Meself back side toolin' with the 118's blades when he comes lurkin' around...sniffin' the U-2 like a dog in heat, till I tells him to bug off! Fuckin' starch ass! Like I wasn't needin' introduction, knowing he was collaboratin' with the 'Cong' when T.S. was flyin' cover with your daddy over 'Nam. Like I has to keep close lip, what with T.S. fearin' I'd get after him with me wrench! Same time, not to worry for the analyzer, Keithy. There's no way he can trace the circuits, unless he attacks the bird with a chain saw while I'm back side for a pee!"

"So where is he now?"

"Ain't seen him yet this morning, man! Most likely sacked up, seein' he hit the bottle when he heard the madam bought the park! Fotis sayin' she was clobbered curbside at Hellinikon; like maybe you didn't know?"

Hard put to phrase a quick answer, realizing he knew Willitts and I were aboard the same flight, I opted to play it laid back…so as not to elaborate the gory finale. Allowing we were searching for a taxi when the Opel exploded and the shit hit the fan!

"Fotis have anything else to say?" I furthered, curious if he'd caught a description of Amalia's assassin or Bruno's means of escape?

"Negative, Keithy! ''Cept Fotis' sayin' it appears the madam was on the lam when she was cut down, like maybe he knows more than he's admittin'! But I ain't seen him around since last night, the lieutenant sayin' he's busy scoutin' quarters for Nokomo's bevy of secretaries. What with the tides flooding the city, they's up to their armpits an' sleepin' top their desks! Nokomo leavin' it to Sabina to carry on with what they's supposed to do! Like she had good sense to bed down in Schumann's office when their FAX machine went out to sea! Brings to mind, you'll need me spare bed, Keithy! Seein' Frankenstein latched on to Willitts' sack when the madam split for Nirvana, God bless her soul!"

I glanced quickly at my watch, noting it was close to high noon and I'd yet to touch base with Schumann and Ingrid, the latter foremost in mind. MacDougal allowing they'd most likely split for lunch at the village, aside from Dr. Sigurdesson who seldom left her desk, he added, when I questioned her health and well being.

"Judge for yourself, Keithy man! For me, she's top mark, but I'm noticin' she's coughin' blood last couple days…judgin' from her Kleenex coming back side with the trash!"

Sigurdesson smiled wearily from her console when I entered the lobby, her ever-present mug of coffee at hand. She appeared to be completely exhausted, her bangs matted with sweat; a braided girl seated beside her copying notes, the lobby otherwise deserted. The girl caught my eye and winked. I nodded politely, walking to the window to view the ramp, allowing Ingrid a moment of privacy to apply a touch of lipstick, as ladies are prone to do.

Like Hellinikon, a sense of urgency prevailed the scene outside. Their duties mostly done (aside from block-testing the engine), the mechanics were gathered in rapt conversation beneath the U-2's portside wing, pointing now and then to the curl of smoke rising from the horizon; their tools and spare parts neatly stacked on a pair of dollies, the spare engine hoisted to its carriage. The cavernous C-130 imminently due. My interest was drawn to the change shed where the space suits were stored, noticing the door was ajar and there obviously was a presence inside.

"I've decided to become a geophysicist," the young lady declared. "Dr. Sigurdesson has chosen to recommend me to her college in Stockholm, Mr. Slater. My, you seem upset! Have you become involved in an accident?"

"That's nice...I mean, not to my knowledge!" She tossed her braids aside and frowned, not knowing of my part in the sequence of events.

"The tremors have worsened," Sigurdesson interrupted, pointing to the seismograph readings on her screen. "Quickening between mean and low tide, if you take note of the timing, Keith, approaching 7.9 at the moment. We'll sense the shock momentarily," she added. "Now then, Keith, it's urgent we consider the facts."

I pulled a chair to her console, but she was wary of the youngster's ears, waiting until she'd disappeared to transmit her notes on Schumann's fax machine. Then, pointing to a slide she'd been studying under a microscope, Ingrid laid it on the line!

"Dr. Schumann collected a specimen of pumice from the roof several hours ago," she said. "The venting is definitely Plinian, Keith. We alerted Major Fotis and advised Athens of our findings, but we've a problem gaining their immediate response, indicating a bureaucratic delay!"

"Nokomo?" She rolled her eyes, flung her pencil to the floor.

"That fatuous idiot! Would you believe he as much as told us to mind our business and send our particle count to his office, not to confide directly with Athens?" Sigurdesson coughed, put a hand to her face, peering apologetically from her fingers.

"I do not understand this man," she whispered. "Athens is conferring with us on an emergency basis, and he insists on burdening us with trivialities and meaningless delays! He seems to be at odds with what we are about, insisting we contain ourselves to the particle count over the Sudan. Frankly, I believe he's bloody frightened! Bloated himself to thinking he can ward it off with his pencil point!"

"Not so stupid to call in a charter," I said. Sigurdesson nodded.

"I was apprised of the fact. Good riddance, perhaps, but it doesn't alter the equation," she added. "I wasn't wanting to alarm my assistant, but if the chimney velocity continues to accelerate, the end is near!"

"Prediction?"

"I believe a paroxysmal explosion will occur within the next 36 hours, Keith."

"You're calling a mean shot!"

"I am fatalistic by nature, Keith. Let us pray an early collapse will choke the venting. If not, I recommend you terminate your flight at Gianaclis, not here. The tides will be full ebb tomorrow evening and I fear for the worst. I have already told you my theories and you have been most patient, but I'd hope to obtain the velocity and infrared readings by tomorrow noon."

"Does Athens agree with your prediction?" I questioned, pondering what she'd said.

"They have requested that we monitor the situation closely, but not to discuss it openly on the cell-phone. They are fearful of the media, I assume. As for my predictions?" She put her fingers to her eyes, wearily shaking her head. "I am a woman, Keith, a secondary voice in a man's world. They don't seem to realize the tremendous force the moon exerts on the Earth's crust. Every major eruption has followed such an alignment; history tells us so!" She toyed with her wedding band, lowering her voice.

"There's another matter that concerns me, Keith. I was hesitant to tell you, but Mr. Gunnar has been acting strangely since yesterday afternoon." I exhaled and stared at the floor.

"Was he upset?"

"Terribly! He was incoherent during our six o'clock briefing. I do believe he was intoxicated."

"When did you see him last?" I questioned, curious if he'd stirred from his sack.

"He locked himself in his room last night and we haven't seen him since, Keith! Odd sort to say the least, cold and mechanical. I do hope you'll get along. The others have gone to Antimahia for moussaka and tea," she added, turning again to her screen. I patted her gently on the shoulder and excused myself to collect my brief case from the jeep. Intending to borrow a change of duds from MacDougal...hopefully a quickie shower before they returned. The jeep close at hand when, true to Ingrid's prediction, a quake rumbled the under-strata and rippled the ramp. Fotis' sirens echoing from the distance when my legs rubbered and I sprawled on all fours!

Like a wave breaking on a reef, the force was spent and I quickly regained my feet. The mechanics clinging to the U-2's entry ladder dusted themselves silently, accepting the tremor as a matter of form. Myself noting Gunnar's space suit had been withdrawn from the change room door, presumably while I was conversing with Ingrid. The door conspicuously ajar! It was then I spied my 'would be observer', first time ever!

Obviously shaken, Gunnar stumbled from the shed, not certain of his footing, expressing a face his mother would have shunned. The saber scar livid across his cheek whilst he mouthed an array of stainless steel teeth...Smoke thin, not so tall as I, he was dressed in khakis fresh from the shelf; his shirt buttoned tight to the throat, his brownish hair carefully combed and parted in the middle. His sideburns, shaved to the tops of his ears, augmented his spindly neck. He apparently recognized me, but had good sense not to extend his hand, realizing I was not receptive. Knowing I was confronting an absentee murderer, I made no attempt to disguise my disdain.

He introduced himself in fluent English, scrutinizing my face sideways with pale blue eyes, as if he'd catalogued my measure but was uncertain of what he had.

"Dr. Horst Gunnar here," he said, raising his voice above Fotis' sirens. "And, you would be Major Slater?"

"Mr. Slater," I corrected, attempting to establish eye contact, but he'd have none of that.

"Yes, of course. I only know you by name, but I was told you held a commission during the Persian war. Presently employed by the UN to fly our U-2, are you not?"

"Subject to my choice of time and conditions," I said, sensing what he was about.

"Indeed? Said conditions do not imply interference with the Project's undertaking!" he rasped. "In that, as your duly appointed communications adviser, I have been denied access to the U-2's electronic devices by your subordinate, Mr. MacDougal, which I deem offensive!"

"You're late on the scene," I replied. "If you're referring to the data-link, Dr. Schumann's taken care of that."

All of this spoken in a mechanical, staccato-like voice, as if he'd memorized his lines by rote. Obviously hung over, he turned away and made straight way to his room. But I witnessed his full measure when the rumbling after shock had the U-2 swaying its long, slender wings. Caught by the quickness, Gunnar clung desperately to the lieutenant's newly planted Solitaire palm, moaning "Mein Gott, not again!" When I regained my balance, I hitched him upright by the seat of his britches, knowing exactly what I had...a distressed and frightened old man!

* * * * * * * *

Obtaining the key to MacDougal's room, I decided first to touch base with Sabina, curious if Stavos had called in from the Helena and might yet be standing by? The possibility of my sacking a change of clothes, not least if he'd caught word of Nina, knowing he was apt to keep abreast of the latest news. Smartly dressed in a loose fitting Jamaican gown, Sabina was busy transmitting Ingrid's notes on Schumann's Fax machine when she recognized my face in the doorway and beckoned me to come in.

"Mighty pleased to see you!" she called over her shoulder, continuing to feed the Fax. "Youngster said you were conversing with Dr. Gunnar when the last one shook us up! Least we're on high ground," she added. "Fucking airhead should have known better than to locate our office down town...what with the tides nippin' our personals day and night!

"Now then," she continued, peering at her notes when I reiterated my questions. "Yes indeedy, Captain Stavos called in to say he was outbound to safe anchorage and would be unable to reach us by cell phone due to its range. You also had a call from Katrina saying Major Fotis moved Auntie Cleo to his tent city in the hills, allowing she can be reached by cellular, Keith! So best to call her when you have a chance. We've also had a visitor inquiring of yourself early this morning, Keith! Pretty English type with freckles and a tangle of curls, cut short like mine. Said she'd been staying north shore since Dr. Petrie returned to the UK...intends to stay on, I believe. Appears you have a 'sweetie' worrying for your blue eyes, Keithy love! Gutsy lady, what with the roads as they are. First time to see a proper lady ride a donkey...aside from myself when I rode 'Old Kicky' to school at Maroon Town in Jamaica years ago!"

"Gunnar made mention of a four o'clock meeting with Dr. Nokomo," I stammered, opting for change of subject, my heart skipping a beat whilst I pictured Lesleigh astride a donkey with an umbrella and her knapsack of belongings fetched astern. My thoughts given to her determined freckled face when she spied me clinging to the walkway at Akrotiri and entered my heart.

"So I understand from the note he slipped beneath my door," Sabina asided, obviously aware of my lingering thoughts. "In fact, I had to lock myself in when the loathsome creature had his full measure and tagged me to the office, assuming you know what I mean! So I'm saying I've yet to contact Dr. Nokomo to confirm, but will let you know as soon as I do! Most likely he's busy inquiring a charter to take his brood to Lagos, once he sees you off! The doctor has good intentions, Keith, but he's out of his drawer when it comes to dealing with volcanoes I've come to believe!"

It was after one when the group pulled in with the lieutenant's MG. Fresh from a shower and a change of clothes from MacDougal's rack, I joined them in the lobby, grateful for the plate of moussaka Winner brought along, assuming

I was aboard the Sea Hawk when we circled from the east. Their immediate concern the conditions I'd observed in Athens, post Schumann's and Ingrid's televised interview when they laid the facts on the line.

Realizing they were genuinely concerned, but remote from the mainstream, aside from the newscast and spasmodic response from Athens, I said it appeared a hasty evacuation was under way, describing the enormity of the flow of traffic jamming the highways leading to the hills. Allowing the shops were tightly shuttered, the streets virtually deserted Hellinikon in process of closing, aside from outgoing flights.

"I also noticed there were others going about their business as usual," I added. "Mostly oldsters, nonbelievers and the confused! Also malingerers eyeing the shops, although it appears the militia is hanging in to keep the ball rolling. But God help the lot if and when you drop the other shoe!"

"And they panic for the heights of the Acropolis, lest they suffer the noxious fumes or be swept to sea!" Ingrid commented from her console. I sat down beside her, intending to share my moussaka, but she was on the horn with Athens, her eye on the seismograph. Fotis' sirens blaring from the distance when she raised two fingers, indicating another jolt was due. We raced outside, not certain of the ceiling, but Sigurdesson remained steadfast in her chair, lofting an umbrella to shield her console from falling plaster. The young lady electing to remain at her desk, casting a weary eye at the ceiling seemingly nonplussed.

More likely a continuation of the aftershock, the tremor was over in a matter of seconds, although the force was sufficient to bring us to our knees. Schumann suffering a snapped suspender which he remedied matter of factly, bandoliering the strap across his chest, his trousers oddly hitched whilst he searched his pockets for a handy safety pin.

"It would appear we've been given notice to get on with measures at hand," he commented wryly, struggling to make do with a paper clip from his sheaf of notes...his eyes drawn to the notations he'd apparently scribbled earlier in the day. His attention given to myself while the group ventured the lobby, observing the ceiling was yet intact.

"Yes indeedy, Keith! Like the tremor and our 'unsolicited' guest, the heavens have also seen fit to reward us with a fall of pumice during the night, which we immediately put to test! Although we've yet to confide in Ingrid, allowing her a moment of peace while we cross-checked our findings over lunch.

"Salinity, hey?" The Dutchman nodded.

"Minute but positive traces, Keith! Indicating the magma chamber is accepting the sea, however lightly. But, come the flood tides a Plinian venting will doubtless occur!"

"And blow the island all to hell!"

"Fear so, Keith! But given the temp and cone velocity, we have a chance to calibrate the timing and advance word to Athens, before the flood tide accelerates the venting. Opting you'll give us a six or eight hour lead once you're airborne and relay your scan on our data-link."

"Sooner the better, hey?"

"Yes of course, Keith! Frankly, we'd hoped you would be airborne at the stroke of dawn, until we realized it takes an inordinate amount of time to refit the U-2, judging from its condition when you probed the volcano and put Dr. Winner to task! In short, we realize tomorrow's flight is not a piece of cake whatever the urgency, Keith! But here again, your scheduled 1800 take off was set arbitrarily before we gave credence to Sigurdesson's prediction. Which is a mite too close to the hour of dread, unless you can prevail upon yourself to do better, given a full night's sleep! Allowing MacDougal time to test the turbo-fan, which he's apparently near about to do!"

I stared silently at the ominous haze veiling the blood red sun, my conscience on line when I spied Ingrid hunched wearily at her computer; realizing the Dutchman was loathe to say it would be 'inordinately selfish and counter productive' to deprive the valiant lady (and Athens) of critical lead time, for sake of what? But, here again, contrary to Schumann's thoughts...my projected 1800 take off was calculated to afford penetration of Turkmenistan at the stroke of midnight...which was not subject to arbitration! Moreover, my calibrated time en route was not likened to a yardstick I could manipulate at my pleasure!

My alternative, of which the Dutchman was quick to agree having pressed me to the brink, was to take on the volcano myself come early morning...provided the U-2 was fit and ready and he monitored the data-link minutely! Allowing I'd need precious time to turn about and 'suit up' for the long turn, which would have me flat on my ass, but nevertheless! Same token, I realized Schumann was aware of the 'multi-purpose' mission, per Keenan's briefing. But to what extent, since he was seemingly unaware I had to play my cards in the dead of night? In short, I was curious if he was knowledgeable of T.S.'s 'time slot' and the wizard's black box? Which he answered in part when I raised the possibility of Gunnar's interference, allowing I'd met him briefly and intended to exercise my prerogatives if he breathed fire from his nose!

"I understand what you mean, Keith! But you must also understand there may be mitigating factors beyond our control, lest you choose to abandon the leg to Iran – which is not opportune considering the urgency of the situation in the Caspian!" I nodded to this, realizing Keenan had him short tether and the burden was on to myself!

"Meaning Gunnar has Nokomo in pocket and I'm stuck with the bastard, like it or not!"

"Would appear so, Keith! Which is inversely fortunate, since the Nigerian insists we track the ash fall according to plan, not believing or accepting Ingrid's prognosis, nor mine! Mind you, Nokomo is well intended, but he's caught up with his ego, thinking the volcano will lessen and come to terms! Which is typical of bureaucratic bliss, despite the flood tides of recent days! In other words, it would be judicious to take Gunnar in stride and be long gone before Nokomo wakens to reality and deems it's useless to track a foregone conclusion! So let's hearken to our consciences, knowing there be two sides of the coin. Be it the Aegean or the Caspian, the U-2 is accountable to millions of lives, although it's not observable to the naked eye! So, that's what you're put to, Keith...like it or not!"

Heroics aside, Schumann's comments were aptly put, considering the apparent need to pay lip service to Dr. Nokomo – which I'd more or less foreseen and thought we could manage! Horst Gunnar something else again, should he be party to a bargain and I had no way out! Provided he 'had a valid medical certificate and proof of flight time in a pressure suit above 50,000 feet'!

"Moot question," Schumann allowed. "So best to bring it up when we meet together with Dr. Nokomo at four o'clock and observe what he has to say! Allowing it's your prerogative to question his status before he joins you rear seat! But first, allow me to advise Ingrid of your change of mind...your change of plans! Knowing she'll be overjoyed which is paramount to all else!" The Dutchman's labored but faultless English precisely phrased as usual. His obvious concern for Sigurdesson sufficing his true colors. His makeshift suspenders and drooping trousers another matter whilst he hastened to confide with the group in the lobby. But thanks to his input, I'd gained focus on the urgent conditions at hand, and adjusted my flight plans in better context without jeopardizing T.S.'s objectives (albeit despite Gunnar's presence) nor my long range plans which had to do with the strings of my heart.

And so went my endless day, with yet another to face, plus a sleepless night at the wheel once I'd obligated my probe of the bloody volcano and returned to suit up for the long turn. But given a full night's sleep, I thought I could hack it, hopefully catching a catnap at altitude with the U-2 on autopilot, realizing I'd need to be mentally alert when I bridged the border east of Tehran. My physical endurance on the line, should I encounter hostile action over the

Caspian...nor could I afford to relax until I drew bead on Antimahia at the break of dawn – not Incirlik – for sake of what I would have yet to do!

My first priority, to advise MacDougal of my abrupt change of plans and visually check the U-2's ranks to ascertain I had sufficient fuel for a two hour flight, plus two in the event of an emergency (say a tremor voided the strip and I had to wait the lieutenant's grader to smooth it out). All of which pleased MacDougal no end, allowing he'd have time to check the 'dragon lady's' blades before he topped the tanks for the leg to Iran.

"Fact is, we're about to test the blades full thrust, Keithy man! So batten your ears when I light the candle and see what we have!"

Assuming he'd give the GE-118 a twenty minute burn, I advantaged the opportunity to examine Gunnar's pressure suit in the shed...knowing the Russians selected their cosmonauts to fit three set sizes; small, medium and large! Gunnar's the 'medium', which I probed at length, searching the pockets he could reach with his gloves, of which there were four...two abreast and one alongside each leg. All sized for tools, which were not included, although I could ascertain a suspicious 'bulge' from a distance, if Gunnar had mind for such!

Next, I examined his parachute which was similar to mine, inclusive of the survival pack, which I determined he couldn't reach unless he ejected; which is not recommended at high altitude with pressure suit inflated (due to risk of rip or tear from the cockpit's ungainly protrusions, thus decompressing the suit to where blood tends to boil without ambient pressure above 65,000 feet). Although he had option to 'fall free', should the U-2 become inverted, which I doubted he'd risk, whatever the occasion! Come next, his flight helmet, which I intended to examine minutely for 'out of order' electronic devices he might activate with his glove! The helmet apparently elsewhere when I scanned the shelf next to mine...presumably contained to Gunnar's quarters, for what reasons?

Wondering about this, my inspection tour was abbreviated with just cause, however, when MacDougal opportuned the moment to spool and ignite the GE-turbo fan at the blast fence. The thunderous thrust scattering stray dogs and debris to the ends of the ramp! The shrieking decibels sufficing to bring Gunnar stumbling from his room, staring blindly at the sun, not altogether awake! And, thinking it wise to avoid a confrontation, I made haste to Schumann's office for twofold reasons...the possibility of contacting the Helena before we met together with Nokomo at four o'clock.

Fortunately Sabina was yet at hand when I reiterated the problem of reaching Captain Stavos aboard the Helena, for reasons left unsaid! The savvy Jamaican on to it immediately, however, suggesting we 'call Katrina and request she give Fotis' single side band a go'! Which Katrina quickly obliged when we reached her at Fotis' office and I handed off the Helena's call numbers; allowing the yacht was beyond the range of cellular and conventional means, would she give it a try? All of this whilst I paced the office, gandering the chart I'd left with Schumann for safekeeping, which we needed to discuss post or during our four o'clock meeting, imminently due!

Fortunately, within minutes, although it seemed hours, we had Stavos' gruff voice audible on our makeshift connection. The old man obviously delighted to hear my own when I questioned his whereabouts...and expressed my concern for Nina in words he 'd understand. Realizing he'd have rabbit ears for the Athens' newscast all the while!

"Come to safe anchorage, but not so far away, Keeth! Same time have plenty con-versation with Cleo, 'til her phone dis-connect! Cleo believe pretty bird come touch with am-nesia and find safe haven in Crete with strange man she see at Arhannes long ago, when Helena come to anchor close by! Same night, she have strange mix-up dream...and Nicholas find her walk in sleep with bad storm, Cleo theenk! Place not far from Helena reach, once deluge come an' sub-side, Keeth! Old man keep watch for long bird with white feather, come plenty quick when see light flash from Kefalos!

"Come time now, pray for safe return," he added. "Not forget holy medal old man receive from Nicholas when we bring ship to safe harbor, before Nina came to be!" And with that, Stavos signed off, having said all that need be said! Myself fingering the St. Christopher's medal I'd nearly lost in my pocket of loose change. Katrina's apt ears not a problem, since both she and Major Fotis regarded Nina and myself as members of the family!

* * * * * *

Our four o'clock meeting came to be when Dr. Nokomo arrived in his festooned Hummer, fit and proper in his starched khakis, his swagger stick at hand, like the second coming of General Patton! Visibly nervous, however, his jaw flinching involuntarily when the volcano belched a hideous thunder clap from its maw, indicating a problem with its indigestion! But then I realized the man was scared shitless and trying to make the best of it, so not to be scorned!

All together there were nine of us seated at the table adjoining Ingrid's console, inclusive of MacDougal, who'd successfully tested the turbo fan and advised me aside; also Horst Gunnar, conspicuous by his presence and demand-ing ways. Schumann verbalizing in German to set him right, whilst he complained of the re-edited language of our data-link to English. Not to be put down, however, he immediately produced a chart allowing the vectors the U-2 was to track during the continuing leg to Iran, allowing the update was approved by the UN! At which point Schumann caught my eye and put a finger to his lips, indicating he knew otherwise, but cautioning me to hold tight!

"Major Slater has also to bide my instructions when we parallel the northern border of Iran should we veer off course!" Gunnar went on to say. "Otherwise, I am duty bound to report a 'mis-endeavor' to the UN and parties concerned!"

I stared at the man but held my water! He'd inadvertently clued me to the back side of his mind...either by slip of lip or believing I was incredibly stupid! Schumann also made silent note, his temper obviously on the rise!

"First matters first Colonel Gunnar, albeit 'Herr Gunnar' according to the FAX that came late to my attention wherein I was apprised of your appointment to monitor our data-link with the U-2, in lieu of the late Dr. Gomulaka's absence. But it is up to the pilot in command to perceive and adjust to conditions that may vary in flight! Not yourself, since you are neither a meteorologist nor a volcanologist, as stipulated in the terms of Captain Slater's contract with the UN!" Schumann added. At which point Nokomo rose to his feet.

"Speaking as the Project's administrator, I find that irrelevant, Dr. Schumann! Dr. Gunnar was chosen primarily to monitor the relay of the U-2's electronic findings to Doctors Sigurdesson, Winner, Edwards and yourself. Also to provide council to Captain Slater should he wander off course and provoke an international incident, as I understand it!" Nokomo added, Schumann quick to cast eye to Fraser, wanting to ascertain he was recording the conversations as the project's historian, before he proceeded further before he proceeded further.

"Fair enough, Dr. Nokomo! Provided Captain Slater agrees to set provisions and Dr. Gunnar understands he's not to interfere with the U-2's flight path in any way! Inclusive of demanding we adhere to the charts he saw fit to bring along...which may or may not compare with the flight plans approved by the UN!" Schumann added.

"I've also been informed it's necessary for Herr Gunnar to provide proof of flight wearing a pressure suit above 50,000 feet, as a precautionary measure, so's not to dislodge the dual controls with the boots, Dr. Nokomo! Which requires ground tests whilst the suit is fully inflated, minding one's blood tends to boil without protection to ambient pressure above 60,000 feet! It's also required he present a valid medical certificate attesting to his physical condition, before given entry to a sustained flight in the U-2," Schumann added, peering at the notes I'd scribbled in my behalf.

If there was ever a smirk on the ready, Gunnar had one in pocket when he [produced an official appearing manila envelope from his attaché case and handed it to the taciturn Dutchman. Schumann scanned it briefly and turned it over to Dr. Sigurdesson, knowing she was fluent with the Russian language from when they'd researched the volcanic regions of Sakhalin Oblast, years back. The weary Swede reaching for her glasses, translating into English.

"The log book, signed by the Adjutant at Ramenskoye attests: Ex-Comrade Horst Gunnar has been given a series of ground tests in an inflated Cosmonaut pressure suit for indications of vertigo, prior to accomplishing 8.5 hours of dual control (rear cockpit) with an assigned M-17-B reconnaissance aircraft, above 16,000 meters. Three flights, no landings! As for his medical, which is initialed by the flight surgeon at Ramenskoye, it appears Dr. Gunnar has a detectable heart murmur, the condition waived, lest he exerts himself unnecessarily or suffers physical fatigue!" Ingrid commented wearily, seemingly detached from the proceedings whilst she turned again to her computer.

So there we had it! Gunnar livid of face, saying she'd misinterpreted the surgeon's remarks! Myself curious of the wording 'indications of vertigo'? Schumann allowing it was my prerogative to accept or reject a physical liability, considering the twelve-hour flight! Nokomo non-committal but, giving to his priorities, I deemed it wise to carry on for sake of the long turn. Knowing what I'd have rear seat cockpit would be subject to 'procedures' I'd learned from my dad, should Gunnar come unwound!

I also allowed Gunnar was welcome to fly my rear seat come morning when I probed the volcano close up! An offer he promptly rejected, as I thought he might. My purpose, to show his stripes to Dr. Nokomo, realizing he was having second thoughts of the bastard's ongoing intent! And fortunately, Fraser had the 'conditions' on record...should it come to a flap with the UN, when it was all said and done!

That done, but not out of mind, we dispersed for other parts, waiting a catered dinner from the village promised at eight o'clock. Nokomo departing with his Hummer, Sabina trailing with a lorry borrowed from the militia, presumably to collect his bevy of secretaries to the abandoned terminal, where they'd bed down until the chartered C-130 arrived to take them to Incirlik. Edwards and Fraser to be included, their objective to set up a temporary base until the remainder of our staff and equipment arrived aboard an Air Force C-130-J, the Hercules programmed to hold on until the U-2 was airborne over Cyprus, provided the volcano held the same!

Of this, Schumann and Nokomo resolved as a matter of common sense, although the Nigerian was adamant about his misconception of the volcano's activity, however…until Schumann put it to him gently, referring to Ingrid's analysis matter of factly. Nokomo most likely worried his judgment might be faulty and he lose face with the UN! The Nigerian agreeing he was duty bound to hold his charter in abeyance until his charges were safely off to Incirlik. No mention of his intentions thereafter, however, but at least he handled it in good faith as a gentleman! And I had better understanding of the man, despite his stubborn bureaucratic ways!

Horst Gunnar, something else again! But I'd gained the tilt of his number, realizing what I had to contend while he stalked to his quarters with his attaché case underarm. Presumably for a nip of Schnapps while he groused his thoughts of the day that lay ahead. Conceivably thinking of Amelia, which I couldn't fault! The black side of his mind and his intentions, a self-serving ego trip, in a noxious sort of way!

* * * * * *

Next, and hopefully last, Schumann and I had immediate need to discuss the vectors I needed to track, once the U-2 lay east of Tehran!   Assuming Keenan had briefed him to the purpose of the 'midnight intrusion' of southwest Turkmenistan, before turning west to regain the allowable border of Iran! The niggling question, was he aware of the intention to ascertain and relay the transmissions of the robot tanks and command posts via the wizard's black box to an AWAC-E8 loitering nearby? Thus pinpointing the viable targets for T.S.'s combo of stealth B-2s and proximity fused bombs? The latter part conjecture, of course! But like Willitts, I ventured a wild ass guess, knowing T.S.! My basic problem, to reduce the equation to Schumann's understanding, once we compared Gunnar's charts with mine!

"Note, the charts are identical, aside from a series of Nav Aids in south-west Turkmenistan shown on Gunnar's…which we know for certain don't exist!" I said, comparing the charts side by side. "The 'approval', authorized by the UN, on the margin, is also identical, the signatures the same, no change of date. Indicating there are two 'official versions' for the taking! One of which is obviously forged and subject to slip of hand, presuming the pilot is out to lunch!"

"Appears Gunnar's motive is interlocked with the U-2's intrusion into Turkmenistan, Keith! Which I'm led to believe is intended for electronic surveillance of the troubled areas, covertly at high altitude…of which he's apparently unaware? Frankly, I find Gunnar's dossier repulsive, a discredit to the UN! But I fail to understand the paralleling 'intensity' to arrive at the same juncture in the middle of the night! Unless Gunnar intends to capitalize a 'misadventure', of which I know naught?"

I nodded silently to this, realizing Keenan hadn't clued him to the bottom line, despite Schumann's hard-nosed guess! Most likely respecting the Dutchman's neutrality in regards to the UN.

"First, I have reason to believe the so called Nav Aids are either mobile or pre-fixed to divert and challenge the U-2 to set down, most likely an air strip bordering the Caspian, abandoned by the Soviets some time back!" I added, when Sabina was out the door and gone with the military lorry. "Which is absurd, since I'll know the U-2's exact GPS position all the while! Nor do I believe they have means to threaten the U-2 with a surface to air missile capable of 70,000 feet...which would be counter productive! Leading me to believe Gunnar intends to 'incapacitate' me in some way and land the bloody U-2 on his own!"

"Lordy, Keith! How could he possibly do that? And for what purpose, since you'll be in communication with our data-link at Antimahia...or Incirlik, whatever the situation?" (Also with the E-8 Joint Stars, without my saying.)

"Don't think I haven't given it thought, Doctor! Could be he's a genius with a screw driver and scotch tape, not forgetting we'll be on auto pilot...which he can't abort from rear cockpit! Although it cancels automatically when the U-2 buffets a stall...which is food for thought!"

"So, let's say you're asleep at the wheel and he wrests control, attempts a landing! Again, for what purpose, Keith?"

"Could be to give the insurgents an excuse for a 'call to arms', provoke an international incident and embarrass the UN, should the U-2 come to hand! The oil regions in Azerbaijan and Baku the name of the game...once they have foothold and carry on! Gunnar a convenient tool to their ends, as I see it, Doctor! De facto KGB with an axe to grind, a SAM specialist with the Viet Cong, a top dog operative for the KGB in Silicon Valley...until they spun out and he resurfaced as a displaced East German with the UN!

"The brains, most likely a gaggle of ex-Soviet Generals...opportuning a cache of high tech tanks developed secretly in east Turkmenistan during the phase out of the Cold War!" I went on to say. "In other words, it appears they're aggressively bent and ready to roll...the timing apparently waiting the U-2's leg over Iran! Which was programmed before Dr. Gomulaka disappeared, give note!

"So let me elaborate to give picture of Gunnar's involvement, Doctor! In that, it so happened Gomulaka's disappearance 'coincided' with Gunnar's absence, while he was doing his thing at Ramenskoye – for what reason? The turn of the volcano unexpected at the time, of course! Although it serves unholy means to divert attention of what they're about! So, let's take it from there, Doctor...once I'm over the hill there's no time for second thoughts!"

The Dutchman raised eye at the note; he'd obviously been clued to Gunnar's dossier, but not of the ongoing specifics, since Stash's photos came late to Keenan's briefings. My candid remarks seemingly lending credence, however, when he turned to re-examine the subject charts! Adjusting his spectacles, whilst he studied the area, unwittingly smudged by my thumb!

"Well now, Keith! Appears Gunnar's foot fits the shoe, as I see it now! The 'shoe' apparently the abandoned air strip short of Cheleken you bring to my attention! Understandably, the point of Keenan's interest when he obliged to lend hand to your double-fold mission, Keith! But from thereon, I'm somewhat at a loss, although he confided Gunnar's dossier when we met briefly in Amsterdam. Following his request to firm up the project as a volcanologist, in lieu of Ingrid's illness and Dr. Nokomo's...lack of scientific proficiency!"

"Okay. So let's tally what we know for certain and play it open jaw, Doctor! What with our satellite scan picturing a fleet of motorized barges lying close in to Cheleken, it goes without saying there's an objective in the works! The 'objective' presumably to load and transport a bevy of robot tanks across the Caspian after dark, while the convoy can't be seen or detected by satellite, until the break of dawn!

"The tanks and their mode of communication the leading question, as I understand it, Doctor. Since they're housed in radar reflecting sheds in daytime, and emit no infrared signature when they maneuver during the night. But come morning, their tracks in the desert are open view by satellite! Intelligence's means of determining their size, optimum range, and where they're serviced during the day. Their means of communication with the Command Posts up for grabs, however...the technology unknown! Do you follow me thus far?" I added, curious if Schumann's briefing tallied with mine.

"Yes and no, Keith...although what you say makes sense! Frankly, Keenan gave hint of the so called 'robot tanks', which I laid to science fiction since they defy imagination! I'm also curious as to how they can be loaded and transported across the Caspian, presumably at night, without being detected, since the motorized barges would pulse infrared, like so many fireflies, when they put to sea!"

"This they'd realize, of course! So, let's equate with their time schedule and take it from there, Doctor! First, the barges needn't fire up their engines until the tanks are aboard and they're ready to put to sea, which would take at least a couple of hours since the barges are widely dispersed...the tanks most likely consigned one to a barge, judging from their size! All of this after dark, once they know for certain the U-2 is airborne, assuming they have means to intercept our data-link! Which is no big trick once they know the frequency...here again, possibly Gunnar's hand? So let's say the lot's all together in the lee of Cheleken waiting signal to carry on! Presumably waiting Gunnar to play his role when the U-2 comes to the scene at 80,000 feet!

"That's the way I see it, Doctor...allowing the U-2 is equipped with optical and infrared imagery which produces and relays a computerized picture of the proceedings to interested parties, at touch of glove! Which they may or may not know, or care less, since the tanks are obscure in read-out due to their stealth mode of communication!"

"I understand what you say, Keith, and God help your perseverance! Frankly, I wasn't aware of the significance of your projected 'time slot' when I persuaded you to skim Santorini first thing in the morning. Which you saw fit to remedy to Ingrid's advantage...unselfishly, I must say!"

"Mutual advantage, Doctor! Nor would I call it 'unselfish', since there are thousands of lives in the offing, be it in the Aegean or the shores of Azerbaijan! But, unlike Santorini, we've a chance to nip the problem in the bud!"

"Carry on, Keith...I'm 'open jaw'!"

"Okay. So let's say the convoy makes it across the Caspian without interference. Now, what do we have but a regional war that could spread to the Black Sea! Of which not only the Azerbaijani, but the Iranians, Georgia and the Russians have a vested concern! So what's affordable, deploying thousands of troops as we did in the Persian Gulf, or applying a 'pre-emptive strike' which was effective in Kosovo, due to advanced technology!"

"I gander your point, Keith! Allowing the Iranians have given lip service to the U-2's passage during the night, I dare say I'm not opposed to pre-emptive surgery, given just cause! But, unlike the Balkans, the desert regions are remote and lack logistical support! So how can a flimsy U-2 play the hand of God? Aside from transmitting an 'image of activity' at a specific time and place! But little else, judging from what you say. Lest there be plans afoot to carpet bomb the area, to which I'm violently opposed considering the needless loss of life, cruelty to goats, camels and the like!"

"Carpet bombing's old hat, Doctor Schumann! The present swing, to detect and destroy singular targets, exclusive of goats and camels, since proximity fused bombs are effective within a half meter, once the target is identified and the weapon takes it out! Otherwise, I believe you're on track, Doctor! So, let me speculate further and I'll explain the 'options' provided by Lockheed when they assembled the hybrid U-2!

"First off, the timing is the critical issue, of course! Once the convoy puts to sea, it's a mite late to target the fleet...and, prior to that, the singular targets are obscure! So let's back track to my options when we breach Turkmenistan and come on the scene...considering the occupant peering from rear seat!

"First option, to cancel our data link, which is not manageable or reversible from rear cockpit! So now we're Scot free of our known tethers, so to speak! The U-2, all but invisible in the light of the full moon, at 70,000 feet! Gunnar presumably at odds with his charts when the 'read out' fades from his console! His means of communication via the data link also cancelled, although we can converse by inter-phone, to put it mildly!

"Mean time, the U-2 stays on course, since it's coupled to the auto pilot which is slaved to our GPS Nav system, which in turn tracks our computerized flight plan, correcting for drift, forward ground speed and altitude at all times! Needless to say, the autopilot is also not available rear console, although it automatically shuts down should the U-2 approach an abnormal flight maneuver! Which is possible, should the throttle and flight controls be deliberately forced by either the pilot or rear cockpit observer!

"So bear it in mind when we enter the 'no fly zone' and I activate the U-2's optical and infrared imaging systems...hopefully without interference, Doctor! The picture inclusive, as you say, aside from fixing a time and place by independent means!

"Now then, Doctor! Following the curve, comes next a breach of secrecy I'll share in confidence...considering the odds and Gunnar's intentions! Unbeknownst to all, aside from certain parties, Sergeant MacDougal and myself, an ultra-sensitive listening device was installed in the U-2's wingtip while she was on line at Lockheed's Skunk works! Designed to detect, locate and decode transmissions from the tanks and their command posts in the field. It instantly translates and relays the vectors to an airborne jam resistant computer bank! Be it a RC-135 'Rivet Joint' or an E-8 'Joint Stars', loitering close by, they'll have the 'singular targets' instantly placed!

"All of this available at touch of glove to a pressure point beneath my seat, Doctor! A blinking light responding from my console, indicating the 'analyzer's' in the green! Self-recording and put to repeat for duration of the spool!

"So now you have it from the horse's mouth, Doctor! The moot question, the system is yet untried...for my part, I intend to be out of there, should a pair of stealth B-2s appear out of nowhere and release their proximity fused bombs! Conjecture, of course! All else failing, could be I'll end up on display with the U-2 on the streets of somewhere! Tarred and feathered, bearing a sign 'Gratis of the UN'!"

"Perish the thought, Keith, unless Gunnar sups on dried apples and water, explodes mid air!"

"And messes up my rear cockpit? No way, Doctor! At least I'll have you on my Z-band frequency while they unravel the wreckage and you explain matters to the UN! Not to mention the 'analyzer', however...should I survive and they decide to hang us together, while they lower the flags and sound taps on BBC!"

And so went my endless day...beginning with Petrie's Cortina gasping its last; T.S.'s florid face; the Commander's knowing stance; MacDougal at odds with the GE-118's blades; the incredible Swede fixed to her console, her eyes shot with pain; the creature with stainless steel teeth I had yet to contend! My gain, the intellectually bent Dutchman, who fortunately was at hand when I was down with my divers and seeking common sense!

The sun long gone behind the ominous cloud on the horizon when the Moussaka for the group arrived from Antimahia, with appropriate jugs of Santorini's excellent wine! Gunnar late to the scene, obviously recovering from a strung out hangover, although he devoured the Moussaka like a hungry dog from the streets...but not the wine!

As for myself, I supped on the U-2's high altitude provisions and hydrated with Gatorade, knowing my physical limitations at 70,000 feet. Totally exhausted, I bedded down on MacDougal's spare mattress, dreaming of Nina, her impish smile while we plunged the surf at Lyford Cay. Her eyes sparked with fury later that night, when she levered the family candelabra and I caught her arm before she clobbered Tony Metexas! Then, a fleeting glimpse of her sandals lodged beneath the wall at Kavouri...Nina's purse and Uncle's revolver nearby, the sound of her voice when she joined me in the depths, saying, "I love you, Keith, never give in!" My heart low ebb, however, when I spied a strange craft with red sail waxing down stream with Nina's scarf trailing in its lee! Then, inexplicably, I found Lesleigh Butterfield standing beside me, her freckled face expressing concern while I stared at the image of Nina, recently retraced on the walls of Akrotiri, my curiosity drawn to the artist's tools of trade and a freshly peeled orange husk nearby?

"Deuca comes from Praisos," she said. *"A tiny village deep in the moun-*

tains of eastern Crete. A place where the historian Staphylos told of people called the 'Eto-Cretans', whereto found in his day!"

The C-130 landed at midnight, its thunderous reverse thrust augmenting my spurious dreams! But then, by then...I was honed to the clatter of the Stearman's perky engine whilst I skinned the hills of western Tennessee!

* * * * * *

CHAPTER 25

"Rise and pee, Keithy! The world's on fire!"

"Lemme go!"

"Not on your life, it's 0600 and you need to be on target before the thermals set in!" I located the floor with my feet and sat on the edge of the bed to clear my mind...opting for the thermos of coffee MacDougal had the foresight to fetch from the pantry.

"So how's the weather, man?"

"Six knots from the north-west an' snowin' pumice like Christmas Day! Fact we covered the bird with a tarp overnight, but I ran your pre-flight at 0500, Keithy! Figurin' you'd need your full turn of sleep, what with twelve hours to roll once you skin the fucking volcano!"

I stumbled to the bathroom to ease my obligations, examined my growth of beard in the mirror, tested the shower with my toe...found it lacking hot water! Double fold reason to shave later day before I suited up for the long stretch, I thought. The icy shower sufficing to bring me fully awake whilst I searched blindly for the soap.

"Any sight of Gunnar since last night...damn it to hell, where's the soap?"

"Ain't seen him yet this morning, Keithy! Fact Winner and Schumann been taking turns watching our Com system, fearin' he'd be prowlin' around...find the soap where you used it last, eh?" I bridged my toes and located the soap on the shower floor, inquiring of Ingrid. Had the young lady arrived to look in on her yet?

"Stays with her all night, last couple of days. Helps her to the johnnie to fresh up...like Ingrid's walking death till she's had her shots! Hangin' in though, like that volcano's given her spirit to carry on!" I toweled down, allowing I'd look in on her before I took off. My uniform of the morning, the NASA flying togs I'd brought along from Mount View, not requiring the pressure suit, although I'd be borderline at 50,000 feet.

Unfortunately, neither Sigurdesson nor the young girl was seated by the console while I breakfasted on a protein tube and a glass of juice for low residual reasons...looking ahead! The girl presumably leading Ingrid to her quarters for a quick nap. Winner and Schumann also somewhere apart; Edwards saluting briefly from the console when MacDougal jigged my arm, pointing to the ramp!

"Let it wait until you get back and have a couple of hours on the side, Keithy...seeing as Dr. Winner's filed your flight plan with Athens Center last night and they requested your transponder fix at 0800, so they can advise commercial traffic when you're airborne vicinity of Santorini!"

I'd forgotten I'd programmed a 0730 take off, which was close at hand, although the U-2 appeared fit and ready; what with MacDougal's ground crew air hosing the last of the pumice from the turbo jet's intake, the forward canopy open for access and my entry ladder in place. Winner and Schumann were also at hand, likewise unshaven, indicating they'd been up most the night! The four of us an unlikely sight with the pristine U-2 highlighting the early morning sun! MacDougal had pre-flighted the bird but, by force of habit, I conducted a 'walk round' to make certain the rudder lock had been removed, the status of the tires, the possibility of a misplaced wrench?

The threesome accompanying me while we circled to the ladder, Winner briefing me to the morning satellite scan, indicating the ash drift was continuing to the south-east, my approach from windward clear as a bell! Schumann commenting privately of another matter when he drew me aside!

"Had chance to put your chart to task last night, and discovered an area of interest we need to discuss when you return, Keithy lad! Specifically, a recently constructed agricultural airstrip alongside a sparse roadway betwixt Okaren and Cheleken! Which I noted was superficially erased, or not appearing on Gunnar's chart?"

"Otherwise it'll wait, so first thing, Doctor! Watch his eyes and his hands should he show face while you're on to our data and vocal links; he's apt to have interest in our Z-Band module whilst I communicate with parties apart! In fact, it would behoove you to pocket the 'chip' until we're off for the long turn, since we'll be communicating open channel until then!" Schumann nodded silently, myself assured of his confidence when I climbed the ladder and buckled in.

With a makeshift green light from the tower, I spooled the GE and taxied to the runway, applying heavy rudder, the single main landing gear not steerable,

313

the dual tail wheels apt to digress. Fortunately, the C-130 was out of reach of our 116 feet wingspan while I lined up the runway, facing a miserly six-knot head wind. I noted the C-130 was already boarding Nokomo's gaggle of secretaries and their gear, our forward group presumably last aboard, exclusive of our mainstay s waiting the Air Force C-141, which had yet to appear!

All the while, MacDougal pacing our wingtip pogo wheels with his jeep, so he could remove the safety pins, indicating all was clear when he raised his hand! The U-2 lightly loaded, with ballast rear cockpit, leapt like it was sprung from a springboard, and was airborne with a run of 600 feet! The remaining runway yet beneath us while the U-2 climbed through 10,000 and we broke clear of the haze of pumice to greet the early morning sun. The agile bird continuing to climb 9,000 feet per minute at 100 knots, until I leveled off at 40,000...all told, less than five minutes since I released the brakes and traveled full throttle thrust!

Obviously over-powered, the hybrid U-2's extended wings and added fuel cell most likely designed to enhance its ultimate reach and range before it became obsolescent! My advantage, its capability of cruising above 80,000, burning less fuel than we had whilst taxiing for take off! The enhanced electronics, including the wizard's Black Box added later. Hopefully not a test bed for battlefield conditions!

The U-2's transponder was blinking its assigned numbers when I pressed the 'indent' and called in to Athens Central ATC, requesting clearance to skin Santorini at flight level four zero thousand and return to Antimahia, round robin two hours! Obviously in tune, Athens responded immediately.

"Roger, White Dove, we have your 'indent'! Proceed with caution above flight level three five and maintain vocal contact for ATC relay. Advise no observable traffic within a fifty nautical mile radius of Thera (Santorini) at present time! Also advise Hellinikon closed to all traffic! Airdrome at Spata, one seven miles north of Athens, available in event of an emergency if need be!"

Factually, I had the volcano's fiery glow in view when I activated the U-2's data link and called in to Schumann to confirm the readings via our vocal link. The Doctor responding in turn.

"Yes indeedy, Keith! Present time, we have you sixty-two nautical miles south west of Antimahia at 41,000 feet. We also have a shadow on our screen!" he added quickly, indicating Gunnar's presence, whilst I reduced throttle to correct the U-2's altitude within reasonable doubts. The cockpit pressurized to the equivalent of 8,000 feet, communications arranged, free of the cumbersome pressure suit and gloves...although the outside temperature read -50° Celsius. I activated our onboard sensing devices (the readings instantly relayed to

Sigurdesson's console) and drew bead on the windward side of the inferno, agonizing its growth and intensity since Winner and I had scanned it last!

Off my portside wing, the volcano was a horror story beyond comparison. Its base engulfed the entire northern portion of the island, its shank veined with incandescent lava, the ancient caldera a witch's brew of boiling brine immersed in a mist of sulphurous steam. The plume topping 120,000 feet I judged from 40,000...the shaft, not unlike a spike of red neon, feathering green to purple, wrenched with static lightning to the reaches of the troposphere! Never had I seen or dreamt of anything so awesome; nor had the world, since the days of Pliny the Elder!

Hand flying and descending from 40,000, I engaged our side screening radar and called in to Schumann, approaching the volcano apprehensively, watchful of the U-2's sideways drift from my down looking periscope, not wanting to be sucked in by the high rising thermals!

"So, how does it look, man? Ten miles from the epicenter, I'm reading 850° Centigrade, cone velocity over the hill!" In fact, I could hear the mounting decibels above the turbo jet's continuing whine.

"Okay, we have it!" Winner called back. "No need to pod the ash, Keithy! Ingrid says it's definitely Plinian on the upside, so best haul ass...like she's calling in to Athens to spread the word!"

"Did you read the feedback from Antimahia?" I questioned Athens Central.

"Affirmative, White Dove! Things look plenty bad, hey?"

"Yeah, man, the cone velocity would blow your mind! Have you a fix on my position on radar?" I shouted when a thermal lofted the U-2 to other parts! The altimeter winding through 50,000, the U-2 nose high when I disengaged the auto-pilot and manhandled the controls, fearing a compressor stall! Although the turbo jet seemed content to mush along when I forced the yoke forward and gained level flight!

"Affirmative, White Dove! We have you ten nautical miles west of Thera's epicenter, your angular altitude approximately 53,000! Have you a problem, sir?" I acknowledged as much, re-engaged the auto-pilot and made haste to sip pure oxygen...the unbelievable 13,000 feet ascent beyond my comprehension! Having experienced the side effect of a cone velocity exceeding the speed of sound, I stated my intention to make an immediate 180° turnabout and descend to 10,000, vectoring Antimahia!

"Roger, White Dove! Permission granted to conduct a procedural turn to the north and descend to flight level ten! Again, no observable traffic in your vicinity! Proceed with caution below ten thousand, however! Considering the probability of low flying helicopters beyond reach of our radar! We also wish to advise best regards from Athens Central, Captain Slater...God bless!" This I took warmly to heart! Realizing the U-2's findings would enable Sigurdesson to announce the grim facts and predict the inevitable, before the onslaught washed the shanks of the Acropolis, the capital city of Kos no less!

Completing my turn, I retarded the throttle to idle, lowered our landing gear, raised the spoilers and deployed speed brakes to help unload the wings and effect a near power off glide ratio of 28:1 at 110 knots (indicated air speed)...I needed the sixty minute stretch to contact T.S., knowing he'd be off the wall when my data link was decoded in Riyadh!

Riyadh presented a problem when I contacted the Base on my Z-Band military frequency, however. The operative not receptive to a non-military aircraft answering as 'White Dove', much less when I insisted he put me on the horn with General O'Brien.

"Out of your mind, you asshole! This ain't no 'bird farm'! So try the Royal Palace!"

"Okay, so read my data-link!" I called back, pressing the probe.

"Yes sir, we have it! Man, you're a thousand miles out, at 48,000? Name and rank of pilot, sir? Also type of aircraft, like we're reading 110 knots?" I thought it best not to say, not wanting the U-2 to be subject of conversation when they split for lunch!

"So check your data-link work schedule as of 2200 GMT, specifically points north-east of Incirlik AB to northern Iran!"

Long minutes for the NCO to absorb and tally his computer.

"Yes sir, we have you now, but not where you're supposed to be at 2200 GMT? Request your code name, sir? Like we have a NASA bird on record, but White Dove doesn't match up with the computer!" I wracked my brain, short of an answer. Willitts? Questing the same when we met at the downtown Athens café?

"Okay, try 'Turtle Dove' and see what you have!" The operations officer, obviously summoned or standing by, came on the horn momentarily.

"Colonel Imparato here, Keith! Stand by and I'll put you in touch with the old man!" The name I recognized from somewhere in the past. Down to 35,000, I gave further note to the hybrid U-2's extended wings, the stability of her glide I'd possibly need, the panorama of Kos and the coast of Turkey...hopefully again in view at break of dawn! Then an audible click from my earphone, T.S. obviously aroused from his nap! Not anticipating I'd be airborne before sunset, allowing for his all night vigil, I presumed!

I was greeted with an obligatory 'chewing out', of course, his nibs wondering what the shit? Until I fed back the recording of my conversations with Athens Central I'd had the foresight to hold at ready, so at least he'd realize conditions in the Aegean before he sounded high C! I also allowed my six o'clock take off was on schedule, compliments of the UN! The general's reaction was unusual, knowing he habitually sounded off with whomever or whatever was at hand!

"Glad you dared put it to me, lad! Had no way of knowing since Willitts took leave! The Z-Band not for latecomers, aside from the Dutchman Keenan sent along last minute! So best play it by ear, my boy...for my part, the candy's with 'Bell Jar' if you need instant help! God bless, Keithy lad!"

'Bell Jar' the code call for the E-8, or conceivably a RC-135 Rivet Joint recon tracking the U-2 to all points! That I knew without paining my brain. T.S.'s 'second part' the moot question, considering the availability of the B-2s based at Riyadh and the minimal distance to the Caspian at supersonic knots!

Down to 10,000, I signed off with Athens Central, canceled my data-link and called in to Antimahia to make certain the runway was yet intact. MacDougal responding from the makeshift tower, allowing there was a recent bulge midway, which the Lieutenant's bulldozer was in process of clearing...would I hold off for ten minutes? No problem for my part, allowing for the U-2's incessant glide. An opportunity to make a long banking turn over the island's easterly reach, hopeful for the sight of the motor sailer, which was for naught! The outlying hulls a matter of interest however, realizing Lesleigh Butterfield was bedded down in the vicinity, the sparse roads kin to a donkey's four wheel drive!

"Clear to land, Keithy man!"

Heavy on the rudder at 80 knots, the yoke at my stomach, I skinned a row of olive trees, holding off until the mainstay wheels spun gravel. MacDougal racing alongside with his jeep whilst I planted the tail wheel on the tarmac, all the while flexing the ailerons so as not to drag a wing tip until his crew had the pogo wheels attached. The GE winding down while I trailed the lot to the ramp. No sweat, not unlike the tail dragging Stearman I'd soloed years before!

Winner and Schumann first out whilst the crew detached the ash collecting pods for their inspection. Myself down the ladder, wanting a quickie pee and a Gatorade to slake my thirst! The C-130 apparently long gone to Incirlik. Edwards and Fraser no longer in view when I stripped to shorts and made haste to the change room for a quickie shower and what I had yet to do!

The lobby was noticeably quiet in lieu of Edwards' and Fraser's absence. They'd also taken our standby data-link system in total, intending to activate the system at Incirlik prior to Schumann's and Winner's arrival. Hopefully in tandem with the mainstay at Antimahia, once the U-2 was aloft at 1800; my fix at Antimahia up for grabs thereafter! Depending the availability of a knowledgeable hand to con the vocal-link before the Base disappeared altogether!

My thoughts given totally to Dr. Sigurdesson, however, when I spied the gallant lady from the doorway. Seated at her console as usual, she ignited a weary smile and made point to greet me 'thumbs up', indicating she'd analyzed the feedback from the U-2...advised Athens of her findings, presumably! Indeed, the radio in Schumann's office was blaring martial music together with terse announcements of the evacuations underway!

Disheveled and obviously dog-tired, Ingrid's blondish hair clung damply to her forehead, her blue eyes circled with red, her shirt matted with sweat. She'd apparently spent the night at her desk, peering at her computer. The young girl sat beside her, copying Ingrid's notes on a yellow pad. Fresh with the morning, her hair neatly braided, eyes alert, following beyond my shoulder to stare pointedly at the door behind me! And, noting Ingrid was again preoccupied, I made way to the glaring sunshine, the young lady by my side.

"She won't leave her desk, Mr. Slater! We are to evacuate to Incirlik when our transport arrives, but she insists on staying on, no matter what! Adamant, Mr. Slater...unless we take her forcibly, which is not our desire!"

"Is she taking food?"

"She's had nothing but black coffee for the past two days. She goes to her room to rest every three hours; been taking injections, I think - the splotches of blood on her arms, you know what I mean?" I nodded grimly, I'd noticed the scars before.

"You're going along to Incirlik, I take it?"

"Yes, definitely! Dr. Winner invited me, phoned my parents after you'd gone to bed. I believe she had a hand in the thing, had me copying her notes since yesterday afternoon. I have a feeling she intends I take them along to Sweden when I pursue my graduate studies, possibly on her behalf...since I plan to be a volcanologist one day!"

The determined young lady fixed me with her wide brown eyes while I glanced sideways at the ramp, noting MacDougal and Dr. Schumann were studying the U-2's slender wings! I myself curious if I'd popped the rivets when I was flung aloft.

"Please...you must talk to her now, Mr. Slater! You are the only person she will listen to, and there's so little time!" She turned away, her eyes brimming with tears. I followed her inside and sat down beside the stubborn Swede, allowing myself a sip of coffee from her thermos cup. Sigurdesson eyeing me warily, shaking her head.

"I know what you're going to say, Keith. Don't be difficult...despite your feelings, I intend to stay!"

"Don't be an ass, Ingrid! You'll be set up at Incirlik long before midnight!"

"It will be too late!" she snapped. "I know what I have to do; I'll have my instruments and Fotis' radar is beamed on the cone. If there is a paroxysmal explosion, we can radio an instant warning." She doodled on her yellow pad, shaking her head. "There have been 574 tremors since we arrived here, Keith...sixty-two have approached magnitude 6 on the Richter scale. Yesterday's was 7.9. If we provide a few hours warning, we might save millions of lives, if they will only LISTEN! Tel Aviv, Alexandria, Tripoli, Venice...the entire eastern Mediterranean will be inundated if the catastrophe approaches the magnitude of 1628 BC. The coastal cities are so dreadfully exposed; sea level is much higher now than it was then, yet the outside world doesn't seem to *comprehend!*" She paused to bring a tissue to her lips, turned, and coughed heavily to her hand.

"If I stay at my post they will have cause to listen," she whispered through her fingers. "The monitoring devices on Santorini are gone; Athens is too remote to detect the cone velocity. If I give a few hours warning, I will have justified my existence. I haven't long, Keith; you know that as well as I." She turned again in her chair to grip my arm.

"Does it really matter if this is my choosing...a few more hours, isn't that my right? The generator is fueled, I have my instruments and an open line to Athens. If the sea is to carry me away, I'd as soon it take me at my desk...

"...I have written a little note to my children," she continued, pointing to a blue envelope tucked beneath her pad. "If Sergeant MacDougal would post it from Incirlik, I'd be most grateful." She smiled weakly, linked a finger with mine. "Kiss me, Keith," she whispered. "Good luck, God speed, and please don't look back!" I bent to kiss her and quickly walked from the room, turning the envelope in my hand. There was no return address; a dollar bill attached to the back side for postage.

Schumann had spread my charts on a table when I joined him in his office, leaving the door ajar to view the hallway. Metric ruler in hand, he sketched a radius from my projected turning point at the juncture of the Iranian boundary with Turkmenistan. The radius, I noted, was inclusive of my covert flight to Nebit-Dag and the western Caspian, which obviously was what he had in mind.

"Here you may encounter a problem, Keith! Judging from Gunnar's vectors, it appears he intends to have - or draw - the U-2 140 nautical miles east of your projected flight path, when you parallel the border of Turkmenistan. Which would place you midway between Ashkhabad and Cheleken, should you adhere to his vectors once you penetrate the border...of which he's seemingly apprised!"

"More like they seized the opportunity when Iran agreed to the over-flight, Doctor. Factually, I was assigned to fly the long turn before Intelligence caught the drift and laid it on the line when I stopped over in New York!"

"Was the wingtip analyzer installed at the time?" I gave thought to that, realizing he was on to a leading question...my second thoughts when I collared T.S. in the elevator!

"Could be opportunity knocks twice, Doctor...the ways and means at my disposal, if I read you rightly!"

"Of that we're in coherence, Keith! So let's consider Gunnar's other intentions, should he force the U-2 elsewhere and bring it down. The analyzer would not only be a hi-tech 'door prize', but also an incalculable discredit to the UN, once it's brought to light!" I gave thought to Gunnar's presence in Silicon Valley when he was pulled over by the police...the accessibility of Hughes and Lockheed, and their network of computers! Stash Obolensky's part until he met up with Dr. Gomulaka and turned himself in! T.S.'s part, when he hastened Stash off to Vienna as a double agent, and Stash managed the photos of Gunnar at Ramenskoye! The tragedy unfolding when Stash sent coded word to my digs in New York, obviously in trouble when an unknown friend brought the photos to my address in the city. Myself none the wiser until I found him dead in the lobby!

"You appear upset, Keith! Might we have touched a bag of troublesome thoughts?"

"Mixed bag of truths, Doctor! First part, a sense of being used...which I accept and intend to follow through! Second part, I've an axe to grind with that bastard on my own terms!"

"Vengeance is not your nature, Keith!"

"So let me put it this way, Doctor. If you had a known murderer in your back seat, would you play 'pussy cat' and let him take it from there?"

"Of course not!"

"So bear with me, man! Name of the game, to pinpoint the action south of Cheleken; from there on it's a matter of one's conscience – or 'vengeance' – to settle scores in the field of his choosing, should I luck out and go on from there!" The Dutchman not commenting of that end, but fortunately, he'd reintroduced salient features I'd nearly forgotten, which firmed my resolve!

Arriving silently, until it grounded and reversed props, and Air national Guard C-130-J spun gravel whilst it turned midway the strip and taxied to the ramp. MacDougal and his jeep quick to greet the updated Hercules, the pilot tracking the jeep's 'follow me' sign to a far side parking area so as not to interfere with the laddered U-2 and the mechanics checking its blades. The aft loading ramp descending immediately to disgorge the crew. MacDougal's iced six pack of Bud readily at hand! The crew, normally based at Charleston, S.C., on extended duty at the time.

They had little time for shop talk, however, what with Sabina standing by with the stake-back lorry and the Project's files, Nokomo's Mercedes in tow. The spare GE turbo-jet and his mixed bag of tools MacDougal's concern when I joined him by the U-2.

"They'll take all, includin' the Hummer, Keithy. But they want it first in, Nokomo's Mercedes no way! Now then, been wanting to say the blades test OK, but appears you sprung the wings a wee bit! Negative thrust, Keithy man...like you came to grief with a thermal and bent the spars? But seein' you ain't popped the rivets, I see no problem, less you tries it again!"

"So how about a 'Split-S' to straighten things out?"

"I'll tell the jokes, man! Less you have the bastard rear seat when you pull six Gs! Like the SOB's been hangin' close in, askin' questions concerning the U-2's electronic circuitry, like he knows more than he's admittin'!"

"Nose for the analyzer?"

"Could be, Keithy. So judge for yourself, like he's due for a cockpit checkout at 1300, according to Sabina." I wasn't aware of this until I borrowed MacDougal's key, intending to stretch out for a nap, and found Sabina's note pinned to the door! Which I took literally, allowing I had forty minutes of peace.

* * * * * *

Conceivably my mental clock, more likely Dr. Nokomo's chartered Lear 55 turning off at the Commercial terminal, brought me awake at precisely 1300. The Tower operator peering from his window, obviously advised by ATC with their limited means. No indication of Nokomo or the Hummer, I noticed whilst I hurried across the ramp to acquaint Gunnar with the U-2 and its high riding rear seat!

The cockpit ladders already in place, as was the man himself, glancing pointedly at his watch! Dressed as usual in spotless khakis, freshly shaved, his hair parted neatly in the center, his long neck emphasizing his ears and birdlike brow. Not altogether a pleasant sight, with his teeth glinting ominously in the sun! Polite, however, he made do to shake my hand and we conversed on even terms while I conducted a 'walk around' of the tethered bird, explaining its external functions, of which he seemed apprised. He also seemed aware of the protrusions conducive to the imaging SAR, EQ camera and signals sensors, but made no comment, to my relief. His curiosity taciturn, but apparently aroused when we rounded the extended portside wing panel containing the 'analyzer', but again no comment, although he made his point when he shrugged and eyed me warily when I allowed it contained an added fuel cell to extend the U-2's range, to MacDougal's apparent relief!

Our inspection tour complete, aside from the 'Q-Bay' containing the U-2's advanced electronics array, of which Gunnar expressed immediate interest! Noting the bay was conspicuously lacked and not available to the ground personnel, might I have the key?

"No way!" I said, shouldering him aside to the rear cockpit entry ladder. "The Q-Bay is strictly off limits, man! No bloody secrets, but it takes a qualified top dog from NASA to maintain our electronics, myself excluded!" I added, noting MacDougal was conspicuously elsewhere when Gunnar gave him further thought.

Animals possess empathy, but I wondered about Gunnar -- the cruel twist to his mouth – although he'd displayed remorse for Amalia. Scented liberally with nervous sweat, his breath reeking of medication, his hand unsteady when he grasped the windscreen and lowered himself to examine the controls.

Competent at what he was at, but not relaxed, he exercised the yoke and rudder mechanically, as one might steer a tractor, flexing trim tabs, inquiring of the power and flap settings, and gear rotation speeds. He nodded silently when I pointed to the placards. Last, inquiring of the autopilot system, he quizzed my face when I explained the system was not operable from the rear cockpit. His eyes dilated noticeably with the explanation that the raised rear cockpit was designed primarily as a student pilot feature, the meteorological console added later. The U-2's navigational system essentially the command pilot's chore.

I pointed to the slaved ECM GPS (guidance system) which he could monitor, but not alter, once I engaged the autopilot, stressing the rear cockpit was basically equipped for low altitude transition, mainly takeoffs and landings while the autopilot was disengaged. Neglecting to add the latter would disengage automatically at a critical air speed or power-down situation.

"Ja, I understand," he said, noting the oxygen and communication connections. "And what is this?" he added, peering under seat.

"Your ejection toggle, Mr. Gunnar, but I'd advise you not to try it above

40,000 feet."

"Ah, yes, but my suit is better equipped," he replied, canceling a hopeful thought. "I have also experienced transition in like airplane and you needn't fear my hand with the controls," he added testily. "Although I presume Dr. Nokomo has informed you of my accreditation from the Russian Republic?"

"I wouldn't have you aboard if I wasn't aware of your flights at Ramenskoye, *Colonel* Gunnar!"

"Apparently so, apparently so," he repeated to himself, "but then you would have known from my flying suit I was prepared to offer my services, yes?" I shrugged it off, intending to rattle him further.

"It's your age I fear, not your hand on my controls! Your medic states you have high blood pressure and a hyper heartbeat. So what happens if your ticker gives out? You're inclined to vertigo and we'll be flying in the dark. Have you thought about that?"

"Jesus! Take it easy!" MacDougal muttered

"Strength of will!" Gunnar sputtered. "I was schooled in the fatherland and my saber scar is a badge of courage! You Americans lack the blood strain and determination of the rightful heirs to the cause! I also intend to follow our prescribed flight plan," he added hurriedly. Throttling back, he realized he'd overshot; his face livid with anger, a stainless steel tooth protruding his salivating lower jaw.

"So long as you know I'll be tracking my own charts, Gunnar, not yours, nor the ones faxed to the UN. I also plan to terminate our flight at Incirlik or Kos, if conditions warrant, not somewhere en route if you fuck up! Do you understand?"

"We shall see!" he hissed. "I have right to request an emergency landing should you violate UN intentions! Also, I insist my right to examine your forward cockpit and query the purpose of the extended wingtips!"

"Gentlemen, please!" Schumann called from the base of our ladder. Fotis alongside, I was quick to note. "We've only a few hours and we've matters to discuss, Keith!" I took the hint and turned to MacDougal.

"Let him look it over, aside from the Q-bay," I cautioned. "You may pound on the wingtips if you like," I added, addressing Gunnar. "We need the wingtips to accommodate your ass, but not your overnighter," I continued, pointing to the ditty bag he'd deposited rear seat.

"I've the right to carry what I wish, you insolent pig!"

"But not a sidearm!" I reminded, handing the bag to Schumann when I dropped to the ramp.

"You are not to inspect my personal belongings!" Gunnar shouted, noting the doctor was puzzling the weight.

"So cool it and suit up!" I said, indicating he could take it or leave it, once he disclosed what it held!

"Lordy, I thought you would come to blows," Schumann asided. "You baited him mercilessly, Keith. Is that what you intended?" I nodded, suddenly weary of it all.

"He's a demented old man, a sad sack neo-fascist out of touch with reality," I commented when we returned to the lobby. "Up against it, lost his woman, and I know how he feels! All of a sudden I feel sorry for the bastard. Strange, hey? Inside every living thing there's a soul intending to survive."

"Self-serving in Gunnar's instance! Don't wax philosophic, Keith. From what I've seen and heard, he has no soul; his ego is something else again. Demented or not, he's full of tricks!"

"Figures...but I'm also intent on survival!"

"May I have a quiet word with you, Captain Slater?" Fotis interrupted, pointing to the Lieutenant's office. I stopped short, realizing he'd observed the confrontation and was on to something else.

"Word of Nina?" I blurted, tailing him to the Lieutenant's office.

"Not really," he said, closing the door behind us, "but I must caution you, Keith. Despite my personal feelings, Athens has requested her apprehension for questioning. And there's no way I can invalidate or erase their computers."

"Meaning it's embedded for all time?"

"Meaning Athenian law is often macho inclined and women have secondary rights," he said. "There is also likelihood of a cover up to avoid charges of corruption in high places. In short, they're apt to hang her before the facts are logically examined!"

"Jesus Christ!"

"Word to the wise, Keith! If you should find her, don't let it be known until the emergency has passed and I've time to prepare a proper defense from the facts that have recently come to light. I speak to you as a lawyer and a loyal friend of the family," Fotis added. "Nina is dear to our hearts. God speed your safe return!"

* * * * * *

Gunnar lasered me with his bloodshot eyes when I entered the air-conditioned change room, deciding last minute for a quickie rub down with a hot towel

324

before I donned my thermal underwear and suited up for the duration. Swearing profusely, Gunnar was having a problem with his Russian pressure suit and elongated neck. White of skin, not unlike his thermal underwear (or a sack of damp flour), he required the assistance of a brace of militiamen to fasten his enclosures. His helmet came next; and again he required assistance to attach and seal his visor. Quick to attach his oxygen bottle, however...he flexed his arms and stumbled about like a woebegone gooney bird. Eventually settling in a reclining chair to breathe from his oxygen bottle, whilst I underwent a similar procedure.

My pressure suit, unlike Gunnar's, was a custom-sized, full body type, identical to those worn by the SR-71 and Space Shuttle pilots, capable of surviving ejection up to mach 3 and 120,000 feet. Suit up and pressure checks routinely take thirty minutes. With the pressure helmet attached and the visor sealed, we would breathe pure oxygen to purge a maximum of nitrogen from our bloodstreams as a precaution against 'the bends'. Our climb-out at 80,000 feet would be rapid after we relayed a final reading from Santorini. In Gunnar's instance, his intake of oxygen should be soothing solace to his furtive mind.

Gunnar contained himself to his chair while MacDougal sealed my boots and gloves. I eyed his knee pouches warily, but they seemed to hold nothing more than his chart and a sequence of notebooks he would require en route. An outsized chronometer was attached to his shoulder pocket by a nylon cord, and I gave the item thought when his back was turned. He seemed nervous and fidgety, thumbing it several times with his glove.

"Beats the hell outta me," MacDougal muttered. "Like he doesn't trust me panel clocks. Came up with it while you was talkin' to Major Fotis. Want me to check it in the shop?" I shrugged it off. Time was short; I had other things in mind!

"Most likely Nina left the keys to the van under the mat. If you've time, check it out and stash them in my locker. Also a bright-glow flashlight," I added, thinking of a possible rendezvous with Stavos and the *Helena*.

"Anything else? It's soundin' like Finnegan's Wake!"

"I'm worried for Lesleigh Butterfield, Mac! She's sacked up in the hills east part of the island, since Dr. Petrie pulled stakes...hopefully with family, like she intends to hang in!"

"Wouldn't worry it, man! Fact, she came by this morning while you were jawboning with Athens; loaned her me baseball cap, seein' the donkey was chewin' her straw! Pretty little thing; reminds me of me wife when I was crewin' the 99th! Stubborn like Nellie, no way we could talk her into boarding the flight to Incirlik; like she has pangs for your heart, methinks! Anything else, Keithy man?"

"Ingrid! She hasn't long to go! Don't upset her, but make sure the generator has an extra tank of gravity fed diesel. I'll call in when we're over Cairo West, but from thereon it's beggarman's guess!"

"You ain't intendin' to set down at Incirlik, ole buddy! I know what you have in mind; ain't foolin' me, kid! I got eyes in the back of me head." I turned on my oxygen bottle and stood by the window while he checked the suit for leaks. The U-2 had been dusted with an air hose, the canopies opened.

The sun was an orange blob peering from the west; trees and fields reflected white against the distant gray hills. The scene was reminiscent of wintertime in New Hampshire...feathery pumice falling like virgin snow, hooded militiamen gathered around. It was 17:30 local time. Come midnight, my reluctant dragon and I would be sharing our moment of truth.

Dr. Nokomo strode to the ramp when we were driven to the U-2. Dressed to the teeth in a spotless tunic, his baton underarm, Sabina by his side. He waited patiently by the scaffolding while we were buckled in, then climbed the ladder as I was energizing the GE. Reaching over to pat my shoulder, he dazzled me with his freshly brushed ivories.

"He says he came to wish you luck. I think he wants to apologize, Keith," MacDougal offered from the long cord intercom connection. I winked and raised my glove. Hell, he was well intended.

I saw him waving from the gantry while it was wheeled away, his ebony face beaming. He was a likeable ass; stubborn, officious, a typical bureaucrat, out of touch with reality. We were never to see him again. The Lear disappeared from radar over Tel Aviv at 45,000, a little high for its critical thin wing. The time? 1900 Athens local time.

I took a squint at my backseat companion. Other than the mirror, this would be our last visual until termination. Gunnar stared beyond me from the visor, his eyes seemingly dilated, as if he were under sedation. I buckled in with mixed emotions, detached the zero delay parachute lanyard from the D-ring, and called back to see if he was following our check list. His voice was thick when he answered. I prompted him in German; his reply was long in coming and hesitant. Under normal conditions, I would have aborted the mission, but the situation wasn't normal, and I had to be content with a tranquilized tiger eyeing my controls.

MacDougal preceded us to the runway and pulled off to the side to wait until we lined up the active. I ran a transponder check with the tower, squawked

4460. The lone operator acknowledged the 'Ident' and cleared us for takeoff at 17:48. I spooled the GE and centered the runway for the twelve-hour tour. Procedures much the same as my morning flight, allowing I had Gunnar's ass for ballast, intending to give him a view of the seething volcano to ease his bowels.

The pogo wheels dropped away and we were airborne immediately...climbing to 70,000 with a banking turn towards Santorini eight minutes later! Leveling off, our cruise speed mounting, the GE full thrust, I activated the side viewing radar and infrared sensors to give Ingrid a final shot!

"How does it look?" I called back to Antimahia.

"Terrible, Keith! The infrared is beyond belief! Might you give it another try?" I edged a few miles closer, the U-2 bucking its displeasure when we pierced the gritty fall-out, the peripheral scanning radar and sensors continuously in tune...the U-2 IFR!

"That's it, honey, we're twenty-five miles north of the cone, turning due west!"

"Mein Gott, not so close!" Gunnar interrupted from the intercom. Hand flying the U-2, I sensed his boot on the rudder and gave it a kick to warn him off.

"So toggle the pods and get off the intercom, I'm talking to Dr. Sigurdesson, you asshole!"

"I cannot see, you have lost the horizon!"

"Name of the game!" I shot back, switching again to our open line. "Do you have it now, Ingrid? The cone's past our beam and we can't focus it much longer!"

"We have it on screen," Schumann responded. "Image vivid and clear, infrared above 950 degrees! Best of luck, Keith...unfortunately, Ingrid insists she's staying on, but we'll monitor your data-link from Incirlik by 0200!" Indicating the base evacuation was presently underway.

"Okay, that's it!" I called back, canceling the probes. "We'll call in over Alexandria, but at the moment we're IFR!"

As was Cairo West and Tel Aviv when we topped the drift at 80,000. The outside air stable by then, I engaged the auto-pilot, fixing 80,000 as our cruise altitude when I notified Tel Aviv we were above their commercial play. Their reply,

"God speed, White Dove! We have you over El Fayum (Egypt) at the moment! Advise you to check your GPS for deviation, sir!" That I did, noting the autopilot was deviating degrees east of my computerized flight plan?

"Affirmative!' I said, advising our next checkpoint would be Medina, Saudi

Arabia, would they advise Antimahia since we'd out-ranged their transmissions! There was an understandable delay, of course; a mixed bag of translations, the southern shore of the Red Sea under wing when Tel Aviv replied.

"Feeble signal from Antimahia, White Dove! Female stating the Base is unattended as of now! Messages, Captain Slater...we can barely hear with our sirens full bloom!"

So what to say on the black edge of space, the sun fast disappearing in the west, the bloated full moon rising in the east!

"Tell her we love her dearly, and I'll see her tomorrow morning, to please hang in!"

"Will relay, White Dove...we know what you mean, judging from Athens ATC! Same prayer, man!" the operator added, his accent Brooklynese. "Fact we're about to close shop with visibility down to zero, fuckin' pumice swirling like snow! Same token we've lost contact with a chartered jet bound to Lagos! Last report, calling for radar vectors...like he didn't know where he was, his turbos ingesting ash!" Hopefully not Dr. Nokomo, his wives and children, I thought, picturing a power off glide to the desert in the dead of night!

All peaceful at 80,000, however, and dropping our useless pods over the Red Sea, I allowed the U-2 to find its wishful altitude; the GE-118 in agreement when we leveled off at 87,000, our ground speed exceeding 450 knots, the ash plume drifting to the south west, per Winner's prediction! With this in mind, I elected to the great circle routing to points east of Tehran, savaging an hour of wasted time!

"You are deviating from our intended course," Gunnar reminded from the intercom; and indeed I had. The Saudi desert was beneath us while I was tracking an elliptical course over Medina, pointing for Bahrain and southern Iran.

Over Medina and Riyadh, I was once again in familiar territory, although I shuddered at the thought of my last sortie...the F-15 tumbling out of control over the desert, the agonizing bail-out and terrible hours I spent avoiding Iraqi patrols, their search pattern narrowing until a Pave Hawk helicopter gunship scattered the lot!

Undoubtedly, T.S. had our fix when I called to Medina...more so when I avoided the air space over missile happy Riyadh. From here on, AWACS would have us on screen, T.S.'s B-2s most likely in abeyance nearby; stealth types, at low altitude during the night, undetectable by Iran's primitive radar.

Far beneath us the burn-off from the oilrigs glowed like a carpet of lively fireflies; then came the opalescence of the Persian Gulf, shimmering the reflection of the full moon. Aside from their oilrigs, Iran was in total darkness until I determined the lights of Shiraz off our portside wing, and called in.

Forewarned by the UN, Shiraz acknowledged our predicted position, although there was a difference of longitude when I checked my GPS, which I thought a bit odd. The operator advised us to contact Mashhad before we commenced out turn to the northwest. Altogether routine, although I had reason to wonder if Tehran was venturing lip service or aware of the circumstances that would yield to a takeover in the southern Caspian.

Gunnar was strangely quiet, his helmet barely visible from my mirror. Possibly asleep during the two hour stretch? Myself wide-awake, sipping coffee from my tube, I checked his oxygen supply and found the flow in green. But my heart did a flip-flop when I noticed our auto-pilot was playing games, deviating to the east when I cross-checked our position with the unflappable GPS!

Wondering 'what the shit?', I compared our bearing with my charts and calculated a slippage to the east! Noting it was minor, but at odds with the autopilot's normal displacement of 1/6 degrees. Thinking there was a possible malfunction, I examined our heading minutely. True, the auto-pilot was correcting our elliptical course, but its bearing would have us twenty miles west of Ashkhabad (Turkmenistan), two degrees, 120 miles east of my critical turning point! The malfunction most likely the 'expertise' of the bastard rear seat!

My first reaction, to manually reset a corrected heading…he'd obviously hot-wired the circuit with his electronic bag of tricks! My only option, to disengage the autopilot, but he'd already seen to it that my yoke button offered no response! He'd also wedged our power quadrant, I noted, when I attempted to adjust the setting. In essence, he had me locked in while the U-2 maintained his selected course!

"Easy does it," I murmured to myself, refraining from hammering the intercom. Never before had I heard or experienced such a thing, much less at the edge of space! I could manhandle and force the controls, but there again, he'd wedged the rudder with his boots; the yoke immovable when I tested it with my glove. I had a low hold card available, however, a wild chance! Nearing the analyzer's optimum range, I decided to hold tight and determine what he was about.

All the while, AWACS would be puzzling the diversion, knowing the U-2's exact position; T.S. at ends, no doubt. The U-2 was also wanting to climb, I noticed, Gunnar apparently unaware or without the means to cap the altitude fix. I also observed a faint pulsating light from the U-2's rear radar warning system, indicating we had a presence following at low altitude, miles behind.

Thirty minutes out, in a cold sweat, playing Gunnar's game to the hilt, I called to Mashhad to announce our predicted GPS position, knowing it was at odds with our continuing deviation. Mashhad responded quickly, seemingly anticipating our contact, the operator spoke hesitantly in broken English.

"Confirming your position, longitude 58°, 36° latitude, White Dove," he replied, without questioning the obvious difference. "I am further advised you are to home ADF frequency 396," he added, as if reading from notes. I blipped my response and set up 396 on the ADF. I illuminated my kneepad to compare my chart with Gunnar's forged notations; the latter continuing his silence, my controls rigidly blocked.

The ADF needle wavered, the signal weak, possibly mobile and well over the horizon. My chart allowed there was such, but it was circled and noted on the forged addendum! The name of Gunnar's game, I thought, glancing at the panel clock. Ten minutes from our critical turn, he'd have us 120 miles to the east of the analyzer's intended target, 60 miles short of its maximum range!

Clever bastard! He'd apparently been tipped off when the analyzer was installed at the 'skunk works', possibly by a hand at Lockheed who had access to the U-2's electronics and the autopilot's circuitry. Nevertheless, he had me short end and presumably intended to force a landing! The advantage: a multi-million dollar prize of super secret technology, to say nothing of an international flap if the U-2 was seized where it definitely shouldn't be!

"So now you observe we are directly on course, despite your intentions!" Gunnar hissed on the intercom. "It is also my right to declare a violation and demand an emergency landing," he furthered, switching to Mashhad's frequency to repeat what he'd said. The autopilot continuing to track course...verging the ADF's bearing, while Mashhad acknowledged, stating they'd copied. As would AWACS, inclusive of the ADF's frequency!

I quickly scanned my chart, noting the ADF signal had firmed and would have us in the vicinity of Kizl Arvat, a major road junction between Krasnovodsk and Ashkhabad. A Notam from Intelligence I'd circled hastily on the chart, indicating an airstrip under construction near Kazandzhik, a remote village strad-dling the oil pipelines and roadways a few miles west of Kizl Arvat.

"Bingo!" I murmured to myself.

"Now then, we shall reduce power in accordance and descend immediately to 2000 meters at 1500 a minute," Gunnar commanded, releasing the power quadrant but not the autopilot or his boots on the rudder controls. Calculating his rate of descent would have us over Kizl Arvat in 20 minutes, I seized the moment to reach under my seat and activate the analyzer!

A pinpoint of light appeared immediately on my panel, indicating the system was in the green. At that moment, we were miles apart from the target area, but nevertheless the game was on! The U-2 nose high at 92,000 feet, the compressor verging a stall; the autopilot wavering, disengaging when the throttle slipped to idle. Gunnar, seemingly oblivious, appeared to be scrutinizing his chart.

"Ja, I have it now," he muttered on the intercom. "Once we have vector beneath 2000 meters, we shall turn 290° and descend at 140 knots. My colleagues will have illuminated the field with flares and you shall land at my command!" he added gleefully, obviously savoring his colleagues' delight!

"Fuck you!" I said, tightening my harness.

"We shall see to that!" he hissed. It happened then, totally unexpected.

A loud shrill came from *inside* my helmet! I lurched against my harness straps, shaking my head, fumbling with my earphones. The piercing sound continued unabated, like a dentist's drill gone berserk! The excruciating pain became unbearable; my senses reeling, saliva dripped from my mouth, the taste of acid! I flailed my helmet with my gloves, pounding the radio console. The console blurred and spun, the moon wheeled overhead, rising higher and higher! I tore at my helmet, convulsed, arched my back and screamed! The shrieking suddenly stopped.

"You shall bide instructions without question, else I raise the decibel level until your brain explodes!" Gunnar shouted from the intercom. I nodded numbly, gagging for breath, senses reeling.

"Ja, I test again until you answer your master's voice!" he rasped sadistically, raising the decibels to a shrilling high!

I grayed out, semi-conscious, clutching the yoke to my chest as would a child with his teddy bear. I was only vaguely aware of the U-2 hurtling skywards, of the moon careening violently, my helmet banging against the canopy, of Gunnar screaming "Nein, nein! Mein Gott!" Then a veil of velvet darkness overcame me and I blacked out...completely!

* * * * * *

How long was the recurring nightmare of my F-15 tumbling out of control over hostile Iraq? Perhaps seconds! When I regained consciousness, I was hanging by my restraining straps, the moon peering between my knees. My helmet pressed the canopy; the U-2 spiraled gracefully in an inverted spin!

How it came to be, I'll never know. Possibly a power-on hammerhead stall, caught with Gunnar's boot lodged in the rudder controls. His unearthly shrilling had ceased, however, and all was quiet rear seat. The GE had flamed out, of course, but there was sufficient battery power to keep my panel aglow; the altimeter winding through 70,000 and continuing! Sot with fuel from the venting bladder tanks, the wheel loose in hand, I tried a mixed bag of flaps until the wheel gained leverage and we had sufficient knots to break the stall. The rudder next! Lunging to reach it with my boot, I applied opposite rudder and stabilized the spin. The U-2 recovered a few turns later...nose down, busting 200 knots! Fearful of a wing bending 'split S', I rolled her out. Her long wings responded ever so gradually, until she came fully upright on a floating descent. Our altitude 48,000, the panel clock reading four minutes past midnight Athens time! Outside, all was black aside from the moon, which fortunately had relocated a few points to the west.

At 40,000 feet, I managed to re-ignite the turbo jet and, spooling minimal cruise, hand flew the bird until I could determine what I had; Gunnar hopefully immobilized, no longer on the horn! Disoriented, my charts at a loss, I picked up a northwesterly compass bearing, discovered his ADF bearing had remained in general terms, firming all the while. Vectoring Ashkhabad, I had a fix to compare with the GPS. I determined we were straddling the border of Turkmenistan...80 nautical miles short of Kizl Arvat!

The cockpit re-pressurized, I opened my visor to cleanse what I'd expelled, continuing to inhale oxygen as I checked Gunnar's flow gauge. His supply was in the green, but the flow was unmoving, although he'd have an emergency bottle at hand. Unconscious? Or playing games? My head throbbing, I warily maintained the course; peered from my ear view mirror, rising to look astern when I detected no movement, only the sheen of the backside of his helmet by the light of the moon. Nor did he evidence any response when I clicked the intercom. He'd panicked, that I knew; suffered a heart attack possibly?

Gunnar had set up a VHF frequency on his communications console, most likely intending to contact his colleagues at Kazandzhik when he blasted my ears. Realizing AWACS also had ears and would home the response, I activated the channel and hoarsed "...vier, drei, zwei, eins!" on the VHF transceiver.

The response was immediate, seemingly anticipating; a faint, long count in guttural German, their signal weak and over the hill. All the while, the self-sufficing analyzer's light continued to glow, as did our rear radar warning system, indicating I had company close behind! And all the while, AWACS would have our fix, although they'd be puzzling the U-2's spiraling descent and my choice of language on open channel!

With seconds remaining, I decided to make the big turn...Kizl Arvat was close beneath us, but ominously blacked out! Banking to 292°, I called in to

Gunnar's collaborators, versing my very best NATO German, indicating we'd had a compressor problem and would they ignite the flares.

Surprisingly, the reply was affirmative in garbled German; my voice was likewise garbled with the VHF's low yield. And, upon rolling out, in the distance I sighted a two-mile string of igniting flares, a brilliant green light indicating the windward approach. Straight in, as they would have it, but maintaining 40,000 feet, I set up AWACS on the Z-band and broke radio silence.

"Bell Jar, Turtle Dove here! Do you read me loud and clear?"

"Affirmative, Keithy boy! We have a multiple fix, man! First off, a mobile ADF and a mess of flares."

"So take them out...my regards to T.S.!"

The result was instantaneous! The ADF needle faltered and spun uselessly; seconds later the illuminated strip disappeared in a glow of blue-white fire! Turning due west, I was greeted with a sequence of like explosions appearing north of the U-2's needle nose, a secondary blast in the vicinity of Nebit Dag! Toggling the U-2's aperture radar system, I gave the boys at Riyadh (and presumably the Pentagon) a vivid screening of what they'd wrought!

The multiple flashes continued to occur towards Cheleken, a continuing array alongside the eastern Caspian, presumably the heavily laden barges pointing for Baku. The black velvet night prevailing, aside from the flashes south of Cheleken, most likely contained to the remnants of the warehouses and the command posts in the field. In effect, in less than six minutes, the B-2s' proximity-fused bombs had reduced the threat to shambles, and they'd disappeared as quickly as they came. In time, the world would cease to wonder from whence, but at that moment I was witness to the scenario at 40,000 feet; midway across the silvery Caspian when I remembered to cancel the U-2's data link and was strictly on my own!

Sickened by what I had endured and seen, distrustful of the autopilot, I continued to hand fly the U-2 due west. The fellows at Beale and NASA would be disbelieving. The U-2 is not prone to aerobatics, but that's the way it was! I vectored Trabiz and picked up a heading to Kayserit, Turkey; two hours out by my indicated air speed, Ankara a half-hour further west. All the while, AWACS continued to maintain contact, questioning my status and plans. Most likely prompted by T.S., but at the time I could care less, not wanting to indicate what I had in mind!

Somewhere over central Turkey I allowed myself a catnap, the yoke locked between my knees, the forgiving U-2 obliging a point or two, but continuing to maintain altitude. The GE-118 in agreement, having experienced a near mortal wound when we turned turtle over Kizl Arvat.

Miles south of Elazig, Turkey, I was awakened by a flash of brilliant light from the southwest; the horizon illuminated, a horrendous yellow glow silhouetting the descending moon. An eerie luminescence clung to the sky like a gigantic aurora borealis loosened from the Arctic. I stared unbelievingly as it began to fade, flaring anew momentarily; like the colors of the rainbow, from bright orange to deepening purple, fading to an iridescent green...clinging, clinging, until the black of night overcame it.

"Jesus Christ!"

"Good God, what was that?" shouted Bell Jar on open channel.

I knew what it was long minutes later, when the shock wave lifted the U-2, my earphones caught with a blast of celestial static. The panel clock read 0348 GMT, Sigurdesson's prediction no longer in question. Santorini had blown its bowels, and the worst was yet to come!

My first thoughts centered on Nina's conceivable landfall, but I reckoned northern Crete would be devastated; Kos my best bet, provided the Helena remained afloat. AWACS had other thoughts, however, insisting I terminate at Ankara, or Incirlik AB, according to plan! Most likely prodded by T.S., The U-2's top secret electronics in mind, although he had reason to suspect I had continuing priorities! For my part, the lack of transportation once land locked at Incirlik a concern, which I'd fortuitously foreseen.

AWACS was also quick to indicate they had a change of venue; Bell Jar advising they'd been re-assigned to monitor the Sixth Fleet flat tops for emergency operations. The fleet apparently well offshore, requiring the E-8 Joint Stars radar and communications systems at altitude, since the shoreline ground stations were no longer available, which was altogether ominous! They had my fix, 300 nautical miles south east of Ankara, however. Confirming the U-2's data link and GPS readings when they signed off! Which was helpful, what with my autopilot completely useless!

Continuing due west, I calculated I'd have Kos within reach in an hour and twenty minutes, plus an hour of burn, although I was distrustful of the fuel gauges and the quantity we'd sloshed hanging inverted over Iran. I had a glimpse of early dawn from the east, but not for long. West of Kayserit, we encountered a fallout of pumice, and the going was brutal IFR; the GE sneezing spasmodically and no way could we climb above the plume topping 200,000 according to Bell Jar's last scan!

All of this at 40,000...hand flying the gauges, my nerves raw edge, and presumably a dead man rear cockpit. Then again, the unexpected! A secondary shock wave rocked the U-2, flinging us skywards, whipping the super thin wings like balsa sticks! The yoke loose to my hands, the altimeter winding through 45,000 when the shock wave passed on, Sigurdesson's words echoing in my ears... *'The initial blast will weaken the volcano to its root,'* she'd said. *'The second will signal its total collapse; the emptied cavity will draw the Aegean from all points, until the cavity overflows. This will result in a horrendous tidal wave that will put Krakatoa to shame!'*

AWACS E-8-C also had been tossed about, presumably over western Turkey; their comments akin to my worst fears.

"Damnit, what a banger!" Bell Jar shouted. "The coast has had it, man...like it got hit with a 20 megaton cherry bomb! Same with Crete! All we can see is smoke broadside the mountain range!"

"Kos?"

"Okay...we have it on radar scan. Doesn't appear as bad, 'cept the harbor's messed up and there ain't many buildings left to tell; lots of fires. Same thing with Rhodos, Keithy! Gotta sign off now. Seems the fleet's having problems; we have your fix tenner east of Konya, and that ain't headin' to Ankara, ole buddy!"

I continued due west without commenting, descending on a long float when I broke clear of the pall. The sun was a half orange in my rear view mirror. Turbulence was moderate to heavy; the U-2 recoiling with the incessant thermals, visibility clearing somewhat when we passed over the mountain lakes of Isparta twenty minutes later. Kos lay 180 nautical miles beyond on a bearing of 250°; the island obscured by a rise of billowing smoke. My concern at the moment, the obsolescent fuel gauges indicating the bladders were borderline and fast approaching my emergency reserve.

"Heads up, you idiot! Where in hell do you think you're going?" a voice thundered from the open channel. I knew who it was, visualizing his grotty cigar. He had a fucking nerve!

"Answer me, damnit!"

"I'm setting down for a cold beer, you old fart!"

"Don't smartass me!"

"You've got what you want; get off my back!"

"Turn back to Incirlik! The U-2's high risk and I intend it be properly secured!"

"Don't threaten me, you rank-happy bastard! I've got a wife out there and I intend to look around!"

"Get on with it then!" another voice said. "If need be, spot a high level field and we'll prompt a 'copter to pick you up, my son!"

I knew immediately who it was. I had no idea where they were, but the sound of their twin Pratt Whitneys was altogether familiar. I anticipated a visit momentarily! Muting the volume when T.S. continued to sputter, I continued my heading with a fuel-saving descent. I had other thoughts to grind; hopefully a glimpse of Crete!

The smoke thinned as I crossed the last of the Turkish ridges; the early morning sun a globe of deep orange, eerie, not unlike that fateful morning in New York. Visibility so-so when I crossed the coast eleven hours and six minutes since we'd rotated from Kos.

The scene that lay before me was unimaginable! The Turkish coast had been totaled by the paroxysmal blast, and seared by a hurricane of fire. Smoldering villages and broken highways, forests laid and ignited like straw, hills and fields ablaze from the water's edge to the ridge behind me, stretching the coast as far as I could see, billowing acrid smoke from the offshore islands hanging the sea.

An enormous doughnut of rising steam shrouded Santorini, convulsing upon itself, drawn to its torrid center by the onrushing sea! A spectacular 200,000-foot genie of pumice was drifting with the stratospheric winds hundreds of miles to the east, its foothold detached from the fragmented volcano, curling the Aegean to Tel Aviv. Eighty cubic miles of white-hot magma had been expelled from the cavity to blight the Northern Hemisphere for years to come! Santorini's orgasm was complete!

Looking down, I had Kos on my port wingtip, a 40-minute burn left in the tanks; an 80-mile dead stick glide when the turbine emptied its cup. Crete lay 340 nautical miles to the west. I considered the odds; the seething rise of steam I'd encounter; the turbulent mass of unstable air, and the pumice-laden sea streaking for Santorini's emptied womb.

"Give it up, Keith!" a familiar echoed as if attuned to my thoughts. I spun in my seat; a tiny speck was gaining from the east.

They half-rolled my canopy seconds later. I had a fleeting impression of an inverted F-15E as it thundered overhead and rolled into a long turn from the north. They came alongside a moment later, their speed brakes extended; desert brown, two seasoned helmets in tandem! The rear seat observer raised a glove and pointed to the north.

"Take it back to Incirlik, son! There won't be an airstrip left to the Aegean in the next half hour!"

I strained my harness, shielding my eyes. The sea was draining the coast on all quadrants, the offshore shelf cascading to the depths like the falls of Niagara. The Aegean had fallen 50 feet since I'd crossed the coast.

"If you flame out, you haven't a fucking chance!" T.S. rasped. I reassessed my priorities. He was right; if the GE sneezed, I'd be boiled alive!

"I'll circle for a while. If Kos clears, I'll set her down."

"Take her to Incirlik or I'll have your fucking hide!"

"If I have a problem, I'll spot a high level field."

"Do what you believe is right, son. And it goes without saying, I admire your guts!"

"Who asked you to say that?" sputtered T.S.

"Take it from an old buddy, asshole! The kid's shook up and you put him through a mess of shit!"

"Would you check my rear seat?" I questioned. "I think it has rigor mortis!"

"Affirmative. He's head down in his harness," T.S. snapped.

"Double Eagle one eight!" AWACS intoned.

"OK, what is it?" T.S. thundered.

"We have a ground report of 8.4 along the Anatolian fault. Yerevan's been wiped! SACEUR wants a picture spread if you have sufficient fuel!" The F-15, rising swiftly above me, turned to the east. T.S. would be on the horn with SACEUR in Brussels. I was temporarily forgotten.

I banked to the north and followed the coast of Kos with mixed emotions. I had a dead man in my back seat, and a wife hopefully alive in the mountains of Crete. If I landed otherwise, I'd be hard put to arrange transport for the duration. I gave heavy thought to the Helena bobbing the tortured sea, the terrible mound of water rising on the horizon. Would Stavos be able to ride it out? I prayed then, eyeing my alternatives.

The Crusaders' fortress rose beneath my starboard wing like a battleship gone aground. The parallel breakwaters were high and dry, the harbor emptied. Convulsive quakes had ripped the core of the demolished town, strewing the ancient marbles like confetti on a forgotten street. I flew on, sickened at heart for what was sure to come. Had Fotis managed to take Cleo to the hills, to part Sigurdesson from her desk? Had they lasted the initial blast? The scorched cliffs, brush fires, and the blackened tower faded behind me. There was hope, however, in the mirrored reflections from the mountain shanks...ant-like strings of vehicles winding the valleys; Fotis shepherding his flock to the hills.

I elected for a 10-minute float to bide my time and harbor fuel; leveling off at 10,000, I inched the throttle to maintain minimum cruise. The cockpit stifling from the greenhouse effect, my pressure suit rank with sweat; my back itched, my limbs stiffened. I unfastened my helmet to wipe my brow, then unfastened my gloves, loosened my boots and opened the vents to freshen the fetid air. Kos fell behind; the coast of Turkey curling beneath the U-2's wing. Izmir lay 90 miles to the east; Athens 100 miles to the west. My fuel tanks hovered the red line. Far below, the ebbing sea had come to a standstill, gathering itself for the finale!

The compass rolled 270°; my air speed indicating 140 knots. Athens came up on the U-2's nose as a pyre of smoke illuminated by the morning sun. I leveled off momentarily, drawn in part by morbid curiosity, shielding my eyes to the bloody sky. The GE droned on, smoke broadening the horizon. My hand tightened the wheel, an icy sense of doom wracking my spine. I blinked and shook my head. The scene unfolding was of unimaginable devastation...3,500 years of ancient history, the tragedy of 1628 BC was evolving before my eyes!

Plato's unfinished story echoed in my mind; Solon's words, the description inscribed by the Saite priests! Butterfield's description of the receding sea when the Israelites crossed to the Sinai; the deluge that fell upon the Sea of Reeds to inundate the Egyptian chariots. I breathed deeply from my oxygen, examined my face in the mirror. Had I been rapturing since I discarded my helmet? Was I quite myself? Red of eye, pale and drawn with shock, frightened by the unworldly scene; the raw truth is a terrible thing when it comes to be!

Athens had been an uninhabited valley then; Piraeus a simple fishing village of other name. Time had filled the valley with Grecian temples and skyscrapers, the harbor with a maze of piers and ships. But it was all undone. The quakes had devoured 3,500 years of history and laid it all to waste.

The harbor was a clutter of toppled ships: super tankers, cruise liners, freighters all lay together on the rocky bottom like discarded toys. The piers afire, gas mains torched the deserted streets, dense smoke rising from the tank farms and refineries adjoining the coast. The shoreline and Marine Drive were saw-toothed with collapsing multi-story buildings. Hellinikon was remarkably unscathed, but there were no aircraft drawn to the gates, only a twisted few littering the deserted ramp.

Kavouri passed beneath my wing, but there was little I could determine from 8,000 feet. Villas were destroyed or soon to be. I gave thought to the brief moments Nina and I had shared there...our night on the town, the Alstir, her Jaguar abandoned in the garage...memories embedded in my heart. A thermal jolted the U-2 as I turned to the south, the starboard wing rising to afford a hideous glimpse of central Athens. I recoiled, man-handling the controls, appalled by the scene below.

The temples beneath the Acropolis had been reduced to naked stone; the Parthenon's lower reach black with desperate Athenians. One building remained above the five-story level...the Grande Bretagne Hotel...its upper terraces a temporary refuge to the citizens clinging to its walls. Nearby buildings crumbled to the Boulevard of Flowers. Neo-classical edifices were no more; the graceful arches and classic statuary completely destroyed.

Vehicles jammed every outbound roadway...automobiles and buses lay abandoned in the streets; the pavements creviced and blocked by debris, flooded by bursting mains. The late leavers would be afoot; the unbelievers, the looters, the infirm, the helpless...for them, it was too late.

The sea had come to seek them out!

Slowly it returned to the harbor...turning ships, flooding Marine Drive, rising and rising as it came...an awesome mountain of rolling green. Streets disappeared; the massive tide mounted the Grande Bretagne and cleansed its terraces. The Acropolis flooded to the base of the Parthenon. Oily water swept the city, carrying whatever would float...rooftops, wooden buildings, boats, denizens of the streets clinging to the debris like insects riding a nest of weeds.

An overturned freighter spewed oil in its wake as the wave reached up the valley to lick the hills. Great boils of air rose from the submerged buildings; a power station exploded and ignited the maelstrom as I clung to the canopy and stared. Within minutes, the valley had become an extension of the Aegean Sea. The 900-foot rise of Mt. Lycabettus was all that remained of the ancient city; there were no signs of life that I could see as I descended through 6,000. Aside from the reflective glass of vehicles ringing the hills!

I banked to the southeast, counting seconds. The mass of water clung momentarily to the hills, then began its retreat as the force behind it subsided. Slowly at first, then as a raging torrent, sucking its contents like a millrace, claiming the broken ships and whatever remained. On it went, swirling whirlpools of muddy water, escaping the valley with a roar that deafened my ears.

The base of the Acropolis reappeared, shedding sheets of brine, its barren sides washed of those who'd sought its sanctuary. The Grande Bretagne emerged as a crumbled mess of brick and stone. No pattern to the streets...sodden mounds of marble marked the graves of the ancient temples. The city of Athens was a scene of crumbled concrete and twisted steel; a valley of mud and rubble; a valley of death.

I rolled out on 135° and set up a shallow climb to exchange air speed for altitude. I'd lost a thousand feet and the GE was sipping its last. The receding tide swept beneath me, Kea and Kinthos cascading their burden, and on it went until the horrendous sweep met a secondary wave emerging from the abyss. The head-on collision resulted in a catastrophic undercut. An awesome comber rose and toppled, racing outward in a widening perimeter, a 400-foot wall of frothing water far more destructive than the initial rise...pounding, grinding, shredding all that lay before it.

I stared, disbelieving its magnitude as it exploded upon Parox and Naxos, surging on and on, collecting Cape Sounion, thrusting the archipelago, and belting the hapless villages. A third and fourth came, successive waves of diminishing strength, belched from the swirling caldera of Santorini. The Aegean slowly subsided to roll with the prevailing winds; Santorini's wounds washed and cleansed. The worst was done.

An immense horseshoe of sodden pumice was all that remained of the island. A newborn caldera embraced the sea to the west; the islet of Therasia had disappeared. The enormous blast had cleft the 1,600-foot rise of Mt. Haghios to its subterranean base. Phira and Akrotiri lofted to the stratosphere. Thera and the fishing villages on the easterly reaches were buried beneath the burden.

A feast for future archeologists, the stratified remains of the twentieth century awaited the spade with the residue of the Minoan culture.

I stared long at the boiling inferno riding my wing, marveling its incalculable depths. A chunk of real estate the size of Manhattan, *eighty cubic miles of volcanic rock,* had been dispersed to the sky. Its collapsing shell – the paroxysmal explosion – had rocked my wings from 600 miles to the east, radiating instant death with an avalanche of fire, unleashing a tidal wave to curl the Straits of Gibraltar!

History told me that the hills of Crete, which should be on the horizon, were ablaze, its temples leveled, and that the sea had splayed its mountain valleys. Nina! Had they made it safely to the flanks, climbed the tortuous trail to Karphi? What might I find? Was she alive and well? Had she given her blood to a ritualistic knife? Were her uncanny dreams entwined with the deadly offering at Arhannes? Was Deuca the simplistic man Butterfield had led me to believe?

The GE coughed and brought me upright in my seat. The power reading plummeted; the fuel gauges had swallowed the red line. I hit the aux pumps, the engine sputtered and caught momentarily. I agonized the few seconds remaining in the sumps, agonized the coast of Kos. Ankara was out of the question. Amorgos lay beneath me, but its lonely ridges were curled with fire. I had 8,000 feet, a glide ration of 28:1, a 20-mile float when the engine was done, 30 nautical miles until I had Kos under keel. And what might I find?

Leaning forward, I rowed with my arms like a galley slave. Two minutes went by and the GE continued to whine. The hazy outline of Kos emerged in the distance; a windswept column of smoke identified Astapelia to the south. I eased the throttle to wring the last ounce of fuel from the tanks, warning lights ablaze on the panel. The turbo jet coughed and tendered its resignation then!

An abrupt silence descended the cockpit as the turbine spooled down; then, the soft whispering airflow from our long, tapered wings, the GPS guidance system clicking obediently by my side. Airspeed dropped rapidly. I rolled the tab to stretch precious knots; a man alone with his steed, a mile above the tumultuous sea.

I canceled the systems to conserve battery power, keying the Z-band military channel. A crackle of static sounded...a muffled voice from some faraway place, perhaps the flight deck of a carrier. Another burst of static, then a military jet with a 'mayday' over Malta. No response from AWACS on my third and fourth tries. I was definitely on my own!

We slipped quietly through 3,000 feet. The island continued to grow until I'd established its length. The central ridges came to view, the rugged plateau that lay beyond, Antimahia and the winding road leading to the base. The burden of water had eased from the midlands when we glided through 2,500...ten miles, six, then the eroded cliffs of Kamari and Kefalos. Butterfield? Has she heeded Fotis' sirens? Stavos and the Helena?

I uncurled my toes when I had the coast under wing, studying the rise to Antimahia and the broken highway leading from Kardemena. The tailing wind gave me a gentle loft, a blessed 300 feet to clear the final ridge, then a downdraft to combat when the rocky spine reached for our starboard wing. Antimahia lay dead head. I banked to the west for a bird's eye view of the base at 1200 feet. The strip was a sea of glistening mud; the ridge had stemmed the secondary wave, but there was damage enough. The tower was gone, terminal buildings reduced to their foundations, the abandoned road grader midway alongside the rutted runway.

I leveled off with the airspeed clinging 105 knots, jettisoned the canopy to peer from the side, and studied the soggy strip minutely when we crossed over at 800 feet. An open area alongside the buckled ramp seemed relatively clear of debris, the offering hazardous and pooled with water. I nodded to myself and banked to bring the ungainly bird around in a continuous approach to the northeast.

The U-2's zero fuel speed was 70 knots, and the tanks were empty. The retracted gear would raise our stall speed a couple of knots, and the near sea level barometric pressure would give us additional float. I gauged the flattening sea beyond Mastiharion; we'd have 10 knots on our nose when we completed our approach, 10 knots to slow us down if we 'bellied' a 60-knot slammer! The remaining question, to belly in and risk the ship, or drop the gear and hope for the best? I opted for the latter, extending the bicycle gear last second, switching off our battery power and tightening my harness.

We crossed the threshold nose high at 70 knots; from there on it was up to the U-2's immense rudder to guide us along the debris strewn runway...double action for my part, ailerons and rudder to avoid a calamity. Light of load, the U-2 ballooned; mid-strip passed us by; last second, the ungainly road scraper reaching for our starboard wingtip. Averting this by crossing the controls, the U-2 nose high, she stalled a foot or so above the strip and I slammed her down. The wheels grinding mud until our portside wing skid-touched turf and we came to a mushy ground loop...full stop. Yards short of the end of the strip, the U-2 resting on its wheels and portside wing skid, more or less intact!

CHAPTER 26

ot quite believing we'd made it back, I patted the faithful bird's pitted skin.

She'd taken me far and returned me to the uncertainties that plagued my heart...*silver footed ironies, deciphered in the skies; to trust the soul's invincible surmise!'*...remembered words I'd read long ago.

An unearthly silence prevailed the crackling turbine and its downing blades. I sat for a minute in the cockpit, head reeling, my legs quivering like willow wands from the harrowing splash down and mind-bending shock of what I'd seen. To the east, the vaporous sun was peering defiantly from the Turkish hills, adding its heat to the stifling cockpit and the steaming morass of weeds and dead fish recently torn from the sea. I unbuckled my harness mechanically, bent to lock the controls when the rudder swung gently on its axis, retrieved my helmet and oxygen mask from where they'd fallen beneath my seat.

Of my helmet I had avid interest, but at the moment I was disconcerted by the fetid stink wafting from Gunnar's enclosure, the hideous fix of his sightless eyes when I stood to look astern. A dog howled somewhere nearby. I turned quickly about to focus on the immediate surroundings, conscious of other sounds; a screeching vulture overhead, a siren sounding from the hills twice over – hopefully indicating an all clear. Sounds of diverse meanings, but repulsively close at hand, the gaseous utterings from the corpse in my high riding rear cockpit.

Shuddering, I unfastened my boots, kicking them aside; underwent the tedious fastenings of my pressure suit to savor the cooling air. Sat for a moment with my helmet in my lap, remembering only too well the ear-piercing shriek that had me semi-conscious with my brain about to explode! An innocuous thing when I probed the helmet and it came to my fingers. The size of a quarter,

343

fastened with a strip of adhesive to the inner lining, a deadly thing when released to my ear! A miniaturized amplifier, cleverly set to a cadmium battery, and triggered remotely from Gunnar's pocket of tricks. Not unlike the activator MacDougal had installed to prep the wizard's black box. In a sense, we'd played the same game! The moral issue for whom to decide?

The humidity was unbearable; Santorini's lingering heat upping the high 90s while I struggled from my pressure suit, discarding the thermal underwear when I dropped to the U-2's wing in a pair of soggy shorts and a scivvy shirt. From there down, I was greeted with ankle-deep mud. My intent, the depleted base buildings, the dog trapped in its upper reach whining gratefully when she sighted me testing the creviced ramp.

Our change shed was long gone; the AV truck on its side where the lobby had once been, the truck dribbling fuel to the terminal's littered floors. Why it hadn't flamed was a mystery, the blackened ceiling beams indicating passage of fiery heat. Ever so carefully, I trudged through the shoulder-high remains, examining the wreckage as I went. Sigurdesson's desk, her seismograph lying buried amongst the rubble: a dead cat, a sodden chart from Winner's wall. I probed about with heavy heart, came upon the teenager's folding chair, her limp yellow pad; but no trace of Sigurdesson, no arms or legs protruding from the debris. Where might she be?

I found the van lodged against the security shack, miraculously upright, where MacDougal had seen fit to move it from the lot across the field. A last minute gesture apparently, a thoughtful gift, realizing I'd be in need if I terminated where his instinct reckoned I'd be! The van, axle deep in mud, was no way driveable, but plausibly dry inside when I pried the door. My brief case and khakis atop the seat next to a case of Bud he'd thoughtfully provided, blessed liquid for my dehydrated soul!

I popped a can and drank it down, opened another then set it quickly aside when I gave thought to the whimpering animal. Requiring a desk and chair to reach where she floundered, she came to my arms, her tongue lapping my face. A ragtag mongrel, endowed with Hennessey's taste for potable beverages, we shared a portion of MacDougal's parting gift.

Near to nine o'clock by then, I set my khakis to dry on the van's windowsill; my companion peacefully asleep rear seat. Mindful of the U-2's security, I trudged the further mile to where she lay. The sun a vengeful orb, radiating heat from the weed strewn mud, the lot drawing flies and bloodthirsty mosquitoes, the going unpleasant. Judging from the wreckage and the van's upright status, I determined the onslaught from the sea had been no higher than two meters when it overran the strip. Its driven force something else! The unsheltered lowlands would have had it, of course, but the island's mid spine would have absorbed the worst. My attention drawn again to the circling vulture, and I realized where I'd find Sigurdesson when she had been swept from her desk!

Gagging when I released Gunnar's canopy before he broiled where he sat, I retrieved my parachute pack and tossed it on the wing. Its contents included a survival kit...emergency locator, rations, signal gun, 9mm pistol. The ELT I activated immediately, thinking AWACS had lost our fix; the 9mm I pocketed in my waistband, just in case. Springing the chute, I collected the billowing fabric underarm and made haste to a pile of weeds where the beady-eyed vulture was circling his intent.

Unlike Gunnar, Ingrid's face was not caught with agony. She evidenced a peaceful smile, seemingly relieved; most likely she'd passed away before she was swept from her desk. The ever-present notebook clasped to her chest by a thin white hand, Her wedding band gleamed softly while I murmured a prayer, then covered her gently with my parachute for a shroud. A valiant lady! Her later years had been given to geophysics and her untested theories...now no longer theories; her genius no longer challenged by her peers in the scientific world. Her future given to the equally bright teenager she'd seen fit to subsidize at the University of Stockholm who, I had no doubt, had inherited Ingrid's courage. And, like myself, realized the depth of her soul.

Turning away with the dog at my heels, I gave thought to the matter of security. The U-2 would have been seen when we descended over Kefalos and made our 270° approach to Antimahia; no mistaking, despite its silence while we glided dead stick from the northwest. Its enormous wingspan would be recognizable to the islanders who'd survived in the hills. I anticipated a visit momentarily, assuming word had passed around, hopefully alerting Major Fotis. Lacking a CB, I had no means of contact; the U-2's radios of no use.

Forlorn at first glance, the U-2 was remarkably intact, and would wait its turn until the strip was cleared and a C-17 became available. In the interim, it would appear to be a piece of salvage, its priceless electronics for the taking, redeemable on the black market! Wary of looters with such thoughts, I elected to stand guard with a weather eye on Ingrid's shroud. My orange pressure suit would alert a friendly search party to my presence; I draped it lengthwise on the U-2's needle-like nose. Next, I gathered the remains of my survival pack containing rations and potable water sufficient for several days; the U-2's uplifted wing served as shelter from the blazing sun. The steamy morass firming to hard-packed sediment by then; endless swarms of flies were drawn to the rotting fish, although a whiff from my kit took care of that! The pack also contained packages of Iranian and Turkmenistani notes, silken maps of like areas, and a packet of South African Krugerrands...trading material for the beleaguered! Last, it held a pair of cyanide tablets (why two?) and a miniature brandy. But no biscuits for my hungry dog!

Promptly at eleven, I beeped my emergency locator again, but there was no response: AWACS would have the blip onscreen and I'd worry it out till nightfall, but what then? Attempt to liberate the van and its tempting reclining seats?

It was high noon when I sighted the first of my visitors...curious children, filthy and tattered from venturing the nearby fields. Smiling and waving, approaching ever closer, one with an unlikely camera, another responding in reasonable English when I warned them to stay clear of the U-2.

"You fly the big bird?" the boy questioned. I nodded to that, asked if he'd seen Major Fotis.

"Papa say Fotis big man," he replied.

"Fotis nearby?" The boy shrugged; apparently he didn't know.

"Dead man give plenty stink," he said, pointing to Gunnar's hatch. The others obviously agreed, pinching their noses as they drifted away, pausing to prod Ingrid's shroud. A flare from the signal gun scattered the lot, but then the flare was highly visible, and a half-hour later I had another visitation...a pair of barrel-chested locals in tandem aboard a high-wheeled tractor. One I recognized as a recently discharged mechanic.

They maintained a respectful 20 meters apart from the U-2 when they noticed the 9mm in my belt. Circling in low gear, their attention was given to the van. They departed quickly when I offloaded another flare.

"Come night time, we take you out!" the mechanic promised, cursing my mongrel, who'd taken a liking to their tires. *Come nightfall I'd be riding forty hours without sleep!* I thought.

My third visit was heartening, a salve to my groggy soul, and strangely reminiscent of a scene from 'Out of Africa'. In a single, ragged line, a hundred meters apart, Fotis unarmed militiamen were descending from the hills, calling to one another, not unlike a line of African game drovers prodding the bush for a kill; the militia prodding the fields for the living and the dead. Their ongoing pattern was possibly a kilometer in length; their intent most likely the cluttered highway leading from Antimahia to Kos. Island wise and methodical, they were screening the hills to where the massive devastation occurred by the sea.

More or less in line, they investigated the commercial terminal and crossed the strip until they came upon my billowing parachute. Determining what lay beneath, they paused to establish a marker flag; they had more in hand, I noticed, when a sergeant approached the U-2. Our conversation was quick and very concise, in fractured English. The sergeant, holding a CB, established contact with Fotis immediately, remarking of the fly-attracting scent from the U-2's rear seat.

Understanding as usual, Fotis allowed he'd observed the U-2 from Pilion, where he was hung up with a broken axle; the roads not yet acceptable when he diverted to Antimahia. Grateful to hear his voice, I gave him a quick rundown, explaining Gunnar's status but not the alleviating circumstances.

"Roger, Major Keith. I've had reason to wonder of this, but mainly you're safe and sound. We directed the militia to check the strip as soon as possible, thinking you may have encountered a mishap."

"Not as yet," I replied, "but the U-2 has expensive hardware and I'd appreciate an armed guard, if possible," I added, realizing he was up to his ass with multiple problems.

"The militia's not armed, Keith, but I'll direct them to establish a presence, realizing what you mean."

I returned the CB transceiver to the sergeant who, nodding to Fotis' instructions, beckoned a pair of militiamen to stand by until Fotis deemed otherwise. Proceeding then, he motioned his troops to continue their westerly sweep, allowing the van and the terminal were to remain untouched.

With a catnap in mind, I sought the comfort of the van's reclining front seat, the guards examining Ingrid's generator whilst I levered my seat full back and fell into a deep, dreamless sleep.

* * * * * *

Awakened somewhat by a dog barking in the distance, I gave immediate thought to Hennessey plunging the surf, tailing a coconut or a scurrying crab? Thinking I'd fallen asleep following our morning swim, curious of my surroundings, I noted the oppressive humidity, the sodden ceiling of whatever I was in? I turned my head to stare, disbelieving the condition of my seaside cottage, thinking my tenant had gone berserk whilst I was helping Nina sort out her house at Lyford Cay? And looking seaward to locate myself, I spied a white sail in the muddy morass, and came instantly wide-awake! Realizing it was the U-2's high-standing white rudder, no less!

"Lordy, I've slept three or four hours!" I thought, judging from the slant of the sun! The militia men obviously elsewhere, most likely searching for dry spares, having dismantled the generator in part. All the while, the dog continued to bark far side the ramp...and I realized I had yet another oncoming visitor approaching from the northeast! And, reaching for my flare gun, I held in abeyance when I sighted a lone figure astride a donkey in the distance, the donkey laden with blanket rolls fore and aft. The lone rider wearing an unlikely red baseball cap and tattered shorts, the cap shading a freckled face festooned with grime and a square-toothed grin!

"Butterfield?" I stammered. My heart pounding while I spilled from the van, not quite ready to believe.

Her blanket roll fell to the ground when I helped her down; a flood of tears flooding her cheeks when she pressed her grimy face to my chest. Completely shaken, I held her tightly, my fingers caught in her mop of hair. She'd come from nowhere, like the breath of spring...the warmth of her yielding body easing the trauma of days on end!

Wondering at my reaction, my thoughts flitted immediately to Nina. Why my overwhelming desire to hold this tiny girl close to my heart? Nina and I had shared like moments; was I overreacting to events? Was my heart telling me something I was reluctant to accept?

"I came to be with you, knowing you would need me," Lesleigh murmured, seemingly attuned to my thoughts. "I sensed it at Akrotiri, in your eyes when Nina wandered to the dig, then again when we said goodbye, realizing you were distraught, in need of someone to know your heart!"

There we were, two lonely creatures clinging together in times of stress. Not altogether alone; the donkey brayed to be fed, not content with Butterfield's hat. In the distance, the militia cordoned the U-2 with yellow warning tape, seemingly knowing who she was and from whence she'd come.

I made no mention of Gunnar while Butterfield unfolded a sheaf of hay from her blanket roll. She'd braved the catastrophe uncomplaining, observed sufficient for her lifetime, clueing me in while the donkey munched contentedly on a toss of hay.

Lesleigh allowed she'd taken shelter in a stone cottage located on a hill with a view of Cape Loannis; the owners an elderly couple who maintained a herd of goats. Fotis had visited recently, seeing fit to equip the area with an internet of CBs, expecting others would take refuge from the low-lying coasts within hours of Athens' last warnings; the lot had streamed to the hills about the time I rotated from Antimahia.

"I watched from the roadside until the U-2 disappeared in the east, Keith," she said. "Such a lovely sight, its long white wings caught by the glow of the setting sun. Although I feared for you, knowing you would be flying throughout the night. Towards evening, I began to wonder why the sun had yet to set. The sky was a brilliant orange, and I hurried on as best I could, realizing the volcano was verging an explosion, the sky reflecting a raging inferno. And then Fotis' sirens began to wail! Stupid of me to tarry by the roadside, but you are not to press my reasoning, Keith, else I shall come to tears!" I nodded dumbly, gripping her freckled hand firmly, not questioning her guts or determination.

"Once to the cottage, I remembered Dr. Sigurdesson's prediction," Butterfield furthered, her voice faltering to a whisper. "Her warnings of a super-heated fireball following a Plinian explosion. Realizing it was indeed about to be, I convinced the elderly couple to find us refuge beneath an outcropping in the lee of their ridge. There we spent the night, Keith, among the others with their animals. It was pastoral in a sense, with the moon soon overhead, but never forgetting the terrible sky. The animals were as deathly frightened as we were; their instinctive sense knowing something was amiss. I prayed for you, Keith, realizing the worst was yet to come; also for Dr. Sigurdesson, having heard she had refused to leave her post."

"I found her over yonder," I said, pointing to my parachute atop the clutter of weeds.

"Oh no! God in heaven...I wondered where she might be! Would she have suffered, Keith? The ghastly fire came so quickly!"

"She died peacefully, Lesleigh, most likely sheltered by her desk...minutes after the blast. Suffocated without knowing, probably, and that's the way she'd have it; her prediction was a reality before she passed away."

"God bless her soul, Keith! From our shelter, the explosion was a terrible thing to see," Butterfield murmured, pressing her tears to my sleeve. "Shortly after midnight, we were jolted awake by an ungodly tremor; the sky suddenly bright, like the midday sun. Then a horrendous flash of fire had us gagging for air; the shock wave was unbelievable. It was quick to pass, aside from the fires along the coast. We knew there was more to come, a secondary blast minutes later. And, come dawn, the unbelievable devastation along the coast, the sea receding all the while, leaving a clutter of hulks that hadn't seen light for hundreds of years."

"I was over Athens at the time, Lesleigh, the harbor draining to the outer wheel, tankers on their sides in the muck."

"For me, a page of ancient history, Keith. Shades of the Egyptian empire on a like occasion in Minoan times...the fast-draining Sea of Reeds near the terminus of the Nile, the passage of Israeli slaves with the Egyptians in hot pursuit...followed by the returning sea which decimated the Egyptian chariots, leaving the Israelis free to wander thereafter."

Butterfield's description of the massive tsunami was not dissimilar to what I'd seen from the air. The fast-draining Aegean was drawn to the abyss until it overflowed and compounded a mountain of water, racing outward at 600mph to whence it came; the worst of it when the rise met the coasts and exploded a devastating curl upon the cities. Its force reached inland until it spent itself, retreating as a torrent of mud and debris. Ships at sea rode it out with a degree of safety coast-wise, end on end.

At Kos, the refugees had maintained contact via Fotis' CB, Fotis advising them not to stray from the hills. His radar had been demolished by the blast, but he realized the receding sea had reached its apogee.

"It came so quickly, Keith, higher than the horizon. The dreadful mass of murky water inundated the coast, then was upon us as a frothing comber swirling beneath our hill, its lick spilling to the northeast. Surely Antimahia, I thought, when we spied your beautiful aeroplane overhead, as if answering my prayers!

"I burst into tears, knowing you'd returned safely, but where to land?" she furthered. "Fotis pleaded with us not to stray. The sea returned once more, but not nearly as high. When I saw you circling Kefalos somewhat later, I gave heart to your intent. Heart in mouth, love, I made haste to board my donkey, the roads not being passable. So here I am, a frazzle of myself! If you were a gentleman, you would offer me another beer!"

* * * * *

With the heat and humidity becoming increasingly unbearable, vapor rising from the strip inundated with the stench of rotting fish, the van became a haven for the rebounding flies. We set about scrounging what we could from the flattened barrack buildings, myself realizing a 'copter would be unlikely to risk the twilight should it come from a flattop at sea. Of the intent I harbored no doubts. The analyzer's cassettes confirmed the bilateral action of AWACS and T.S.'s B-2s; the U-2 of no less importance.

We recovered the soggy mosquito netting from the remains of Winner's cot, as well as his grubby towels and spent soap. From Beneath Edwards' cot came his long-sleeved shirts and a bottle of Scotch he'd hidden for another event. Fortified, we sallied forth to investigate the shoulder-high catch tank alongside the lieutenant's depleted latrine. The water remarkably fresh, not caught by the tide; Butterfield first up, stripping to the buff. Twirling with glee, she doused her hair when I severed the plastic hose with my knife. Quick to join her, we splashed about like a pair of naked kids beneath a neighbor's hose, until it became evident it would lead to something else.

In the interim, we had a change of guards, the latter arriving in a battered truck from Pilion. There they were, armed and smiling politely, when we emerged from our bath wearing Edwards' shirts, our reservoir thoughtfully corked with a piece of wood. Spreading our clothes to dry atop the van, we battened its windows with mosquito netting and made a meal of sorts from my rations, splitting the brandy (the cyanide tablets long since ground underfoot). We spent the night there, clinging together for security, my thoughts not uncertain at the time. Butterfield, obviously aware, snuggled closely and murmured, "I came to be with you, Keith, knowing you would need me. My heart tells me so, no matter what you say – or what we do!"

Throughout the night the dog slept peacefully alongside the van; the donkey asleep on her haunches, her tail warding the flies. The guards enjoying a smoky fire whilst they finished the last of Edwards' Scotch.

* * * * *

Early dawn was beautiful to behold; the sky a golden hue to the east. The volcano no longer an earthly threat, its carcass reduced to a miniscule drift of vaporish steam. In its wake lay an uncountable loss of lives and the near total destruction of the coastal Aegean. Kos, 120 miles to the east, had been spared the worst. Thanks to Fotis and Ingrid's warnings, the islanders had taken to the hills, but damage to crops and livestock was immeasurable. A tourist haven no more, the capital city would need to be rebuilt. And I dreaded the thought of Athens, where the tsunami had funneled its worst. In Rhodos and Crete in ancient times, the survivors were the shepherds in the hills; the Minoan civilization became a page of legendary history, its temples never rebuilt. Hopefully, in the highlands, Nina was alive and alert.

Such were my thoughts as I joined the guardsmen to share their morning brew. They'd also undergone the ordeal, most likely miles apart from their broods. Butterfield, stirring awake to peer from the van, drawn by the heady aroma of coffee. Appearing in her long-sleeved shirt, toothbrush in hand, she passed us with a canister to replenish from our reservoir. The unmistakable 'flap' of a fast-approaching helicopter next upon us from the east.

351

The Sea Hawk hovered directly overhead, then gracefully settled midway between the van and the U-2, its turbine idling down. The pilot's expertise I recognized immediately; his toothy grin when he discarded his helmet and dropped to the ramp.

"Seems like I've been here before," Whitehead commented, extending his ebony hand. "Top brass wanted us to come get you last night, but I was dead beat and figured you'd make out. Like we had word from Riyadh you'd slicked her in, fat ass and happy. They're also wantin' an appraisal of the strip. Maybe yon grader can be put to work so's they can land a C-17."

"Anything else?" Whitehead nodded.

"Yeah, man! Admiral said Riyadh's wantin' something you know about; didn't say what, but they want it hush hush! I'm also instructed to fly you directly to our flattop, Keithy, orders of General O'Brien."

A team of medics were fast out with a stretcher and body bag, another underarm when I pointed to Ingrid's shroud. The Commander jotted her identity on his tally pad while I explained the circumstances. Whitehead grinning in disbelief when Lesleigh appeared with her toothbrush and a mug of the guardsmen's brew.

"Reckon we met before, and I'm grateful for the coffee, ma'am! Week or so back, hey? You came along from Akrotiri with your team of archeologists, hey?"

Whitehead's crew chief joined us with a portable VHF radio transceiver. The VHF module intended for the militia to establish communications with the C-17. They'd also brought along rations and medical supplies from the carrier's stores, together with a white Red Cross tent, identifiable from the air. The team of medics intended to stay on as a gesture of goodwill. In the interim, they'd secured Sigurdesson aboard the idling 'copter.

Butterfield stared in disbelief when they popped Gunnar's hatch.

"God in heaven!" she gasped. "I never realized you had someone back seat!"

"My observer, Lesleigh. Dr. Gunnar suffered a heart attack over Iran; died on the way back."

"Good Lord, Keith! Don't tell me he's been there all night!"

"Where else? Short of activating his ejection seat!"

"You do have a weird sense of humor!"

"Name of the game," Whitehead commented. "Less said the better. I heard tell Keith had a shitty trip and was lucky to make it back!"

Less said the better! Appropriate under the circumstances, I thought, although Butterfield was obviously suspicious and I suspected the Commander knew more than he divulged.

Leaving Lesleigh to ponder the situation, we proceeded directly to the U-2; Whitehead's crew chief bringing his tool kit. The tools were unnecessary, however. With MacDougal's instructions in mind, we rounded the grounded portside wing. The extended portion available to the chief's knowledgeable hand, its upper inspection plate concealing the wizard's black box and spent cassettes. The lot deposited immediately into a high-priority satchel bag the chief retrieved from the Sea Hawk.

"Hadn't figured we'd be on a question and answer session," Whitehead commented when I made certain the satchel was secured with his copilot, a noncommittal Marine lieutenant colonel, his ears bent to the communications console, obviously anxious to be off!

"'Battle-ass' is pissed off 'cause the C.O. insists I do the flyin'," Whitehead commented while we returned to the van. "He knows I'm due my fourth stripe and no longer a minority with his smartass marines! Once we set up tent, we're out of here, man. The fleet's flank speed for Athens and we've a mess on our hands!"

"So where was the fleet when the shit hit the fan?"

"Strung out on red alert, 240 nautical miles northwest of Crete...holding 20° longitude and 36° latitude, with our skipper sweatin' bricks! Man, what a blast, Keithy! Sky lit up like Fourth of July night; the shock wave hit us broadside before we could heel to the east. Lost a pair of F-14s over-side! Next minute, the sea was drawin' our flattop to the maelstrom, and we were sleddin' downhill with our engines full reverse! Then comes the heavy green and we're riding the swell full turn, like hangin' ten at Malibu Beach! Never seen the like of it, but come morning the fleet's still together and the water's dead calm. Like it never happened, except we were ankle deep in pumice and the sea's pasty white like a can of mushroom soup."

"Fatalities?"

"Not aboard our flattop, but the fleet has twenty unaccounted for, and we've been pullin' bodies since yesterday afternoon. Couple more this morning," the Commander added, pointing to a pair of rigid body bags stacked inside the cavernous Sea Hawk, plus Gunnar and Sigurdesson. A guardsman tugged my sleeve and handed me his CB.

"Fotis?" I questioned. The guardsman nodded.

"Want helicopter to wait, Mister Slater."

Fotis was aboard a lorry with a child in need of immediate surgery, possibly a half-hour out, depending on the road to Antimahia. He also had word from

Katrina saying Cleo was safe; possibly word of the Helena, which he'd yet to confirm!

True to his word, Fotis pulled in a half-hour later, mother and child front sear in the dilapidated lorry. The child's head swathed in bandages, the mother staring fretfully at the enormous helicopter; Fotis an authoritative presence despite his gaunt and weary appearance, sporting three days beard stubble and sweat-drenched khakis. The guardsmen respectfully saluted when he leapt from the truck and grasped my hand.

"Seeing is believing, Keithy! You're a sight for anxious eyes!" he said, turning quickly to Commander Whitehead to press his immediate needs.

"We've a child with serious head injuries, Commander. At the moment, we haven't the means for delicate surgery, nor source of medication, which we believe, is available aboard your Sixth Fleet carrier. I have come to plead with you, sir, a child's life in the offing!"

Whitehead reacted immediately, summoning his medics to attend the child and decide if the youngster was transportable in his mother's care. The young-ster, a boy of perhaps six, was semi-conscious, a brown eye peering from his bloodstained bandages. The Commander in a quandary when the medics insisted they accompany the child during the two hour flight. Whitehead worked it out, his appraisal of Fotis apparent when he said he'd take the lot aboard, leaving the U-2's security in the Major's hands! The two becoming friends while they went on to inspect the tent and its measure of supplies. Fotis was near tears, the Commander's ebony face expressing like emotions.

"Man, it takes a pair of honest hearts to trust what it's all about," he said. "I've been hearin' what you've done, Major. Now I'm believin' all I heard!"

I stood by for a private word with Fotis while they littered the youngster to the Sea Hawk, followed by his mother. The lieutenant colonel studied his watch; the crew chief checking weights and balances with- his remaining fuel. Butterfield eyed me quietly, her blanket roll underarm, when Fotis drew me aside.

"Katrina confirm word from Cape Loannis, Keith. Say folk sight Helena's sail fetching Paraskevia, early morning. Come from northeast, with plenty fishing craft…trusting Captain Stavos' ways!"

"Thank God! I've been sweating the old man! Figured he'd ride it out! Popped a sail? Means he's up and able and downwind to Kefalos!"

"Would appear so, Keith, but I wouldn't trust the roads if that's what you have in mind."

"Double feature, Major. If the old man's agreeable, we'll play the other reel. I've a wild-ass hunch Nina's somewhere in Crete!" Fotis nodded thoughtfully.

"Odd you should say that, Keith. Officially I'll not concur, but old wives' tales often ring true, if you're not offended by local gossip."

"So try my other ear!"

"Old folk come to believe Nina flee to Karphi. Knowing Nina as a child, think maybe she bide ancient legends when Thera came to mess. Seek sanctuary in the hills, not knowing what she do! Why they believe this, who's to say, and you darest repeat! But should you have reason to search Karphi, word not come from me!"

"All aboard!" the Commander shouted, gathering Butterfield in his stride. Moral issues aside, I realized the pangs in my heart then!

"Did you hear me rightly?" Whitehead questioned, pointing to the Sea Hawk. We had an immediate confrontation, of course; Lesleigh searching my eyes when I declared my intention to hang in.

"General's orders, Keithy! Don't cause me no problems, man!"

I laid it out the way it was. I'd done my bit for the UN. The shitty part went without saying, knowing the Commander was wise to the action. Lesleigh listening attentively, wide-eyed when I said I intended to search for Nina, the Helena as means of transport, the possibility she might be somewhere in Crete.

"Nina disappeared a couple of days back," I explained, skirting the circumstances as best I could. "So far, without a trace, but lacking communication, no way I can lay down until I know she's okay. T.S. will know what I mean; we hosed it a while back! If not, he can jolly well fuck off! I'm not obliged to obey his orders, and you may quote me verbatim!"

"Mind your language, Keithy! He allowed you had a problem, but calling in from Riyadh, he was spare with words, 'cept to explain what we did! Seein' you made up your mind, and no way I can twist your arm, take pleasure in tellin' him what you said. Knowin' he'll be hard put to holler back!"

Not so Butterfield; her apt ears had caught the drift and she spun about furiously, completely wound up!

"God in heaven, Keith, must I believe what you said? Nina was en route to London when I dropped Dr. Petrie at Olympic! Said she had business with Sotheby's, so how in God's name did she just up and disappear? Crete, no less! Lordy, she was long gone before the catastrophe, when I saw her board the flight to Athens! Dressed prim and proper...first class! Had you thought of contacting Sotheby's, or have you lost your mind?" I had no immediate answer, but Lesleigh was not deterred!

"Now you arrive with a corpse in the back seat, no plausible explanation . . . our airplane all crooked and bent. So don't tell me you had a nice ride! Next,

I find you totally exhausted and suffering with a hungry dog. Implying you landed in this godforsaken mud to search for your wife, not knowing where she may be? Worst of all, the anguish in your eyes, the need for someone to hold close to heart when all was done! True love is not a mysterious and one day you will realize this, Keith! Until then, best we part. I'll let you know where to find me, because – I just know!"

With that, she raced to the Sea hawk, her blanket roll first in, her freckled legs threshing for a foothold while the chief helped her aboard.

"Heavens to Betsy, man! Haven't the foggiest what that was all about, but do what you intend to do, Keithy, man! You did your bit! Your old man come to agreement, I think. Fact we heard he came flashin' by, just to see how you was!"

Whitehead rotated the Sea Hawk, turning overhead to give us a wash of breeze from his blades; they picked up a southeasterly heading and disappeared behind the spine of hills. My heart a piece of mud!

"Lovely girl!" Fotis commented.

I gave serious thought to the van when we pried it from the muck, realizing the roads to Kelosa would be deeply rutted, the van not equipped with four wheel drive! My alternative, Lesleigh's donkey which I'd promised to take in tow . . . more or less following the direct course over the spine of hills, a two to three hour jarring ride? Fotis in total agreement, now that I was equipped with a CB. Myself down to minimal needs, my flying togs and charts long gone with the Commander's chopper. I had my basic survival kit, however . . . my flare gun and sidearm within reach, together with the compass and a half dozen gold Krugerrands I might need along the way.

My attire complete when I gathered the last of Butterfield's hay, rolling it in the blanket we'd shared, strapping it aft. My composite kin to Don Quixote I reckoned, when I mounted the complacent animal, my shoes within inches of the ground! Fotis amused...last minute handing me a canteen of potable water and MacDougal's wide beam light I'd nearly forgot.

"Keep in touch with Katrina and sally forth!" he called out, whilst I allowed the donkey to take the lead, my means of guidance limited to a twist of rope.

* * * * * *

And so it went within an hour of Lesleigh's leaving. The donkey retraced her route until I held her short tether to offer my beloved U-2 a final salute from the brow of the hill! Hopefully to fly her once again, when Lockheed and NASA were acquainted with the conditions she'd survived at the edge of space! The updated GE-118 also a blessing to a future breed in times to come!

And, what with the mongrel tailing alongside, my hopeful landfall was the grove of ancient cedars and tumbled cottage where I'd come ashore...that fateful morning I'd flown to Athens with Willitts and Amalia, God rest her soul! By highway from Antimahia, an hour at the most...but peering from the ridge, the remains were a mass of rubble and fallen trees, impassable by vehicle, or donkey at present time! Myself allowing the animal her cautious detour as a matter of practical sense, although it meant following shepherds' ancient paths, which she seemed to know. Here again, Lesleigh's common sense, since she'd come from Kefalos the self-same way.

Rough going for me, but not for the sure-footed animal on the angled paths. We often stopped for a drink from a rainfall, but the old girl was content to carry on, possibly thoughts of her like in a barnyard somewhere in the hills. And, what with the blazing sun, I had my spare T-shirt draped over my head and shoulders...strictly Ben Hur!

Finally from a hilltop, I sighted the stand of cedars by the sea. The sea seemingly placid, but no longer blue; awash with debris and mud scoured from the northerly shores. No sight of the Helena's sail, however...but I had high hopes for nightfall when I reached Katrina on my CB and she said,

"We've established contact by single side band, not to worry, Keithy! Appears he's full reach by sail, expecting to sight Kefalos by sunset, advising you to stand by with a ready light!"

Gladdening news, but unfortunately the donkey had other thoughts when I hastened her down the hill. Call it a confrontation of sorts...the old girl, wanting to continue her path, would go no further despite a dig to her under parts together with words I'd learned in Grammar school. The mongrel, taking sides, nipped her hindquarters, to the dog's discomfort! The end result, it was I who led our entourage down the hill, the beast, jawing her displeasure, as donkeys are prone to do! There was no certain path, of course. The brambles we managed to skirt, but there were moments I had to rely on my compass, until the stand of cedars came readily to view.

Below us, the roadway leading to Kefalos was pooled with the muddy residue, but appeared to be passable by foot! Her 'nibs', sensing I had it more or less right, laid back her ears and, jawing her tether full length, down the slippery ravine we went! The donkey's forelegs straight forward, her ass for a toboggan, she careened the slope and landed on all fours! Myself...leap, skid, jump...miraculously upright when I splashed beside her, the tether yet in hand!

The stand of cedars appearing at the turn of the road as we wallowed along side by side in ankle deep brine.

"Lordy," I thought, glancing at my watch. 'It was precisely forty-eight hours since I buckled up and rotated from Antimahia! Five unbelievable days since I'd come ashore from the Helena to search for Nina!'

Yards ahead, where I'd waited for MacDougal's jeep. The ancient cedars were forever blighted by the rise of the sea, their skeletons hopefully Captain Stavos' guide posts to where I'd come ashore. No sight of the Helena to seaward as yet. But, turning a trace of the lane, we came on the unexpected, the dog racing before us!

Sheltered by a makeshift tarpaulin on the cottage's foundations, an old man and his wife, a gaggle of grandchildren, grimy like myself, together with a bevy of goats they'd apparently rescued from high water, were obviously set for the night, a smoky fire burning nearby. Myself apprehensive, but unlike my stand-off with the tractor at Antimahia, we were greeted with open arms; the children delighted at the sight of the friendly mongrel, not caring from whence he'd come!

The old lady, hand on hip, studied our approach...my unlikely appearance, with a flickering grin! Turning to point at a chicken she'd prepared on the spit, when I addressed her in faulty Greek.

"Most welcome to join us for supper!" she replied in fluent English. The old man, noting my thatch of blond hair, in apparent agreement. His grasp of English understated but liberally spiced with Greek.

"Americano, hey? Maybe same fella fly big sail plane?"

"I'm a friend of Major Fotis," I asided guardedly. The old man grinned and leapt forward to grasp my hand!

"Fotis say you big hero, 'Kelly Slaver'! Athens radio also say same damn thing! God bless you, sir...not for Fotis and UN, plenty many people never come see another day!"

Out came a bottle of Ouzo, the old man extracting my promise to relate my story to his wide-eyed siblings. The old lady apt of ear, allowing they were long retired from Civil Service, tending the family olive groves near by Kefalos, as their ancestors had! Their son and daughter-in-law intending to practice medicine at the University of Hippocrates; last heard, okay! Myself noting they were equipped with Fotis' CB, thoughtfully out of reach of the children and inquisitive goats.

Fortified by the Ouzo, striving to get my surname straight, all the time keeping an eye to seaward, it was indeed a pleasure to describe the joy of flying an aeroplane, as my Dad had often done when I was near about their age. The oldster interpreting from time to time, although my audience seemingly understood my gestures whilst I explained the workings of stick and rudder, the use of ailerons to bank gracefully like a bird, once aloft. Extending my arms to emulate the U-2, which they'd apparently seen when I circled to land at Antimahia. And, utilizing the smoky fire for the volcano, I described the force of its updraft that had the U-2 at ends fifteen kilometers in the sky! Admitting I was totally frightened when I called in to Athens, advising of what I'd seen!

"Big boom come next?" the eldest of the three questioned, apparently a young girl, judging from her braids.

"Flash in the sky come later when we were fast asleep!" the old man asided, sparing me a description of the awesome aftermath I'd witnessed come early morning. His siblings sheltered in the lee of the ridge when the onslaught bridged the island of Kos, the mounting green seas falling short of the caves where the ancient had fled!

End of my story then, not wanting to frighten the children with the gruesome scene I'd witnessed of Athens...of which they'd learn in due time. Their experiences vivid in mind later day, when they'd give note to the pages of ancient history! Their homeland semi-submerged by the sea, the capital city no more; but thanks to major Fotis, they'd come out of it lightly, my part long forgotten, as it should be. Twilight by then, the children scattering for the beach to look out for the Helena at the old man's bidding. Myself with an eye to the northeast, noting a mast-topping light on the distant horizon?

The old couple in confidence while I described the unholy scene I'd witnessed of Athens...allowing my decision to land at Antimahia had to do with the intention of searching for my wife in the high lands of Crete. Captain Stavos and the Helena, my only option and means to that end!

The clatter of a spoon on a pan sufficing to bring the group together. The donkey savaging the last of Lesleigh's hay whilst we shared the chicken Negresco from the spit, rice pilaf, a heady helping of field vegetables, a round of baker's bread and a round of local wine, served over shoulder from a goatskin bladder. Altogether, the finest meal I'd experienced since I'd supped with Nina and Auntie Maris at Kavouri! Blessed the ongoing conversation with the intelligent pair whilst we shared the last of the Ouzo and discussed our futures, in lieu of the unworldly events. The children, noting the green and red running lights of a vessel approaching from the seaward, disengaging to run come see!

"Big boat, Keithy Slaver!" the young girl called back.

And there the Helena lay, silhouetted by the sunset, her masthead lights ablaze...idling cautiously under power to where she could drop anchor, her sails

359

unfurled and flapping uselessly in the listless breeze. Noting the splash of the forward anchor, I raced to the beach, arcing a 'greenie' from my flare gun to the children's delight; Stavos responding with a bull horn from the bridge.

"That be you, Keeth?" I beamed MacDougal's torch light in reply, continuing the beam from the bridge aft, noticing the motor skiff was no longer on its davits; the inflatable raft also appeared to be missing when I swept the beam forward.

"Take plenty heavy sea!" Stavos shouted. "No way to fetch you, Keeth!" Meaning I was in for a 300 yard swim, which I thought I could manage.

Flashing a 'dit-dah-dit', I assessed the situation, near to total darkness by then. First, Lesleigh's donkey, which the old man remedied, allowing he knew where she came from and would gladly take her in tow. Also the dog, since the mongrel was peaceful with the goats, to the children's further delight! Expressing my gratitude for their forbearance and hospitality, I offered the old lady a pair of gold Krugerrands from my trove, one of which she accepted, saying they'd keep the other as a souvenir of the occasion and, "God bless you, Keithy Slater!" Lesleigh's blanket roll and the remainder of my rations she accepted with pleasure.

My personal belongings, inclusive of passport, UN credentials and toilet kit, together with the Krugerrands and usable currency, I inserted in the pockets of my survival pack, which was fortunately watertight and equipped with back straps, although its buoyancy was uncertain for my 300 yard swim. The 9mm hand gun last in, realizing I might need it along the way. Not so the flare gun, however, knowing the Helena was so equipped. Fotis' CB another matter. The old man suggesting I take it along, what with Captain Stavos relying on his bull horn at the moment!

Not certain the CB would survive my swim, I called in to Katrina last minute, however. The response, a busy signal and multi voices calling in. Realizing Stavos had use of his single side band, I handed the CB and MacDougal's flashlight to the old man. I stripped to my shorts and scivvy shirt, the survival pack strapped to my back, my pockets emptied of all except for a jack knife and a plastic 'ident' card I discovered rear pocket and let be.

And so we proceeded to the beach, the children and the dog scampering ahead, the old man flashing MacDougal's wide beam behind us, myself not unlike a character from Jules Verne, treading the shallows to the sea. Waist high in the waters when I waved adieu to the collective family, a side stroke my means to gain the Helena, the survival pack popping up to afford additional flotation!

Factually, it wasn't all that difficult when I gained the Helena's stern ladder and grasped Stavos' reaching hand. The old salt on to his bull horn, advising the group he had the situation 'okay'! The old man standing beachside blinked his understanding, his group dispersing to the residue of their fire.

What with the Helena firmly at anchor, the old salt bent and weary from his sleepless days and nights at the helm, we agreed to discuss past and future matters come morning. Myself intent for the aft state room, where Nina and I had spent our last night together. Stavos nodding wordlessly from his sack on the bridge, whilst I tossed the sodden knapsack aside and, downing the aft stairs, stripped to the buff, to sprawl headlong on the bed, mentally and physically spent. My long journey at questionable ends.

Fitful dreams of Nina, of course. Her clutter of pillows, the lingering scent of her lavender, ever present when I turned my head from one pillow to the next, the bloated moon peering from the transom, sot to other thoughts; and, to echo Homer, 'Darkness came to rest on the quieting sea.'

* * * * * *

Dawn, blessed dawn flooded the windows with its golden hue. This and the aroma of freshly brewed coffee drew me awake; my eyes, casting about the familiar cabin, settling on Nina's neatly hung dresses, her shoes tidied alongside her vanity case, which she'd apparently left in her haste. Heartrending thoughts, but nevertheless, the beginnings of a new day. Sabbath Sunday, judging from the clang of makeshift church bells from Kefalos, the tower ost likely reduced to rubble by the flood. The locals, dressed in their Sunday best, would be flocking to the Orthodox service with thankful prayers for their deliverance from the catastrophe. Myself offering a silent prayer to parts unknown.

My benefactors ashore were obviously gone before daybreak, I noted when I joined Stavos on the bridge; his eyes moist with tears when we compared notes. The Helena's skiff had been torn from its davits by the raging sea; the radar scope gone from the forward mast, indicating the Helena had taken the heavy green broadside, flooding the diesels to where he lost power. All of this while he endured the crest single handed with jury sails, splicing the mainstays with his stern and bow lines to save the masts. Fortunately, he'd managed to snag the line of a semi-submerged fishing skiff and tied it astern as a sea anchor when he bent with the winds. The craft yet on line nearby, I noted, a plausible pump job and buckets of sweat!

Most of the damage occurring when the rising sea inundated the shores of Turkey and returned as a cresting surge that had the Helena on her ends! The waters stabilizing near about the time he spied the U-2 in the catching rays of early dawn.

"First not believe high tiny speck from the east be the U-2, Keeth! Old man plenty busy then, but later I see your big white bird when she come low from the west and make long turn over Kos! Make haste then to add sail and steer for Kefalos, knowing it be you!" Fortunately, he'd kept in touch with Katrina by single side band, and here we were once again...three days to the hour since I'd slipped ashore to catch Olympic, the old man knowing why. Omitting the bloody confrontation at Hellinikon, I described what I'd discovered at Kavouri the self-same day. Nina's handbag and Uncle's revolver, noting there was one spent cartridge, the bag reeking of cordite, the residue on one's hand? Leaving me no choice but to swim offshore and secret the lot, hopefully for evermore!

"Come then believe Neenie shoot Metexas dead and flee to Kavouri with 'blank out mind', not knowing what she do?"

I elaborated on that, noting she'd tossed her handbag seaside with no apparent thought; next searched the villa and cabana for her childhood toys in a semi-conscious state of mind, most likely confused by the lack of familiar furniture in the abandoned villa, darkness on to her by then. Like the night at Arhannes, when her Daddy found her wandering the decks of the Helena in a walking nightmare! Furthering, I added comment of the cook's sighting a 'strange craft' loitering offshore the previous day. Myself on to the awesome truth of Nina's footprints leading to the seaside ledge, but not returning?

"Cook mention same craft when she talk with Cleo, Day before Neenie come to Athens and disappear, Keeth! Cleo think maybe same craft belong to 'strange lad' who appear at Arhannes when Neenie young girl. Maybe see Neenie picture in family gathering at Kavouri, and sail to come look see!"

Thunderous thoughts for my part...the ironic circumstances of the newspaper clipping attached to Deuca's easel when he painted Nina's likeness to the frescoes at Akrotiri; his craven face watching from the shadows later days, when she alighted from the Sea hawk, seemingly drawn to the ancient digs when the tremor occurred and we ran to fetch her. Lesleugh's voice sounding beside me: 'Deuca came to us from the highlands of Crete...his boat lies at anchor in the cove!' The boat, when we flew overhead, a double-ender rigged with a lanteen sail, the source of my recurring dreams!

Be it conjecture, or in terms of the occult, the make up made sense. If Deuca was drawn to Kavouri by his image of Nina, he would have found a tall distraught young lady, with shoulder-length hair, standing at the water's edge in the dark of night, obviously alone. Possibly he called out when she was yet on

362

the verandah, noting she was frightened by the rumbling volcano on the horizon. What else but to take her aboard and sail for his homelands? As would I, given to like conditions...twelve hours too late, the deed already done.

Crete in mind all the while, I questioned Stavos if they'd had time to reach its lee before Santorini let loose its super-heated volley of suffocating fire.

"Tend to believe so, Keeth...three days sailing would have them shield by high mountains, the deluge next worry! But wise to what was to come, most certain then make haste for high lands...and there we find people who would know and see! Helena ready and able once we fix diesel engines and aft stays, Keeth! Maybe two day sail. Reply next question, my son! Old man think it wise invite Auntie Cleo aboard Helena and come help search for Neenie! Cleo have smart head, Keeth! Understand Neenie's 'strange ways', Nicholas many time say."

Not much for monologue, Stavos said all that need be said betwixt his second cup of coffee. Cleo's presence a foregone conclusion if she was willing, but where and how to pick her up? The roads to Kos impassable, the status of the harbor should we lay in with the Helena?

Fortunately, Fotis' tent city was within reach of Stavos cell-phone with the clarity of early morning; the incessant static from the volcano's last throes at low ebb. Katrina on the horn first try!

"Read you loud and clear, Keithy! In fact, we received your input on single side band last night and advised Cleo you were aboard the Helena with Captain Stavos.

"Now then," she went on when I popped the next question, "at the moment we have transport to the city, but the city itself is a mass of rubble, the Crusaders' fort no more. The concrete pier appears to be firm, however...no water, electricity or fuel, of course. Advise your intentions, Keithy. If you plan to tie in, you'll be the first vessel to arrive, and we'll bring out the big brass band!" I held her on the line while I queried Stavos, relaying what she'd said.

"Take couple hour fix stays and prime diesel engines, Keeth! Say we hope reach city before sunset...not want to founder in channel with no harbor lights to find way." All of which I relayed to Katrina, allowing we intended to set sail for Crete come morning! Would she advise Auntie Cleo the aft stateroom was ready!

"Intend to search for Nina, Keithy? I can read between the lines!" Altogether in terms of close family, I thought, when I clicked off and sized what we had yet to do.

Restarting the diesels was a lost cause for my part, realizing they had to be primed and the cylinders heated with a blowtorch, Stavos more apt than I. But splitting our chores, I refastened the stays so that we'd have serviceable bow and stern lines when we tied in at the pier. The fisherman's dory came next, should we ground or swamp unexpectedly. The inflatable raft long gone, the outboard engine in the forward locker, fortunately. Indeed, with a manual bilge pump, I managed to bring the dory reasonably afloat! The chattering diesels music to my ears when I drew the dory astern and fixed its lines full length.

Next chore, we tested the Helena's fuel tanks with a measuring stick, Stavos – like myself - not trusting the gauges! The tanks reasonably full, due to the old man's savvy use of the sails, like myself with the U-2. Also, no indication of water bedded in the tanks when he withdrew the stick to test for salinity. Indeed, with the throttles near idle, jury sails fixed fore and aft, we were en route to the channel by high noon. Stavos at the helm, myself on to the sails when we caught a helping breeze, all the while watching for the flotsam we encountered along the way. The channel between Turkey and Kos clear of shipping; most likely so for weeks to come.

And cautiously we rounded the horn, with no markers to guide us, until we came full view of the decimated harbor and dropped sails. The city reduced to rubble, as Katrina had said. The Crusaders' fort on to its ancient history...the Greco-Roman columns ravaged by the Crusaders glistening in the sun; of note, the vestige of a street leading uphill to Fotis' tent city had been cleared recently by a bulldozer.

"Plenty many people come look for belongings!" Stavos asided. True, but there were no red marker flags indicating the dead; Fotis' warnings obviously effective when Sigurdesson called out her last!

Our arrival was also apparent, judging from the crowd rushing to the harbor when Stavos blasted the Helena's horn. The militia quick to cordon them off, fortunately, whilst the old man maneuvered the motor sailer alongside with his diesels. Myself forward with the bow line, hoping to lasso a cleat, when I spied a ready hand the militia had seen fit to let through! Stavos immediately shouting to his former deckhand in Greek, obviously pleased no end, whilst I raced aft to cast out stern line to the lad. Once we had the spring lines in place, Stavos quit the bridge to unfold our gangplank to the pier; the lad first aboard, clasping the old man with tears in his eyes, his wife and family apparently okay.

But that wasn't the last of it, however. Horns blasting in unison, we were greeted by the sight of Fotis' jeep, top unfolded, Auntie Cleo resplendent rear seat, her parasol full sprung, followed by like ladies with gifts for the Helena. The militia dropped their cordon to allow the lot to stream to the pier.

364

The Greeks love to party; the Helena's tall standing masts the occasion...the fleet of visiting yachts no longer tied in, the bistro across the way washed to the hills! Music and moussaka aplenty, however, musicians strumming the balalaika while they came aboard to share what they had, and the last of the Helena's excellent Santorini white wine.

With naught but hand torches to guide them when night fell, the group dispersed reluctantly to the hills; Fotis, Katrina and Cleo's ladies last down the gangway. Fotis and I confiding privately with Cleo when I tendered Nina's passport she'd forgotten to take along. No way she'd journeyed to Paris, Cleo's last hope. The old gal a bit unsteady, but clear of mind when I led her to the starboard stateroom and allowed what we were about, come early morning.

And came the rosy hue of dawn in the eastern sky...Stavos complacent with his new found deckhand, Cleo yet asleep, we raised quiet sail and cast off from the pier to catch a fetching breeze, Stavos at the helm. Our GPS heading coupled to the autopilot, knowing where we were bound.

* * * * * *

THE FINALE

We had indication of their passing when we anchored off Lebana and questioned a fisherman casting his net from the beach at early dawn. He remembered it well: a strange craft approaching from the east on the eve of the catastrophe, pathing the moon. A solitary steersman tended its long reaching sweep as it disappeared in the darkness toward the village of Lasaia.

And there we met a villager combing the ruins, the first to try the venture since the deluge washed the hills. He spoke of a red sail furled at the mast, of a strange craft at loose anchor on the morning of the catastrophe; it lay at anchor beyond a rounded rock that bore inscriptions from the past. He seldom went there; it was 'the place of ghosts', he said. He spoke of a path that led from the place, a faint path that skirted the road to Pombia and went beyond. To where, he did not know.

It was at Pombia that we came upon an old man, a stubborn old man who had stayed when the wave entered his valley.

"They passed close to my cottage," he said. Deuca was known to him: a 'painter of walls', who sometimes came from the mountains for salt and oil; who sometimes sailed from 'the place of ghosts' in a craft with a crimson sail. To where, he didn't know; when he returned, he returned by night and followed the path that skirted the road.

"Was it there you saw him, on the eve of the catastrophe? Was there a woman dressed in white?"

"Possibly," he said, but there were others who sometimes used the path, and his eyes were very tired.

An old woman who lived by her window, an old woman dressed in black, described Deuca's companion.

"She was tall and beautiful, as I once was myself. She had lovely green eyes and wore a robe embroidered at its claspings with a design from the ancient vases – and little else from what I could see. Strange people, those who live in the valley beyond Karphi. Would you have tobacco? My pipe is empty," she said.

A wrinkled shepherd had seen them in the highlands, following a path beyond Kerveri where the road came to an end.

"The path follows a mountain stream," he said. "Sometimes I tend my flock in its grasses. It was late morning, the morning of the catastrophe, when I saw them in the distance. Then they turned to follow another path, a path that leads to a misted ridge beneath the 'nail', past a stone escarpment bearing very old inscriptions in the Greek alphabet and in the Greek fashion, but not in the Greek language...the language of the palaces, it's said. This I have not seen since I was a very young boy."

A young boy had seen them, a tall young boy with hazel eyes unlike the Cretans in the valley below, Anatolian in stature. He was guiding his sheep from the trail when we came before him.

"Deuca and his woman were resting when the sky exploded," he said. "Deuca knew it was to happen; he told me to scatter my flock to the west and wait in the shadow of the 'rock' until it was done. Deuca is my cousin by my mother's father," he added. "He is a good man. Sometimes he brings me books from other lands; it is only recently that I learned to speak the Greek language. Sometimes I go to Kerveri to buy sweets. Once I was inside their school; they thought I was odd because I hold my nose. They stink of fish," he said. "My, what a lovely knife! May I have purchase? I have earned many drachmas tending our goats."

He pointed to the trail that wound beyond his village, beyond the escarpment with inscriptions his grandfather had said were written in the language of his forefathers, the language of the palaces, from whence they came. The palace of the 'bulls', the temples of Knossos and Arhannes, where their ancestors lay at rest. Of that he knew.

"And beyond the 'rock' you will come upon a valley, some five kilometers to the west. You will find Deuca's cottage at its end. But the light is fading, and the old lady riding the donkey seems tired of eye. Best rest the night in my village; you are most welcome. We have excellent wine and cheese. My father would be happy to talk of other places. I shall lead you there once I settle my flock; they seem frightened of the old sailor who wears no shoes."

On the morning of the seventh day, we reached the escarpment and saw the inscription cleft on its oxidized face, deeply cut, eroded by time. It was a Rosetta-type stone, two thousand years old, from when the Minoans' ancestors fled to Karphi, written in a language that preceded time; thoughtlessly carved beneath the inscriptions was *J.B.D. 1884.*

We single filed the rocky trail that led to the valley beyond, a lush green valley divided by a gurgling stream. The stream's source was a spring near a tiny whitewashed cottage with bound straw for its roof. A curl of smoke rose from its chimney. My heart quickened and Cleo shaded her eyes. The donkey brayed softly and balked. He would go no further; the grass was green and sweet to his nose. I helped Cleo from her saddle and took her hand, Stavos staying behind. We walked the knotted grass, came upon a tiny bridge, and crossed the gurgling stream. And when we were yards apart from the cottage, I called Nina's name.

Deuca came first to the doorway, blinking from the sunlight. When his eerie eyes fixed to mine, there was instant recognition, a flicker of knowledge. He spoke soft words to his side, to Nina as she emerged from the shadows, smiling, bowing, happiness written on her face; her long black hair white at her forehead, and gathered at her neck with a length of twine.

Cleo spoke softly in Greek, calling Nina's bedding name, as she had when she was a child. I tensed; there was no recognition, none at all. She shook her head and continued to smile; then Deuca spoke words I understood.

"Her name is Pyrrha," he said. "She is not of your kind. She has come with me to be my wife. It is best you leave or you'll destroy all that is before."

My shoulders tensed; I stepped forward and Deuca backed into the shadows. Nina's eyes widened and she cringed by his side. Cleo caught my arm and stepped between.

"You mustn't, Keith. He is but a simple man who harks from the past."

"Nina's my wife, damnit! Let's see who's the painter of walls!"

Deuca faded into the shadows as I bounded the steps. Cleo caught my waist and we came to a tangle inside the doorway, Cleo clinging to my belt when I fell to my knees. Pleading with her eyes, she pointed to Nina cowering by the hearth.

"Let them be, Keith! She's deathly frightened, do you not understand?"

I tested my feet and adjusted my sight to the dimly lit interior, to the low flame burning from the hearth, to the steaming kettle on a grid work of stone. Deuca disappeared through a low-hung doorway to other parts. Nina huddled against the chimney, agonizing my intention. Seemingly bewildered, arms clasped to her breasts, she bowed from the waist when I lowered my eyes.

Cleo spoke gently in Greek, but the response was the same. Nina replied with her lips, as if the words were strange to her ears. She ventured a frightened smile and glided to a wooden table laid with earthenware and a vase of wine. I hesitated further steps. A cold awareness entered my heart when I realized what she was about.

"If you love her, Keith, you must let her be," Cleo whispered. "She's confused. She's trying, don't you see?" I turned to face the sunlight, raising my eyes to the stony face of Karphi, to the clearing mists trailing from the escarpment. Would she recoil from my arms when fast asleep, slip again to her mysterious dreams when thunder echoed from the sea? Had I the right?

The fire was gone from her eyes. Gone was the mischievous tilt of her chin, the lighthearted defiance I'd known since Big Sur, her long-stemmed stride. Now she took short, sure steps, a hand to her belled skirt. A sense of inner peace and tranquility glowed from her face when she came quietly to the threshold and offered her tray of wine.

I lingered a moment when Cleo had gone to the bridge to wait. She quizzed me with her eyes when I returned the cup to her tray, smiled for her of words. I realized she was being kind to a wretched man she had never known.

And when I looked down at her fingers, she raised them for me to see. Our wedding ring was nestled above a serpent ring, a symbol of the past she would never know. When she tossed her hair aside and called softly to Deuca in the entryway, I murmured, "I love you, Nina," and turned away.

* * * * *

Printed in the United States
68294LVS00001B/1-9

9 789768 184818